Philosopher, Teacher, Musician:
Perspectives on Music Education

Edited by Estelle R. Jorgensen

University of Illinois Press
Urbana and Chicago

Illini Books edition, 1993
©1991, 1993 by the Board of Trustees of the University of Illinois
Manufactured in the United States of America
P 5 4 3 2 1

This book is printed on acid-free paper.

The essays in this book originally appeared in the *Journal of Aesthetic Education*, volume 25, number 3 (1991). Publication of the issue and this book was supported by a grant from Indiana University.

Library of Congress Cataloging-in-Publication Data

Philosopher, teacher, musician : perspectives on music education /
    edited by Estelle R. Jorgensen. — Illini Books ed.
        p. cm.
    "Essays . . . originally appeared in the Journal of aesthetic
education, volume 25, number 3 (1991)"—T.p. verso.
    Includes bibliographical references.
    ISBN 0-252-06349-X (paper : acid-free paper)
    1. Music—Instruction and study—Philosophy.   I. Jorgensen,
Estelle Ruth.
MT1.P512   1993
780'.7—dc20
                                                            93-3328
                                                              CIP
                                                              MN

Contents

Introduction

ESTELLE R. JORGENSEN

The appearance of Bennett Reimer's *Philosophy of Music Education*[1] following closely upon Abraham Schwadron's *Aesthetics: Dimensions for Music Education*[2] heralded an era in North American music education sometimes described as the aesthetic education movement. Reimer's philosophy, widely read internationally, remained largely unchallenged by philosophers of music education in the intervening years.[3]

During this time, an extreme form of positivism came to characterize music education inquiry. Increasingly, music education researchers thought of themselves as social scientists instead of artist-philosophers. Without the benefit of a concerted effort to divorce philosophical discourse from advocacy, a scholarly community of philosophers interested in music education, and a strong and well-established tradition of critical examination of ideas within the music teaching community, philosophical teaching and research in music education languished. The relatively few philosophers of music education found themselves increasingly marginalized within their research community. A need developed for an international symposium that would bring together those interested in the philosophy of music education to share their ideas and move philosophical discourse in music education forward.

Moreover, though Reimer's ideas had enriched the profession and his argument for the relevance of aesthetics for music education had pointed music educators toward finding philosophical bases for their activities, other perspectives emerged. Some, such as those articulated by Keith Swanwick and Christopher Small, offered different theoretical and philosophical perspectives.[4] Others, such as those espoused by David Aspin and David Elliott, pointed to the need for a reconsideration of the ideas that had guided the music education profession during the past few decades and the development of alternative paradigms for music education.[5]

Estelle R. Jorgensen is professor of music and chair of the music education department in the School of Music at Indiana University, Bloomington. She has published theoretical and philosophical essays in leading research and professional journals in music education and has contributed to various essay collections.

On 8-12 July 1990, *The Philosopher/Teacher in Music: The Indiana Symposium on Research and Teaching in the Philosophy of Music Education* convened on the Bloomington campus of Indiana University. This landmark symposium attracted an international group of participants and represented the first time that music educators interested in philosophy had met with each other, philosophers from other fields (general philosophy, aesthetics, music, education, and art education), music theorists, and musicologists to discuss the philosophy of music and music education. The essays in this book are based on the papers presented at this symposium.

Several themes emerge in the essays. A first concerns epistemological issues related to the nature of the understanding(s) that music brings and the way(s) in which music is known. Leading a quartet of pieces, Iris Yob suggests that in the context of Tillich's ideas about how and why the arts access realities not always available through other means, music may be approached as a way of understanding and a symbolic language that has its distinct semantic and syntactic features that are collectively and individually understood. The issue of the nature of the knowledge music conveys is then examined from two points of view reflecting a persistent philosophical tradition of dividing musical knowledge into *musica practica* and *musica theoretica*. Focusing on the practical aspects of music making, David Elliott explores the epistemological implications of a particular sense of "music" he believes to be philosophically and practically useful, "musicing," or the making of music through performance, arguing that musicing is both a form and a source of knowledge. From a theoretical perspective, Wayne Bowman posits that music is also understood formally and that contrary to their past characterization in music education thought, philosophers such as Kant, Hanslick, Gurney, and Meyer provide important insights into the nature of musical experience. Rounding out this quartet is Mary Reichling's exploration of the attributes of aesthetic and artistic imagination in music, with particular reference to Dewey's ideas. Her analysis suggests some possibilities for the role of imagination as a means through which music is known.

The theme of the second group of essays concerns the place and nature of music in education, and education in music, particularly music as a humanity in the academy. Peter Kivy's search for philosophical reasons why music should be included as a compulsory subject among the humanities within the academy leaves him somewhat skeptical. He suggests that a justification deriving from music's role in "tribal rituals" may hold promise. Alternatively, John Shepherd sees music's role as crucial in understanding humanity, and on this basis he suggests how musical education in the academy may be revisioned in a way that directly faces the current rhetoric of instrumentalism and forges alternative ways of thinking about and doing musical education. The thread of music among the humanities is further drawn by Ralph Smith, who develops, in line with ideas by Meyer, Levi, and Beardsley, reasons why music should be envisaged humanistically and proposes that this view of music need not exclude musical composition and performance. Finally, taking up the problems inherent in musical canonicity and its impact on musical education in the academy, Austin Caswell describes how the canon developed and offers some suggestions about what should be done about it that are in line with an inclusive view of music making.

A third theme concerns philosophical perspectives on music curriculum and instruction. Keith Swanwick tackles the problem of how to build a music curriculum structured around musical experience utilizing particular musical *features* rather than generalizable musical *concepts* as the basis of curricular structure. From an international perspective, and taking African music as her exemplar, Elizabeth Oehrle finds a discontinuity between African music education based mainly on Western music making and indigenous African music making. She suggests that musical instruction would be enriched by more inclusive attitudes to world musics and musical traditions. Looking inwardly in his phenomenological account of whole/part relationships in music, particularly pitch relationships and the implications for musical instruction, Douglas Bartholomew sees individual musical experience in the context of both self and world as the object of music education.

A fourth theme concerns the nature and place of philosophy in music education and its contribution to research and practice. Bennett Reimer clarifies his views on the characteristics of aesthetic education in the context of events during the past few decades, and traces his journey of changing understandings of aesthetic education. Reimer's ideas are then set in philosophical perspective by Philip Alperson, who offers an analysis and critique of three possible strategies by which philosophies of music education might be built. The tie-in of philosophical research with various forms of descriptive and experimental research is illustrated in an essay by Hildegard Froehlich and Gary Cattley, who discuss the implications of language use in music education research, particularly metaphor, analogy, and model and the limitations and strengths of each. Rounding out the collection, Gerard Knieter reflects on the present situation of philosophy in American music education, its appropriate role in the advanced training of music educators, its objects and principles of course content, and how philosophical thinking in music education might be enhanced in the future.

Taken as a whole, the essays in this issue reveal that a variety of views of music education has now emerged. These ideas have yet to be systematically criticized. It remains to be seen how philosophy will develop in music education and what its future directions will be. We have in these essays, however, a glimpse of some of the possibilities.

NOTES

Several people have helped make this book possible, and I wish to acknowledge their assistance: Charles Webb, Dean of the School of Music, and George Walker, Dean of Research and the University Graduate School, Indiana University, for funding *The Philosopher/Teacher in Music: The Indiana Symposium on Research and Teaching in the Philosophy of Music Education* and providing a subvention to assist in publishing the essays in book form; Janet James, for her invaluable assistance in coordinating the symposium; Ralph A. Smith, editor of *The Journal of Aesthetic Education*, for inviting the papers and publishing them in a special issue; and Carole Appel, senior editor, University of Illinois Press, for bringing this book to life.

1. Bennnett Reimer, *A Philosophy of Music Education* (Englewood Cliffs, N.J.: Prentice-Hall, 1970).
2. Abraham Schwadron, *Aesthetics: Dimensions for Music Education* (Washington, D.C.: MENC, 1967).
3. The *Journal of Aesthetic Education*, the *Bulletin of the Council for Research in Music Education*, and the *British Journal of Music Education* have been among the principal forums for discussing philosophical issues in music education.
4. See Keith Swanwick, *A Basis for Music Education* (1979; repr. Windsor, Berks.: NFER-Nelson, 1981), *Music, Mind, and Education* (London and New York: Routledge, 1988); and Christopher Small, *Music-Society-Education*, 2d. rev. ed. (London: Calder, 1980).
5. See David Aspin's essay "The Place of Music in the Curriculum: A Justification," *Journal of Aesthetic Education* 16, no. 1 (Spring 1982): 41-55; and David Elliott's review of the second edition of Reimer's *A Philosophy of Music Education* in *Philosophy of Music Education Newsletter* 2 (1989): 5-9.

The Arts as Ways of Understanding: Reflections on the Ideas of Paul Tillich

One may wonder how it is that the German-American Paul Johannes Tillich (1886-1965), theologian primarily and philosopher by training, comes to be included in a discussion of research and teaching for music educators. The wonder may be exacerbated when one also discovers that music is an aesthetic endeavor to which he gave little or no attention. He seldom mentions it, or dance and drama, in his voluminous writings and innumerable papers, and often when he does, they appear in parentheses as though he sensed they somehow belonged to the arts but did not quite know what to do with them once they were admitted for consideration.

His father was an amateur performer and composer, but the son's artistic desires drew him first to literature and then to painting, sculpture, and architecture which, under the disapproving eye of his minister-parent, became a constant source of inspiration and reflection throughout his long professional career. Even then, he laid claim to being "neither an artist, an art historian, an art critic, nor even a philosopher whose special subject is art"—but simply to being "a philosophical theologian."[1]

However, I believe that Tillich warrants our attention because he struggled with many of the same issues, confronted the same challenges, and sensed many of the same possibilities in the study of the visual arts as those who are engaged in the study of the aural arts. He reflected, among other things, on the kinds of understandings paintings, sculptures, and architecture could impart as distinct from those of science and mathematics. And he analyzed the elements of artworks to discover how they function to produce their own distinct understandings. A study of Tillich, therefore, may lead music educators effectively into a search for answers to their own similar questions: Can music be regarded as a way of understanding? If so, how do the elements of music function to impart understandings?

In pursuing his version of these questions, Tillich alerts us to promising

Iris M. Yob is an Assistant Professor of Education at the State University of New York—Geneseo. She has most recently published in *Religious Education*.

ways of thinking about the arts, although his answers are limited by the assumptions of German idealism and the predominance of expressionistic artworks in his analysis. Our critique will build on and offer alternative perspectives to his original contribution.

Are the Arts Ways of Understanding?

As a young man, Tillich served as a German army chaplain during the First World War. It was, he declares, "the dirt, the horrors and the ugliness" he experienced in the trenches more than anything else that induced him "systematically to study the history of art and to collect as many as possible of the cheap reproductions available" to him on the battlefield. On furlough, he visited a Berlin museum where he discovered Botticelli's *Madonna and Child with Singing Angels*, an experience for which he reports he had no better name than "revelatory ecstasy."[2]

To describe the experience as one of ecstasy indicates that it was an intensely emotional one, still memorable over thirty years later and a whole continent removed. But the qualifier "revelatory" suggests its significance had to do with more than feelings, powerful as these may have been. It suggests he also learned something from the experience, and in fact he indicates that in this "one moment of beauty," as he later called it,[3] he gained a new understanding, a decisive insight, which remained with him from that time. It gave him, he declares, "the keys for the interpretation of human existence" and along with "vital joy" brought him "spiritual truth."[4]

From his analysis of the human situation, Tillich identifies certain inescapables: awareness of our own finitude and the anxiety and fear that this produces. He describes anxiety as "the state in which a being is aware of its possible nonbeing" or "the existential awareness of nonbeing."[5] The threat of nonbeing may have been sharpened by the trauma of some of his early experiences, but on continuing reflection he came to understand it not only as the anxiety of having to die, but also, in a preliminary way, as any experience of meaninglessness, guilt, or condemnation in our daily lives.[6] And when being is threatened with nonbeing, he reasons, human beings are driven to ask "the ontological question," "the question of being." This, he claims, is the universal question—the central question of philosophy as well as of myth and the arts.[7]

Although the question of being arises first in the personal experience of existential anxiety, Tillich argues that it is pursued through a number of levels, including inquiry into the nature of being as a part of everything that human beings encounter, evolving eventually into a search for what he calls "the ground of being," "the power of being," or "Being-itself."[8] Between his first formulation of the question and the last lies a vast distance, moving as it does from personal experience (concern about our own mortality) to philosophy (inquiry into the nature of being) and ultimately to religion (the search for Being-itself), but he regards Being-itself as the ultimate answer to the original question of our being. The search for this answer he describes as "ultimate concern,"[9] the driving, shaping, integrating feature of individuals and societies.

It is in this setting that he finds the arts have an indispensable role. They are an active expression of ultimate concern. They explore the nature of being and at some level reveal to us in our existential *angst* how we may find "the courage to be."

As a way of understanding these things, art performs three interrelated functions, according to Tillich. First, it expresses. That is, it expresses humankind's fear of the reality it discovers, the finitude, meaninglessness, and isolation in human experience. But in its expression, art transcends both "mere objectivity," for it gives more than a camera record of reality and also "mere subjectivity," for it is more than just an "outcry"—it may also express a level of being or reality beyond the immediate.

Art also transforms. It transforms ordinary reality "in order to give it the power of expressing something which is not itself." That is, art takes givens and makes them into symbols. So the gold ground of Byzantine or early Gothic pictures is not merely decorative but is symbolic of the heavenly spheres beyond, and the landscapes in Dutch paintings are not the landscapes we meet in an ordinary encounter with trees, fields, roads, and wide horizons.

Finally, art anticipates. It anticipates the possibilities that transcend the given in both its portrayal of perfection and also of distortion. It is able to find a kind of harmony in the disharmonious or, in effect, courage in the experience of anxiety, finitude, meaninglessness, and estrangement. In other words, art anticipates salvation.[10]

When science examines something, he explains, it discovers the thing's structure and appearance but, he indicates, this does not show what the thing means for itself. The tree registered and explained by Linnaeus does not give us the kind of knowledge that a Van Gogh painting of the same tree would give. In art, he says, we experience "the dynamic power of being which is effective in the life and struggle of the tree." We can "discover its inner meaning, the way in which it expresses the power of being which is present in everything that is."

Of course, he recognizes the arts and the sciences have much in common. They both transform elements of the perceived world around us into images so they may become objects for our reception. Both art and science are rightly labelled *theoria*. But, he adds, in its "cognitive" or scientific capacity, *theoria* gives an analysis of what things are in their relation to each other; in its "aesthetic" capacity, *theoria* gives the vision of what things are in their very being.

He continues, the kind of knowledge that science gives depends on a degree of distance and detachment from the object, but art unites us with and relates us to its objects. Consequently, "intuitive participation in works of art liberates us from the loneliness of our separated existence in a much more radical way than cognitive participation can."[11] That is, art can do what science cannot. By means of scientific transformation and reception, we can learn nothing more about an object, a tree, an animal, or whatever, than "its calculable internal and external relations";[12] but art "uses pieces of the ordinarily encountered reality in order to show a meaning which is mediated by the given object but transcends it."[13]

Apparently Tillich recognizes that the arts no less than the sciences contribute to what we know of the world we live in and who we are, and yet they contribute different kinds of knowledge. While he reserves the expression "cognitive function" for the activity of the sciences and related disciplines and "aesthetic awareness" for the arts, he nevertheless prefers to call the products of both "knowledge."[14] Art, like science, he proposes, "discovers reality. It is theoretical in the genuine sense of *theoria* but it is not cognitive."[15]

It produces knowledge, it brings awareness, it is theoretical, but it is not cognitive. What is Tillich saying here? We inhabit a world we have constructed largely on scientific assumptions, by means of scientific method, and according to scientific findings. Science has criticized and often overturned the old myths about who we are and what we know—thankfully, irreversibly. But Tillich is reminding us here that all that can be known is not the result of scientific activity alone. He is reclaiming "knowledge" from the exclusive use of science and sharing it among all the activities of searching, thinking, theorizing, expressing, meaning-making human beings. He is reminding us that all we can know is mediated not only by the scientific enterprise but also by aesthetic, philosophical, and religious endeavors.

It seems that Tillich has the same problem with the term "cognition" that he believes others may have with the term "knowledge," although neither "knowledge" nor "cognition" need exclude "aesthetic awareness." We may prefer, however, to regard music as a "way of understanding" or a "form of thought."[16] But whatever music may be called, the important point is that some knowledge may not be propositional in character—it may be "awareness" (to adopt Tillich's term) that is mediated by means of the intuited, the expressive, the allusive, the imaginative, the emotional, or the spiritual.

While we may applaud Tillich's pointing us in the direction of regarding the arts as serious makers of meaning, we may not be satisfied with his description of the meaning that they make. His moment of "revelatory ecstasy" in contemplation of *Madonna and Child with Singing Angels* may have found best expression for him in an exploration of the themes of finitude, being, and the ground of being, themes that he could pursue with vigor in theology and philosophy. However, in his enthusiasm for these ideas, he sometimes lost clarity. Being-itself is said to "embrace" not only being but also nonbeing.[17] It is the "ground," "power," and "structure of being" and "the really real," but is not a thing.[18] It is something we are at once separated from yet participate in. It is God and it is beyond God and secularized. It is our ultimate concern, but it is nonpersonal and amoral. Ontologically speaking, it is "Being-itself," psychologically speaking, it is "ultimate concern," theologically speaking, it is "God," but this blurring of distinctions gives rise to many questions.

Leaving aside the difficulties raised by the notions of being, nonbeing and Being-itself, the significant feature of aesthetic productions, according to Tillich, is that the realities they refer to have to do with who we are, what we fear, and wherein we may find hope and courage. That is, they provide cognitive access to fundamental issues lying at the heart of human experience, some of which, it is possible, cannot be empirically explored.

Scientific knowledge too is frequently of transcendent realities, if by "transcendent" we mean outside the reach of observation, measurement, and other means of experimental verification, for science deals with putative entities such as black holes, electrical charges, quanta, and subatomic structures. However, art has always had a particular affinity with religion because it is often the most adequate means, if not the only means, of representing or expressing the transcendent realities that religion is attentive to.

Whatever it may be that art productions reveal, it is, Tillich proposes, something that without art otherwise "would be covered forever." This suggests that the arts are both indispensable and irreplaceable in the sum total of human knowledge and also that they are irreducible. Their revelations are not always accessible by any other means and cannot be expressed in any other medium without loss. This does not mean that talk about the meanings of artworks is impossible or pointless, but simply that, for great art at least, such talk is not exhaustive for something will always be lost in the translation. Tillich's work testifies to this fact when one peruses the voluminous works in which he continues to explore the insight he gained originally from the Botticelli. Maybe the most adequate and meaningful response to art is more art.

Although he has collapsed together existential, ontological, aesthetic, and religious notions, and although his own argument is sometimes more bewildering than enlightening, Tillich is at least attempting to indicate that aesthetic productions have meaning that is arguably important in our understanding of ourselves, of the world, and of the transcendent. This meaning is, he suggests, not accessible to other ways of understanding. Others agree and on these grounds, a substantial body of literature proposes that the arts are an essential part of a well-rounded liberal education.[19] As an irreplaceable, indispensable, irreducible way of understanding, they belong in the curriculum. The task of teachers and their students is to discover the revelations and insights of particular art productions and communicate these discoveries in ways that faithfully reflect the medium that embodies them. And this leads us into our next consideration.

How Do the Arts Impart and Shape Our Understandings?

That which sets human beings apart from the nonhuman, Tillich maintains, is their capacity for language. In encountering a particular tree, he explains, we experience more than just the tree—we experience at the same time "treehood, the universal, that which makes a tree a tree." And, through language, we give this universal a name, liberating ourselves from the particular. But language, he notes, is not bound to the spoken word. It may be written or read. And more than that, "It is present in silence as well as in talk. It is effective in the visual arts, in the creative as well as the receptive act." As he observes, "Only that being which can speak can also paint." In a painting, he proposes, meaning is expressed through the choice of colors, grades of light and darkness, forms of balance, and structural features[20]—all of which may be symbolic elements.

Tillich heartily welcomed the renewed philosophical interest in symbols, believing that only with more profound understandings of symbolic functioning can we comprehend without distortion the meaning of alternative "languages" (that is, verbal and nonverbal symbol systems). He is particularly anxious to avoid the derogative "Only a symbol!" For him, it is instead a matter of "Not less than a symbol!" because he regards symbols as "the most revealing creations of the human mind."[21] While his approach to symbols can only loosely be called a theory, he nevertheless identifies with those who recognize that different kinds of understandings "demand different approaches and different languages."[22] As an introduction to the specific languages of religion in which he was primarily interested, he variously specifies six characteristics of symbols in general[23] which he believes are foundational for any understanding of symbolic languages.

First, he indicates that symbols point beyond themselves to something else. The implication is that not the symbol itself but that to which it points is the focus of interest. In this way, he proposes, symbols are like signs: just as the sign of the red traffic light does not point to itself but "to the necessity of stopping,"[24] so we employ some "symbolic material" to point to something else. This "material" need not be verbal, he notes, but can be pictorial, dramatic, concrete, or abstract. And just as colors, shapes, shades, and balance may be visual symbols, so, this suggests, rhythm, pitch, tone, volume, and the other elements of musical works are potentially aural symbols. Whatever the symbolic material may be, Tillich has identified here a basic "pointing" function of symbols—a symbol is something that stands for, refers to, points to, denotes, or represents.

In elaborating this first characteristic, Tillich goes on to indicate to what a symbol may refer: a symbol is anything which refers to the transcendent, extraordinary, and ultimate. That is, a symbol "points to something which cannot be directly grasped but must be expressed indirectly"—to that which transcends empirical reality or to "a dimension of reality which is not open to an ordinary encounter" or to "ultimate reality."[25]

The second characteristic of symbols he identifies is that while many things may "point," symbols are able to point or refer because they "participate in the reality and power" and "the meaning" of that to which they point. Nonsymbolic pointers are such things as mathematical signs; the letters of the alphabet because they do not participate in the sound to which they point; a word such as "desk" because the desk itself has essentially nothing to do with the four letters d-e-s-k; and the red light which summons the driver to stop but which bears no intrinsic relationship to stopping.

In contrast, he identifies as symbols the representatives of a person or institution because they "participate in the honor of those they are called on to represent"; liturgical and poetical languages because they have built up over time "connotations in situations in which they appear so that they cannot be replaced"; and the flag because it "participates in the power of the king or nation for which it stands."[26] Because they participate in what they symbolize, he adds, symbols have a certain irreplaceableness and an "organic connection" with that to which they point. Nonsymbolic pointers, on the other hand, are arbitrarily chosen, merely conventional, and readily replaced if ever it is expedient to do so.[27]

Participation, developed within idealist and romantic traditions, has been a rather indeterminate notion.[28] In one respect it is too narrow, in another too broad, to explain clearly how symbols work. It is too limited in that it depends on metaphysical considerations and assumptions that are inherently problematic. Primarily, it assumes that if there is a symbol, then there is something which is symbolized and in which it participates. As Peter Fingesten points out, however, this is particularly open to question when one recalls the symbols of prehistoric and forgotten religious art. The Egyptian term *Ka* and its bird symbol, for instance, are no guarantee that the shadow soul which they symbolized actually existed. "One can make a symbol of anything," he warns, "but only at the expense of its objective reality or by inventing a symbol like the Ka which may have no reality at all."[29]

Further, since Tillich regards participation in ontological terms, he implies that a symbol participates in several realities, each dependent on what it is a symbol of. But what is the real nature of a rising crescendo if in

various musical pieces it may symbolize power, triumph, mounting excitement, deepening agony, or simply a change of intensity in whatever mood
is being portrayed? If it participates in the being of all the realities it points
to, how are these various beings interrelated within the ontological structure of the symbol itself? These troublesome questions can be eliminated
only if participation is redescribed in terms that avoid narrowly defined ontological claims, as we shall see.

In another sense, the notion of participation fails as an explanation of
how symbols work because it claims more than it can deliver. Primarily, it
does not distinguish symbols from nonsymbols. As William Rowe rightly
points out,[30] our response to a ringing fire alarm, which in Tillich's analysis
is not a symbol, is the same fear and flight that would accompany our
response to an actual fire. As he enumerates other instances, the distinction
between nonsymbol and symbol on the grounds that nonsymbols are conventional, arbitrary, and replaceable begins to break down, for these signs
also come to be inextricably related to what they signify.

Moreover, some things Tillich identifies as symbols, Rowe points out,
are not as organically connected with their referent as he may suggest. A
nation's flag is such a symbol—it is accepted through a process that typically begins with a number of artists' designs, which are deliberated over and
evaluated at many levels, until eventual agreement and final approval is
reached by vote or general consensus. Such a selection process would be
unnecessary if in its very being the symbol "radiated the power of being
and meaning of that for which it stands,"[31] as Tillich claims.

And yet, to describe symbols as participating in another reality does
seem at times to coincide with our experience of them: we treat sacramental
wine and bread differently from other wine and bread, the flag differently
form other pieces of fabric, a king's representatives differently from other
people. We tend to regard these things with the same reverence, care, and
even awe that would apply to what they symbolize; we develop elaborate
procedures for properly handling them; and should we ever see one of our
highly regarded symbols being treated without proper respect, we would
become duly upset, as Tillich indicates.[32] Similarly, the symbolic elements
of a musical performance may induce in us an imaginative experience of
hope, fear, the joy of victory, grief, awe, or relief that rivals the actual experience of such moments. If the relationship between a symbol and its
referent cannot be adequately explained as ontological participation, how
can it be explained?

I suggest a fruitful line of exploration is to attend to the observable
rather than the supposed differences in *modus operandi* of the things Tillich
identifies as symbols and nonsymbols. That is, if we look at how the symbols actually work, we may avoid problematic metaphysical assumptions
and implications, and we may find a way of describing the relationship be-

tween symbol and symbolized that does not depend on speculation about covert symbol properties. Clearly, red stoplights, the letters of the alphabet, words used in what he calls their "ordinary" sense, and mathematical notation function differently as pointers from the way the flag, the king's designate, and a great deal of poetic, liturgical, artistic, and musical languages do. The former, or what Tillich regards as nonsymbols, are nothing more than labels or indicators to be read literally. They simply name, indicate, predicate, or describe, and once learned, they involve no cognitive strain or insight but are taken as referring in a direct, straightforward, and uncomplicated way.

The latter, or what he calls "symbols," make different cognitive demands. They refer indirectly and require some imaginative effort on the part of the symbol maker and symbol user because they employ figurative processes. For example, when a symphony expresses feelings of tragic loss, it does not literally have those feelings, nor are the feelings expressed literally those of the composer, the performers, or the listeners. Rather, they are feelings perceived to be present in the work itself, and since a work does not literally possess feelings, they must be present figuratively.

In *Death Set to Music*, Paul Minear examines how four masterworks express various meanings of death in human experience. As he takes each of the works apart movement by movement, it is apparent that the message of the music depends significantly on nonliteral symbols. To illustrate, we can look at his discussion of the statement in the second movement of Brahms's *A German Requiem*:

> the grass withers and the flower falls
> but
> the word of the Lord abides forever.

Central in this statement is what he calls "one of the most decisive 'buts' in all music." From the mournful words of the first phrase there is an abrupt change to the positive affirmation of the second phrase, a transition that is expressed equally in the musical qualities as in the words. The first phrase is sung as a dirge—slowly, in the lower voices—but at the "but" there is a marked acceleration in tempo and a brighter mood. He attributes the "brightness" of mood to the more animated and exuberant voices of the higher ranges taking over from the somber tones of the voices in the lower pitches, by the coming into play of the whole orchestra, and by the interplay of musical lines in a fugue. The combined effect of words and music in this context is the sober recognition of the transience of life even in the course of one summer's wait for "the latter rains" contrasted with the endless patience and permanence of God.[33]

Seen in this light, participation is less dependent on a symbol's literal embodiment of what is symbolized than on figurative embodiment. When a musical symbol expresses a feeling, an idea, or a state of affairs, it points to what it expresses through the characteristics it possesses, characteristics that are understood metaphorically. In the context of Brahms's *Requiem*, we hear the slow rhythm and low voices of the first line as mournful and the interplay of exuberant, high, accelerated voices in the second line as bright because we have learned how to interpret the figurative qualities of the music. In both lines, the music directs our thought to particular notions and emotions because it metaphorically embodies them.

In recasting the idea of participation this way, however, we are not countering some of Tillich's valuable insights. He has rightly recognized that not all "languages" can be reduced to the equivalent of literal labels or pointers,[34] but may in fact "participate" in the meanings they refer to, if not in what they are, then at least in how they represent and express. That is, aesthetic symbols must be evaluated by standards different from those of literal pointers—they must be seen appropriately to embody that which they symbolize for those who have learned the "language." Because aesthetic symbols figuratively incorporate or embody what they express, their interpretation requires attention to their nuances, their possible overlays of meanings, their subtlety, in general, their suggestiveness.

The third characteristic of symbols he identifies is that they open up levels of reality that otherwise are closed to us. Artistic symbols, he suggests, are particularly apt in this function—an artwork "expresses a level of reality to which only the artistic creation has an approach";[35] a painting "mediates" something that "cannot be expressed in any other way than through the painting itself."[36] In fact, the "ecstatic," "expressionistic," and "spiritual" elements are the very features that enable art most effectively to refer to the ultimate, the transcendent, or the extraordinary[37] which are otherwise beyond the descriptive capacity of ordinary, literal, direct language. In referring to the transcendent, the symbols of art and music are most effective pointers simply because they suggest without delineating and describe without circumscribing.

Again, he believes this mediation is made possible by the participation of the symbols in that which they symbolize. Here too, however, the participation need not be literal; it can be nonliteral, providing aural figures to point beyond the ordinary to the extraordinary. Reference is none the less powerful for being nonliteral, for the capacity of musical symbolic language to be as sad, triumphal, excited, fearful, militant, and so on, at the figurative level as its referents are at the literal level makes it an especially appropriate accompaniment to patriotic occasions, celebrations of various kinds, funerals, and religious ceremonies.

The third characteristic of symbols is intimately tied to the fourth; namely, symbols also open up dimensions and elements of our soul that correspond to the dimensions and elements of reality. At the least, in their cognitive capacity symbols are not always employed detachedly or neutrally. They have an impact on the symbol maker and symbol user, either by way of cognitive surprise or affective response. More than this, in making symbols we make ourselves, for our reality is that meaning which through our symbol systems we have imposed on the world around us.

Of course, Tillich intends more than this when he speaks of a correspondence between our soul and the dimensions and elements of reality. His cosmological understanding of the world is that "the knower and that which is known is united," since everything is ultimately derived from the unity he calls "Being-itself."[38] One does not have to go as far as this, however, to appreciate that the central symbols of our various discourses make our self-understanding and in so doing touch us profoundly and determine us personally. This is as true of aesthetic symbolisms as of scientific symbolism.

The fifth characteristic of symbols in Tillich's summary is that they cannot be invented—rather, they grow out of the collective unconscious and function only when they are accepted by the unconscious dimension of our being. The term "collective unconscious" is borrowed from Jungian psychology, but Tillich uses it somewhat hesitantly. He qualifies it by admitting, "I would say out of the womb which is usually called today the 'group unconscious' or 'collective unconscious,' or whatever you want to call it—out of a group which acknowledges, in this thing, this word, this flag, or whatever it may be, its own thing."[39]

This implies that symbols are not a private matter but are socially rooted and socially accepted. They are not a matter of individual preference but arise in a community of users. Although he also expects they are best understood within that community, it should be noted that their meanings should not be regarded as forever exclusively accessible only to the group in which they originated even if others reject those meanings. In dialogue, a wider public may be persuaded by or can bring pertinent critique to the discourse of a particular group.

Tillich leaves open the question of how, if symbols are not invented, they might grow out of the collective unconscious. Artists, scientists, philosophers, religious thinkers, and other symbol makers are certainly embedded in a cultural milieu by which they are influenced, but against which they must sometimes react if they hold a place at the cutting edge of thought or artistic expression. But whether they are reflecting or rejecting current cultural understandings, there is no reason to insist that they do not invent any new symbols. Tillich shows some confusion on this very point when he speaks of symbols as the "results of a creative encounter with reality."[40] What is "creative" about the encounter, as he puts it, if nothing is created?

Anybody, it seems, could invent a symbol, but as Tillich explains,[41] invention does not guarantee general acceptance. The artist at work, although a responsive member of a larger community, creates or invents the symbols of an artwork, but these may or may not be accepted by the public at large. Here the "collective unconscious" makes a determination,[42] if by that we mean the group decides on the work's appropriateness, insightfulness, usefulness, or simply its "goodness of fit."

As the sixth and final characteristic, Tillich proposes that symbols, like human beings, pass through a life cycle of birth, growth, and death. In their development, they are dependent on their environment—they grow "when the situation is ripe for them and they die when the situation changes." Their existence depends on their ability to "produce a response" in the group where they originally find expression.[43] He holds that symbols cannot be destroyed by criticism, but they will cease to be effective as symbols only if the relationship between the group and the symbol significantly changes. "In the moment in which this inner situation of the human group to a symbol has ceased to exist, then the symbol dies. The symbol does not 'say' anything any more."[44]

It is not clear, however, what he means when he speaks of an "inner situation." If it refers to an emotional commitment to a symbol, he could be noting the psychological attachment people may have which maintains the symbol even after good reasons for its continuation have ceased. Many Australians, for instance, are loyal to their flag with its Union Jack, although the country's increasing independence from Britain was signalled by Federation at the turn of the century. But emotional attachment to a symbol does not insulate the symbol from historical, scientific, aesthetic, or philosophical criticism. And sooner or later, such criticism can affect what is considered acceptable as a symbol or schema. Again, Tillich has tended to fall back on an obscure notion like the "death" of a symbol and one's "inner situation," and to speculate about covert processes and situations. Alternatively, and more straightforwardly, it could be said that at times accepted symbols prove to be inappropriate, and favored explanations no longer "fit" changing situations. At that point, they fall into disuse, without there being anything particularly occult about it. But certainly he is right in noting that new times abandon old symbols in favor of new ones, and in fact, new times are ushered in by new symbols.

Tillich's theory of symbols depends on a number of indeterminate or unclarified terms such as "participation," "organic connection," "mediation," "levels of reality," "opening up the soul," "inner situation," and "collective unconscious." Many of his claims about symbols and symbolic functioning are based on assumptions that, rather than clarifying the nature of symbols, raise a number of new questions. Nevertheless, he describes well our existential involvement with significant symbols when he illuminates their role, tenacity, and influence in social groups. His theory of symbols is also more convincing when it recognizes the complexity of symbols, especially in figurative modes and changing interpretations to meet changes in context. And he alerts modern thinkers to the challenge of dealing with symbols that no longer vitalize and energize us.

By way of practical application, he advises that the role of educators in respect of symbols is threefold: conceptualization, explanation, and criticism.[45] That is to say, their task involves the presentation and exploration of symbols as symbols; the interpretation and exegesis of them; and in understanding how symbols relate to each other and to that which they symbolize, the discovery of adequate symbols and the rejection of inadequate ones. In consequence, he believes symbols will be protected from profanation and valued for their capacity to disclose at some level the mystery of life and the meaning of human experience.

Critical Questions for Music Educators

From our conversation with the ideas of Tillich, a number of questions and implications emerge for music educators. In the interests of simplicity, I would like to suggest two sets of questions, one revolving around the concept of musical understanding and the other around the related notion of musical symbolic language.

Is music legitimately regarded as a way of understanding? If it is not, then music may be nothing more than the enjoyable experience of sound, a disembodied and ungrounded emotional event, or a display of technical skill with an instrument—in which case it no more belongs in the liberal arts curriculum than eating ice cream, recreational napping, or mowing lawns.

If it is a way of understanding, then the experience of its sounds, its emotional events, and the technical skills that produce it combine to provide cognitive access to notions, ideas, structures, and relationships that may not be accessible in other ways; in giving form, it may also give meaning to the emotional and spiritual moments in our experience; and it may contribute to our perception of ourselves, our society, and possibly something beyond.

If music is a way of understanding, then educators may seriously consider their role in the "conceptualization, explanation and criticism" of music. At the least, the study of music will involve them and the learner in an experience of music as music, symbolic element as symbolic—an immersion in the musical sounds, forms, nuances, moods, voices, and shapes of a musical work. It will also involve them in an analysis of that musical experience, an interpretation that articulates in words or re-expresses in related aesthetic forms its insights in search of its distinctive and multilayered meanings. And to complete the learning, it will involve them in an assessment and evaluation of those expressions and meanings for their existential relevance and veracity. Beyond these minimal considerations, it may also encourage students of music to look for and even contribute to musical meaning making on the growing edge of our cultural understandings.

Is the nature of music properly understood as a symbolic language? If not, then one may overlook the relationships among its elements and neglect the coherence within an individual work and its interdependence with other aesthetic products. If music is not a symbolic "language," then it may very well not have a "message" or be a way of understanding.

If music is regarded as a "language," we have a schematic organization for approaching the phenomenon of music which can be insightful and productive in a number of ways. The term "language" brings with it a particularly rich network of associated notions such as "words," "sentences," "grammar," "figures of speech," "punctuation," "mood," "tone," "idioms," and so on, which in turn suggest two possible lines of study in music: semantics and syntax. Where the "semantics" of music refers to *what* meanings or understandings music may afford, "syntax" refers to *how* music makes its meanings. Students who are "fluent" in music will have a working knowledge of both.

If music is a symbolic language, its syntactical structure may be analyzed and learned. The question is, How does music function as a symbol system? Our discussion of Tillich's ideas suggests that music may express meaning because its combined elements are figurative embodiments of the notions and emotions it refers to. This kind of expression may very well be a significant syntactical feature of musical functioning, but other possibilities should not be overlooked. If sounds and sound qualities are to musical language what words are to verbal language, and if words and combinations of words may function in a variety of ways, both literal and nonliteral, music may also exhibit a similar variety of syntactical forms and functions. In fact, Peter Kivy has recognized various degrees of literal depiction in what he identifies as musical pictures or musical representations: the simulation of the cuckoo call in Beethoven's Sixth Symphony, the clash and whir of machinery in Mossolov's *Iron Foundry*, the chugging of the train engine in Honegger's *Pacific 231*, and the buzz of flies in Handel's Israel in Egypt.[46] An exploration of possible, even simultaneous, literal and figurative levels of expression may contribute to our understanding of how music makes its meanings.

Tillich may have speculated on how aesthetic symbols achieve results in ways that prove problematic, but there may be something the music teacher will find worth exploring in his claim that these symbols are the "most revealing creations of the human mind, the most genuine ones, the most powerful ones."[47]

NOTES

1. From an address given at the Minneapolis Institute of Arts in 1952. Entitled "Art and Society," this three-part address now appears in the collection edited by John Dillenberger and Jane Dillenberger, *Paul Tillich: On Art and Architecture* (New York: Crossroad, 1987), pp. 11-41.
2. Ibid., p. 12.
3. Tillich, "One Moment of Beauty," in *On Art and Architecture*, pp. 234-35.
4. Ibid., p. 235.
5. Tillich, *The Courage to Be* (New Haven, Conn.: Yale University Press, 1952), pp. 35, 36.
6. Ibid., p. 41.
7. Tillich, *Biblical Religion and the Search for Ultimate Reality* (Chicago: University of Chicago Press, 1955), p. 9.
8. Ibid., pp. 6-13.
9. Tillich, *Systematic Theology*, three volumes in one (Chicago: University of Chicago Press, 1967), vol. 1, p. 14.
10. Tillich, "Art and Society," pp. 18-21.
11. Ibid., pp. 15, 16.
12. Ibid., p. 27.
13. Tillich, *Systematic Theology*, vol. 3, p. 71.
14. Tillich, "Art and Society," p. 26.
15. Ibid., p. 27.
16. Nelson Goodman and Catherine Elgin, *Reconstructions in Philosophy and Other Arts and Sciences* (Indianapolis: Hackett, 1988), pp. 3-5, propose "understanding," suggesting that it comprehends cognition in all of its modes: perception, depiction, and emotion as well as description and that it can be imparted in verbal and nonverbal, literal and metaphorical, descriptive and normative systems of understandings. Israel Scheffler, *Reason and Teaching* (Indianapolis: Bobbs-Merrill, 1963), p. 37, adopts the expression "forms of thought" because it may involve, among other things, inferring, categorizing, perceiving, evaluating, deciding, attitude forming, and expecting.
17. Tillich, *The Courage to Be*, p. 34.
18. Tillich, *Systematic Theology*, vol. 1, p. 189.
19. For instance, Paul H. Hirst, *Knowledge and the Curriculum: A Collection of Philosophical Papers*, International Library of the Philosophy of Education, gen. ed. R. S. Peters (London: Routledge and Kegan Paul, 1974); Elliot Eisner, ed. *Learning and Teaching the Ways of Knowing*, Eighty-fourth Yearbook of the National Society for the Study of Education (Chicago: University of Chicago Press, 1985).
20. Tillich, "Art and Society" p. 23.
21. Tillich, "Religious Symbols and Our Knowledge of God," *Christian Scholar* 38 (September 1955): 193.
22. Ibid., p. 189.
23. Tillich, *Dynamics of Faith* (New York: Harper and Row, 1957), pp. 41-43; "The Meaning and Justification of Religious Symbols," in *Religious Experience and Truth*, ed. Sidney Hook (New York: New York University Press, 1961), pp. 3-5; "Theology and Symbolism," in *Religious Symbolism*, ed. F. E. Johnson (New York: Institute for Religion and Social Studies, 1955), pp. 75-77, 108-16; "Religious Symbols and Our Knowledge of God," pp. 189-92; "The Religious Symbol," *Journal of Liberal Religion* 11 (1940): 13-15; "Art and Society," pp. 36-37.
24. Tillich, "Religious Symbols and Our Knowledge of God," p. 189.
25. Tillich, "Meaning and Justification of Religious Symbols," p. 4.
26. Tillich, "Religious Symbols and Our Knowledge of God," p. 190.
27. Tillich, "Theology and Symbolism," pp. 108, 109.

28. Plato, adopting the term from the Pythagoreans, first applies participation to the relationship between ideal forms and their instances, suggesting it has to do with cause, essence, and naming. (*Phaedo*, 100d.ff., Jowett translation.) S. T. Coleridge uses the notion of participation to distinguish symbols from other forms of figurative representation. Where other figures are merely translations of abstract notions into picture language, he sees symbols being characteristically "translucent": by participating in the reality to which it points, a symbol "abides itself as a living part in that unity of which it is the representative." (*The Statesman's Manual* [New York: Harper & Row, 1853], pp. 437-38.)

29. Peter Fingesten, *The Eclipse of Symbolism* (Columbia: University of South Carolina Press, 1970), pp. 126, 127.

30. William L. Rowe, *Religious Symbols and God: A Philosophical Study of Paul Tillich's Theology* (Chicago: University of Chicago Press, 1968), pp. 108-26.

31. Tillich, "Meaning and Justification of Religious Symbols," p. 4.

32. Tillich, *Dynamics of Faith*, p. 42.

33. Paul S. Minear, *Death Set to Music* (Atlanta: John Knox Press, 1987), pp. 70-71.

34. Tillich, "Religious Symbols and Our Knowledge of God," p. 190.

35. Tillich, "Theology and Symbolism," p. 109.

36. Tillich, "Religious Symbols and Our Knowledge of God," p. 191.

37. Tillich, "Art and Ultimate Reality," in *Art, Creativity and the Sacred*, ed. Diane Apostolos-Cappadona (New York: Crossroads, 1986), pp. 217-35.

38. Tillich, *Systematic Theology*, vol. 1, p. 94.

39. Tillich, "Religious Symbols and Our Knowledge of God," p. 192.

40. Tillich, "Theology and Symbolism," p. 109.

41. Tillich, "The Religious Symbol," p. 14.

42. Tillich, "Religious Symbols and Our Knowledge of God," p. 192.

43. Tillich, *Dynamics of Faith*, p. 43.

44. Tillich, "Religious Symbols and Our Knowledge of God," p. 192.

45. Tillich, "Theology and Symbolism," pp. 111-13.

46. Peter Kivy, *Sound and Semblance: Reflections on Musical Representation* (Princeton, N.J.: Princeton University Press, 1984), p. 59.

47. Tillich, "Religious Symbols and Our Knowledge of God," p. 193.

Music as Knowledge

DAVID J. ELLIOTT

Is music a form of knowledge? Is music a source of knowledge? Since "music" and "knowledge" can be taken in a variety of senses, and since the identifiable senses of these terms are slippery at best, the concept of music as knowledge is rich with possibilities. One might argue, for example, that some form of knowledge is imparted by each kind of music, or only some, or by every kind of music in combination, or by the very fact of music's existence. Following this, one could argue that music imparts knowledge to music makers, or to some of the listening public, or to all music makers and listeners everywhere, and so on. Furthermore, music's status as a source of knowledge might be considered its primary value, or a secondary value, or merely incidental.

It is not my intention to rehearse the major themes from music as knowledge. Neither will I trumpet a new theme of my own composition. Instead, I intend something akin to what a jazz pianist might do given a classic bass line as the impetus for a solo. I will highlight the importance of a fundamental line of thought about music by spinning out some of its vertical and horizontal possibilities. Put directly, my purpose here is to explore the epistemological implications of one particular sense of music.

The following discussion is divided into three parts. Part one states my "bass line" sense of music together with the tenor of my thoughts on its importance to music educators. Part two examines this grounding sense of music as a *form* of knowledge. Part three pursues music as a *source* of knowledge.

David J. Elliott is Professor of Music and Chair of Graduate Studies in Music Education with the Faculty of Music, University of Toronto. His articles have appeared in such journals as the *Bulletin of the Council for Research in Music Education, The International Journal of Music Education,* and this journal. He is currently writing a philosophy of music education for the Philosophy of Education Research Library and has had several compositions and arrangements published.

Part One: A Basic Sense of "Music"

There is a doctrine about the nature and value of music education that has become so widespread among scholars during the last forty years that it deserves to be called music education's official philosophy.[1] It is more commonly known as the philosophy of "music education as aesthetic education" (or MEAE).

At the core of the MEAE philosophy is a cluster of eighteenth-century theoretical concepts original to that small group of thinkers (including Baumgarten, Shaftesbury, and Hutcheson) who founded aesthetics and the aesthetic concept of art. According to the aesthetic concept, music is a collection of autonomous pieces, works, or aesthetic objects that exist to be contemplated in abstraction from their contexts of use and production. On the basis of these idiosyncratic social/historical notions, the MEAE doctrine claims that the payoff of aesthetic listening is a specific kind of knowledge. To explain the nature of this knowledge, MEAE repeats the central claims of Susanne Langer's widely disputed theory of music.[2] According to Langer, musical works are "presentational symbols" that offer "insight" into the general forms of human feeling. On the official view, then, music=objects, and the goal of music education is to develop the ability of listeners to gain the knowledge these objects are alleged to offer.

As I argue elsewhere, the philosophy of music education as aesthetic education is severely flawed.[3] Its central claims do not pass the test of critical analysis. In short, music education's official doctrine fails to provide a reasonable explanation of the nature and value of (i) music and (ii) music education.

Nevertheless, and in the absence of any alternative philosophies of music education, the practice of music education in many localities has shifted its focus from musical performing to musical consuming: from the active making of music in accordance with standards of excellence to the perception of recorded music during "listening episodes" (some of which include musical "producing" activities). Again, the official doctrine claims that the knowledge to be gained from music is to be found *not* in the actions of musical performing, but exclusively in the "aesthetic qualities" of musical aesthetic objects. In fairness, MEAE does proffer that "performance is a creative act and that the performance curriculum exists to involve students in that act."[4] But the logical weaknesses of MEAE's concept of "musical creation"[5] together with its insistence that performing is an "actualization process"[6] (something that serves "a piece awaiting actualization") only reaffirm that, on the official view, musical performing is secondary and subservient to "music-as-object." Moreover, in an attempt to bolster the notion that performing ought to remain secondary and subservient to awaiting pieces of music (that performing ought to be a means rather than an end in music education), one advocate of the doctrine takes it one step farther. In the proceedings of *The Crane Symposium* on the teaching and learning of music performance, Harry Broudy maintains that musical performing conceived as an end in itself is merely a matter of "skills" in the sense of "using a wrench or piling brick upon brick."[7]

In sum, music education's official philosophy, like aesthetics in general, neglects the epistemological significance of music making. It fails to acquit the *art* of music. Due to its myopic focus on music as a collection of isolated and autonomous objects, MEAE overlooks the more fundamental and logically prior consideration that music is something that people do and make. Put another way, music is a verb as well as a noun. As Nicholas Wolterstorff reminds us, "Before ever there were *works* of music, there was music."[8] Indeed, even in the West where the composing of "works" is an important aspect of what music *is*, composing and its outcomes exist *not* in isolation from musical performing, but *in relation to* the elaboration and development of musical performing.

The failure of MEAE in the above ways is unfortunate for at least three reasons. First, music is unquestionably an *art* in the classical Greek sense of the term. Music is an organized set of informed actions and understandings, transmissible by instruction, directed to making changes of a certain kind in materials of a certain kind.[9] Music, at root, is what musicians know how to do. On this view, the art of music is both a form of knowledge and a source of knowledge. For it is the art of music that potential music makers must learn. And to the aspiring music maker (performer, improvisor, composer, arranger, conductor, and so on), music is the body of knowledge that is the source of what he or she will know. More broadly, and as I will attempt to explain in a moment, musical performing offers an even more fundamental kind of knowledge.

Second, to many music educators in North America (and to many educators outside North America) music is equally a verb and a noun. Musical performing is conceived as a viable educational *end* for *all* children—something worth doing for its own sake. In terms of the MEAE philosophy, however, performing is never more than a *means*, even in performance-based programs. Performing, says Bennett Reimer, is "*the* major means for musical experience" in the performance program; in the general music context "it is a major means."[10] The aesthetic doctrine does not allow the possibility that musical performing could be an *end* in itself: that musical performing could be a form of thinking and knowing valuable for *all* children. Again, MEAE conceives performing as something that *serves* music by actualizing awaiting pieces of music.[11] In educational terms, then, MEAE conceives performing as a "*means* behavior,"[12] something that *supports* the development of aesthetic sensitivity.

Despite the dominance of the official philosophy, a large number of music educators (perhaps the majority) continue to see themselves as choral music educators, jazz educators, band directors, Suzuki string educators, and so on. The focus for many of these music educators continues to be music education through musical performing and the concomitant achievement of recognized standards of musicianship and musical excellence. Indeed, according to *The Crane Symposium*, music education conceived as musical performance is still "the biggest single preoccupation" of the profession."[13]

Unfortunately, many music educators continue to labor in the absence of a critically reasoned position on the rich and complex nature of musical performance. Put differently, many teachers for whom musical performing is a central pursuit have been left cold, or out in the cold, by music education's official philosophy.

Is it possible to argue that musical performing is an educationally viable *end* for all children? I believe it is. Moreover, and in addition to the possibility of providing alternative justifications for music education, more attention to music as *musicing* may offer something of equal importance: an improved understanding of what "performance" really is.

Third, and much more broadly, consider that what professional music schools offer in rigor they often fail to offer in practical relevance. For example, an important part of what aspiring music educators need to learn—namely, how "to music" and how to teach others "to music"—is just what too many professional music schools have the most difficulty teaching. Of course, music schools are not alone. Parallel forms of this difficulty haunt professional schools of medicine, architecture, law, engineering, and so on. Where do the problems lie? The central problem, says Donald Schon, is "an underlying and largely unexamined epistemology of professional practice."[14] In other words, there is a critical lack of understanding about what successful practitioners actually "know" when they *know how* to do something well. On one hand, we have little difficulty identifying surgeons, basketball players, singers, teachers (and so on) who *perform* well. We recognize quality in practical performances when we see it. On the other hand, we understand little about the nature of such performances. The tendency in the literature is to dismiss such practical "doings" in one of two ways: either coldly, as matters of mindless "skill" (in Broudy's reductionist sense of "using a wrench or piling brick upon brick"), or warmly, as the outcomes of talent, intuition, inspiration, and so on.

Unfortunately, such weak forms of thinking do nothing to open inquiry; they simply close it off. They are a convenient means of junking phenomena that elude our traditional assumptions and methods of research. More fundamentally, they combine to support a longstanding but false assumption:

that the physical actions involved in practical performances do not involve thought.

For the above reasons, it seems appropriate to spend a few moments considering "the art of music" as it manifests itself in musical performing (or what I will often call "musicing") as both a form of knowledge and a source of knowledge.

Part Two: Musicing as a Form of Knowledge

If musicing is a matter of making changes of a certain kind in materials of a certain kind, then the actions involved in musicing are neither natural nor accidental. The actions of musicing are taken up deliberately or "at will." But to act intentionally is to do something *knowingly*. For if (say) Jessye Norman is engaged in singing a song, then she knows she is doing it. She knows it because she decided to do it. And once having decided to do it, her choice of a particular course of action (singing a certain song in a certain way) necessarily required her to select a particular pattern of actions from many possibilities.

Now deciding and selecting require that options be considered and judgments be made. More importantly, deciding, selecting, and judging are all aspects of thinking. Deciding, selecting, and judging require a person to conceptualize what counts (and what does not count) in a certain context. In other words, the intentional actions involved in any kind of musical performing are thought-*full*.

More specifically, the thinking-acting relationship involved in musical performing is *not* a simple two-step sequence of think-act, think-act, and so on. Contrary to popular wisdom, action is not a matter of alternating mental and physical events.[15] If it was, then thinking would count as a primary action which would, in turn, demand its own preceding action thereby creating an endless regress.[16]

In musical performing, thought and action are interwoven like themes in a fugue. Intention not only governs action, it accompanies action. Saul Ross makes the same point in this example.

> A surgeon operating on a patient, moving his [or her] scalpel, is engaged in a form of behavior which is both theoretical and practical at the very same time. Each thrust of the scalpel, a movement which is done intentionally, is one wherein thought and action work tog' ther, not as two separate additive components nor as two consecutive events, one mental and the other material, but as one where the mental and the material components are interwoven. An action is a piece of overt behavior that cannot be detached or separated from the thought which motivates and directs it.[17]

John Macmurray describes intentional action as a process integrating the whole Self:

> The Self that reflects and the Self that acts is the same Self; action and thought are contrasted modes of its activity. But it does not follow that they have an equal status in the being of the Self. In thinking, the mind alone is active. In acting the body is indeed active, but also the mind. Action is not blind. When we turn reflection to action, we do not turn from consciousness to unconsciousness. When we act, sense, perception and judgement are continuous activity, along with physical movement. . . . Action, then, is full concrete activity of the Self in which all our capacities are employed.[18]

In musical performing, and in every case of intentional action one might care to name, the knowledge of the agent or practitioner (musician, surgeon, sculptor, skier, and so on) is *not* manifested verbally but *practically: it is manifested in the actions themselves*. Intentional actions are practical, nonverbal manifestations of thinking and knowing. Gilbert Ryle makes the point succinctly: "Overt intelligent performances are not clues to the workings of minds; they are those workings."[19]

That the intentional human action we call musical performing is cognitive, or thought-*full*, is the first step in expanding our understanding of what counts as knowledge. It leads us to a new epistemology, one in which knowing is not restricted to words and other symbols, but is also manifested in *doing*. In such an epistemology, one's actions are an expression of one's intelligence. Indeed, knowing, thinking, and conceptualizing are *not* limited to verbal means of expression. People know many things and hold many concepts that cannot be reduced to conventional language terms. On this view, music makers need not translate their practical form of knowledge into words to be deemed "knowledgeable" or "intelligent."

The above reflections bring us to a crucial distinction.

Knowing How and Knowing That

Almost fifty years after Gilbert Ryle published his seminal paper on "Knowing How and Knowing That,"[20] the concept of procedural knowledge (or knowing how) still lacks a secure place in philosophy generally and in music education philosophy particularly. The notion that thinking is a purely "mental" phenomenon, that thinking is only expressed verbally, still dominates many philosophical considerations of epistemology and cognition.

More broadly, centuries after the nature of practical knowledge was probed by Plato in *The Statesman* and by Aristotle in his writings on *acrasia*, and years after it was singled out for attention by William James, John Dewey, and Martin Heidegger (among others), practical or procedural knowledge remains secondary to propositional or declarative knowledge in the minds of many educators. Accordingly, music is most often conceived as a "branch of knowledge" in the traditional sense: as something one learns *about* and cognizes purely "in the mind." What these notions overlook is the concept of "knowledge" as a body of practice or a form of rational action. Let me explain.

Procedural knowledge and propositional knowledge are logically separable: one does not imply the other. For example, although knowing how to perform a composition on the trumpet requires that I understand how certain procedures produce certain results, such knowing does not imply or require that I be able to *say* why or how my actions produce the desired results. Understanding in the sense of verbalizable knowledge or propositional knowing-that may or may not be a feature of someone's overall understanding of what they know *how* to do. Indeed, no less an authority than Plato reminds us that the consistent quality of a person's doing and making is the only valid criterion of a person's rationality, not his or her ability or inability to *explain* his or her actions.

Of course, knowing how to do something effectively always implies an understanding, either tacit or verbal, of the *principles* that underpin the repetition of successful actions. Our ability to do something successfully on succeeding occasions demonstrates that we are able to distinguish, select, and redo what it is that works in our successful actions. Understanding, then, makes it likely that we can both apply and extend our proficient actions in future situations which will inevitably combine both old and new challenges. These ideas lead us to two important points.

First, the integration of a specific body of informed actions and understandings is the essence of "music" conceived as a verb. For whatever kind of musicing it is—Gregorian chanting or chamber musicing; blues singing or bluegrassing; ragtiming or rock and rolling—the musical outcomes we call chants, string quartets, blues, rags, "works of art," and so on are possible *only* because particular sets of informed actions and understandings are *portable*.[21] Every form of music (in whatever product forms we find it) is possible only because specific sets of informed actions and principles are carried over and adjusted from one situation or occasion to another. Every form of musical outcome owes its existence to actions that are "informed" in the fullest sense of being reliable, flexible, and *critical*.[22] The person who really knows *how* to sing or play the trumpet possesses *critical* competencies of assessment and adjustment.

Clearly, the proficient musical performer, like the proficient surgeon, must learn by experience and practice how to put principles into action. For, as Gilbert Ryle observes, "the intelligence involved in putting the prescriptions into practice is not identical with [and cannot be reduced to] that involved in verbally grasping the prescriptions."[23]

People who make music well through performing or improvising certainly have rules and principles in mind (either in the foreground or background of their awareness). But they also have broader and more flexible understandings which enable them to transfer and adapt what they know to meet the demands of new musical performance challenges and opportunities. In sum, it is not the case that for every informed action of musicing there is one verifiable principle that always applies and always works, and that can always be reduced to words.

The second important point here is that what we have been calling musical know-how involves a wide array of actions and understandings that mesh together like the wheels of a gear to impel us forward in our doing and making. Although the doublets skill and knowledge, rational action, cognitive skill and procedural knowledge suggest sharp distinctions, the suggestion is misleading.

The form of knowledge that musical performing represents is more aptly thought of as a continuum of knowing ranging from what can only be demonstrated in action ("sing the phrase like this . . .") to what can be fully explained in words ("the reason for doing this is that . . ."). In other words, says Vernon Howard, musical performers understand how to do something by their actions, by what works in their actions, and propositionally as their knowledge is expressed in the jargon of their practice or in more formal or scientific explanations.[24] Additionally, however, a music maker's understanding includes more than can ever be formulated in words (either technical or theoretical) and more than can ever be reduced to so-called "trained procedures."

The contrast between knowing-how and knowing-that has to do with the different contexts in which they are validated. Both Francis Sparshott and Vernon Howard suggest that to count as propositional knowledge, a person's beliefs must be supported by logical reasoning; to count as procedural knowledge, a person's ability must be exercised successfully in the appropriate circumstances.[25] Logical evidence validates knowledge *that*; practical success validates knowledge *how*. Unlike propositional knowledge, then, rational action cannot be assessed in abstraction from its context of use.

In sum, to continue talking in terms of musical know-how, or procedural musical knowledge, is both awkward and incomplete. Though useful, these double terms only perpetuate the misconception that musical performing is a matter of thought followed by action. They fail to communicate the complex *integration* of knowings that underlie artistic musical performances. Is there a single word that will do? Five possibilities come to mind.

Aristotle's single term was *techne*: "the ability to execute something with apt comprehension."[26] Unfortunately, we have no single word in English today that captures Aristotle's concept completely. The modern term "technique" will not do because one *techne* (one form of know-how) includes many techniques as well as many habits, routines, facilities, abilities, and so on. Similarly, although "skill" (from the Old Norse *skil* for understanding or competence) comes close to what we need, one kind of know-how involves a wide array of procedural and critical skills. "Art," in the original Greek sense, would be ideal. But the tendency today to use "art" as shorthand for "fine art" in the aesthetic sense only blurs the important distinction we are trying to make. Craft, from the Teutonic word *kraft*, meaning strength or manual dexterity, is a subset of skill.[27] Although craft later came to mean practical knowledge as well as discrimination and understanding, its old-fashioned sense of manual dexterity persists to the point that "musical craftsmanship" seems less than an appropriate term to communicate the wide range of capabilities (from habits to critical skills to problem-finding abilities) that the fluent demonstration of procedural musical knowledge includes.[28]

Perhaps other terms ought to be considered. I would be grateful for suggestions. Until then, I propose musicianship as the most apt term to cover both the horizontal range of capacities that constitute procedural musical knowledge and the vertical sense of competency, proficiency, or artistry we intend when we say that someone "really knows how" to make music. On this view, a masterful level of musicianship, or musical artistry, would be distinguished not only by a higher level of proficiency, but by an even wider range of abilities on the horizontal plane of musicianship (principally in the area of critical abilities).

At this point we have much of what we need to explain why and how musical performing is not only a form of knowledge but also a source of knowledge. The next requirement is an understanding of what it is that musicianship actually achieves.

The Concept of Performance

To cognitive psychologists, musical performances are quintessential examples of cognition in action because they require a performer to match a detailed cognitive representation of an auditory event with an equally complex mental plan of action. Nigel Harvey explains:

> A singer is to perform a song. She must learn the score (the stimulus array) off by heart as she will not have the opportunity to sightread it during the performance (resulting action). Here action cannot be directly controlled by a parameter that has been directly extracted [perceived immediately] from the environment. An internal representation (memory for the score) must act as a mediator. It is this internal representation that specifies the parameters that tune the function generators subserving singing performance.[29]

What Harvey's description leaves out, and what this essay has omitted until now, is an explanation of musical performing as something in and of itself. For musicianship is not organized and deployed merely to *produce* musical sounds. Musical performing clearly involves more than producing or actualizing awaiting "pieces" of music. What more?

A useful way to answer this question is to compare what a performer does when performing a composition with what a speaker does when he or she speaks in certain ways. Thomas Carson Mark has explored this comparison in a previous publication.[30] It is to him that I am indebted for several points in the following discussion.

Suppose I am playing tennis with a friend called Terry. After winning the third of three straight sets, Terry runs to the net and says: "David, do you give up now?" In reply, I utter these immortal words: "I have not yet begun to fight!"[31]

What have I actually done? First, I have quoted John Paul Jones. Quoting has two aspects: (i) producing another person's precise words and (ii) deliberately intending that one's own words match those of another. It is the deliberate *intention* to match someone else's precise words, says Mark, that makes an utterance a quote rather than merely a statement or an accident.

Second, in deciding to reply to Terry with the words, "I have not yet begun to fight!" (instead of simply saying "Yes" or "No!"), I am not merely quoting John Paul Jones, I am doing something more. I am using his precise words to *assert* something. I want my partner to understand clearly that I will not surrender as easily as she might think. Thus, says Mark, for a quotation to be also an assertion the speaker must deliberately intend that his or her quotation be understood as making some sort of pertinent point.

Quoting and asserting have important parallels in musical performance. When we say that a pianist is performing Bach's English Suite no. 2 in A Minor what we mean, in part, is that the performer is producing the precise sounds indicated in the score and deliberately intending that the sounds he or she makes are those that Bach stipulated. To this extent what a musical performer does is analogous to what a speaker does when he or she utters a quotation.

But there is obviously more to a performance than this. Producing music in the sense of quoting the score of Bach's English Suite no. 2 (or producing a musical work completely from memory) by actually sounding the indicated (or remembered) sounds is only part of what makes something a performance.

The "more" lies in the distinction between quoting something and asserting it. To be a performance, a performer must not merely quote what a composer has indicated, he or she must also intend to assert it in the sense that a speaker intends that a quotation be taken to mean something to his or her listeners. Mark explains:

> As is the case of assertion in language, the principal requirement for assertion [in musical performance] is intentional: . . . in music, the performer intends that the sounds he produces will be taken as having cogency, as articulating how things musically are. . . . The intention of a performer—the intention that makes his production of sounds a performance—is that his listeners will take the sounds produced to have this authority, this claim to attention which is analogous to the claim made on our belief by sentences that purport to be true.[32]

Quoting John Paul Jones to assert a point demands that I first understand what Jones means (that I interpret Jones correctly) and that I consider how Jones's words will be understood in context when I quote them to my tennis partner. Merely repeating words that one does not understand, or using them inappropriately in a given context, does not count as an assertion. Here is the critical point.

Performing a musical work, says Mark, is parallel to quoting someone else's words in order to assert something.[33] One produces the notated sounds of a musical composition (as one might speak Jones's precise words) in order to express one's concept or interpretation of the composition (as one might assert one's understanding or interpretation of what John Paul Jones meant by his words). Performing a musical work, then, is matter of understanding and interpreting as well as producing.

From this we see that what a musical performance offers is *not* simply an audible reproduction of what a score indicates or what a previous performer has done. Musical performing is not the auditory equivalent of reproducing a numbered copy of an original print. If it were, then any competent production of a musical composition would be deemed as important as any other. And this is not the case in actual performance practice or listening practice. Performing is not merely a means of actualizing musical compositions for people who cannot hear notation in their heads.

Musical performing, like asserting a quotation to make a point, projects a particular conception of a remembered or previously notated composition into a specific context in such a way that the performance *itself* is open to the criticism of others. A musical performance is something in and of itself: it is a personal conception of a composition projected through a performer's intentional actions which can be focused upon and scrutinized in terms of the actions themselves.[34]

So, in addition to knowing how to produce a given composition, a performer/conductor must build an informed and personal conception of a composition which he or she then "asserts," or projects, or communicates *not* verbally, but in his or her musical actions. Although Peter Kivy does not talk in terms of assertion or projection, he means something akin to this when he characterizes the musical performance of a composition as the "ultimate nonverbal description of the work."[35] Similarly, Alan H. Goldman calls the musical performance of a composition a nonverbal "explanation" of what a performer considers to be the important relations and values in a composition: "[A] performance . . . instantiates, exemplifies, or implicitly conveys the performer's interpretation. What it exemplifies or implicitly conveys is an explanation of the work and its elements, one that reflects the performer's view of the values inherent in the piece."[36]

A musical performance is a setting forth of a performer's/conductor's personal understanding and evaluation of a given composition. Through performing, a performer conveys his or her overall conception of a composition in relation to (a) what the composer must/could/should have intended, or (b) what past performers must/could/should have intended, or (c) what one thinks one's audience would expect to be brought out in a composition, or enjoy hearing brought out in a composition, or (d) some combination of all of these.

Altogether, then, a musical performance (in the classical Western tradition, at least) involves not one but *two* works of music. When pianist Ivo Pogorelich performs Bach's English Suite no. 2 in A Minor we have (i) the musical composition which is Bach's English Suite no. 2 in A Minor (BWV 807) and (ii) the musical work of Pogorelich: the knowledgeable, informed actions of the artist-pianist Pogorelich which project the Pogorelich performance/interpretation of Bach's English Suite no. 2. Thomas Carson Mark sums the point: "The performance is not simply an interpretation (though it requires or involves one) or a presentation (thought it requires that too since it includes producing an instance of the work): it is *another* work of art."[37]

Part Three: Musicing as a Source of Knowledge

The most common belief underlying the pursuit of music performance in music education is that musicing or performing is a *means* to an end. According to official doctrine, if students re-construct the steps involved in producing a musical work, then students will enhance their perception of and response to the work. As far as it goes, this notion of performing gets some things right. Producing, reproducing, or re-constructing a musical work (like quoting or reading lines from a play) *does* give students a sense of the intelligence involved in the construction of a musical work. Second, producing a musical work may also provide a basis for understanding the basic structure of similar works or aspects of dissimilar works. In this way, being able to produce sounds from notated scores, as students might learn in general music contexts, does breathe life into what might otherwise be studied and misunderstood as a collection of precious but distant objects. Unfortunately, the aesthetic concept of performing as a means overlooks some key points.

A person who deploys his or her musicianship in performing a score follows rules and principles developed by previous practitioners, but he or she is also free to adapt these principles. During performances, unforeseen circumstances are always a possibility. Therefore, every action or idea conceived must be evaluated in relation to a host of criteria that are not strictly aesthetic but social, practical, historical, artistic, and so on.

Something akin to this back-and-forth interaction of idea and outcome exists in all types of performances and in all fields of endeavor. In every human performance deserving the name, deliberate intentions are mobilized in actions that are at the mercy of possibilities beyond rules and predictions. Thus, while *producing* musical sounds provides an understanding of the predictable procedures of a practitioner's practice, interpreting and performing a musical composition enlighten students about how a musical performer copes with musical decision making, unpredictable opportunities, problems, influences, and so on. In short, real musical/interpretive performing involves both *generative* thinking and *evaluative* thinking.[38] Because the results of performing cannot be guaranteed in advance, the understanding gained during musical performance is not merely a duplication of procedures, it is a *live* deployment of the *whole* Self. The performer deploys musical thinking-in-action, knowing-in-action, and reflecting-in-action.

The upshot of this is that the educational value of music-as-musicing, or music as musical performing, is *not* secondary to the aesthetic concept of "music" as a collection of autonomous objects. If we shift our focus back to performing itself—to interpretive musical doing and making conceived strictly as the outcome of the doing and making in question[39]—we realize something rather important. We realize that the teaching and learning of musicianship provides students with *direct* knowledge of that "other" musical work: the interpretive musical performance itself. To understand, appreciate, and evaluate the intelligence or stupidity of a given musical performance requires an understanding of musical performing itself. This understanding, in turn, comes from learning how and knowing how to perform musically. Gilbert Ryle makes the same point: "Understanding is a part of knowing how. The knowledge that is required for understanding intelligent performances of a specific kind is some degree of competence in performances of that kind."[40]

In other words, learning to listen to music only by listening, without the benefit of learning how to perform music in the ways discussed above, provides only indirect knowledge of music as a "performative presence."[41] Although one can learn what to listen for in a composition without knowing how to perform music, learning what to listen for in a musical *performance* of a musical composition requires musicianship.

John Dewey makes a similar point in *Art as Experience.* To Dewey, what holds for the education of the musical performer holds also for the education of the listener. Dewey points out that in contrast to someone who is merely *able* to do something, the cognitive action abilities of the person who really knows *how* to do something renders the latter's perception of a given situation "more acute and intense and incorporates into it meanings that give it depth."[42] "But," says Dewey, "precisely similar considerations hold from the side of the perceiver."[43] To know what to listen for in a musical composition requires what Dewey calls "readiness" on the part of the listener's cognitive action abilities (or, in Dewey's words, "motor equipment").[44] Dewey puts it this way: "A skilled surgeon is the one who appreciates the artistry of another surgeon's performance; he [or she] follows it sympathetically, though not overtly, in his [or her] own body. The one who knows something about the relation of the movements of the piano-player to the production of the music from the piano will hear something the mere layman does not perceive."[45] To Dewey, the development of cognitive action abilities or procedural knowledge (or "motor preparation") is "a large part"[46] of any form of arts education.

In sum, as Dewey points out and as Vernon Howard reminds us, proficient performers embody within themselves the attitudes and critical skills of perceptive listeners as they deploy their musicianship in practical performances.[47] Proficient performers know what to listen for in a given work and, also, what to listen for in a musical *performance* of that work.

If we sustain our attention on music *as* performance a moment longer we gain another important perspective. To borrow an example from Israel Scheffler, consider that a child learning to play baseball will view the game quite differently if he or she understands what we mean when we say: "It's not whether you win or lose, it's how you play the game."[48] To be aware and give attention to *how* things are done—to deportment, style, quality of action, to traditions of performance practice, to one's actions as "a performance"—is to modify one's perception and understanding. Students so informed shift their sense of responsibility and the locus of their energy. A game is no longer simply a means to an end, but something in itself: *a process to be lived.* Playing a game takes on added meaning if one does it with style, sportsmanship, innovative strategies, and discipline. Even a game lost in the context of such awareness has value because it was played properly and well.

The above thoughts point us toward an understanding of why and how musical performing may be conceived as a source of knowledge that is both necessary for all and available to most through music education.

Musicing for Its Own Sake

The human species is defined, in part, as the species that "musics." Ethnomusicologists inform us that regardless of time and place, significant numbers of people in all cultures take up and pursue music making and the form of knowledge that music making involves. More often than not, music makers around the world are not professional musicians. In short, regardless of what kind of musicianship is involved, people tend to find musicing an enjoyable and absorbing experience for its own sake. Why?

To answer, we must consider a subject that is more fundamental than music education's official philosophy has considered: the existence and role of the conscious Self in human action.

According to Mihalyi Csikszentmihalyi, the evolution of individual consciousness depends upon our engagement in active pursuits that order consciousness or increase "constructive knowledge." These pursuits are experienced as more satisfying than normal experience because they are congruent with the goals of the Self. By investing our powers of attention, awareness, and memory in challenges that are not based exclusively on purposeful drives for biological and social satisfaction, "we open up consciousness to experience new opportunities for being that lead to emergent structures of the self."[49]

Now the conditions required to bring order to consciousness are essentially two: something to do (a challenge), and the capability to do it (know how). Put another way, the universal prerequisite for achieving constructive knowledge and its affective concomitant, enjoyment, is a *match* between the challenges one sees in a given situation and the know-how one brings to it.[50]

True, any challenge to which a form of know-how can be matched has the potential to yield constructive knowledge to the participant. At the same time, says Csikszentmihalyi, no activity can continue to offer constructive knowledge or sustain enjoyment for long unless both its challenges and its requisite know-how become more complex. For an activity to continue to offer constructive knowledge it must have an inner dynamism: it must be capable of providing the participant with increasing levels of challenge to match the increasing levels of know-how that come with pursuing the actions one enjoys. In other words, enjoyment occurs more often in endeavors that have a clear structure and progression of complexity. These conditions allow for the control and balance of challenges and developing know-how.

Musical performing is a major source of constructive knowledge because musicing provides progressive levels of challenge and complexity together with ways of improving one's musicianship to meet musical challenges. Musical performing provides the performer with knowledge about his or her own actions—their quality and affect—and, therefore, a sense of who he or she *is*.[51] The kind and quality of the actions an agent deploys, and the changes that his or her actions make in materials, contexts, audiences, and so on, provide "constructive knowledge" to the agent about his or her personal Self and the relation of that Self to others. Csikszentmihalyi explains: "Constructive knowledge is information about agentic powers (one's power to control one's life). Constructive knowledge is perhaps the most meaningful information that any of us can get."[52]

The musicianship one acquires and deploys in musical performances is the key to ordering consciousness, to gaining constructive knowledge. Through musical performing, students learn that their intentional actions result in significant changes and, therefore, produce achievements that would not have existed without their efforts. In each instance of performing/interpreting done musically, students invest their whole selves (including their cognitive action abilities) in the pursuit of molding a medium that has the possibility to model the whole range of ways that humans think about and experience reality.

The paradox of constructive knowledge lies in the fact that many of the things that people do to achieve it—to achieve the enjoyment of doing things for their own sake (e.g., musical performing, painting, writing, inventing, and so on)—produce practical outcomes of great interest, satisfaction, or usefulness to others.

On this view, one of the major contributions music education can make to students is to develop their musicianship. Because musicianship is a unique form of procedural knowledge, it is also a unique source of constructive knowledge. In this sense, making music for its *own* sake means making music for the sake of the Self. Moreover, musicing is limitless in the amount of constructive knowledge it can provide and, therefore, in the amount of *enjoyment* it can provide.

In sum, there are at least three general conditions to consider in music curriculum development. First, dabbling in musical producing activities will *not* yield any valuable knowledge about the Self.[53] Growth in constructive knowledge is correlated with growth in procedural knowledge: "The more refined and diversified one's skills are, the more information about the self's existence one can produce."[54] In a word, *depth* ought to take precedence over breadth in music education.

Second, music education ought to make the development of musicianship meaningful by enabling and permitting students to generate and evaluate musical performances that are personally meaningful and sequentially developmental. When student musicianship is carefully challenged with musical opportunities for personal interpretation, students are likely to achieve the enjoyment that comes with doing something that is worth doing for its own sake.

Third, it is essential that students develop their musicianship in the contexts of specific musical practices. That is, students must receive appraisals about their developing musicianship from teachers who *know how* to make music musically and who are themselves *connected* with the music-making procedures and principles of a given musical practice (e.g., choral singing, jazz improvisation, and so on). This might be called learning by "induction." That is, in the process of developing their musicianship, students become inducted into specific ways of musical thinking and specific goals and standards of music making.

Indeed, as Nicholas Wolterstorff points out, the internal goods (intrinsic values) of musical practices are available only to those who take part actively in the relational knowledge formed *around* and *for* the musical practice in question.[55] This is also what Csikszentmihalyi means when he says that "the most effective kind of constructive knowledge is that provided by the social environment."[56] Experienced members/teachers of a given musical practice legitimate the actions of each other and their students through their knowledge and preservation of appropriate reference norms, standards, and ways of being musical.

From this perspective, to enter into and take up a musical practice is also to be inducted into "a musical world." The musical world as a whole, and each musical world on its own (the jazz world, the choral world, and so on), rests on long traditions that provide the musical practitioners/teachers/students of these practices with constructive knowledge about who they are in relation to themselves, to each other, and to past others.

Indeed, the musical actions underlying the performances we value are themselves connected to long traditions of practice. To learn to make music is to resonate with the purposes, efforts, trials, and achievements of musicians and musical learners past and present. In learning how to perform/interpret music well, students not only come to understand the objective "aesthetic" qualities of works, they do much more: they connect with the efforts and contexts of composers and performers present and past. Hence they tend to empathize with these efforts and to connect with these musical practices and practitioners.

Conclusion

Is music a form of knowledge? Is music a source of knowledge?

Taken as a verb, music in the fundamental sense of musicing or musical performing is both a form of knowledge and a source of knowledge. To know how "to music" musically, to possess musicianship, is to possess a rich form of procedural knowledge. People who know how to interpret and perform musical compositions know these compositions as both products and performative presences. Musicianship provides direct access to the musical work (the composition) and to the art of *musicing* the musical work (the performance-interpretation of the composition).

Even more fundamentally, musicing is a major source of the most essential kind of knowledge a human being can gain: constructive knowledge. In this sense, musicing is an end in itself. Musical performing is something worth doing for its own sake. What this means, in turn, is that musicing is worth doing for the sake of the individual Self. A central task of music education is to make constructive knowledge accessible to students through the development of individual musicianship.

Can this be done? It is already being done; it has been done for decades by music educators who conceive musical performing not merely as a means, but as something worth doing by all students for its own sake. Such practices only need to be carried out more widely and more effectively.

How can music education philosophers contribute? If it makes sense to teach "music" as a complex process-product continuum, as a diverse human practice, then perhaps it is time for music education philosophers to help practitioners by paying more scholarly attention to the nature and value of musicing. Perhaps it is also time for music education philosophers to give more consideration to the kind of knowledge possessed by those music educators who already know how to induct students into the interplay of informed musical actions, understandings, practices, and traditions through the development of individual musicianship. More fundamentally, perhaps it is time for music education philosophers to put forth alternatives to music education's official doctrine.

In conclusion, consider the following words of Israel Scheffler. In emphasizing the vital connection between making and understanding in all areas of education, Scheffler provides an eloquent summary of the epistemological importance of musical performing in music education.

> To view past works—whether of art or science, or architecture, or music, or literature, or mathematics, or history, or religion, or philosophy—as given and unique objects rather than incarnations of process is to close off the traditions of effort from which they emerged. It is to bring these traditions to a full stop. Viewing such works as embodiments of purpose, style, and form revivifies and extends the force of these traditions in the present, giving hope to creative impulses active now and in the future. To value such traditions requires an emphasis on process. Conversely, the strength of our emphasis on process is a measure of the values our education embodies. Appreciating the underlying process does not, by any means, exhaust

the possibilities of understanding. But the understanding it does provide is a ground for further creativity in thought and action.[57]

NOTES

1. The resemblance between this sentence and the first sentence of Gilbert Ryle, *The Concept of Mind* (London: Hutchinson, 1949), is intentional for reasons that will become apparent shortly.
2. For a critical examination of the philosophy of music education as aesthetic education, as well as Langer's theory, see my article "Music Education as Aesthetic Education: A Critical Inquiry," in *The Quarterly of the Center for Research in Music Learning and Teaching*. In press.
3. Ibid.
4. Bennett Reimer, *A Philosophy of Music Education*, 2d ed. (Englewood Cliffs, N.J.: Prentice Hall, 1989), p. 193.
5. For a critical examination of MEAE's concept of creativity, see my article, "Music Education as Aesthetic Education: A Critical Inquiry." See also David J. Elliott, "The Concept of Creativity: Implications for Music Education," in *Proceedings of the Suncoast Music Education Forum on Creativity*, ed. John W. Richmond (Tampa: Music Department, University of South Florida, 1989).
6. Reimer, *A Philosophy*, p. 187.
7. Harry Broudy's statement appears in *The Crane Symposium: Toward an Understanding of the Teaching and Learning of Music Performance*, ed. Charles Fowler (Potsdam: Potsdam College of the State University of New York, 1988), p. 196.
8. Nicholas Wolterstorff, "The Work of Making a Work of Music," in *What Is Music? An Introduction to the Philosophy of Music*, ed. Philip Alperson (New York: Haven Publications, 1987), p. 115.
9. Cf. Francis Sparshott, *The Theory of the Arts* (Princeton, N.J.: Princeton University Press, 1982), pp. 25-57.
10. Reimer, *A Philosophy*, p. 169.
11. Ibid., p. 169, 187.
12. Ibid., p. 167ff.
13. Fowler, *The Crane Symposium*, p. viii.
14. Donald A. Schon, *Educating the Reflective Practitioner* (San Francisco: Jossey-Bass, 1987), p. 8.
15. Ryle, *Mind*.
16. Saul Ross, "Epistemology, Intentional Action and Physical Education," in *Philosophy of Sport and Physical Activity*, ed. P. J. Galasso (Toronto: Canadian Scholars' Press, 1988), p. 135.
17. Ibid., pp. 134-35.
18. John Macmurray, *The Self as Agent* (Atlantic Heights, N.J.: Humanities Press, 1957), p. 86.
19. Ryle, *Mind*, p. 57.
20. See *Proceedings of the Aristotelian Society*, vol. 46 (1945/46): 1-16, reprinted in volume 2 of Ryle's *Collected Papers* (London: Hutchinson, 1971), pp. 212-25.
21. Cf. Sparshott, *Theory*, p. 31.
22. Ibid., p. 26.
23. Ryle, *Mind*, p. 49.
24. V. A. Howard, *Artistry: The Work of Artists* (Indianapolis: Hackett, 1982), pp. 49-50.
25. Sparshott, *Theory*, p. 33; Howard, *Artistry*, pp. 49-50.
26. C. B. Fethe, "Hand and Eye—The Role of Craft in R. G. Collingwood's Aesthetic Theory," *British Journal of Aesthetics* 22 (Winter 1982): 43.
27. Arnold Whittack, "Towards Precise Distinctions of Art and Craft," *British Journal of Aesthetics* 42 (Winter 1984): 47.

28. Howard, *Artistry*, p. 26.
29. Nigel Harvey, "The Psychology of Action: Current Controversies," in *Growth Points in Cognition*, ed. Guy Claxton (London: Routledge, 1988), p. 70.
30. Thomas Carson Mark, "Philosophy of Piano Playing: Reflections on the Concept of Performance," *Philosophy and Phenomenological Research* 41 (1981): 299-324.
31. Ibid., p. 309. The example of quoting I use here is original to Mark.
32. Ibid., p. 312.
33. Ibid., p. 317.
34. Sparshott, *Theory*, p. 41.
35. Peter Kivy, *Music Alone: Philosophical Reflections on the Purely Musical Experience* (Ithaca, N.Y.: Cornell University Press, 1990), p. 122.
36. Alan H. Goldman, "Interpreting Art and Literature," *Journal of Aesthetics and Art Criticism* 48, no. 3 (Summer 1990): 207.
37. Mark, "Philosophy of Piano Playing," p. 321.
38. Israel Scheffler, "Making and Understanding," in *Proceedings of the Forty-Third Annual Meeting of the Philosophy of Education Society* (Normal: Illinois State University Press, 1988), p. 73.
39. Sparshott, *Theory*, p. 154.
40. Ryle, *Mind*, p. 53.
41. Howard, *Artistry*, p. 124.
42. John Dewey, *Art as Experience* (New York: G. P. Putnam's Sons, 1934, 1958), pp. 97-98.
43. Ibid., p. 98.
44. Ibid.
45. Ibid.
46. Ibid.
47. Dewey, *Art*, pp. 48, 50; Howard, *Artistry*, p. 185.
48. Scheffler, "Making and Understanding," p. 74.
49. Mihalyi Csikszentmihalyi, "Introduction," in *Optimal Experience: Psychological Studies of Flow in Consciousness*, ed. Mihalyi Csikszentmihalyi and Isabella Csikszentmihalyi (Cambridge: Cambridge University Press, 1988), p. 29.
50. Ibid., p. 30.
51. Mihalyi Csikszentmihalyi, "Phylogenetic and Ontogenetic Functions of Artistic Cognition," in *The Arts, Cognition, and Basic Skills*, ed. Stanley Madeja (St. Louis: CEMREL, 1978), p. 122.
52. Ibid.
53. Ibid., p. 124.
54. Ibid.
55. Cf. Wolterstorff, "The Work of Making a Work of Music."
56. Csikszentmihalyi, "Phylogenetic," p. 125.
57. Scheffler, "Making as Understanding," p. 77.

The Values of Musical "Formalism"

WAYNE D. BOWMAN

For decades the orientation called "absolute expressionism" has reigned virtually uncontested over North American music education philosophy. Leonard Meyer introduced the phrase in 1956[1] to describe the middle ground between two untenable and unpalatable extremes: "referentialism" and "absolute formalism." There are two senses in which we speak of musical expression, he reasoned; two ways in which feeling terms are commonly applied to musical experience. One construes expression as a designative or associative affair, and insofar as the feelings with which it is concerned are not strictly implicated by perception of the musical object, it is not truly musical. But a certain range of felt experience is authentically musical: that which is felt as one anticipates, follows, and experiences music's unfolding sonorous patterns.

Most of the wrangling as to whether music's essential meaning is expressive or formal arises from a failure to recognize the crucial distinction between musical and extramusical feeling, reasoned Meyer. Those who deny the possibility or relevance of emotional responses to music mistakenly assume all expression is referential by nature, a transitive affair in which the music itself serves as a springboard to associative or introspective indulgence. But since some expressive experience is indeed rooted in the perception of events objectively or "absolutely" in the music, one can profess both absolutism and expressionism without contradiction.

In Meyer's estimation, the real difference between "absolute formalism" and "absolute expressionism" was rather slight: adherents of the former focus upon musical relationships, while proponents of the latter focus upon the felt response to those relationships. Both are "actually considering the same musical processes,"[2] only from different perspectives. Formalist and absolute expressionist simply look at different aspects of the same thing, a

Wayne D. Bowman is Professor of Music Education at Brandon University, Manitoba. His most recent work has appeared in the *NSSE Yearbook: Basic Concepts in Music Education* and *The Quarterly* (Center for Research in Music Learning and Teaching). He is also a former contributor to this journal.

fact that "should make them allies rather than opponents."[3] In effect, Meyer's theory postulated a fundamental, dialectical relationship between feeling and form (between the subjective and the objective) in musical experience. The felt aspect of experience properly considered musical is wed to the perception of music's temporally unfolding formal "events."

The theory had its rather thorny problems, a fact which led Meyer to modify his original stance in important ways in ensuing years. But North American music education appropriated the early version for its philosophical base—with surprisingly little regard for Meyer's subsequent work. Judging from the use to which it was put, it seems the profession's primary attraction to absolute expressionism may have been the vindication of feeling as music's essence. What was originally a subtle theoretical position degenerated into a political slogan and, in the process, lost its essential relationship with musical form. All too often, absolute expressionism was presumed synonymous with expressionism,[4] a position frequently equated with the utter rejection of formalism.

Curiously, then, espousing absolute expressionism came to mean dismissing formalism. The effort to delineate a unique if somewhat restricted range of felt experience as genuinely musical became something of an ideological haven for those who wished to maintain, against a formalist foe, that the "essence" of music is feeling. Meyer's contention that there was "no diametric opposition, no inseparable gulf, between the affective and the intellectual responses made to music," that they were "complementary rather than contradictory positions,"[5] appears to have collapsed back into the very dichotomy he was trying to dissolve.

But the "formalism" described by advocates of absolute expressionism is a position espoused by no *musical formalist* of whom I am aware, a fact that seriously compromises music education's understanding of a profound and provocative body of musical philosophy.

In what follows, I do not intend to vindicate formalism (or anything else) as "the" philosophical base for music education. But we do need to be reminded that formal perception is a crucial feature of a great deal of musical experience and that we owe to philosophers of the formalistic bent many profound musical insights with equally profound educational implications. Toward that end, I will undertake glosses of the thought of four formalists: Kant, Hanslick, Gurney, and Meyer.

Formalism in Music Education Literature

Lest I be perceived as resorting to straw-man tactics, I feel obliged to substantiate my rather sweeping claims about musical formalism's misportrayal.

Even Meyer's original exposition contributed modestly to the problem, describing formalism (used synonymously with "absolute" formalism) as the rejection of "the possibility or relevance of any emotional response to music."[6] His objective was to show the excessive nature of pure formalism and to demonstrate its compatibility with absolute expressionism. But I want to suggest here that musical formalists did not really require this correction: their formalism was hardly as "absolute" or destitute of feeling as Meyer implied.

Still, a formalist arch-villain is quite a useful thing to have when it comes to demarcating ideological borders. Bennett Reimer's celebrated philosophy, for instance, tells us that the formalist's conception of musical experience "is primarily an intellectual one," one concerned with "the recognition of form for its own sake." For the formalist, music's significance is wholly self-contained, its beauty unlike any other, and the "so-called" musical emotion "is a unique one—it has no counterpart in other emotional experiences."[7] It follows, the explanation continues, that "the purer the appeal to intellect," "the freer from ordinary emotions," the better the work. In "the rarified realm of pure form, untouched by the homeliness of ordinary life, Formalists find their satisfaction and their delight. They do not expect to find much company there."[8]

Now, Reimer concedes that explicit commitment to this ultraformalistic position may not be all that common. But evidence of its implicit acceptance by music educators is, he apparently believes, fairly common. Formalists construe music primarily as "discipline" and teach isolated formal elements "for their own sake." Their notion of musical experience "consists primarily of using the mind to ferret out all possible tonal relationships." They endorse "teaching the talented and entertaining the remaining majority."[9] Since the formalist's musical experience is "a fragile thing suitable for some people but irrelevant for most,"[10] it is "a matter for the artistic elite, and it provides those few a special intellectual pleasure unlikely to be considered essential by any but that chosen few."[11]

I have quoted Professor Reimer rather selectively, in a way that may not be entirely fair to his exposition.[12] But the tenor of the message is clear: musical formalism is extreme, exclusive, elitist, cerebral, feelingless, and its values are inimical to the practice of musical education in an egalitarian democratic society.

Nor is Reimer alone. Foster McMurray, despite assurances that music education consists in the "cultivation of a capacity to attend to and to hear with understanding the kinds of music that qualify as serious,"[13] apparently doubts that formal perception is particularly relevant to that effort: "Anyone who makes serious music a significant part of his life will feel uneasy about this," says he.[14] Form is merely a technical means to the more important end of experiencing "*sensuous* esthetic quality."[15] Undue emphasis upon formal discrimination is due, he urges, to the pernicious influence of Platonic realism, which fails to recognize the primacy of "the sensuous excitement, the flowing line, the tensions and climaxes, the sometimes passion and always the contents of feeling or emotion that provide an aesthetic experience." Form, in short, is but "a naked mannequin waiting to be clothed."[16]

These brief remarks will suffice as a point of departure. To Reimer's list of formalism's deficiencies, McMurray adds a putative preoccupation with recognizing forms and the notion that formal phenomena are merely vehicles for the transmission of aesthetic (or sensuous, or expressive) content.

Let us examine what formalists themselves have to say about all this.

Kant

Since the theory Kant developed in his *Critique of Judgment* is particularly notorious for its formalistic propensities, it is a logical place to begin. Kant's formula for the purely aesthetic experience was "purposiveness without purpose" or, alternatively, formal subjective purposiveness. It consisted in a state of mental gratification afforded by exemplary unity and design, a pleasure altogether distinct from considerations of utility, sensory gratification, or conceptual understanding. Aesthetic experience was on the one hand *disinterested* and, on the other, *conceptless*.[17] The tenet of disinterest was intended to underscore the experience's essential freedom: he was anxious to disallow the seeming determinism of empirical accounts on which aesthetic pleasure was triggered by some "appetitive" stimulus, a mere state of sensory arousal and gratification. The tenet of conceptlessness, on the other hand, distinguished the aesthetic from the intellectual, stressing its freedom from reason's logical constraints: being purely and wholly subjective, aesthetic judgments contribute absolutely nothing to knowledge.[18]

And yet, in marked contrast to other subjective experience, that subjective experience which is aesthetic in nature claims a kind of universal validity.[19] Unlike purely personal judgments, the aesthetic judgment imputes agreement to all humans who apprehend the same thing in the same (contemplative) way. This it can do because all human minds work in the same fundamental manner, striving to wrest coherence and meaning from confusion and randomness. Reason is an auspicious product of such mental activity, but not the only one. In aesthetic experience, the imagination embraces a phenomenon in which it finds unity, completeness, and formal integrity—features characteristic of mind's rational constructions. The pleasure of the aesthetic moment, then, is due to the free play of these two cognitive powers, reason and imagination.[20] Aesthetic judgments are grounded in the feeling of pleasure which attends this play; but there are equally grounded in the *formal* relations which excite this play. Thus, Kant's aesthetic experience defies reduction to either sense or reason; it is rooted in feeling, but remains a cognitive activity rooted in the perception of form. Aesthetic pleasure is pure, contemplative pleasure, untainted by sensual, practical, or intellectual intrusions.

This perspective offers several noteworthy contributions to the topic at hand. First, here is a formalism that is not indifferent or hostile to feeling: indeed, feeling is a constitutive feature of aesthetic judgment. Nor is such experience purely cerebral: on the contrary, Kant goes to great pains to distinguish it from intellectual experience. Since beauty is what *pleases in form*,[21] its pleasure is cognitive yet not conceptual: it consists in a distinctive satisfaction grounded in perceived pattern and relationships; its source is formal, and its pleasure unique, arising from the harmonious free play (one is tempted to say "resonance") of the mind's cognitive faculties.

To be sure, Kant's aesthetic pleasure is a unique kind of felt experience, distinct from sensation, from everyday emotion, and from whatever pleasures attend conceptual activity. But since aesthetic experience is rooted in mental functions all humans share, there is little reason to consider it an exclusive, elitist affair.

But of course, this account has conveniently omitted Kant's rather disparaging remarks about music itself.[22] Music was not, as we might reasonably have expected him to conclude, the perfect example of conceptlessness, of formal subjective purposiveness. It was too fleeting and sensuous, too transient and intrusive to sustain the disinterested contemplative pleasure he called aesthetic. Music is an agreeable art rather than a fine one; more a matter of enjoyment than of culture.[23] But one aesthetic defect (so to speak) music shares with all the "arts": since its proper experience rests upon an understanding of *what kind of thing it is supposed to be*, some estimate of its *perfection in kind*, its beauty is dependent or adherent, not purely aesthetic.[24]

Genuinely musical beauty is not conceptless in the way natural beauties are. It is grounded in, among other considerations, stylistic awareness: were musical experience purely aesthetic, awareness of the particular kind of music being experienced would be irrelevant; one would deploy the same kind of interpretive schemata for plainsong as for jazz or a fugue. This kind of (purely aesthetic) musical experience is clearly possible; but it is only marginally musical (if that).[25] If we take this as establishing the insufficiency of aesthetic pleasure to judgments of music (a position that seems consistent both with Kant's concept of adherent beauty and the extra-aesthetic basis of many of his criticisms of music), it is not unreasonable to speculate that even Kant may have found his formal "mannequins" a bit underclothed when it came to art.

It would seem to follow (although here we take leave of Kant) that, to the extent a truly musical understanding implicates something of a dialectical relationship between aesthetic judgment and awareness of appropriate stylistic practices (to say nothing of myriad other contextual concerns), an adequate account of it is obliged to embrace both aesthetic pleasure and mind. If this tips the scales toward the intellectual pole, it neither renounces feeling nor declares it irrelevant. Kant did not proclaim music a *purely* intellectual affair: indeed, its most severe shortcoming as aesthetic object was precisely an overabundance of feeling. In any event, to this formalist, form and the felt pleasure of its experience were inseparable. That he found music too "feelingful" was unfortunate for him, but hardly an indication of its total denial in his theory.

Hanslick

In *On the Musically Beautiful*, Hanslick argued that music's only true content is its "tonally moving forms."[26] His caustic characterizations of expressionists are legendary. They preferred feeling music to hearing it; they swayed and wallowed in trancelike states which might as well have been drug-induced; their experience of music was purely sensory, more animal than human.[27]

Music is neither about the arousal nor the representation of feelings or emotions, he argued: these are adventitious effects and resemblances, not what music essentially is. Feeling theories spawn musical distortions of two kinds: the logical and the pathological.[28] In the former, speculation and presuppositions contravene or distort full perception;[29] the latter consists of little more than introspective emoting, fueled by "flickering impressions." Roses are fragrant, he reasoned, but that hardly establishes the representation of fragrance as their content. Nor does one learn what is particularly important about a wine by drinking it to the point of intoxication.[30] In short, both the logical and pathological expressionist fallacies divert and distract us from what they purport to explain. Music's true content is nothing but sonorous, tonal forms; music "speaks not merely by means of tones, it speaks only tones"; and genuinely musical experience is a contemplative "enjoying," not an "undergoing."[31] Music must not be misconstrued as a revelatory window on anything but itself, as meaning anything beyond itself, or as a springboard to any but a range of feeling that is uniquely and distinctly musical.

So entertaining are Hanslick's attacks on musical "enthusiasts," his positive thesis often gets lost in the fray. The proper focus of genuinely musical perception, he urged, is "just this one particular beauty."[32] Its distinctive pleasure consists in a state of mental alertness (the "worthiest and most wholesome" manner of listening)—the mental satisfaction which derives from actively anticipating and following music's unfolding designs, "here to be confirmed in [one's] expectations, there to be agreeably led astray."[33] Its significance resides not in subjective musings, but in a sonorous, "tonally moving" pattern. Simply put, feeling is not sufficient to musical experience. Unfortunately, Hanslick often sounds as though he were arguing feeling has absolutely nothing to do with musical experience, as if it were altogether dispensable and beside the point.

On the contrary, Hanslick was acutely sensitive to music's felt nature. He did not seriously question music's capacity to arouse feeling, only the musical relevance of many or most emotions so aroused. He appears to have been quite surprised at the uproar his book created: far be it from me, he says in effect, to underestimate the significance of musical feeling,[34] to denigrate the marvelous "otherworldly stirrings" it awakens "by the grace of God."[35] He also concedes the possibility of congruence between music's tonal motions and those of certain aspects of emotion; only, he urges, similarities simply do not implicate the kind of conclusions of which expressionists are fond.

Hanslick himself made generous use of expressive predicates in his own musical criticism.[36] But such language is a kind of metaphorical shorthand, he thought, justified by its economical utility for describing what is ultimately ineffable (or more precisely, *purely musical*).[37] Music's pleasure and its meaning are strictly its own, and we must be vigilant against assumptions and practices that would lure us away from the audible patterns of tonal motion that are music's true essence.

It is tempting to portray Hanslick as an arrogant elitist whose conception of musical experience is abstract, cerebral, and inaccessible to any but a gifted few. And yet, it seems to me he would urge that both his moving forms and the "otherworldly stirrings" they awakened were there for anyone who would listen in an unbiased and undistorted way. His considerable disdain for musical "enthusiasts" was based, it seems to me, not so much on their *incapacity* as their *disinclination* to listen musically. Perhaps his contempt was directed less at the common man than the aesthetician, the critic (might we add the music educator?): people who should know better yet persist in deluding an unsuspecting public.

Nor were Hanslick's forms empty, cerebral abstractions—skeletal affairs, unclothed mannequins. They were concrete, kinetic, vital.[38] They *moved*. Like Kant's, Hanslick's formalism embraced both feeling and mind, yet steadfastly refused to be reduced to either. Despite its obvious excesses, it sought middle ground between barbaric sensationalism (the "pathological" extreme) and the speculative extravagances of idealism (the "logical"). The *properly musical* experience must have as its focus perception of sonorous pattern, since what is uniquely musical about its "feelings" or "ideas" is far more important than anything nonmusical it stimulates or resembles.

Hanslick argued the necessity for a perceptual focus in musical experience while, in his own inimitable fashion, denying conceptions of music as stimulus or reference. His forms were not conceptually abstract, but perceptually rich. They were not empty and skeletal, but replete and vital. And the experience they (music's tonally moving forms) engendered was not the affectively barren, intellectual achievement of the specially endowed, but one available to all who would listen.

Gurney

Edmund Gurney's *The Power of Sound* was far more evenhanded than Hanslick's combative treatise. In a manner surprisingly like modern philosophical method, Gurney patiently explored the use of words for subtle sources of confusion and drew upon ingenious musical examples in support of his points. Music, according to his view, was "Ideal Motion": a phenomenon positively distinct from the experience of sound and one which was ultimately inexplicable since, he contended, one's sense of musical "rightness" arises from a discrete musical "faculty" of mind. Any intellectual account of musical beauty can as easily generate trite music as beautiful, thought he.

Gurney drew a sharp distinction between higher and lower senses. Unlike lower sense organs, the human eye and ear have a unique capacity to grasp their perceptua in more-or-less discrete units which may be proportionally combined to achieve pattern or form. This relational, constructive activity is essential and unavoidable in the exercise of the higher senses: only rarely is their activity purely sensory. The pleasure we derive from use of the higher senses is inextricably wed to the perception of *form*: indeed, "the world of Beauty is preeminently the world of Form."[39]

Beyond a common capacity for quantitative perception, however, eye and ear diverge radically. The characteristic achievement of sight is distinct, external objects. Sounds, on the other hand, "present no certain group having the character of an object."[40] Because of this, Gurney thinks, everyday visual experience rightly claims superiority to hearing. Yet when it comes to the experience of Beauty, the eye's superiority is usurped by the ear. In *musical* experience, the ear is no longer concerned with mere auditory acuity, with the nonsonorous associations so crucial to our experiences and uses of "unformed sound." In auditory experience *which is musical*, one enters an "otherwise unimaginable world"[41] in which mind and sense achieve wholly unique integration, through the perception of sonorous form.

Gurney draws a further distinction between representational and presentational arts. In the former, a subject matter "exists externally to and independently of" the work. As a presentational art, music is encumbered by no obligation to extra-artistic subject matter. The auditory forms music presents to sense do not *convey* subject matter; rather, they *constitute* it.[42] Music's content is its form. Music is not "about" a subject matter, it consists of *musical subjects*. Nor is sound the material of which music is constructed: rather, its material is a system of notes. Thus, music's subject matter, music's materials, music's forms—all are absolutely and exclusively musical. Nothing like them exists anywhere outside music. All the fuss about musical expression obfuscates the essential truth that before it can possibly be *expressive*, music must first be *impressive*.

An "abstract form as addressed to the ear,"[43] music is a wholly unique phenomenon to which we apply visual metaphors at considerable peril. Visual and spatial terms like symmetry, line, mass, contour, and color subtly distort what they purport to describe, because visual and musical experience are so profoundly different. Where, for instance, is the visual counterpart of melody? Not line, says Gurney, for it lacks melody's distinctive transience, its moment-by-moment progression, not to mention the proportional temporal and pitch relations between each melodic tone and every other. Music's forms are fundamentally processive and have none of visual form's "impression of conspiring parts all there at once." And musical form is far less tolerant of alteration than visual form: it has, Gurney says, a "greater definiteness." There is in music "nothing analogous to an *outline* or skeleton of lines, capable of being presented or imagined alone";[44] in fact, the effort to represent a beautiful melody, even by its contour or most prominent pitches, yields "not an *imperfect* notion, but *no* notion of the actual form."[45] What is mere ornamentation in visual form is essence in musical form.

Gurney's musical form is emphatically not architectonic. This sense of form ("rounded binary" or "rondo," for instance) "has no beauty or meaning for us, no ideal place in our imagination. . . . [It has] little essential connection with the individual beauty of the forms which it embraces and unites." Indeed, these are not music's essential forms at all, only abstract conditions within which real musical form may be presented. Unlike visual form, musical form "makes only occasional and temporary appearances on earth, and builds there no permanent habitations or temples; being literally the 'queen of the air.'"[46]

Even motion is not, except in a very peculiar sense, something of which music is capable. Music's motion is not physical, but purely ideal. So once again, music's resemblance to things nonmusical is radically overestimated. Music is representative in neither the iconic, imitative sense, nor in the metaphysical, revelatory sense. It is simply a phenomenal presentation. Its forms "cannot be abstracted from the continuous process . . . which constitutes our perception of them." This patterned, sonorous, "ideal" motion that constitutes musical beauty is absolutely unique: it has "no parallel outside Music."[47]

As to Gurney's conception of how ideally moving auditory form is perceived, I cannot possibly improve upon his own words: it presses forward

> through a sweetly yielding resistance to a gradually foreseen climax; whence again fresh expectation is bred, perhaps for another excursion . . . round the same centre but with a bolder and freer sweep, perhaps for a fresh differentiation whereof in turn the tendency is surmised and followed, to a point where again the motive is suspended on another temporary goal; till after a certain number of such involutions and evolutions, and of delicately poised leanings and reluctances and yieldings . . . the sense of potential and coming integration which has underlain all our provisional adjustments of expectation is triumphantly justified.[48]

Musical form is also unique in its remarkable capacity to create in us a "sense of entire oneness with it, of its being . . . a mode of our own life."[49] And though, like speech, music's forms give the remarkable impression of being "*something said*, an utterance of imperative significance," their essential significance does not extend beyond themselves. "So far as they are impressive, [music's forms] are each new and unique things, not like new expressions or postures, or alterations and reminiscences, of known things: each fresh melodic presentation which is profoundly felt is felt as till then *wholly* unknown."[50] In short, "We can yearn, triumph, and so on in purely musical regions";[51] and certain affinities to extramusical feelings notwithstanding, the emotions implicated in any given piece of music will invariably resemble more closely those encountered in other compositions by the same composer than anything else.

Gurney's is an elegant, impassioned plea that we not lose ourselves in "barren generalities" that "imply no vestige of beauty or vitality," that are as descriptive of the dead as they are the living.[52] No naked mannequins here. Nor, so far as I can discern, any elitism or unfeeling intellectualism. To be sure, Ideal Motion is an achievement of mind; only in contrast to intellect's conceptual freedom, music has a "much shorter tether." Nor can intellect ever presume superiority over musical perception's instinctive and inexplicable sense of cogency and rightness. Musical beauty is no achievement of mere intellect, but a rare and precious jewel "which must often be long and diligently searched for."[53] And the musical faculty of mind, to which that search must be entrusted, is the birthright of all. What Gurney calls the "indefinite" way of hearing music—the predominantly sensuous response, in which music is primarily a "congenial background for . . . subjective trains of thought and emotion," just "so much moving and coloured sound"—may accompany, yet never replace, the perception of musical form. If Gurney's "mode of hearing which follows and distinguishes the motives as they pass"[54] is relatively rare, it is not so much because it is a capacity given only to a gifted few, but rather because it requires cultivation. The "definite" way of hearing music is difficult "not in the sense that an average ear cannot comprehend" but in the sense that it is rarely achieved merely "at a glance."[55]

Meyer

The decision to include Leonard Meyer in a collection of formalist sketches will seem curious to anyone whose acquaintance with Meyer's thought is limited to his early work, since the confusion surrounding his doctrine of "absolute expressionism" was, after all, where we began. But no less an authority than Meyer himself has characterized much of that early work as "Romanticism in quasi-empirical garb."[56] In the ensuing thirty years, his thought became unabashedly and unapologetically formalistic, with little concern for the issues of musical "emotion" or "meaning." Music is, he was eventually to conclude, a "nonsemantic art."[57] Meyer's earlier fondness for psychological speculation gave way to musical criticism, an undertaking that, as he puts it, seeks to "understand and explain the relationships among and between musical events, not the responses of individual listeners. Those we must leave to . . . the psychoanalysts."[58]

An exhaustive inventory of the problems which plagued absolute expressionism is well beyond the scope of this modest essay.[59] But among its more important problems was a persistent gravitation toward subjectivism, such that musical value was a function of a listener's expectations (or later, "anticipations"). Not just any listener's feelings and responses are musically relevant, Meyer eventually decided: only those of the *competent listener*, one who is stylistically fluent and whose attention is occupied by qualities, events, and relationships discernibly there, in the music. Listen to the music, to the presentational facts, Meyer appears to have concluded, and feeling will take care of itself.

Accordingly, Meyer's mature theory is concerned not so much with listeners' expectations as with music's *implications*.[60] It does not dismiss the listener's complicity in music, but does insist the competent listener's anticipations be grounded in objective musical "universes of discourse," in *musical styles*. To one who understands[61] a musical style, different alternatives for pattern continuation are attended by varying probabilities: not in a strict mathematical sense, but some are more likely and some less so. For the fluent listener, then, stylistic assumptions and constraints constitute sufficiently objective facts to justify calling what they generate implications. Genuinely musical pleasure consists in the appreciation of the ingenuity, or the economy, or the elegance, or the richness of particular solutions to what one might call stylistic problems. Accordingly, one may marvel at a particular turn of musical phrase again and again: instead of becoming banal, particularly imaginative musical ideas are cherished all the more as they become familiar. On this account, musical pleasure consists in "neither the successions of stimuli *per se*, nor general principles *per se*, but the relationship between them."[62] Thus, genuinely musical appreciation entails implicit awareness of compositional or performance alternatives. Appreciating the ingenuity or elegance of a particular musical event is equally a function of one's awareness, however tacit, of choices not made, of roads not taken.

Nor did the structural-syntactical basis of Meyer's early expressionist theory satisfactorily account for music's kinetic or corporeal dimension: its activity, its vitality, its energy. An important feature of his later theory, then, is an explicit recognition of the *motion* that figured so centrally in Hanslick's and Gurney's accounts. An essential feature of musical pattern lies in its processive nature. Processive relationships, both proactive and retroactive, keep Meyer's musical forms alive, prevent their reduction to abstract skeletal affairs.

Meyer's formalism is built upon the interactions between and among what he calls syntactical and statistical musical parameters: interactions that may be implicative, conformant, processual, or hierarchical in nature. The labels are cumbersome, but the basic thesis is clear and self-consistent: music consists of sounds perceptibly patterned, formal arrangements grounded in and undergirded by stylistic interpretive schemata. The most musical of musical pleasures consists in the discrimination and appreciation of these relationships, a kind of "goalless mental play."[63] That this threatens to dehumanize the musical response, transforming it into an excessively intellectual affair, Meyer flatly denies: quite the contrary, "to entertain ideas—to see pattern and structure in the world—and to be entertained *by* ideas is both the most human and the most humane condition to which man can aspire."[64] Music should be valued for its "elegance of design and ingenuity of process,"[65] for its "relational richness."[66] Its principal pleasures derive from "the fun and fascination of exercising that faculty which is most peculiarly ours: namely the human mind."[67]

Meyer's theory does not categorically deny the relevance of felt responses to music. But neither does it enshrine affect or feeling as musical essence. He readily concedes the existence of associative, ethetic, and even referential responses, but these are neither necessary nor sufficient to musical experience; *perceptibly patterned sound*, on the other hand, is at the very least *necessary*: "It is not that art no longer represents, it often does; or that it is no longer expressive, it frequently is; or that it has ceased to be socially relevant, at times it may be so. Rather . . . content and meaning are no longer considered to be definable and explicable apart from the specific materials of a work of art and their structuring in that work."[68] Apparently, such things as representation, expressiveness, and social relevance are characteristics music may or may not have. Form, however, is necessary to musical experience.

Formalism Reconsidered

It is time to stop and consider what this visitation of four prominent formalists may have shown us, aside from the folly of attempting to do justice to subtle and complex ideas in such cursory fashion. To begin, I think we must conclude that formalism of the "absolute" variety (if by that we mean one given to the purely intellectual contemplation of abstract forms) is principally a fabrication of formalism's detractors. The fact that a "pure" musical formalism of this type is untenable means little if no one espouses it. None of the theories examined here insists on the absolute irrelevance of feeling to music. When formalism denigrates emotivist or expressionist accounts of music, it does so primarily for the salutary purpose of establishing the uniqueness and autonomy of a range of feeling that is genuinely musical. To say that music is a closed system is not necessarily to proclaim all feeling totally irrelevant. The formalist's concern, rather, is to distinguish between the musically contingent and the constitutive, between music's effects and the music itself, between what music may be and what it must be. Sonorous form, perceptible pattern, argues the formalist, are necessary to musical experience. Music may be (and often is) expressive, but expression (or even having "expressive" character) is neither a necessary nor a universal musical attribute.

The form espoused by musical formalists is neither a Platonic abstraction nor an architectonic skeleton. Musical formalists are not concerned with "recognizing" general forms, but with perceiving the richness of relationships within and among sonorous events against an interpretive template of the stylistically possible or probable. The musical formalist's forms are, as Hanslick insisted, not empty but *full*. And music's forms *move*, even (if Kant is to be believed) to a fault. Musical form is a fundamentally processive thing, something experientially rooted, something through which one lives. As Arnold Berleant puts it, musical form is not "the structure within which figures or themes are placed and developed" so much as it is "the processive shape of auditory experience."[69]

Finally, it seems clear that musical formalism does not necessarily implicate elitism. Many musics are indeed fragile, subtle, and demanding; but according to the formalist, musical perception derives from universal human capacities and propensities—from psychological universals. Such capacities may require and benefit from cultivation, but they are there in us all. The necessity for cultivation, I feel certain the formalist would urge, is something one would expect an educational profession to embrace with enthusiasm rather than suspicion. After all, many of life's deepest pleasures are acquired tastes.

While formalism's detractors portray it as an extreme position, its advocates conceive it as a centrist one—the reasoned alternative to reductions of music to pure sensation or pure cerebration. Grounding musical experience in perceptible pattern differentiates it from sensation and at the same time distinguishes it from abstract reasoning.

Given its resolve to let music be what it is instead of engaging in flights of fancy inspired by things it may resemble, one might argue with some justification that formalism is *potentially* more ideologically neutral than certain other philosophical orientations:[70] that, to the extent it makes fewer assumptions as to what all music should be or do, it may be more descriptively pluralistic and flexible. Instead of referring judgments of musical value to metaphysical assumptions or extramusical emotion, for instance, the formalist refers them to systems, relationships, structures, and conventions; to stylistic assumptions, priorities, and imperatives; to intramusical concerns. So the formalist's method is more likely critically exploratory and descriptive than sensually indulgent or interpretive.

But formalism's relative neutrality only goes so far. There is, after all, no such thing as complete value neutrality or knowledge without a viewpoint. What are formalism's biases? We might well expect it to prefer the conscious over the mystical and intuitive, the explicable over the ineffable. It clearly values order over chaos, perceptual awareness over blind sensation. It does tend to value complexity over simplicity (although apparent simplicity may be an extraordinarily complex affair). As an "aesthetic" orientation, it tends to value contemplating music over "doing" it. It tends to value structure over process.[71] And, I think, it sometimes tends to underestimate the sociocultural embeddedness of musical experience—overestimating, that is, the universality of human perceptual/conceptual styles.

We might concede, then, that formalism's tendency to focus upon the "objective," artifactual side of music can and often does lead to the underestimation of its experiential aspect: the living-through, the fact of human agency, the joy of "doing" music.[72] But is this a fatal defect or only a tendency of which to be wary? Notably, each of the *musical formalists* whom we have examined has attempted to maintain a dialectical relationship between these two polarities, such that musical form remains *vital form, processive structure.*

What might be the implications of a formalistic perspective for music education? Once more, the scope of this essay will allow us to do little more than hint of possibilities. First, it seems rather doubtful that a formalistic educational perspective based on the views explored here would extensively indulge currently fashionable notions like music's presumed isomorphic relation to patterns of sentience or music as a "teacher of feeling." One might expect formalism to espouse as its goal the enhancement of musical perception rooted in musical patterns and processes, on the assumption that to the extent this occurs, feeling will take care of itself.

Formalism need not deny the expressive quality of a significant range of musical experience. Nor need it dismiss the interesting similarities among the arts upon which general aesthetics is fond to speculate. But, I think the musical formalist would insist, neither a fascination with feeling nor parallels among the various arts should divert instructional efforts from the wholly and uniquely musical. This focus, together with a tenaciously descriptive/critical instructional method, would (I am confident the formalist would maintain) enhance the credibility and nobility of music education—not undermine it.

Second, formalists might well argue that in contrast to intuitive, mystical theories on which "insight" simply comes in a flash, their perspective offers music education both something teachable and a way of teaching it. Formalism maintains the cultural objectivity of stylistic conventions, constraints, and values: phenomena that must be learned and can be taught. Cultivating perception of musical implications, relationships, and patterns seems more compatible with the instructional enterprise than, say, the intuitive grasp of "expressive import," failing which one has few choices but to back up and have another go at it. Instead of abstract metaphysical or general aesthetic principles, a musical formalism would refer judgments of worth to questions of musical style. An indispensable feature of musical instruction would thus consist in the careful consideration of stylistic criteria applicable to the particular music in question, and their revision as perceptual discrimination grows in its sensitivity.

Third, while it is not an intellectual orientation in the sense its detractors would like to have us believe, musical formalism does hold musical experience to be the exercise of a distinctive human cognitive capacity. A reasonable corollary for musical education would be a commitment to developing that capacity to its fullest, to enhancing its sensitivity to and delight in what are deemed the worthiest of its objects. Musical formalism, then, would be committed to nurturing a preference for musics (plural) which are the very best in their kinds. But this is elitism only in a very peculiar sense since, after all, the democratic ideal is more given to equality of access to the best than universal access to mediocrity. The formalist holds that all human minds are similarly structured, that the appreciation of pattern and coherence is a universal human propensity—not that these are the endowments of a talented few. I see little reason to accuse the formalist of proposing, as did Aristotle, one grade of music for the nobility and another for the masses. If what formalism believes to be purely musical listening is difficult to sustain (and who among us never lets attention stray?), this does not detract from its value as an educational ideal or as a valid means for distinguishing (at least with regard to certain musics) sensitive musical judgments from naive self-indulgence.

Fourth, however circumspect it may be of claims to expression as the constitutive feature of all music, formalism need not be cold and unfeeling. The otherworldly stirrings Hanslick described are no small part of music's enduring human importance. Its experience delivers us from the obnoxious dualisms of everyday life, often conferring upon experience a wholeness, a richness, a unity encountered nowhere else. And in this limited sense, the formalist can concede that the felt quality of musical experience is indeed life serving. Yet, such feeling is musical feeling, one intimately wed to music's uniquely moving sonorous forms. Feeling undergirds *all* human experience, even the formalist's; but it is the *distinctiveness* of musical feeling that is important, not spurious or adventitious resemblances.

In 1956, Meyer characterized musical understanding as a "matter of grouping stimuli into patterns and relating these patterns to one another."[73] It may well be more, the formalist concedes, but this much it must be. To be fully understood or fully felt, music must first of all be fully perceived; and musical formalism is obstinate in its determination to rivet attention to the music.

The question remains (though it is not quite the one we set out to examine), Does all this ultimately discredit "absolute expressionism"? When the latter serves as an ideological banner, I rather hope so: anything that threatens to restrict our access to such important insights as have been explored here I believe we can do without.[74] But of course the excesses of a position's advocates do not totally negate its validity. This much, at least, I think we must concede to the absolute expressionist: music does stir us, move us—if in purely musical realms. But it is crucial to note that to live up to its claim to "absolutism," this account of musical expression must remain to a significant extent formalistic. It is a cognitivist theory, not an emotivist one. The particular range of feeling implicated in the absolute expressionist's "expression" is necessarily circumscribed by musical perception, which is to say, perception of sonorous and processively unfolding patterns, configurations, and relationships. Enhancing sensitivity to these is thus among the paramount concerns of music instruction.

NOTES

1. Leonard B. Meyer, *Emotion and Meaning in Music* (Chicago: University of Chicago Press, 1956).
2. Ibid., p. 4.
3. Ibid.
4. It was this, I presume, which motivated rather precarious efforts to forge a syn-

thesis of Meyer and Langer—despite a rather stark contrast between the fairly circumscribed range of feeling which interested Meyer and Langer's everything-that-can-be-felt thesis.

5. Meyer, *Emotion and Meaning*, pp. 39-40.
6. Ibid., p. 3.
7. Bennett Reimer, *A Philosophy of Music Education*, 2d ed. (Englewood Cliffs, N.J.: Prentice-Hall, 1989), p. 23.
8. Ibid., p. 25.
9. Ibid.
10. Ibid., p. 26
11. Ibid., p. 27. Note that while the formalist makes this unreasonable claim for "special intellectual pleasure," the absolute expressionist holds that music offers "meaningful, cognitive experiences unavailable in any other way" (p. 29).
12. Objections to selective quotation out of context are well founded: I resort to this practice primarily because of the necessity for restricting the length of this essay. I trust, however, that a close reading of the text itself will confirm my conviction that a balanced view of formalism is not presented.
13. Foster McMurray, "Variations on a Pragmatic Theme," in *Basic Concepts in Music Education*, ed. Richard Colwell, 1990 NSSE Yearbook (Denver: University of Colorado Press, in press), p. 7; page citations are from a June 1989 draft.
14. Ibid., p. 15.
15. Ibid., p. 16, emphasis in the original.
16. Ibid., p. 17.
17. Immanuel Kant, *Critique of Judgment*, secs. 1 and 5, 6, 9, 15, and 20. An accurate portrayal of even the major points of this subtly stirring theory in a few paragraphs is simply impossible. I must assume familiarity with its basic features and urge those who may not already have done so to pursue it further. One of the most thorough interpretive analyses is Donald W. Crawford's *Kant's Aesthetic Theory* (Madison: University of Wisconsin Press, 1974).
18. Kant, *Critique of Judgment*, Preface to the 1790 edition, para. 6: "... they do not of themselves contribute a whit to the knowledge of things ..." (trans. Creed). See also secs. 8 and 9.
19. Ibid., secs. 8 and 18.
20. Ibid., sec. 15 (see also sec. 1, para. 2).
21. Ibid., sec. 14, para. 7.
22. Ibid., sec. 53 primarily; but also sec. 51.
23. Ibid., secs. 51 and 53 (compare sec. 44).
24. Ibid., sec. 48 (compare sec. 15).
25. This is one of the important points Carl Dalhaus makes in chap. 5 of his *Esthetics of Music* (Cambridge: Cambridge University Press, 1982).
26. Eduard Hanslick, *On the Musically Beautiful*, trans. and ed. Geoffrey Payzant (Indianapolis: Hackett, 1986), p. 29. On Hanslick's treatment of feeling in particular, see Malcolm Budd, "The Repudiation of Emotion: Hanslick on Music," *British Journal of Aesthetics* 20, no. 1 (Winter 1980): 29-43.
27. Hanslick, *On the Musically Beautiful*, cf. pp. 58-62, for instance.
28. Ibid., p. 5.
29. Hanslick argues vigorously against musical aesthetics' "servile dependence" upon a "supreme metaphysical principle of a general aesthetics ...," ibid., p. 2.
30. Ibid., pp. xxii, 6.
31. Ibid., pp. 78, 63-64.
32. Ibid., p. 58.
33. Ibid., p. 64.
34. On p. 58, ibid., he asserts, "Far be it from us to want to underestimate the authority of feeling over music," continuing that the musical response is concerned with that range of feeling which "unites itself with pure contemplation." In the introduction to the eighth edition, he claims it is "incomprehensible to

me" the way his argument against music representing feelings has been mis-construed to imply "an absolute lack of feeling" (p. xxii).

35. "Joy and sorrow can in the highest degree be called into life by music . . . ," he continues. Ibid., p. 7.

36. R. W. Hall, "On Hanslick's Supposed Formalism in Music," *Journal of Aesthetics and Art Criticism* 25, no. 4 (Summer 1967): 433-36.

37. "What in every other art is still description is in music already metaphor." Hanslick, *On the Musically Beautiful*, p. 30.

38. Music's tonal forms are, in his words, "not empty but filled." Ibid., p. 30.

39. Edmund Gurney, *The Power of Sound* (New York: Basic Books, 1966), p. 14.

40. Ibid., p. 12.

41. Ibid., p. 25.

42. Ibid., pp. 55, 54.

43. Ibid., p. 91 (title of chap. 5).

44. Ibid., pp. 92, 94, and 95.

45. Ibid., p. 92n. This resembles Hanslick's assertion that the only way accurately to describe a musical theme is to sing it.

46. Ibid., pp. 100, 101.

47. Ibid., pp. 165, 168.

48. Ibid., pp. 165-66.

49. Ibid., p. 166.

50. Ibid., p. 175

51. Ibid., p. 346.

52. Ibid., p. 216.

53. Ibid., pp. 227, 229.

54. Ibid., pp. 306, 310, and 311.

55. Ibid., p. 308.

56. A. Schantz, "A New Statement of Values for Music Education . . . ," (Ann Arbor, Mich.: University Microfilms International, 1983. D.A.I. number 8400924), p. 203.

57. L. B. Meyer, "Toward a Theory of Style," in *The Concept of Style*, ed. B. Lang (Ithaca, N.Y.: Cornell University Press, 1987), p. 27.

58. L. B. Meyer, *Explaining Music* (Berkeley: University of California Press, 1973), p. 4.

59. A short list would have to include at least the following: the theory of undif-ferentiated affect (feeling equals arousal; specific emotions are products of cog-nitively interpreted arousal); the conflict theory of emotion (no conflict, no emotion); the equation of complexity and novelty with musical value (and his ill-fated sojourn into information theory); and the failure to use the term "mean-ing" consistently (it denotes both objective relationships and subjective proces-ses, both transitive and intransitive functions, both semantic and syntactic connections).

60. I take these few generalizations do not require specific documentation. They are developed in *Explaining Music* and elaborated in a number of articles and chap-ters, several of which are cited below.

61. Such "understanding" may well be largely tacit: we are not implying it need be an analytical, intellectual affair.

62. B. S. Rosner and L. B. Meyer, "Melodic Processes and the Perception of Music," in *The Psychology of Music*, ed. D. Deutsch (New York: Academic Press, 1982), p. 318.

63. L. B. Meyer, "The Dilemma of Choosing," in *Value and Values in Evolution*, ed. E. A. Mazierz (New York: Gordon and Breach, 1979), p. 137.

64. Meyer, *Explaining Music*, p. 6.

65. L. B. Meyer, *Music, the Arts, and Ideas* (Chicago: University of Chicago Press, 1967), p. 223.

66. L. B. Meyer, "Grammatical Simplicity and Relational Richness," *Critical Inquiry* 2, no. 4 (Summer 1976): 693-791.

67. Meyer, "Dilemma of Choosing," p. 139.

68. Meyer, *Music, the Arts, and Ideas*, pp. 210-11.
69. Arnold Berleant, "Musical De-Composition," in *What Is Music?*, ed. Philip Alperson (New York: Haven Press, 1987), p. 247.
70. "Potentially," because formalism has historically aligned itself so consistently with High Art in the European aristocratic tradition. Although this kind of allegiance contradicts my claim to relative value neutrality, I do not believe it to be a necessary concomitant of formalism. At the same time, it would be foolish in the extreme to suggest that formalism is altogether free of normative assumptions.
71. Despite his provision for "processive" relationships, for instance, Meyer designates his "syntactical" and "statistical" parameters "primary" and "secondary," respectively; the rationale as I understand it is that parameters that tend toward discreteness rather than qualitative continuity generally play more fundamental roles in structural definition.
72. This admittedly becomes a defect of major proportions if formalism is taken to provide not only necessary but sufficient grounds for musical experience.
73. Meyer, *Emotion and Meaning*, p. 6.
74. I hasten to add that I would be equally circumspect of a formalistic position pressed in like fashion to the ideological extreme. While its value orientation has what I hope we can agree are conspicuous assets for music education, it is not, as I have indicated, without its blind spots. My fundamental point, once more, is that as music educators we cannot do without the formalistic value system. I have neither said nor, I hope, have I implied it is all we need. Indeed, its tendency to emphasize the artifactual over the experiential (the structural over the processual and the social) would constitute a major impediment to effective musical instruction were formalism naively taken to be not only necessary, but sufficient as well.

Dewey, Imagination, and Music: A Fugue on Three Subjects

MARY J. REICHLING

The work of Jo Ann Boydston in preparing and editing the writings of John Dewey has been the occasion of a renaissance of interest in Dewey's philosophy. Yet little if any research, earlier or more recently, has explored his aesthetic theory in relation to music. Still less can be found concerning the place of music and imagination. This triple fugue is an effort to begin to explore three subjects that recur in Dewey's aesthetic theory found in *Art as Experience.*[1]

Before presenting the subjects themselves, it is important to examine briefly three motives that are fundamental to an understanding of the nature and place of imagination in Dewey's philosophy of art as experience. These are Dewey's concepts of "experience," "environment," and "art" as used in *Art as Experience.* An exposition of the three subjects follows. Answers and episodic material are drawn from the writings of various composers and philosophers in augmentation or diminution of Dewey's theory as it applies to imagination in the experience of music. The fugue as a whole is offered tentatively, as an exploration, articulation, and synthesis, rather than a critical analysis, of ideas about imagination. Finally, the coda suggests implications for music education based upon the application of Dewey's theory of art to music. Throughout, the applications and examples are my own; the few which are Dewey's are acknowledged as his.

For Dewey an experience is the result of interaction between a human being and some aspect of the environment. He conceives the environment broadly to include other people, ideas, and inanimate objects. In an experience there is not only "undergoing" and "doing," but a relationship is established between participants. This relationship may be thwarted or reach consummation. A unity within experience is necessary for it to reach consummation. In reflecting on an experience after its occurrence, accord-

Mary J. Reichling is an Assistant Professor of Music at Southwestern Louisiana University. Her most recent publications have appeared in *Update,* the *Journal of Research in Music Education,* and the *Philosophy of Music Education Newsletter.* She is also a piano soloist and accompanist.

ing to Dewey, one will find that the unity is neither emotional, practical, nor intellectual alone, for these are merely distinctions one can make and not separate properties. Rather, the unity is effected by a single quality that permeates the experience.[2]

Aesthetic experience is a refined and intensified form of ordinary experience in continuity with life and available to everyone. It is not relegated to museums and the concert hall. Here Dewey distinguishes the physical art product, such as a marble statue, from the *work* of art. An art object must be experienced, not simply sit on a shelf, to be meaningful in the aesthetic sense. Dewey seems to be more concerned with Nelson Goodman's question "When is art?" than with the question "What is art?" In this way, Dewey also avoids R. G. Collingwood's ontological dilemma with respect to the art object.

For Dewey, it is the work(ing) of art, that is, the interaction of an individual person with the artistic product, that he views as a refined and intensified form of ordinary experience, or aesthetic experience.[3] Since every person is unique, the experience is different for each individual and may vary over time. Yet from these varied experiences, certain commonalities do emerge and will appear as our three subjects.

But first it is important to note that the three subjects of our fugue constitute a whole work, even though each subject may be heard individually. Similarly, Dewey does not allow divisions among various aspects of human experience at the practical level. However, distinctions will be made here at a conceptual level to facilitate discussion.

The First Subject

Dewey defines imagination as the fusion or conscious adjustment of *old* and *new* that results in a transformation of all that is past in a person's experience with a vision of the future.[4] What he is saying in effect is that a person's *stored* or acquired wealth of knowledge, the old, joins with some imagined new idea or vision. Acquired knowledge and new idea interact or *consciously adjust* as the work of art is formed. In a sense, then, both the old and new are transformed and fused into the work of art. I shall designate the new as comprising a kind of perception in imagination, or *inner* perception of the new idea or vision, and the combining of the new with the old in external reality as a sort of *external* perception, occurring outside of the person but also involving imagination.

Previous knowledge and new conception unite or are transformed into something else. For example, a composer has knowledge of compositional technique, the old, but there must also be present in imagination some new theme or larger conception, the new idea, that combines with the composer's knowledge of music and animates and transforms that knowledge from static fact to dynamic work of art. Dewey designates this fusion as imagination.

Further, Dewey writes that imagination is not just a power that does certain things, but a quality that dominates and pervades an interaction between a person and a work of art. He seems to be making a separation between imagination as a "special and self-contained faculty," which he rejects, and the notion of doing something imaginatively. Dewey is apparently avoiding the old "faculty psychology" view of the person and mind/body duality in favor of imagination as a function and quality integrally involved in the experience of living. If this is in fact the case, then imagination may have various qualities which suggest different functions. Dewey states that imagination animates all the varying processes of making and observing or, in application to music, of composing, performing, and listening.[5]

Dewey distinguishes the participants involved in the experience of art as those who perceive artistically, namely, the artist in the act of production, which suggests the performer; and those who perceive aesthetically, the beholders. He expresses regret that our language has no single word that encompasses both processes. The designation *artistic-aesthetic* perception will be used here to denote these combined processes. There are commonalities between artistic and aesthetic perception; distinctions cannot become categories. But there clearly are distinctions, which Dewey neglects to make, that need to be taken into account in discovering how imagination functions in artistic-aesthetic perception. Several are pointed out in the application of his theory to music.

The first subject of our fugue, then, is this specialized notion of perception, that is, perception that appears to function imaginatively or in imagination as well as in external reality. Let us explore this subject by offering in counterpoint the writings of composers and performers to illustrate and confirm Dewey's theory or to suggest other ways in which perception might be functioning in the musical experience.

The first contrapuntal line is that woven by the composer. With respect to the creator, Dewey writes that as a work of art is conceived, a period of gestation occurs during which "doings and perceptions projected in imagination," the old and new, interact, modify, and fuse into the work of art. His words *gestation* and *fuse* seem to suggest an activity or process. *In imagination* appears to designate these processes as functions of imagination.[6]

For example, a composer may immediately write an entire work on staff paper directly from the work "conceived in the head." Full development of the musical idea occurs in imagination as both a kind of place and function.

Mozart is a well-known example of this process. A letter attributed to him states that works simply came to him in a flash while he was riding or walking.[7]

On the other hand, the interaction of the imaginative perception of a work and its construction may be undertaken in observable reality. Beethoven is said to have labored over the working out of an imaginatively perceived idea through various stages of development to a completed work of art.[8] The composer is then involved in a process of doing and undergoing as imaginatively perceived qualities of the evolving work interact with its production. Through this interaction the composer becomes a perceiver or listener as well as a creator.[9] As listener, the composer hears the imaginative perception in relation to the developing aural form of the work.

Dewey states that the process of creating a new vision may be acute and intense in the undergoing phases and energetic in the doing phase, but until these are related to form a whole, artistic perception is not fully realized.[10] But the entire compositional process may be far more complex than Dewey's position tends to suggest. The two examples cited do not even touch the problems of orchestration, use of text, opera and its visual components, and so forth. But what can be deduced from the investigation to this point is that artistic-aesthetic perception is of a special sort and is of necessity imaginative. Such perception with respect to the composer might be designated as a quality and function of imagination.

Dewey also assigns artistic perception to the act of production. The performer, then, becomes a second contrapuntal line. Dewey writes that the performer exemplifies the doing and undergoing of the composer where perceptions of old and new meet in a new artistic vision.[11] One can accept Dewey's position as far as it goes, for it is attested to by various musicians and aestheticians who at the same time also point out the more deeply lying differences.[12] However, it is particularly with respect to performance that Dewey's aesthetic theory falls short.[13]

For example, one critical area is the place of the score in the performer's new vision of a previously composed work. If performers have a score to which they adhere, where is there any allowance for a new artistic vision? What is the relation of the performer to the score?

Aaron Copland states that as composers see the score, the performer's mind can exercise itself on a given work although the interpreter does not supply the actual composition. Adolph Kullak writes that there are few works whose conceptions as printed are free from ambiguity. Roger Sessions views the score as a series of symbols into which the composer has translated a musical conception. The performer's function then is neither to reproduce the score with simple fidelity, nor to use the score merely as a vehicle for self-expression. Rather, the performer does participate in a similar sense of discovery about the work that the composer did in its creation and shares aspects of the composer's uncertainty with respect to the nature of the final product in the interpretative process.[14]

Sessions, Epperson, and Ferguson acknowledge that the score contains intangible and ambiguous elements that cannot be completely and clearly indicated, such as contour, climax, rubato, and so on. Yet these make the difference between a good or bad performance.[15] Stravinsky views the score as "verbal dialectic . . . powerless to define musical dialectic in its totality."[16]

Stravinsky and Ferguson in particular seem to point the way toward an analysis of the musical score that presages the work of Nelson Goodman.[17] Goodman offers a penetrating philosophical analysis of musical notation and the musical score. Although his findings are at times open to question, Goodman's analysis helps to unravel some of the ambiguities just noted.

Without repeating Goodman's extensive analysis, I present some of his conclusions that are pertinent here. Because of the syntactical specifications and semantic conditions Goodman establishes for a notational system, certain characters that a musician might label as part of a score, Goodman rejects. For example, notes and rhythms fulfill his requirements; verbal instructions are accepted as auxiliary; but ambiguous elements, such as a crescendo sign, do not comply. His view of the score may be narrower than the musician's, but it does make explicit the distinction between definitive and ambiguous elements.[18] It is the latter where the imagination of the performer is particularly at play.

The agent through which the performer's interpretative task is accomplished, states Sessions, is the imagination or the performer's ability to apply imagination to the score and to develop, through a joining of the certain and ambiguous elements, a new sonorous conception, an inner perception of the work. Similarly, the vision of the work is dependent upon the performer's possession of what Kullak designates as "artistic inspiration," or imagination, and "acute artistic intelligence." These join to form what Kullak calls an "inner perception" that corresponds to my identification of perception as a function and quality of imagination.[19]

In the statements of these writers, one might also recognize the link to Dewey's fusion of the old and new. The new is the artistic inspiration or sonorous image of the work that the performer wishes to achieve, perception as a function of imagination. The old is the performer's artistic intelligence including knowledge of style, structural elements, performance practice, technique, and so forth. For example, Epperson writes that the conductor looks at a score and hears the music. "That hearing, though actually inaudible, is an imaginative projection [the new] based upon past knowledge and experience [the old.]"[20] The new and old interact and fuse as the work is brought to external perception in performance. This is a transformation that, as Dewey suggests, defines the work of imagination.

Much has been offered already with respect to the performer in both criticism and augmentation of Dewey's philosophy of art. Still, there remain further aspects of performance that belie the simple alliance between composer and performer that Dewey implies in attempting to find one word to encompass artistic and aesthetic perception. The techniques of composition and performance differ; consider, for example, the ability to write a fugue, or to set text to music, or the technique of orchestration as opposed to digital dexterity or tone production or conducting.

Performers must adapt to acoustical conditions of the hall, limitations of the instruments, their own physical and psychical states, as well as other elements, which may result in continued adjustments of the sonorous image as the work is brought to life. Here the performer becomes a perceiver as well and listens to the evolving work.[21] Again it is evident that the image of the work that the performer holds in imagination and continually adjusts in the act of performing or practicing gives evidence of perception as a function and quality of imagination or perception as a constituent of imagination.

The third contrapuntal line in this episode is that spun by the perceiver or listener. In Dewey's discussion of art as experience he refers to several kinds of perception that give imagination a greater or lesser position with respect to the beholder. For example, he mentions ordinary perception where attention is diffused rather than being focused and functioning holistically toward an end. It is comparable to Session's first stage of listening when one simply hears tones passing, a kind of passive awareness.[22]

Dewey also describes mechanical perception which he likens to cold, colorless recognition, perhaps comparable to that found in psychological studies or theory exams where listeners recognize physical aspects of sound: intervals, duration, chord function, and the like. Further, Dewey seems to present a kind of analytical perception as possibly a facet of reflective thought where one perceives simply for the technique employed.[23] For example, one may listen for style analysis. Such analysis is separated from a total experience of the art work. Later discussion will show how such analysis may dispose the listener to a more intensified and deepened aesthetic perception.

Imagination does not have a central or significant role in the perceptual processes just described. It is in aesthetic perception, which Dewey reserves specifically for the working of the art object in experience, that imagination has a central and indispensable function. It is at the heart of the listening experience.

Dewey writes that perception for the beholder is artistic as well as aesthetic, since perceivers create their own experiences similar to those which the creator has undergone. The process is the joining into a whole in imagination of details and particulars of an artwork.[24] The work functions in the imagination of the listener as well as in the realm of physical or ordinary perceptual existence. Such perception requires work of perceivers whose abilities to recreate the artist's experience are dependent, in Dewey's view, on their point of view, interest, and ability to comprehend. Dewey's description is similar to Virgil Aldrich's concept of aspect perception or prehension in which perception functions as a facet of imagination in seeing (or hearing) aspects that enliven a particular work of art.[25]

In aesthetic perception there occur both doing and undergoing. In listening, anticipation of what is to come is followed by organizing what is heard in varying cycles of outgoing and incoming energy as "music weaves its web." These processes form a whole consisting of related parts; no isolated aspect is singled out as a means to an external end. The perceptual process is holistic and "exercised in imagination as well as observation."[26]

Before a unified perception that carries an experience to consummation can take place in imagination, there occurs a progressive massing and compressing of impressions that have a cumulative effect.[27] Dewey discusses this experience for the arts but with no attention to the differences among the various art forms. He may be oversimplifying the process.

One important difference between music and art is that a visual art form is located before the viewer all at once, as a whole, unified structure, and remains so. A musical work evolves in time as form and structure unfold without opportunity for review or "relooking." The observer of visual art constantly has the complete form present, even though it takes time to grasp the structure. The music listener has before the ear only that which is currently sounding. In the listening process, melodies, rhythms, chord progressions, and so on, need not and cannot be retained in mind, particularly in long works. These elements are present, compressed or embedded through imagination, in what is currently perceived.

Among musicians, Copland and Sessions both attest to the concepts of compression and condensation in the listening experience. Copland adds the notion of balancing in imagination the simultaneously heard musical elements. In the visual arts one may view one element or another of the work at will and return to something previously observed. But grasping the framework of a lengthy musical work and seeing around it, as it were, demonstrates for Copland "one of the rarer manifestations of consciousness. Here if anywhere the imagination must take fire." Sessions allocates the ability to remake the musical work in imagination in a condensed or concentrated form to quite a sophisticated stage of listening. Dewey adds that what is retained from what has preceded is embedded in what is currently being perceived in such a way that by its compression it actually forces the imagination to stretch forward toward what is yet to come.[28]

In summary, three phases seem to characterize aesthetic perception according to Dewey: anticipation, cumulation, and consummation.[29] These.

appear as cycles that occur and recur within the listening experience and as integrating elements that eventually form a new artistic whole. Aesthetic perception, as well as artistic perception, emerges as a function and quality of imagination.

The Second Subject

Dewey observes that "the proper function of imagination is vision of realities that cannot be exhibited under existing conditions of sense-perception." Such realities include the qualitative meanings that can be actualized only by embodiment in works of art. The embodiment of these meanings represents for Dewey "the best evidence that can be found of the true nature of imagination."[30] Imagination has a dimension that includes thought: that thought which is of a qualitative object perceived in the work of art as an all-pervading unity.

Without this unity of quality, the elements of the work are heard, for example, only as melody, rhythm, timbre, and so on, which, Dewey states, results in the substitution of mechanical formulae for aesthetic quality.[31] Further, he writes that artistic thought is not singular in qualitative apprehension; rather, it exhibits an intensification of a characteristic of all thought. Dewey holds that artistic thought, which is qualitative, occurs prior to analysis and is a directly or immediately experienced quality.[32] Artistic or qualitative thought, then, is the second subject of our fugue.

Dewey writes that qualitative objects, such as pleasure or suffering, are subjective and are imaginatively apprehended while physical objects are external and can be perceived by the senses. Several examples will help to illustrate Dewey's idea of qualitative objects. With respect to the world of nature, Bertram Morris suggests several qualitative immediacies, "the wet of the rain, the heat of the sun, the fragrance of the raspberry." In the work of art, then, it is the notion of a pervading quality to which Dewey refers when he writes about the embodiment and apprehension of qualitative meaning. "The underlying quality that defines the work, that circumscribes it externally and integrates it internally, controls the thinking of the artist; his logic is the logic of what I have called qualitative thinking."[33]

Further, Dewey states that "language fails not because thought fails, but because no verbal symbols can do justice to the fullness and richness of thought." The pervasive, qualitative meaning that unifies a work of art is not speakable, for if it were, the arts of music and painting would not exist. Rather, such meanings are imaginatively evoked and apprehended.[34]

At first reading, Dewey appears to be defining meaning in works of art negatively, as that which is not speakable. But where words have external referents, he writes, "there are other meanings that present themselves directly as possessions of objects which are experienced." For Dewey, art expresses such meanings. These meanings are grasped imaginatively, and the understanding of them is a cognitive act. In developing imagination, then, educators are developing the mind. Qualitative thought might be described as a function of imagination. Dewey has succeeded in freeing himself from "any rigid correlation of thought with verbal language," again attesting to the holistic nature of thought.[35]

While Dewey accords primacy to qualitative thought in the experience of art, analysis, as a function of reflective thought, also appears to have a footing. He paraphrases Croce and states that we become aware of temporal sequence in music only through analytic reflection.[36] Perhaps Dewey is aligning qualitative thought with the functioning of a particular kind of symbol.[37] In any event, a special kind of thought process seems to be functioning in apprehending meaning in a work of art. Further, analytical, reflective thought also has a place among the various functions of thought.

Dewey suggests an emotional as well as an intellectual dimension to qualitative thought. He avoids any dualism by joining intellectual and emotional meanings in the experience of art. "Art is thus a way of having the substantial cake of reason while also enjoying the sensuous pleasure of eating it." He writes that in the experience of art "emotionalized thinking" occurs; artists depend on "emotionalized ideas" and "emotionalized imagination."[38]

For Dewey emotion in the experience of art is a quality, not a simple entity such as anger or joy that may last for a short period of time, nor a "boiling over" or "spewing forth" like a flood of tears that brings relief. In these situations there is not the ordering or shaping of the emotion, an intellectual process that art demands. Through their attachment to the work of art, natural human emotions become transformed by the expressive material. Dewey states that without this emotional quality, the work exhibits craftsmanship. Should the emotion be directly displayed, it is not art either; an artist who is overcome by emotion is really incapacitated.[39]

Our subject, then, thought in the experience of art, seems to be made up of several motives: qualitative, possessing both emotional and intellectual meaning; and reflective, encompassing analysis. It is particularly qualitative thought with its emotional and intellectual dimensions that requires imagination for the apprehension of meaning. Here enter again the contrapuntal lines of other writers to illustrate and confirm Dewey's notion of artistic thought or to suggest other ways in which thought might function in the experience of music.

Copland, like Dewey, rejects the dualism of intellect and feeling, stating that the dichotomy has no reality for a composer. He writes of the need for balance of heart and brain in the compositional process. In discussing his method of composing, Copland speaks of beginning with an "expressive idea" or "generative idea" which is of a strongly imaginative quality. "I put down a reflection of emotional states: feelings, perceptions, imaginings, intuitions." For him an emotional state "is compounded of everything we are: our background, our environment, our convictions."[40]

Another view of the compositional process is offered by Sessions for whom a work begins with a "musical idea" or "train of thought." He states that there is a "quality of feeling" sensed through the cumulative effect of the music. Sessions is attesting to both intellectual and emotional elements. He states the matter even more clearly when he writes that "'structure' and 'passion' are not in any sense mutually exclusive as is sometimes assumed, but that one may, when the occasion demands, be the very essence of the other."[41]

Again, Sessions writes that great art achieves its stature by virtue of its inherent qualities of imagination and constructive order. There seems to be a basis here in Sessions's writing, as well as in Copland's, for Dewey's concept of "emotionalized thinking" and "emotionalized imagination." Sessions also appears to support the notion that qualitative meanings may possess emotional as well as intellectual content. Like Copland, Sessions places imagination at the heart of the musical experience. It is imagination that defines the emotion for the listener.[42]

Copland states that a deliberately selected sound image permeates the entire musical composition and is integral to the meaning of the work. He allows that a work may have multiple meanings, including some that he did not give it. In fact, it pleases him to think that his works might be read in several ways, lest it be said that his music lacked richness of meaning.[43]

Copland's suggestion that others may find new meanings in a work of art has implications for performers as well as listeners. Like the composer, the interpreter begins with a total image, a pervasive quality, with respect to the sound of an already created work. Artur Schnabel describes the experience of the performer as beginning with an "intense penetration of the letter and spirit of a composition," the musical score, which becomes the catalyst for the pervasive sonorous quality of the work. Sessions writes that the agent of the recreation of the expressive gesture of the music is the imagination.[44]

Besides this image of the whole, performers, at each step along the way, must focus on what is occurring in every phrase as well as what is to follow in the next phrase so that the composition "may be heard and shaped in the vivid imagination of the listener with the so-called inner ear." Everything is heard twice, so to speak, each phrase is anticipated and then checked while it is played as a control against what was imagined. Schnabel writes that these two phases are fused: "Conception materializes and the materialization redissolves into conception." Further, technique becomes more than simple physical discipline but is an action that stimulates the imagination.[45]

The position of performers is much like that of composers with respect to the union of emotional and intellectual aspects as a kind of "emotional-ized thinking" or "emotionalized imagination" in the performance process. The description of the performer that Schnabel presents offers support for qualitative and analytical thought processes. His position seems to support the suggestion offered above that various thought processes may interact in the experience of a work of art. Dewey, it will be recalled, accorded primacy to qualitative thought. What remains consistent through all of these writings is that thinking in terms of relations of qualities, whether by performer from score or composer from raw materials, functions in imagination. Dewey identifies this as one of the most demanding modes of thought.[46]

Listeners also participate in the experience of composer and performer through the apprehension in imagination of the all-pervasive, unifying quality of a work of art. At the outset, the listener may encounter an indefiniteness about the work comparable to that which the composer found when beginning to develop the generative idea. It is a sense of not knowing for sure where the idea will eventually go. The work becomes clearer as listening continues, and much as it does for the artist, qualitative unity pervades the working of the art product in experience.[47]

At what Copland considers the highest level of listening, one is able to follow the way in which the artist handles the elements. The listener "is both inside and outside the music at the same moment, judging it and enjoying it, wishing it would go one way and watching it go another—almost like the composer at the moment he [or she] composes it; because in order to write his music, the composer must also be inside and outside his music, carried away by it and yet coldly critical of it."[48] Copland is actually presenting here a discussion of imagination at work in the musical experience. In addition, his analysis shows the functioning of various thought processes: qualitative and analytical. Consequently, listening with understanding requires that imagination function in a thoughtful manner, a kind of intellectualized and emotionalized imagination, to grasp the meanings expressed by the music.[49]

Further, Copland writes that music expresses meanings that cannot be verbally articulated, that meaning is not specific, and that listeners should look for no more than a general concept. However, Copland does suggest some of the qualitative meanings that listeners might apprehend: "serenity or exuberance, regret or triumph, fury or delight."[50]

Copland writes of the "power" of music to move us as a kind of "emotional overtone." The music does not manipulate emotion but somehow gives a "distillation of sentiments, the essence of experience transfused and heightened and expressed in such fashion that we may contemplate it at the same instant that we are swayed by it."[51] Copland is referring to the heart and brain balance which parallels Dewey's notion of "emotionalized thinking."

With respect to composer, performer, and listener, apprehension of meaning in the work of art seems to include cognitive and emotional dimensions of a qualitative thought process. Such thought requires imagination for the discernment of meaning in the experience of music and may be viewed as a function of imagination.

The Third Subject

If thought functions somewhat in the manner just described, then how does this knowing in imagination occur? To say that the felt quality unifying the aesthetic experience is apprehended in imagination responds to a question of what and where, but not to one of how. Dewey writes that the felt quality that pervades and unites a work of art can only be "intuited." Various parts of the work are discriminated, but the feeling of the whole is immediately experienced, that is, intuited.[52] Intuition, then, becomes the third subject of our fugue. Let us pursue more carefully the nature of "intuition" about which Dewey is writing and its relation to imagination in the experience of music.

Dewey states, "Intuition is most properly confined to those acts of knowledge . . . in which we know ultimate wholes." He explains that often we are not aware of the qualities of many of our daily acts such as selections and rejections. We do not attempt to objectify them and analyze them. Yet the sense of rightness or wrongness about these actions is a felt quality that guides decisions. "These qualities are the stuff of 'intuitions.'"[53] Further, Dewey writes, "In practical life, we mean by intuition the power to seize as a whole, in a single and almost instantaneous survey, a complete group of circumstances. It is the power to read off at a glance the meaning of a given situation."[54]

The quality of immediacy that characterizes intuition is not unmediated. Dewey states "that only a twisted and aborted logic can hold that because something is mediated, it cannot, therefore, be immediately experienced." What Dewey is including then when he writes that intuition is found in the conjunction of old and new is that this adjustment, while effected suddenly, is based upon a previous process of mediation consisting of perceiving and reasoning, study and experience, that unite with the experience at hand. The immediate in time is seen here as a result of previously mediated mental acts. Intuition is opposed "not to experience, but to abstract logical reflection."[55]

With respect to the artist, Dewey holds that the unreasoned impression occurs first; it is a seizure, an intuitively apprehended quality. In counterpoint, Copland, for example, describes a kind of intuition that is connected with criticism, implying a position similar to Dewey's. Copland writes that intuition is at the conjunction of perception and reasoning and is not a mystical revelation. Charles Ives uses a term "imaginative-penetrative" to refer to intuitive apprehension in this manner.[56]

With respect to the listener, the grasping of the pervasive and unifying quality of a composition is also an intuitive act. It may vary according to each person's experience with the artwork, store of knowledge, and previous experiences that constitute the Deweyan old and new. However, the immediacy of the apprehension, the intuitive nature of knowing the pervasive quality, is for Dewey absolutely essential to aesthetic experience, for "what is not immediate is not aesthetic."[57]

Whether for the composer, performer, or listener, intuition is effected in a quick and harmonious manner comparable to a revelation. But this event has actually been prepared for through long and tedious effort.[58] Knowledge may be apprehended intuitively, that is, immediately, without abstract, logical reflection. Intuition functions in conjunction with imagination by answering the question of how the pervasive quality is perceived. Intuition might be considered a mode of knowing in imagination.

Now as the fugue nears completion, three subjects—perception, qualitative thought, and intuition—have been sounded. Each appears to be, in some way, a facet of imagination functioning holistically in the experience of music. Many ambiguities still remain, and perhaps there are other subjects yet to be found. Nevertheless, some implications for a theory of musical pedagogy may be offered.

Coda

The coda opens with a pedal point that sounds to the final cadence. The sustained tone represents the development of imagination. Over this pedal, our three subjects return as three broad implications for musical pedagogy toward the development of imagination following Dewey's philosophy of art.

First, artistic-aesthetic perception is a dynamic and holistic process in which the imagination is fully engaged. Composing, performing, and listening are activities that rely on imagination in every phase: anticipation, cumulation, and consummation. There is an interaction between the student and the music; the student is not passive in the musical experience. In a sense, there is no sharply drawn line between musical education and musical experience.

Second, the qualitative nature of artistic thought brings together emotive and intellectual factors as dimensions of the same imaginative process. Qualitative realities inhere, according to Dewey, only in works of art. Thinking in terms of relations of felt qualities is a function of imagination. Consequently, for students to understand the meaning of music, they must use their imaginations. Further, since apprehension in imagination of the felt quality as a unifying whole occurs first, it seems to follow that an instructor would begin with a musical work as a whole. After the whole has been grasped, discrimination of elements occurs in analytic reflection. Analysis evolves out of the whole, part by part, with continued movement back to the whole. These phases of doing and undergoing fuse, and again this is where Dewey finds imagination.

Third, and finally, the nature of the cognition that takes place in imagination is intuitive, that is immediate. If Dewey's description of intuition as resulting from previously mediated acts, such as study and experience, is well founded, then it would seem important that imagination be fed and funded by a wealth of artistic experiences. Dewey views experience itself as dynamic and growing, suggesting that people build their capital through allowing themselves new experiences.[59] As Dewey writes, "When old and familiar things are made new in experience, there is imagination."[60] In addition, expansion of experience may enhance the range and depth of a person's aesthetic experience. That developing imagination is a goal of musical pedagogy in this context can harldy be denied.

NOTES

1. John Dewey, *Art as Experience* (New York: G. P. Putnam's Sons, 1980).
2. Ibid., pp. 3, 37, 43-44. In preparing a new introduction for a reissue of *Experience and Nature*, Dewey stated that were he to rewrite the book he would use "Culture" in place of "Experience" better to designate sociological, anthropological, aesthetic, etc., dimensions of experience. This new introduction was unfinished at the time of Dewey's death. See "The Unfinished Introduction," in *John Dewey: The Later Works, 1925-1953*, ed. Jo Ann Boydston (Carbondale: Southern Illinois University Press, 1988), vol. I: 1925, p. 362. This volume also contains *Experience and Nature*.
3. Dewey, *Art*, p. 3. If art is found in experience, then Dewey has placed art in context, in the particular time, place, and culture of the person experiencing the work of art. Other readings on this point include: Nicholas Cook, *Music, Imagination, and Culture* (Oxford: Clarendon Press, 1990); Rose Trahey Breckenridge, "History and Culture in the Study of Works of Art: The Question of Aesthetic Relevance," *Contributions to Music Education* 8 (1980): 55-71; Christopher Small, *Music, Society, Education*, 2d rev. ed. (London: John Calder), 1980; John Blacking, *How Musical Is Man?* (Seattle: University of Washington Press, 1983); Anne Dhu Shapiro, ed., *Music and Context* (Cambridge, Mass.: Harvard University Press), 1985. For readings on Dewey's concept of experience, see John Dewey, *Experience and Education* (New York: Macmillan, 1963), esp. chap. 3, and *Experience and Nature*.
4. Dewey, *Art*, pp. 272, 275.
5. Ibid., pp. 267, 273-75.
6. Ibid., pp. 51-52.
7. Ibid. Edward Holmes, *The Life of Mozart, Including His Correspondence* (New York: Harper and Brothers, 1868), p. 329. In addition, Einstein writes that Mozart "put a composition down on paper as one writes a letter, without allowing any disturbance or interruption to annoy him—the writing down, the 'fixing,' was nothing more than that—the fixing of the completed work, a

mechanical act. . . . he does not make rough drafts." Alfred Einstein, *Mozart: His Character, His Work*, trans. Arthur Mendel and Nathan Broder (New York: Oxford University Press, 1965), pp. 135-43.

8. Lewis Lockwood, "Beethoven's Sketches for *Sehnsucht*," *Beethoven Studies*, ed. Alan Tyson (New York: W. W. Norton, 1973), p. 97. See also Einstein, *Mozart*, who compares the compositional processes of Mozart and Beethoven.

9. Dewey, *Art*, pp. 48-49. Howard describes this interaction as the craft of musical composition which he also views as creative and imaginative. See Vernon Howard, *Artistry: The Work of Artists* (Indianapolis: Hackett, 1982).

10. Dewey, *Art*, p. 50.

11. Ibid., pp. 46-47. Improvisation joins performance and composition. On this point, see Adolph Kullak, *The Aesthetics of Pianoforte-Playing*, 3d ed. rev. by Hans Bischoff, trans. Theodore Baker (New York: Da Capo Press, 1972), pp. 8-9; and "Improvisation: Methods and Models," by Jeff Pressing, in *Generative Processes in Music: The Psychology of Performance, Improvisation, and Composition*, ed. John A. Sloboda (Oxford: Clarendon Press, 1988), pp. 129-78.

12. Aaron Copland, *Music and Imagination* (Cambridge, Mass.: Harvard University Press, 1952), writes that "creation and interpretation are indissolubly linked," p. 40. Roger Sessions, *The Musical Experience of Composer, Performer, Listener* (Princeton, N.J.: Princeton University Press, 1974), states that "composer and performer are not only collaborators in a common enterprise but participants in an essentially single experience." However, their functions within the total creative process differ, pp. 5, 8-9. Paul Hindemith, *A Composer's World: Horizons and Limitations* (Cambridge, Mass.: Harvard University Press, 1952), discusses several differences between composer and performer, pp. 132-34. Igor Stravinsky, *The Poetics of Music*, trans. Arthur Knodel and Ingolf Dahl (Cambridge, Mass.: Harvard University Press, 1975), holds that between the composer and interpreter "there exists a difference in make-up that is of an ethical rather than of an aesthetic order"; performance does not constitute a "recomposition," pp. 123-24. Malcolm Budd, in *Music and the Emotions* (Boston: Routledge and Kegan Paul, 1985), suggests that the points of view of composer, performer, and listener are not fully distinct but may overlap. If music is something capable of being understood, it must be possible for the participants in the musical experience to share that understanding, pp. 16, 151. Gordon Epperson, *The Musical Symbol: A Study of the Philosophic Theory of Music* (Ames: Iowa State University Press, 1967), writes that "to the extent that he [or she] has a conceptual ideal, the performer measures his efforts against his ideal performance—something corresponding to the composer's commanding form," p. 306.

13. Hein argues that philosophers generally do not give enough attention to performance in aesthetic theory. Traditional aesthetics' failure to provide a distinct place for the concept of performance is a "category mistake." Philosophers fail to make sufficient distinctions in subsuming performance under other categories. Performance is itself an aesthetic category. See Hilde Hein, "Performance as an Aesthetic Category," *Journal of Aesthetics and Art Criticism* 28 (Spring 1970): 381-96. See also Joseph Bensman and Robert Lilienfeld, "A Phenomenological Model of the Attitude of the Performing Artist," *Journal of Aesthetic Education* 4 (April 1970): 109-19.

14. Copland, *Music*, p. 42; Kullak, *Aesthetics*, p. 33; Sessions, *Musical Experience*, pp. 72, 76-77.

15. Sessions, *Musical Experience*, pp. 77-78. Epperson, *Musical Symbol*, p. 287. Donald N. Ferguson, *Music as Metaphor: The Elements of Expression* (Westport, Conn.: Greenwood Press, 1960), pp. 78, 81.

16. Stravinsky, *Poetics of Music*, p. 123.

17. Nelson Goodman, *Languages of Art: An Approach to a Theory of Symbols*, 2d ed. (Indianapolis: Hackett, 1976), esp. chap. 4.

18. Ibid., pp. 127-57, 179-92. However, it might be well to point out that the

dichotomy suggested between ambiguous and certain elements is not so neatly drawn when a score is interpreted. During performance, notes, rhythms, crescendos, rubatos, all elements come together as a whole work of art.

19. Sessions, *Musical Experience*, p. 78. Ferguson, *Music as Metaphor*, speaks about "matter" and "manner" in defining the task of musical performance as one of "high imaginative achievement," p. 78. Kullak, *Aesthetics*, pp. 32, 88.

20. Epperson, *Musical Symbol*, p. 287.

21. The necessity of listening in performance is stressed by Czerny who writes "*that the player should know how to listen properly to himself, (or herself), and to judge of his own performance with accuracy.*" Charles Czerny, *Letters to a Young Lady, on the Art of Playing the Pianoforte*, trans. J. A. Hamilton (New York: Da Capo Press, 1982), p. 38.

22. For further discussion of ordinary perception see Dewey, *Art as Experience*, pp. 135-36, 183, 195-97, 201, and *Philosophy and Civilization* (New York: Minton, Balch, 1931), pp. 188-232. The latter offers an analysis and criticism of various theories of perception. Sessions's four levels or stages characterize the listener as one who is able to hear the tones passing, simply enjoys the music, understands the music, and lastly, is able to discriminate vis-à-vis developing a sense of values and critical judgment, *Musical Experience*, pp. 92-93.

23. Dewey, *Art*, pp. 52-53, 139, 199, 217. With respect to psychological perception, see W. Jay Dowling and Dane L. Harwood, *Music Cognition* (New York: Academic Press, Harcourt Brace Jovanovich, 1986), who write that the basic concerns of musical perception are how pitch, loudness, duration, and timbre relate to the physical aspects of sound waves, p. 19. See also Diana Deutsch, ed., *The Psychology of Music* (New York: Academic Press, 1982); and John Sloboda, *The Musical Mind* (Oxford: Oxford University Press, 1985).

24. Dewey, *Art*, p. 54. Fred Lerdahl discusses aspects of the relationship between composing and listening, especially the constraints experienced by listeners. He introduces the notion of musical and compositional *grammars*. See "Cognitive Constraints on Compositional Systems," in *Generative Process in Music*, pp. 231-59. This is to suggest that Dewey may well be oversimplifying the beholder's participation in the creative process of the artist.

25. Dewey, *Art*, pp. 273, 54. Aldrich writes that a *material thing* may be perceived as physical object or as aesthetic object; the categories are mutually exclusive. For example, one may see a camel in a cloud and retain objectivity by describing those aspects of "camelness" to others (prehension). But the material thing, functioning as camel, cannot be placed under observation as such. It requires imagination to be seen. Similarly, a painting or sculpture may have aspects that animate it and are perceived imaginatively. Aldrich argues that Dewey's theory of aesthetic perception is not discriminating enough because it does not allow for shifting from one mode of perception to another. See Virgil Aldrich, "Aesthetic Perception and Objectivity," *British Journal of Aesthetics* 18 (Summer 1978): 290-15; and *Philosophy of Art* (Englewood Cliffs, N.J.: Prentice Hall, 1963), esp. chap. 1.

26. Dewey, *Art*, pp. 48, 236, 51. Dewey implies synthesis of the categories of observation and prehension (contra Aldrich). This holistic approach to the work of art is representative of a matriarchal aesthetic. See Gisela Ecker, ed., *Feminist Aesthetics*, trans. Harriet Anderson (Boston: Beacon Press, 1985), esp. Heide Gottner-Abendroth, "Nine Principles of a Matriarchal Aesthetic," pp. 81-94.

27. Dewey, *Art*, p. 182.

28. Copland, *Music*, p. 15; Sessions, *Musical Experience*, p. 97; Dewey, *Art*, p. 182.

29. Dewey, *Art*, p. 38.

30. Dewey, *How We Think*, p. 224, and *Art*, p. 268.

31. Dewey, *Philosophy*, p. 103. Dewey suggests that criticism's value is not in judgment of compositional techniques but in heightening and deepening qualitative apprehension.

32. Dewey, "Qualitative Thought" and "Affective Thought," in *Philosophy*. See also,

How We Think; and "An Analysis of Reflective Thought," *Journal of Philosophy* 19 (January 1922): 29-38.

33. Bertram Morris, "Dewey's Theory of Art," *Guide to the Works of John Dewey*, ed. Jo Ann Boydston (Carbondale: Southern Illinois University Press, 1970), p. 174. Dewey, *Philosophy*, p. 103.

34. Dewey, *Philosophy*, p. 102; *Art*, pp. 73-74, 272-73.

35. Dewey, *Art*, p. 84. Keith Swanwick, *Music, Mind, and Education* (New York: Routledge, 1988), p. 46. Swanwick does not make this statement about Dewey in particular but in reference to the arts and the development of the mind.

36. Dewey, *Art*, pp. 184, 60, 70, and "An Analysis of Reflective Thought," cited earlier. Further analysis of thought in Dewey's aesthetic theory can be found in D. C. Mathur's essay "A Note on the Concept of 'Consummatory Experience' in Dewey's Aesthetics," *Journal of Philosophy* 58 (April 1966): 225-31.

37. My purpose is not to discuss symbol theory but merely to say that Dewey has anticipated it. On symbol theory see Budd, Epperson, and Goodman, previously cited; Peter Kivy, *Sound and Semblance* (Princeton, N.J.: Princeton University Press, 1984); Victor Zuckerhandl, *Sound and Symbol*, trans. Willard Trask (New York: Pantheon Books, 1956); Susanne K. Langer, *Philosophy in a New Key: A Study in the Symbolism of Reason, Rite, and Art*, 3d ed. (Cambridge, Mass.: Harvard University Press, 1979).

38. Dewey, *Art*, pp. 258-59, 75. On the question of "meaning" in the arts, see Monroe C. Beardsley, *Aesthetics: Problems in the Philosophy of Criticism* (New York: Harcourt, Brace and World, 1958), esp. "The Meaning of Music," chap. 7; Wilson Coker, *Music and Meaning: A Theoretical Introduction to Musical Aesthetics* (New York: Collier-Macmillan, 1972); Michael Polanyi and Harry Prosch, *Meaning* (Chicago: University of Chicago Press, 1975); Nelson Goodman, "How Buildings Mean," in Nelson Goodman and Catherine Z. Elgin, *Reconceptions in Philosophy* (Indianapolis: Hackett, 1988), pp. 31-48.

39. Dewey, *Art*, pp. 41, 61-62, 69, 77. Further readings on Dewey's theory of emotions include John Dewey, "The Theory of Emotions," *John Dewey: The Early Works, 1882-1898*, ed. Jo Ann Boydston (Carbondale: Southern Illinois University Press, 1971), vol. 4, pp. 170-71; P. G. Whitehouse, "The Meaning of 'Emotion' in Dewey's *Art as Experience*," *The Journal of Aesthetics and Art Criticism* 37 (Winter 1978): 149-56. On cognitive emotions, see Israel Scheffler, "In Praise of the Cognitive Emotions," in *Inquiries: Philosophical Studies of Language, Science, and Learning* (Indianapolis: Hackett, 1986), chap. 8.

40. Copland, *Imagination*, pp. 16, 42-44, 111.

41. Sessions, *Musical Experience*, pp. 46, 24, 54.

42. Ibid., pp. 120, 24.

43. Copland, *Music*, pp. 23-24, 46, 49.

44. Konrad Wolff, *Schnabel's Interpretation of Piano Music*, 2d ed. (New York: W. W. Norton, 1979), p. 15. The author was a student of Schnabel who reviewed and approved the text. The book was originally published under the title *The Teaching of Artur Schnabel*. Sessions, *Musical Experience*, pp. 77-78.

45. Wolff, *Schnabel*, pp. 20-22, 13. Imagination is also functioning as a control in a means-ends continuum. See Howard, *Artistry*, p. 136. For applications to improvisation, see Pressing, *Generative Processes*.

46. Dewey, *Art*, pp. 45-46.

47. Ibid., pp. 191-92.

48. Aaron Copland, *What to Listen for in Music*, rev. ed. (New York: A Mentor Book, McGraw Hill, 1957), pp. 18-23. Copland presents three planes of listening: sensuous, expressive, and sheerly musical. On socially based listener types, see Theodor Adorno, *Introduction to the Sociology of Music*, trans. E. B. Ashton (New York: Seabury Press, 1986); and Alphons Silbermann, *The Sociology of Music*, trans. Corbert Stewart (London: Routledge and Kegan Paul, 1963).

49. Here one is, of course, assuming a valid performance.

50. Copland, *What to Listen For*, p. 20.

51. Copland, *Imagination*, p. 10.
52. Dewey, Art, p. 192.
53. Dewey, *Psychology*, p. 206, and *Experience and Nature*, p. 227.
54. Dewey, "The Study of Ethics: A Syllabus," in *The Early Works*, vol. 4, p. 308.
55. Dewey, *Art*, p. 119; *Psychology*, pp. 205-209.
56. Dewey, *Art*, p. 145; Copland, *Imagination*, p. 43; Charles Ives, *Essays before a Sonata and Other Writings*, ed. Howard Boatwright (New York: W. W. Norton, 1961), p. 14. Other forms of intuition are discussed by such philosophers as Kant, Bergson, and Croce. See especially Immanuel Kant, *Critique of Pure Reason*, trans. Norman Kemp Smith (New York: St. Martin's Press, 1965), A320, B377; Henri Bergson, *Introduction to Metaphysics*, trans. T. E. Hulme (New York: Liberal Arts, 1950); Benedetto Croce, *Aesthetic*, trans. Douglas Ainslie (New York: The Noonday Press, 1969), chaps. 1, 2.
57. Dewey, *Art*, pp. 215, 119.
58. Ibid., p. 266.
59. Dewey, "The Philosophy of the Arts," p. 361.
60. Dewey, *Art*, p. 267.

Music and the Liberal Education

PETER KIVY

Suppose I were to play to an average audience of educated men and women recordings, respectively, of Hamlet's famous soliloquy that begins, "To be, or not to be . . ." and the opening measures of the *Eroica*. It is my hypothesis that almost everyone in such a group would know that the first excerpt I played was from a play by William Shakespeare called *Hamlet* and that almost no one would know that the second was the opening of Beethoven's Third Symphony. This puzzling—some might say distressing—fact is the subject of my essay.

Three questions, I imagine, will immediately come to mind. Why *should* I be puzzled, one may well ask, by the fact that most people can recognize Hamlet's famous soliloquy but not the beginning of Beethoven's Third Symphony? Why, second, should I care about this, even if it is puzzling? And, finally, why should a philosopher be talking about Shakespeare, a poet, and Beethoven, a composer? Why doesn't he mind his own business and talk about Plato, or Kant, or the meaning of life, or whatever it is that philosophers are supposed to talk about?

The answer to the third question will, I trust, just naturally emerge as this essay progresses. But the answers to the first and second I will get to right away; for these questions and their answers will serve, really, as the introduction to my subject.

It is fair to say that *Hamlet* is one of the acknowledged masterpieces of Western literature: perhaps the most famous play in the English language. It is equally safe to maintain, I would think, that being at least vaguely familiar with it—knowing who wrote it, approximately when, who Hamlet and Ophelia are, and so forth—is something we would expect of any educated man or woman. If any of its liberal arts undergraduates were to leave a college or university without knowing a little about Shakespeare and

Peter Kivy is Professor of Philosophy at Rutgers University. His recent books include *Osmin's Rage: Philosophical Reflections on Opera, Drama, and Text; Music Alone: Philosophical Reflections on the Purely Musical Experience;* and *Sound and Semblance: Reflections on Musical Representation.*

Hamlet, I think their professors would see it as some kind of failure on *someone's* part.

But any musician, or musicologist, or just plain music lover will assert, quite rightly I think, that in the world of Western classical music Beethoven's Third Symphony occupies a place of honor and importance equal to that of *Hamlet* in the world of literature. As one eminent historian of music has characterized it, "One of the incomprehensible deeds in arts and letters, the greatest single step made by an individual composer in the history of the symphony and in the history of music generally. . . . [T]he *Eroica* simply dwarfs everything in its boldness of conception, breadth of execution, and intensity of logical construction."[1]

The puzzle, then, is this: Why should an average group of educated men and women almost all be able to recognize "To be, or not to be . . ." as a line from Shakespeare's *Hamlet*, yet not be able to recognize what to lovers of music is an equally familiar and memorable passage from one of the "Hamlets" of the musical literature? And such a group, needless to say, would not be singular in this respect, but representative of the incontestable fact that educated people all over the English-speaking world can recognize at least the most well-known passages from their literature or such works as Michelangelo's Sistine Ceiling and the *Mona Lisa*, but not the familiar passages from the musical masterworks of equal stature and fame. Isn't that something to puzzle over? And isn't it scandalous? Hasn't the system failed as egregiously in producing graduates with a so-called liberal education who cannot recognize the opening of Beethoven's Third Symphony or the preludes and fugues of Bach as it would if it produced graduates who were not familiar, at least on a superficial level, with *Hamlet* and the Sistine Ceiling?

But, you may well object, this is an unfair comparison. After all, music is a special sort of thing, for special sorts of people, like athletics, perhaps, or chess. Every person interested in sports will, of course, know who holds the record for hitting safely in consecutive games; and chess enthusiasts will be familiar with the greatest games of Capablanca. One hardly seems justified, though, in expecting everyone with a bachelor's degree to be familiar with the masterpieces, if I may so call them, of baseball and chess. And no more should we be embarrassed or disturbed to call ourselves educated and yet not know the opening of the *Eroica* or the finale of Mozart's "Jupiter" Symphony.

I think now we are getting close to the heart of the matter. And to bring us to the threshold, note, if you will, that the musicologist whom I quoted a moment ago referred to Beethoven's composition of the Third Symphony as a contribution to what he called "arts and letters." In so describing it, he put the work in just that class of objects that includes such things as Shakespeare's *Hamlet*, Michelangelo's Sistine Ceiling, the philosophical works of Plato and Aristotle, the novels of Jane Austen, the political and economic treatises of Adam Smith and Karl Marx, the histories of Thucydides and Gibbon, the essays of Montaigne—in a word, all of those works one would expect to encounter in what we think of as a liberal education: a course in the liberal arts. One would hardly refer to Joe DiMaggio's hitting streak or the best games of Capablanca as contributions to the field of arts and letters, much as we might admire them. And so the response that it is no more surprising for a liberal arts student to be unacquainted with Beethoven's mighty Third Symphony than that he or she be unacquainted with Joe DiMaggio's unique contribution to Western civilization, and no more distressing, seems to run up against the powerful counterresponse that since Beethoven's Third Symphony is acknowledged on all hands to be squarely within the world of arts and letters, whereas accomplishments in sports and chess are excluded, one would surely expect it and not them to be familiar to educated people and find it both surprising and distressing if it were not, given its monumental significance in the history of music.

This would seem to be the end of the matter. What more is there to say? A liberal arts education should surely give one at least a passing acquaintance with the acknowledged masterpieces of arts and letters. Musical works like Beethoven's Third Symphony and (to take another example) the First and Fourth Symphonies of Brahms are such acknowledged masterpieces; yet it is a palpable fact that nine out of ten educated people would not be able to identify a theme from any of them. This is a distressing failure of our educational system that should be corrected; for it is—or ought to be—as embarrassing to us to send people out into the world whom we certify as educated in the humanities who cannot tell Brahms from Beethoven as it would be if we were to send them out not knowing Adam Smith from Karl Marx, or Homer from Virgil. Certainly many people in music whom I know feel this way.

But as much as I identify with the feelings of my colleagues and friends in the musical profession, and as strongly as I feel myself about the musical masterpieces, the defense I have suggested just now for the inclusion of music as a requirement in liberal arts education seems far too facile and unconvincing. On the face of it, it is just going to seem absurd to most people—students and teachers alike—to maintain with equal force that it is unthinkable for someone to be considered educated in the liberal arts if he or she is not acquainted with the *Iliad* and that it is unthinkable for such a person to be considered liberally educated if he or she is not acquainted with Beethoven's Third Symphony. I do not say it *is* absurd. Indeed, I am much inclined to acquiesce in it. What I *do* say is that it is certainly going to seem absurd to others, and that if it is going to stand up to scrutiny it is going to have to have more of a defense than the argument that the Third

Symphony, like the *Iliad*, is a contribution to the world of arts and letters, is of equal stature in music to the *Iliad* in literature, and therefore deserves equal consideration as a *sine qua non* for an education in the humanities. And now at last I have come to the true purpose of this article, which is to investigate the possibility of such a defense.

If I do not think it sufficient for the inclusion of musical works in the required liberal arts curriculum merely that they are works of art of a sufficiently high order, then something important seems to follow: it is that there must be something *else* about a work of art *besides* its merely being a great work of art that I think justifies our inclusion of it in a proper liberal arts education. What can that be? In asking that question I am essentially raising the whole issue of why works of art are to be studied at all by the humanities student. If it is clear that the *Iliad* and *Moby Dick* are to be on the curriculum and less than clear, perhaps even doubtful, that Beethoven's Third Symphony should be, there must be something that the former possess and that the latter at least appears to lack and which rationally justifies such a serious judgment. What that something might be is a daunting question. And I cannot hope to give even the beginning of a satisfactory answer here. All I can do is make some exploratory probes.

I think it fair to say that two closely interrelated justifications are operative, either explicitly or, frequently, implicitly in our inclusion of works of art as objects of study in the humanities curriculum. To begin with, the Western tradition values knowledge perhaps above all other human goods. It is not surprising, therefore, that the most pervasive and influential defense of art as a necessary part of a humanistic education centers on the belief that works of art are sources of knowledge: that artists, like physicists or philosophers, biologists or economists, are discoverers and teachers of truths.

One must say straightaway that this deep-seated conviction is far from being either clear or uncontentious and has been questioned by philosophers since Plato: questioned by some, I should say, only to be reasserted and defended by others. For every Plato who has come along to cast skeptical doubt upon the pretensions of the artist to wisdom has had his Aristotle to answer him.

What kind of knowledge does the artist possess? How does he or she acquire such knowledge? How is it conveyed to us? These questions have much bedevilled those philosophers and critical theorists who have perceived at least one of the values of artworks to be their "truthfulness" or "insight." But as difficult as these questions have been to answer—and I doubt that we have generally accepted answers to them yet—faith in the artist's claim to be a seeker of the truth and purveyor of it to mankind has refused to die out, particularly among those who read novels and look at paintings not as a profession but as a pastime: in other words, educated laymen.

Of course, the view that the artist is knower and educator has undergone evolution and change since antiquity and has been, there is no doubt, particularly vulnerable to the inroads of the so-called scientific revolution. For as scientific discovery, theory, and verification have increasingly become our paradigms of the knowledge game, it has become increasingly difficult to see the artist as one of the players.

This has meant a certain retrenchment in the knowledge claims made for the fine arts. For where a Roman poet could claim to tell us the nature of the universe, we seek that information today from the physicist, astronomer, and cosmologist. And although we can learn a good deal about cetaceans from chapter 32 of Melville's masterpiece, I doubt it is that kind of knowledge we seek there, nor would we be much distressed, or prone to give *Moby Dick* a literary demerit, if we found that the author's zoology is inaccurate.

What the defenders of the knowledge claims of the fine arts tell us is that we can find in them something that we cannot find in the natural sciences: something called humanistic knowledge or, better, knowledge about ourselves as human beings: self-knowledge, if you like. And that brings us to the second of the two interrelated justifications for the place of the fine arts in a liberal, humanities education.

The Enlightenment dream of science as ameliorating the human condition has brought along with it the Romantic nightmare of science as the dehumanization of human life; and the nightmare as well as the dream have, as we now know, both come true in our century. So if it is art, not science, that can tell us what it is to be human, what it is to be ourselves, then it is art that can bring us, through that knowledge, an essential part of the good life that science cannot. Science and its resultant technology can bring us physical well-being and perhaps, as the *philosophes* thought, freedom from superstitious fears; and those surely are a part—a very important part—of the good and happy life. But they are not enough. They do not bring us human feeling: they do not soften the rough edges. More importantly, what scientific enlightenment fails to do is initiate us into our own culture, our own tribe. And such tribal identify, we now know, as the *philosophes* perhaps did not, is a prerequisite not only for being happy but, indeed, for being human. Rites of passage, then, are part of the function of art. In teaching us about ourselves, our symbols, the metaphors by which we live, art seems to humanize us in a quite literal sense of that word. It makes us human beings by helping us pass into our tribal identity.

How does art do these things? How does it teach and, in the process, humanize us? Plato's answer—which is the only even initially plausible

answer that I know——is by the dual process of representation and emula-
tion. We see human beings and their ways of life represented in plays and
pictures or we hear about them in poetic recitations, and, as they are held
up to us at least implicitly in such representations as examples, we follow
as well as understand them. It is because he thought that people tend to
emulate artistic representations that Plato had such respect for, and at the
same time fear of, the arts. For what we emulate we *become*, on Plato's view;
which means that in emulating the virtuous we become virtuous ourselves,
but—and this is the ominous result—in emulating the wicked we become
wicked ourselves, in emulating the cowardly we become cowards.

In any event, it is some modern transformation of this Platonic view that,
I believe, constitutes the implicit justification for our inclusion of the arts,
particularly the literary arts, in the humanistic curriculum. They impart, so
many believe, a knowledge that the natural and even the social sciences
cannot; and that knowledge, far from being an end in itself, is one of the
principal means of our acculturation, our initiation into our traditions: a
principal means of our achieving truly human happiness.

If this is even a shadow of the truth, then we can see not only why, in
general, the arts are considered an essential part of a liberal education, but
what principle of choice is employed in deciding which individual works
are to have pride of place: which, that is, are to be considered *required* rather
than merely optional for the liberal arts student. Of course the works
chosen are those about whose outstandingly high aesthetic quality a
general consensus has developed through time. But high aesthetic quality is
not the only criterion. Confining my remarks here just to literature, I dare
say that on any liberal arts curriculum, it is the "serious" literary works that
will overwhelmingly predominate. Why is that? Clearly, because it is not
just aesthetic quality that matters in these choices but subject as well. The
works on the "required" list are those the consensus has determined not
only to be literary masterpieces but, in a word, the "profound" ones: dealing with those questions of deep and abiding concern that have troubled
mankind throughout its history: God, the problem of evil, human freedom,
determinism, law, justice, love, knowledge, good and evil, life and death.

And where a comic work makes the grade, which is seldom, it is because
a case can be made not only for its literary excellence but for the "seriousness" of its intent, the comic elements notwithstanding. Only just so long as
the people who make up the required humanities curriculum are convinced, for example, that *Candide* is about Leibnizian optimism and the
problem of evil and is not just a comic romp, as some critics now seem to
believe, will it remain part of the educated person's necessary equipment.
And Sheridan's *School for Scandal* or Oscar Wilde's *The Importance of Being
Earnest*, works of the highest aesthetic merit, will gain entrance to the Pantheon of essential reading only when someone comes along to convince cur-

riculum planners that beneath the frothy comedy of manners there lies some profound existential issue.

With this much said, the question of musical works and *their* admission into the holy of holies can now be broached with at least a tentative proposal in hand for what the ticket of admission might be. If Beethoven's Third Symphony is to make a valid claim on the humanities curriculum, as required reading (if I may so put it), it must be determined to be not merely a masterpiece, a perfect work of art, but a profound work into the bargain. It must reveal to us something about those questions of deep and abiding interest that we think of as vital to our understanding of the human condition: questions especially asked and answered by the humanities rather than the natural and social sciences; questions the consideration of, if not the answering of (which may in the event be impossible), eases our passage into the human tribe. All of this Beethoven's Third Symphony must be, and must do, if it is to lay valid claim to stand with Shakespeare's *Hamlet* and Dante's *Divine Comedy* as a necessary part of a liberal education. If so much cannot be said for it, then I have, it would seem, no more justification for clucking my tongue over the inability of a recent humanities baccalaureate to recognize Beethoven's *Eroica* than over his or her inability to appreciate a stirring move in chess or a well-executed double play.

By this time I imagine you can suspect where this line of argument is leading. For not only is it difficult to see how Beethoven's Third Symphony could be about anything profound, it is difficult to see how it could be about anything at all. For it is merely—if "merely" is the appropriate word for one of the greatest artworks of the West—a magnificent, abstract structure of sound: one big beautiful noise, signifying nothing.

Of course, people have, over the centuries, made some extravagant claims about what music conveys to them; and they continue to do so. I do not know if it was in the nature of a satire of such claims or merely another example of the genre, but in a passage toward the close of his novel *Point Counterpoint*, Aldous Huxley has one of his characters say about the third movement of Beethoven's Quartet in A Minor: "It proves all kinds of things—God, the soul, goodness—inescapably. It's the only real proof that exists; the only one, because Beethoven was the only man who could get his knowledge over into expression."[2]

Now if Beethoven's music could do such things, I don't think there would be any doubt as to its right to be considered essential for an education in the humanities, for it is just those profound questions that so many of the literary works on the liberal arts curriculum raise. But do I really need to play this music for you to convince you that it couldn't possibly prove "all kinds of things—God, the soul, goodness . . ."? And if indeed it is true that, far from being able to speak to us of God and goodness, Beethoven's music, and music like it, is, as I have said, a beautiful noise, signifying nothing, it is difficult to see how it can fulfill the second function of such works as are acknowledged on all hands to be necessary for a liberal education, namely, the function of tribal initiation (as I have been calling it). For it is through the imparting of knowledge, the propounding of profound questions, the propagating of the metaphors and symbols by which we live that works of art can, so some people say, facilitate our rites of passage. But if these latter things are totally absent from the Third Symphony because it totally lacks for content, for subject matter, it hardly seems possible that it could serve the function of "cultural initiation" either. So we are left with the conclusion that Beethoven's Third Symphony, and works like it, are deeply satisfying amusements and nothing more. And though there is nothing against the notion that it is a good idea for the liberal arts curriculum to encourage and facilitate deeply satisfying amusements such as chess, or baseball, or, as the argument seems to suggest, listening to classical music, there is absolutely no justification for making a particular one of those amusements, namely, the listening to classical music, a requirement of the educated person. It would seem like mere snobbery to do so.

But perhaps I have rushed on too recklessly to this skeptical conclusion, in particular to the inference from lack of identifiable content to lack of what more generally might be called "humanizing influence." For it has long been thought that music does have some special influence over the passions and emotions of men and women, in some kind of direct manner independent of any ability to do so by conveying psychological insights or prudential advice. "Music hath charms to soothe a savage breast" is the most well-known expression of a view widely held since antiquity that music exercises some kind of direct therapeutic influence over the emotional lives of human beings. It does so, many have thought, by actually arousing in the listener such emotions as love, hate, anger, fear, joy—what I like to call the garden variety emotions—and, through that arousal, helping human beings, one way or another, to be more emotionally well adjusted.

With the advent of the tradition of pure instrumental music in Western culture, beginning in the eighteenth century, such theories have had very tough sledding, however. Before that time, most music accompanied a sung text; and there was some plausibility to the claim that, for example, hearing someone sing sad words to the accompaniment of doleful melodies and harmonies might make the hearer sad, by a kind of sympathetic reaction. To put the matter plainly, as I might be saddened by the plight of King Lear in the play, so might I be saddened by an operatic heroine singing in plaintive tones of her lost love or by a choir singing the *Lamentations of Jeremiah*. But when it comes to pure musical sound, without any explicit or implied protagonist to identify with, it is very difficult indeed to imagine how such arousal of the emotions might take place. Since the middle of the seventeenth century, when the problem was just beginning to be perceived, a vast amount of philosophical ingenuity has been expended on the problem of how musical sound, pure and simple, without the aid of a text or dramatic representation, might arouse the human emotions. Yet no one, from Descartes and Leibniz in the seventeenth century to the best minds of our own, has come up with a convincing explanation. Indeed, at least so it seems to me, the more we know about the philosophy, psychology, and physiology of the human emotions, the less plausible seems to be the notion that pure instrumental music arouses them, in any interesting sense.

Nevertheless, the conviction that music does arouse the garden variety emotions, and in so doing makes us emotionally more well adjusted and happy, is still abroad. And, after all, we do not need to know *how* music does this to justify our putting the appreciation of musical works on the liberal arts curriculum. All we would need to know is *that* it does, and we surely would have ample reason for insisting that our students study the great musical works of our tradition, as well as the great literary works. For if the reward of musical appreciation were, indeed, emotional health and stability, who would not want to encourage it?

But, alas, there is not a shred of real evidence that listening to music can achieve any such thing. Indeed, a modicum of common sense applied to this question will yield a very skeptical result. Think, for a moment, of what the implications really would be if music appreciation were, indeed, conducive to emotional health and well-being. Surely it would mean, among other things, that musicians and music lovers would be better adjusted than other folks. Is that what your experience has been? Are your friends who listen to classical music more agreeable, less strung out, better able to enter into "meaningful" relationships with others? Are the members of the music department on the whole more emotionally secure and well adjusted than the members of the physics department? Do musicians have a lower incidence of mental depression, divorce, or substance abuse? Are there fewer axe murderers among musicians than in the general population? Whenever such issues come up, it is usual to point out that the Nazi party was born in the cradle of the modern musical tradition and that many of its leaders were music lovers. Of course, I am not suggesting that listening to Wagner can make you a sadist. Apparently, however, listening to Beethoven does not have any discernible tendency to prevent it either. Perhaps the safest conclusion is the one I began with: that there is no evidence of music as conducive to emotional health and well-being. But if you are not completely disdainful of anecdotal evidence, a stronger conclusion is warranted: that there is at least some evidence against it.

I am not denying that having relaxing hobbies and amusements is conducive to mental tranquility and well-being. But one needs, as I have remarked before, a more powerful justification than that for singling out the appreciation of classical music above any of the other relaxing and harmless diversions that are available, like playing chess or collecting stamps. Why should I insist that a liberal arts student be familiar with Beethoven's Third Symphony on the grounds that "all work and no play" is a bad idea? Isn't stamp collecting equally respectable? After all, a great president of the United States was an avid philatelist; and, as I recall, his favorite musical composition was "Home on the Range." Who am I to say he was badly educated? He was a Harvard man!

Thus, it seems, I have come again to the distressing conclusion that there is no real rational justification for requiring students of the humanities to be familiar with such masterworks of the Western musical tradition as Beethoven's Third Symphony. But why should I say that this is a "distressing" conclusion? Why should I not simply accept it with equanimity? Well, that is because I find myself confronted here with something in the form of a familiar kind of philosophical dilemma: a very strong inclination to believe that something is the case; and, not for lack of trying, no acceptable argument to *show* that it is the case. I am a very serious music lover and a serious performer on a musical instrument; and I have spent a good part of my career in philosophy writing on musical subjects. I am up to my ears in music. And the idea that a student should be *required*, for example, to read Voltaire's *Candide* before he or she can be granted a liberal arts degree, but not be required to have even a passing acquaintance with Beethoven's Third Symphony seems to me utterly outrageous. I choose *Candide* as an example not merely because it is on everyone's humanities list but because it is a particular favorite of mine. I love the book and, indeed, have written about it. But to compare *Candide* with Beethoven's Third Symphony is to compare a pop gun with a cannon. Voltaire's classic is a sparkling ornament to the world of arts and letters. The mighty *Eroica* is a monument. And it must be deeply disturbing to someone steeped in the Western musical tradition to think that a student should have been required to know about Pangloss and Martin and Cunegonde before being accounted as educated in the humanities, and yet come out of the process without even being able to recognize the unmistakable opening chords and theme of Beethoven's Third Symphony, not to mention the unforgettable entrance of the French horn at measure 394.

So I have a very, very strong conviction, amounting almost to religious fervor, that an acquaintance with Beethoven's Third Symphony, and musical works of its calibre, is absolutely necessary for a well-rounded education in the humanities. Yet, so far, I have no rational justification for that conviction; and a philosopher who has not learned that the strength of a conviction is no argument for its truth ought to be summarily defrocked.

I confess that when I first began writing this essay I could see no further than the conclusion I have already reached. And I thought merely to lay it out as a piece of unfinished business, badly in need of our attention as humanists: essentially a conviction in search of an argument. But the more I thought about this during the writing, the more I thought it would be a dirty trick to play on musicians to go to all of this trouble to write on music and the humanities, only to state in the end that although I just love music to pieces, I cannot think of a single good reason to teach it to humanities undergraduates. With a friend like me, I don't suppose music needs any enemies.

Of course we have all been taught to value no man above the truth. So I hardly need make an excuse for saying what I think is the case, even though we might all fervently wish it were not so. Nevertheless, along with my growing conviction that we do not have any properly worked-out justification for demanding of the humanities student familiarity with the masterworks of the Western musical tradition has come at least the glimmering of an idea about how such a justification might be fashioned. For it has begun to press itself upon me that although we cannot look to the content of music, as we can to that of literary works and even paintings, or to the somewhat naive and uncritical belief in music's direct influence on the emotional lives of human beings to provide such justification, we can perhaps appeal to some function that it might perform in our social lives, related to its earlier history, before it entered the concert hall and, in our own times, the living room by way of the record player: a role analogous to the one literary works and works of the visual arts play in virtue of their content. Let me suggest briefly what I have in mind.

Now it is no very daring thing to assert that no culture is without what we would all recognize as music; and that in every culture, including our own, music has played various roles in our ritual and social activities: in our work, our dance, our religious rites, our public spectacles. And in all of the instances in which music played a role in ritualistic activities, our relation to the music was not passive. In our work we moved to the music; in religious rites we sang; in social contexts we danced; in public events we marched.

This is in sharp contrast to music in the concert hall, of which Beethoven's Third Symphony has served as my exemplar. Concertgoing is a spectator sport. And the concert hall is the musical equivalent of the museum. As a matter of fact, both institutions, of fairly recent coinage, came into existence at the same time: toward the end of the eighteenth century. We go to the museum to gaze and to the concert hall to gaze with our ears.

The music we listen to in the concert hall is, however, related to the music of our rituals. It grew out of those musics and is, as it were, an aesthetic distillation: it contains, in stylized form, evocations of them: the dance, the march, the hymn, the dirge, and so on. As such, it has very deep reverberations in us.

But the performing of music is itself a ritual, a coming together, whether it is four members of a string quartet, coming together in democratic fashion, as equals, or the one-hundred-odd members of a symphony orchestra under what has been described as the military discipline of the conductor. And concertgoing too is a coming together. The community of performers, the musical work as the aesthetic distillation of ritual, the audience as a congregation of cocelebrants, all make, together, an experience that calls up deep things for human beings beyond the description of music merely as a beautiful noise. It is, I want to suggest, somewhere within this ritualistic significance of the *whole musical experience* that the justification of music, as part of the humanities curriculum, must lie if, indeed, there is to be any justification at all.

Two things should be remarked upon that are relevant to this picture. The first is that the community of the concert hall is now in danger of being utterly destroyed by the isolation of the high-fidelity sound system. For one can now get in one's own living room, not only a performance equal to that of a live performance in regard to quality of sound, but, in some respects, even a better one. Second, the audience for classical music is, for the most part, no longer an audience of musically educated amateurs, capable of making music as well as listening to it, as Beethoven's audience, for example, still was. It is instead an audience of completely passive spectators, not only passive in the sense of being, for the purposes of the concert hall, temporarily listeners rather than players or singers, but permanently so, with no musical activity in their lives apart from the passive one of listening. The result of the first development is that listening to music has become a completely asocial pastime, neither bringing people together in a sense of ritual participation, nor bringing them, in its fullness, the sense of cooperatively wresting order from chaos, society from anarchy that a live performance might convey. The result of the second development, far more harmful even than the first to the listening experience, is to deprive the audience of any real sense of what it is like to make music: what it is like to perform the ritual of bringing musical order out of the anarchy of noise.[3] For not only is the performing of music, in ensemble, a deep and rich communal experience in itself; it enriches as well in ways hard to convey to the nonperformer the experience of musical listening. It literally makes one able to hear what to others is inaudible. In particular, I would conjecture, it renders more audible just those qualities of music having the deepest ritualistic, "tribal" vibrations by a kind of sympathetic response to the performance that only someone who has experienced performance directly can have. At the risk of some exaggeration, to listen to music without having performed it at some level, as a singer or player, is like seeing *Romeo and Juliet* without ever having been in love.

Let me now try to draw these threads together in some kind of conclusion. There is some good news and some bad news.

The good news is that there may well be a viable defense for music listening as not merely a part of a liberal arts education, but an essential part. That defense lies, I suggest, in the deep reverberations of tribal ritual that music, *in the complete institution of music making*, sets up. Participation in the musical experience has the effect, through these deep connections, of bringing people together: it has a culturally cohesive effect.

Unfortunately, of course, bringing people together, making them cohere in a tribe, is not an intrinsic good. For people can be brought together for wicked as well as for noble purposes; and music does not distinguish between them. The Nazis used music as a cohesive force for uniting the German people in one cause; and some of you may remember the concerts that Toscanini conducted, during the Second World War, making use of much the same musical repertoire, to help unite us in another. We may not thoroughly understand it—indeed, I do not think we do—but music has always had, throughout the history of the human tribe, this enormous power of creating cohesion. There is no culture that does not use music to that end.

Thus, there would seem to be, in this enormous and unique socializing power of music, ample justification for our requiring the educated person not only to be acquainted with the literary totems of his or her tribe, but with the musical ones as well. That is the good news. Now for the bad.

The bad news is that, to the limited extent to which we try to teach music to the liberal arts student at all, we do it in a completely inappropriate way, with predictably negligible results. We have chosen the wrong paradigm. We pattern the teaching of what used to be called "music appreciation" on the way the English department, for example, would teach the nineteenth-century novel. But that is to make three crucial mistakes. First, it is to treat music as a "content" art, whereas I have been arguing that it is, rather, a "ritualistic" art, if you will. Second, it is to treat music as a "private" art, whereas, I have been arguing, it is a "community" art. And third, it is to treat music, from the appreciation side, as a "passive" art, whereas I have been arguing that even where one plays the role of passive auditor, it is a "participation" art.

What I am getting at is this. If I were the kind of person who, on at least some of the nights he is at home, curls up with a good novel, becomes engrossed, reads it with pleasure and understanding, comes away having communed with fictional human beings and their problems, having gained emotional insight into the human condition, I think you would say that the English department of the University of Michigan, where I was an undergraduate, had done its work admirably well. And it did its work as English departments do everywhere, by giving me the works of the canon to read, requiring that I take them home to study, helping me understand and appreciate them, and, of course, giving me the ability to read literary works after my graduation. They could do what they did, the way that they did, because novels have meaning above and beyond their formal and syntactical properties, because reading novels has its ultimate payoff in the privacy of the reader's own home, where communion takes place, and because reading is, in a perfectly good and rewarding way, a passive activity. Not, of course, in the sense that the reader does not have to bring things to his or her reading of a text and do things conceptually to a text, but in the sense that the reader need not be a writer or performer. To love, appreciate, and enjoy novels I hardly need also write them or read them aloud.

Music also has its canon. Where the English department wants you to appreciate Jane Austen and Thomas Hardy, the music department wants you to be familiar with Bach, Beethoven, and Brahms. And it proceeds in much the same way, except, of course—and this is a crucial exception—that it has no content to reveal, no message to decode. You will, of course, be told about Beethoven's Third Symphony in class. But few instructors, trained in the modern analytic and musicological traditions as they are, will be tempted to attribute any *meaning* to it or any of the other works discussed. Instead, you will be told, with suitable musical illustrations, about the first theme and the second theme of sonata form, what a minuet and trio is, and a theme with variations, how to recognize the subject and countersubject of a fugue, and so on. You will, no doubt, be given one of the standard, analytically oriented appreciation texts to read; and, of course, you will be expected to do your homework, that is to say, to listen to the works either at home on your record player or, plugged into earphones, in the music department's technically up-to-date listening room, just as you are expected to read the novels assigned to you in English 235. If the instructor is successful, and you cooperate in the process, you will be able to listen to the first movement of a classical symphony and repeat the litany of first theme, second theme, closing theme to yourself or to your fascinated roommate.

But the sad fact is that you will not thereby have tapped into the deep resources of musical culture that I have been talking about. If what I have said about music has any validity, then one cannot directly equate sitting at home reading *Pride and Prejudice* with sitting at home listening to Beethoven's Third Symphony. Something is missing here. Something has gone wrong. The modern musical conscience forbids us burbling on about deep and profound meanings in the great works of our musical tradition. We cannot see God and goodness in a Beethoven quartet; and we should not. So we teach music as pure, contentless, abstract form which, in a sense, it is. But we teach it in a way that is suited instead to works of art that have semantic as well as syntactic properties: meaning as well as form. Some, feeling how empty our teaching of music in the humanities curriculum really is, may well succumb to the temptation to fill the void by giving it a content it does not have. Their feelings are justified, their intentions good.

However, we cannot substitute fantasy for content. It is just intellectually dishonest. What we can do is recognize that what is missing from our teaching of music as a humanistic subject is not a subject matter, which it never had in the first place, but a ritualistic dimension that has been forgotten, that we have allowed to slip away.

I fully believe, again to risk exaggeration, that the way we teach music to humanities students is much like trying to teach the nineteenth-century novel to people who cannot read. To be able to sing or to play is a necessary part of musical literacy. It is, as I have argued, a necessary part of the full listening experience. Literacy is best acquired, whether it is musical literacy or linguistic competence, before a student comes to college. But few students anymore will come to college able to sing, or to play a musical instrument, or to read musical notation. And so what I am saying is that we cannot teach music effectively in the liberal arts curriculum without teaching playing or singing as well as basic musicianship, subjects traditionally given only in the conservatory. It is the only way that we will do justice to the ritualistic, communal, and participatory aspects of music that make it what it is, and make it so different form the literary and visual arts.

There is absolutely no justification at all, then, on my view, for insisting that well-educated humanities students learn music in the way that music faculties today are required to teach it to them. But if they could teach it the way they all really know it should be taught, the justification is strong and compelling. To be able to rattle off "first theme, second theme, closing theme" is a parlor trick not worth the trouble of acquiring. To have Beethoven's Third Symphony in one's blood and bones is a boon beyond compare: part of our rites of passage, part of our tribal identity, an important part, it seems to me, of what makes us human. Of course a *human* life guarantees neither a good life nor a happy one. The best, it seems to me, that we can hope from music is that it help to *humanize*. Happiness and goodness we will all have to work out for ourselves.[4]

NOTES

1. Paul Henry Lang, *Music in Western Civilization* (New York: Norton, 1941), p. 763.
2. Aldous Huxley, *Point Counterpoint* (New York: Harper and Row, 1965), p. 433 (chap. 37).
3. This image was suggested to me by Jacques Attali, *Noise: The Political Economy of Music*, trans. Brian Massumi (Minneapolis: University of Minnesota Press, 1987).
4. The present essay was originally delivered as a public lecture to the William O. Douglas Honors college of Central Washington University in Ellensburg, 11 October 1989, and was written especially for that occasion. It appears here with minor revisions. I am grateful to Jay Bachrach and Barry Donahue for inviting me to speak and to the audience of students and faculty that made it such a stimulating and memorable experience for me.

Music and the Last Intellectuals

JOHN SHEPHERD

Recent years have witnessed an intensification of debate over the role and function of universities in North American society. A central feature of this debate has been an attack on scholarship which, in one way or another, could be described as "critical." The view that too much academic work was being politicized (that is, preoccupied with questions of race, gender, and class) or trivialized (that is, by a fascination with public culture) was made both by the conservative chair of the National Endowment for the Humanities, and later Ronald Reagan's Secretary of Education, William J. Bennett, and by Allan Bloom, author of *The Closing of the American Mind.*

Both Bennett[1] and Bloom[2] have argued against certain forms of criticism that became an important force in university life in the wake of the 1960s. These arguments can be read in the context of political cultures which, in the English-speaking nations of the northern hemisphere, have taken a marked turn to the right during the 1980s. The role of universities is being seen increasingly by governments and funding agencies in terms of the rhetoric of "human resources." Universities and the intellectual life they nurture are increasingly being inserted into the rhetoric of a narrow economic instrumentalism which can only conceive, or is only prepared to conceive, social usefulness and social responsibility in material as opposed to cultural terms. As Bill Graham, president of the Ontario Confederation of University Faculty Associations, has observed: "The university, according to the new mythology, is a key player in the on-rushing knowledge based, information economy. Post-secondary education becomes an engine of economic growth because universities supply much of the basic research needed for growth, and, along with colleges, they supply most of the 'human resources' as well."[3]

John Shepherd is Professor of Music and Sociology and the Director of the School for Studies in Art and Culture at Carleton University, Ottawa. Among his recent works are *Music as Social Text* and *Alternative Musicologies*, a special issue he edited for the Canadian University Music Review.

It is not difficult to muster arguments in support of the view that, if universities are to function as an intellectual resource in society, their role should be inclusive of the full range of human activities, not restricted simply to the instrumental achievement of material reproduction. Any society that consistently and for a long period of time prioritizes the material over the cultural will irreparably damage itself, as recent events in the German Democratic Republic have demonstrated. It can be argued that the collapse of the GDR had as much to do with the failure of a repressive Stalinist regime to ensure a viable and meaningful everyday culture for people (over and above the ubiquitous state-run television service) as it did with the supposedly spontaneous uprising of a people in search of democratic ideals. The situation in the West, of course, is very different. While universities as sites for cultural renewal and cultural criticism are under consistent attack, rich and vibrant forms of cultural expression continue apace outside the academy. It is unthinkable that Western societies will collapse because of the lack of viable and meaningful forms of everyday culture.

The kinds of arguments advanced by Bloom result in a view of the university as a repository for the intellectual capital of the dominant culture. If the university is to become an increasingly instrumental institution, then, in so much as it continues to research and teach "culture," its secondary role becomes that of imparting a capital in terms of which the dominant culture can identify and demarcate itself against those cultures that are not dominant. This strategy for intellectual life within the academy can take root and prosper only because of a significant gap that has grown up between the university and large segments of society. These segments of society have little understanding of the teaching and research that are undertaken in universities and so become easily susceptible to arguments couching universities' social usefulness and responsibility in the rhetoric of instrumentalism. However, if universities as sites for significant cultural criticism have come under attack in this fashion, then it is in part because intellectuals have allowed this to happen. Forced for financial reasons to work in the university as opposed to other places in society, intellectuals have reacted to the increasing professionalization and bureaucratization of the university world and become preoccupied with matters of professional development and security. As Russell Jacoby argues in his book *The Last Intellectuals*, the intellectual's vision has become restricted and inward looking. By the 1960s, he says, "the universities virtually monopolized intellectual work; an intellectual life outside the campuses seemed quixotic . . . many young intellectuals . . . never left school; others discovered there was nowhere else to go. They became radical sociologists, Marxist historians, feminist theorists, but not quite public intellectuals."[4] Since, claims Jacoby, these intellectuals "are occupied and preoccupied by the demands of university careers . . . professional life thrives [and] public culture grows poorer and poorer."[5]

The attack on significant cultural criticism by Bennett and Bloom is understandable, since they are attacking forms of intellectual work that bring contemporary cultural life inside the classroom and therefore undo, to a certain extent, the separation of academic from public culture. So long as this kind of intellectual work remains cloistered within the university and makes little impact in the world of public culture, it will likely be regarded as an irritant: undesirable, unnecessary, misplaced, peripheral, but hardly worth taking seriously, the more so since to take it seriously would give it a profile both undeserved and unwarranted. It is ironic, therefore, that the very market forces that have provided such a sympathetic context for the ideas of Bennett and Bloom have resulted likewise in intellectual areas such as critical theory and cultural studies becoming big business. In those universities that are enrollment driven, courses in communications, critical theory, cultural studies, film, television, and popular culture (including popular music) are hardly suffering. There are significant numbers of students interested in studying the rich and vibrant forms of cultural expression that inform their worlds and their biographies, and in studying them in ways that guarantee a certain distance from the market forces that drive them. As Jacoby observes: "The public sphere is hardly neutral; it responds to money or power or drama, not to quiet talent and creative work. For decades, even for centuries, writers and critics have decried the press for distorting cultural life. Inasmuch as the public sphere is less a free market of ideas than a market, what is publicly visible registers nothing but market forces."[6]

It is our students, or at least some of them, who within the present context of these market forces are creating a situation where critical thought can have an impact, if not on public culture itself, then certainly on an appreciable number of people who are likely to take their place in it. It is important, therefore, that the rhetoric of instrumentalism which is currently being aimed at our universities, and the conservative criticisms of figures like Bennett and Bloom which go with it, be met not with well-worn truisms about the value of cultural inquiry within the academy, but with strategies and programs developed in the light of a realistic appraisal of what it is we should be teaching and why. Social usefulness and social responsibility demand not alternative rhetorical forms, but alternative ways of thinking and acting.

Music and Politics

It is not difficult to make the case that the majority of music education that takes place in our universities conforms either to the rhetoric of instrumentalism or to a perceived need to impart a certain kind of cultural capital. In other words, either we are imparting skills, or we are teaching a certain kind of music in a certain kind of way. Simon Frith has explicitly linked the traditional curriculum of university music departments to a specific class position. The organizing institution of bourgeois music, he says,

> is the academy—the music departments of universities, conservatories, the whole panoply of formal arrangements and practices in which classical music in its various forms is taught. . . . the bourgeois music world is heavily dependent on scholarship, on the accumulation of the knowledge about music history and the compositional process without which score and performance cannot be understood. The scholarly skills developed in university music departments . . . are just like those developed by art historians or literary critics. Their purpose is the same: to establish the canon, to come up with a coherent, linear narrative.[7]

Likewise, Susan McClary has linked the way in which this traditional curriculum is conceptualized in terms of a politics underpinned by, although certainly not reducible to, questions of gender. Most people care about music, she says,

> because it resonates with experiences that otherwise go unarticulated, whether it is the flood of cathartic release that occurs at the climax of a Tchaikowsky symphony or the groove that causes one's body to dance—that is, to experience itself in a new way. Yet our music theories and notational systems do everything possible to mask those dimensions of music that are related to physical human experience and focus instead on the orderly, the rational, the cerebral. The fact that the majority of listeners engage with music for more immediate purposes is frowned upon by our institutions.[8]

The reasons for this disapproval, continues McClary, "are often hidden in the ideology of idealism, in that rigid set of interlocking Western binary oppositions (i.e., culture/nature, mind/body, objectivity/subjectivity . . . bourgeois/working class . . .) that ultimately collapse back onto masculine/feminine."[9] For this reason, she concludes,

> a feminist criticism of any music . . . would have to be concerned with uncovering the dimensions of Western music that are organized according to all of those pervasive and pernicious metaphysical dichotomies. We cannot afford to focus solely on obvious instances of gender—to be one-issue critics—but we must also be alert to the politics of race, of class, of popular culture: those elements that have been relegated to the "feminine" slagheap. Indeed, recent attacks on criticism by . . . Bennett . . . and . . . Bloom . . . make it very clear how much elite culture regards all these threats as interchangeable.[10]

There is, in other words, a socially and politically located philosophy that underpins both the traditional curriculum of university music departments and the way in which that curriculum is understood and taught. However, it is not the only possible philosophy, and it is certainly not a philosophy immune to criticism.[11] It is not my purpose to engage in that criticism here but to suggest that there are other ways of thinking about and engaging in music education at the university level that would result in academic music becoming a less isolated discipline within the academic world and one that could contribute significantly to the revitalization of universities as places where critical intellectual work could begin to make an impact on public culture.

In his book *Contemplating Music: Challenges to Musicology*, Joseph Kerman bemoaned the fact that

> serious music criticism . . . does not exist as a discipline on a par with musicology and music theory on the one hand, or literary and art criticism on the other. We do not have the musical Arnolds or Eliots, Blackmurs or Kermodes, Ruskins or Schapiros. In the circumstances, it is idle to complain or lament that critical thought in music lags conceptually far behind that in other arts. In fact, nearly all musical thinkers travel at a respectful distance behind the latest chariots (or bandwagons) of intellectual life in general. . . . Semiotics, hermeneutics, and phenomenology are being drawn upon only by some of the boldest of musical studies today. Post-structuralism, deconstruction, and serious feminism have yet to make their debuts in musicology or music theory.[12]

Yet, given the kind of feminist agenda for music criticism contemplated by McClary, it is doubtful whether scholars such as Kerman would want to engage seriously with critical theory, whatever the orientation. As McClary observes:

> Recent statements by scholars such as Joseph Kerman make it seem that on the one hand musicology is eager to have instances of feminist criticism; but, on the other hand, the discipline is apprehensive about how far the critique would go and about the consequences with respect to the canon. The ideal form of feminist critiques would appear to be one that contributed new insights but that did not challenge received conceptions and judgements. The great composers and traditional notions of what makes them great would remain securely in place, but we would have yet another reason to pay them homage.[13]

The carefully circumscribed nature of Kerman's anticipated reforms, his desire to maintain the established canon in its traditional form, becomes clear when he considers the implications of social scientific thought for an understanding of Western music (by which he clearly means "classical" music). Despite the fact that many forms of poststructuralism and "serious" feminism are virtually indistinguishable from the social scientific enterprise (both, for example, subscribe to the notion that reality is socially constructed—that there is nothing "given" or "essential" about the realities we so take for granted), Kerman believes that "western music is just too different from other musics, and its cultural contexts too different from other cultural contexts"[14] to be subjected to this kind of examination: "The traditional alliance of musicology has been with the humanistic disciplines, not with the social sciences. . . . This alliance is still the best for developing a contextual framework for Western music. . . . It is one thing . . . to draw on modern historiography, with its ample provision for insights from anthropology and sociology, and quite another to draw on those disciplines directly for the understanding of Western music."[15]

But in what ways "Western" music is so different from other musics remains unclear in Kerman's account. The conventional wisdom within musicology has been that the traditional canon distinguishes itself from other musics in the way in which it relates to "the social," the serious study of which Kerman does not wish to bring to bear on "Western" music. In the words of Line Grenier, traditional theories on music "do not deny the fact that music has, indeed, something to do with culture and society. However, they tend to assert that 'music itself' can be defined without any further reference to social or cultural dimensions. Accordingly, it is assumed that the specificity of music lies exclusively in its sonic materiality (musical 'notes' defined from an acoustical point of view), as well as in its aesthetic, if not formal, nature."[16] A corollary of this position is that any musics whose sonic, aesthetic, or formal qualities are significantly affected by social or cultural forces really cease to be music at all. We are back, here, with McClary's idealism; with the orderly, the rational, and the cerebral; with masculine objectivity. I have argued elsewhere how the dichotomies referred to by McClary generate and underpin a view of music in which musics that display an obvious and undeniable sociality—the majority to have existed on the surface of this planet—are considered not to be worthy of study in university music departments.[17] The musical intellectual is safe in the academy, occupying a position of which Bloom would thoroughly approve.

The implication here is that either music is music, or it is something else, to be read off the surface of social existence. This is clearly the attitude that academic music takes toward the study of popular music, the form of music that musical intellectuals would study if they were serious about forming bridges to public areas of cultural activity and debate. Yet, although different forms of popular music are enmeshed in powerful commercial processes, they cannot be reduced to them. Jacoby makes this point more generally in relation to public culture. If it is true, he says, that "what is publicly visible registers nothing but market forces," then "this observation easily degenerates into a cliché that the ruling ideas are the ideas of the ruling class; cultural studies vanish into economics. Intellectual life . . . is obviously subject to market and political forces but cannot be reduced to them. The impact of network television or national newsweeklies on cultural life can scarcely be underestimated; but it is not the whole story."[18]

There is, in other words, a legitimate object here for departments of music to study, an object that is no less "musical" and no more "social" than classical music, particularly in the way in which the latter is currently produced, disseminated, and consumed. As Frith has observed of John Culshaw, for many years head of the classical division of Decca Records, "His autobiography is instructive in general terms—because he takes for granted that classical music records are produced commercially. The tension between judgments of commercial value and judgments of musical value are ever present in his decisions."[19] If there are other ways of thinking about and engaging in music education at the university level which will lead to a greater academic and public presence for the musical intellectual, then a consideration of the issues raised by the study of popular music in music departments may well be instructive.

The Relevance of Popular Music Studies

Since its inception as a more or less continuous academic tradition since the late 1970s, the field of popular music studies has constructed itself largely around two related tensions. The first has to do with the study of music either from the point of view of context or from the point of view of text. In the study of the established canon, this tension has displayed itself in the lack of communication between the related disciplines of historical musicology and music theory. As Richard Leppert and Susan McClary recently observed, "The disciplines of music theory and musicology . . . cautiously keep separate considerations of biography, patronage, place and dates from those of musical syntax and structure."[20] In ethnomusicology, this tension has displayed itself in increasingly subtle and fertile dialogues between anthropologically oriented and musicologically oriented ethnomusicologists. And in popular music studies it has displayed itself in the different orientations adopted by scholars who come out of sociology, communications, and cultural theory and those who come out of musicology. The second tension has occurred between those who take a more empirical and positivistic approach to their subject matter and those whose approach is rather more interpretive. Neither approach can exist without the other. Interpretation requires information. But conversely, the adducing of information always occurs within particular social and cultural contexts that influence not only what questions are asked, but also the particular premises that shape the asking of the questions and the provision of the answers.

However, the academic study of music has been dominated by an emphasis on the empirical and the positivistic at the expense of the theoretical and the interpretive. If historical musicology has been characterized by the ascertaining of "facts" and the structuring of such "facts" into meaningful narratives, then music theory has been concerned to analyze music as if it were a definitive and nonnegotiable object whose inner workings could be incontrovertibly understood. Kerman has linked this stress on positivism to the inability of historical musicology and music theory to communicate meaningfully with one another. The concentration of musicologists on "limited positivistic tasks," he argues, "has had the decided effect of side-stepping 'the music itself.'" He continues: "If the musicologists' characteristic failure is superficiality, then that of the analysts is myopia. . . . by removing the bare score from its context in order to examine it as an autonomous organism, the analyst removes that organism from the ecology that sustains it."[21] Ethnomusicology has been similarly dominated by an emphasis on positivistic tasks. Area studies have typically undertaken the documentation of musical practices in different parts of the world as an exercise in museology. Again, more musicological approaches within ethnomusicology have sought to understand and document musical systems and musical instruments as objects decontextualized from the social ecologies that sustain them. Interpretive scholars in both disciplines, while certainly not absent, have been scarce. The emphasis has been on the particularities of empirical evidence rather than on broader questions to do with music as a signifying practice within human communities.

Popular music studies has been the exception in this regard. To be sure, it has been possible, since the late 1970s, to discern a distinction between, on the one hand, the empiricists, the historians, and the positivists, located largely but not exclusively in the United States, and, on the other hand, the theorists who have been located largely but not exclusively in Europe and Canada. However, there has been, proportionately, a greater emphasis on interpretation and theory in popular music studies than in either musicology or ethnomusicology. There are two reasons for this. Firstly, most popular music is obviously, evidently, and undeniably social in its significance. Secondly, a significant proportion of the popular music studied by popular music scholars has existed in the here-and-now of its analysis. It has been there to interrogate the academic discourse constructed around it. This has resulted in the first tension, that between context and text, being more inescapably and sharply focused than it has been in musicology or ethnomusicology. The music under examination has not been from other times and places. Not only has this made it difficult for the music to become the pawn of academic discourses. It has also meant that the pressure to examine musical affect as an experience mediated essentially through social and cultural processes has been intense. Questions to do with the relationship between context and text could not be deferred to unfold in the fullness of academic time. The questions have had an urgency that has caused and motivated popular music studies to develop a theoretical trajectory remarkable and sometimes alarming in its speed and directions.

To make these observations is not to claim for popular music studies a special status derived from its subject matter. It is simply to recognize that popular music studies have been led inescapably to ask and attempt to answer some of the more important questions to do with music as a signifying practice within human communities. This particular focusing of popular music studies is important, because the academic study of music has indeed been slow to influence the rest of the academy. Not only has music been marginalized and peripheralized—indeed, feminized—in modern societies, but so also has the academic study of music. This marginalization has little to do with the nature of "music" (a term that itself is problematic, as Grenier has pointed out, because of its "highly polysemic nature" and the fact that it "encompasses distinct notions").[22] It is more of a comment on the nature of the contemporary world and of the way in which that world structures and reproduces itself. Popular music studies could be poised to make a very significant contribution to wider academic discourse. It could establish that, within the humanities and social sciences, the study of music is just as important and just as crucial to the understanding of humanity as any other discipline. I now wish to illustrate how such a case could be made.

Music, the Body, and Signifying Practice

I would argue that "music"—as it is discursively constituted within specific conjunctures of social, cultural, and historical forces—displays unique and specific qualities that become partly constitutive of the signifying practices within which, as "nonlinguistic" sound, it is embedded. This uniqueness and specificity rest not on any one quality, but on a combination of three qualities. Firstly, music makes no direct appeal to the world of discrete objects and concepts. It is nondenotative. It completely elides Julia Kristeva's "symbolic order." Music evokes *directly* the textures, processes, and structures of the social world as that world is manifest in the external, public realm of social interaction *and* the internal, private realm of individual subjectivity. The prime focus of music's evocation distinguishes it quite radically from language as the other mode of human communication based in sound. Secondly, music's appeal is significantly iconic. That is, a strong *but not determining* element of necessity obtains between music as a sonic event and the particular meanings invested in the sonic event. This principle of iconicity again distinguishes music quite radically from language. Thirdly, music's appeal is primarily and initially somatic and corporeal rather than cerebral and cognitive. Music appeals directly and powerfully to the human body as an individual site of utterance (a word I am using purposively instead of "speech") and of political struggle. The corporeal foundation of music's communicative power again distinguishes it radically from language.

A problem in understanding the specificity of music as a social form is that, in the development of the discipline that could contribute fundamentally to understanding the interpenetration of context and text—the discipline, that is, of cultural theory—music has been almost totally absent and language omnipresent. Cultural theory has developed overwhelmingly from the study of language, either through the discipline of literature or the discipline of linguistics. The study of music, however, has hardly affected the development of cultural theory. Because of this, the presence of language in cultural theory or, more precisely, the implications of certain conceptualizations of language for the development of cultural theory, become hidden from view. The implications of certain conceptualizations of music for cultural theory are, on the contrary, rather more visible. To make the kinds of claims I have just made about music as a signifying practice and to make them before an audience of cultural theorists is, usually, to draw accusations of essentialism. To discuss language in terms of "signifiers" and "signifieds" does not, however, draw the same response. Cultural theory, developing in the main from the study of language, has folded within its diverse categories of analysis the "unique" and "specific" qualities of language as a signifying practice. The problem, then, is that to claim that language has specific qualities does not appear to essentialize it, since its study fits comfortably within the categories of analysis deemed appropriate to the study of culture as a wider phenomenon.

The distinctions being made here are important, because there is one possible route to understanding the signification of sound in music that rests on the traditional understanding of how sound in language signifies. According to this route, however, sounds in music work differently in the sense that they do not invoke or call forth signifieds coterminous with the world of objects, events, and linguistically encodable ideas as that world is understood to be structured and called forth by language. Sounds in music are understood to occasion a ground of physiological and affective stimulation which is subsequently interpellated into the symbolic order of language. It is at this point that the sounds of music enter the social world and take on significance. Sound in music is thus equally arbitrary in its relationship to processes of signification as is sound in language, except that, to the extent that sound in music depends upon the arbitrary signifying processes of language in order to take on meaning, it is more distanced from and not as immediately implicated in processes of meaning construction as is sound in language. Sound in music could thus be said to float even freer in its relationship to processes of signification than does sound in language because it is not as directly burdened by the conventions of traditional associations between signifiers and signifieds. There is more of a sense, according to this understanding of signifying processes in music, in which sound in music can take on *any* meanings assigned to it than can sound in language.

The objection can at this point be raised that although sound in music can be argued to be polysemic in theory, it never appears to be in practice. That is, people in specific social and historical circumstances appear to be affected only by certain orders of structures, processes, and textures in the sounds of music. Sound, in other words, does seem to be implicated in processes of meaning construction through music. This objection can, however, be effectively overcome by claiming that certain orders of structures, processes, and textures in the sounds of music are conventionally taken to be meaningful and certain other orders are not taken to be meaningful by people because there already exist embedded within the symbolic order of language, mutual agreements on what is and what is not meaningful among the range of such possible orders. This position on processes of signification in music is, in other words, logically defensible. It has the advantage of explaining how there can be a meaningful relationship between sounds, words, images, and gestures in music—something that is crucial to understanding meaning in popular music and something that has been almost completely ignored by the world of musicology.

Be that as it may, this position on significance in music is incompatible with the one I elaborated earlier on two grounds: (a) it drops the body, and affective states as corporeally constituted, out of the realm of the social construction of meaning as linguistically constituted; (b) relatedly, the symbolic order of language is taken to occupy a primary and exclusive position in processes of the structuring and constitution of meaning in the sense that processes of signification involving media other than language can take on meaning only by being interpellated into the world of language. This "linguistic" approach to understanding the significance of sound in music can thus be understood to drain music of its real signifying potential, to render it a colony of language. Although not without insight into the broader task of understanding significance within popular music, this view is not, however, grounded in the very materials fundamental to the ways in which music connects. Ungrounded consumerism in cultural theoretical accounts of music remains a constant possibility!

That views of music ungrounded in music's material substance can lead in directions that lack rigor can be illustrated by reference to attempts to construct alternative semiologies of extralinguistic discourses. A symptomatic reading of some of the dominant lines of thought within poststructuralism in particular reveals how views of language are not only ahistorical but exclusionary and unsympathetic to processes of social mediation that do not fall easily within their preferred categories. In fact, most views of language within cultural theory *as well as* the position on significance in music that I elaborated earlier are essential—esssential, that is, if one wishes to extrapolate from the placements and practices of "language" and "music" within contemporary conjunctures of social and historical forces to those placements and practices of other times and other places. This tendency to reify and essentialize language affects even the work of those poststructuralists who have sought to ground discourse on extralinguistic forces and dispositions, as Richard Middleton observes in the context of Roland Barthes's writings on music. "Like other French poststructuralists who wanted to ground discourse on extralinguistic forces and dispositions," argues Middleton, "the later Barthes is open to the suspicion that 'anything goes': that along with meaning, the category of critique is abandoned, leaving the field open to political quietism, untheorized spontaneism, or apolitical hedonisms."[23] Either we have language, meaning, discourse, and reality (the orderly, the rational, the cerebral), in other words, or we have the spontaneously unstructured world of ruptured, ecstatic *jouissance*, replete with luscious, Dionysian, hedonistic pleasures.

What is being suggested here is rather different: that music, in complex and multidimensional ways that go beyond language, is both structured and structuring. The pleasures of music are socially and historically situated and, as a consequence, display logics that can speak directly to complex conjunctures of social, cultural, and biographical forces. However, these pleasures are situated nondenotatively, iconically, and corporeally. Approached in this way, the understanding of the functioning of music as a moment of social and cultural negotiation could lead to the kind of understanding of affect that Lawrence Grossberg has recently called for as a future important development for cultural theory. The functioning of music is in a certain sense global, concrete, shaping, forming, and, crucially, internalized within the body. Social configurations are intensely yet dialectically related to bodily configurations, configurations that have both external and internal dimensions. The social body becomes the human body in much the same way as the human body becomes the social body. The internal states of the human body, somatically experienced, become the source of externally uttered movements, as John Blacking has argued:

> Crucial factors in the development of cultural forms are the possibility of shared somatic states, the structures of the bodies that share

them, and the rhythms of interaction that transform commonly experienced internal sensations into externally visible and transmissible forms. . . . The shared states of different bodies can generate different sets of rules for the construction of behaviour and action by means of repeated movements in space and time that can be transmitted from one generation to another.[24]

The internal dispositions and configurations of bodies that find expression in externally perceptible bodily movement affect fundamentally the dynamics of sound production from the most basic and inalienably human of all musical instruments, the human voice. The voice, says Middleton, "is the profoundest mark of the human. An unsounding human body is a rupture in the sensuousness of existence. Undoubtedly this is because vocalizing is the most intimate, flexible and complex mode of articulation of the body."[25] It is also, presumably because the voice, as the most intimate, flexible, and complex mode of articulation of the body, is fundamental to the creation of human societies as quintessentially symbolic. Johann Sundberg discusses the relationships between body movements, human emotion, and the physiology of voice production:

There is a close correlation between body movements observable with the naked eye and hidden body movements. Examples of normally invisible body movements can be found in laryngeal cartilages, most of which are involved in the regulation of pitch. If it is true that a particular pattern of expressive body movements is typical of a specific emotional mode, then we would expect a corresponding pattern of, for example, voice pitch in speech produced in the same emotional mode. In other words, it is likely that expressive body movements are translated into acoustic terms of voice production.[26]

The way in which internal states, somatically experienced, become the source of externally uttered movements and the way in which this dialectic affects the physiology of voice production is mirrored in the production of instruments as extensions of the human voice. Here there is an external, technological manifestation of sound production thoroughly implicated with the external movements of the body. John Baily has developed this theme in arguing that players' movements affect musical structures in fundamental ways. The motor patterns that are implicated in a particular kind of music results, in Baily's view, from interaction between the morphology of the instrument and the player's sensorimotor capacities. Equally, there has grown up an intimate relationship between instruments as imitators of the human voice and the human voice as an imitator of instruments. Middleton discusses *this* dialectic with specific reference to Afro-American music:

One of the importances of Afro-American music lies in the fact that often the voice seems to be treated more as an "instrument" (the body using its own resources to make sound). . . . From work-song grunts through 1930s jazz styles (Louis Armstrong singing "like a trumpet"; Billie Holiday "like a sax") to the short mobile vocal phrases of funk and scratch textures (used like percussion, bass or synthesizer), we hear vocal "personality" receding as the voice is integrated into the processes of the articulating human body. Of course, at the same time, instruments in this tradition often sound like voices. But the often noted importance of "vocalized" tone is only part of a wider development in which "instrumental" and "vocal" modes meet on some intermediate ground: while it is true that the instrument-as-machine (technological extension of the body) becomes a gesturing body (the "voice" of the limb), at the same time the voice-as-a-person becomes a vocal body (the body vocalizing).[27]

Whatever the complexities of the dialectics between body, voice, and instruments, we may nonetheless conclude, with Baily, that "music can be viewed as a product of body movement transduced into sound."[28]

Music, through the body, does not therefore speak of a spontaneously unstructured world of ruptured, ecstatic *jouissance*, replete with luscious, Dionysian, hedonistic pleasures. I find it difficult to agree with Barthes that in music the body "speaks, it declaims, it redoubles its voice: *it speaks but says nothing*: because as soon as it is musical, speech—or its instrumental substitute is no longer linguistic, but corporeal; it only says, and nothing else: *my body is put into a state of speech: quasi parlando*."[29] I would argue that, as somatically and corporeally manifest, music is both structured and structuring. As such, it resonates powerfully within the lived, somatic, and corporeal experience of the listener. To hear a voice, a musical sound, is frequently to know of the somatic and corporeal state which produced it. The reaction is both sympathetic and empathetic. "Listeners," says Middleton, "identify with the motor structure, participating in the gestural patterns, either vicariously, or even physically, through dance or through miming vocal and instrumental performance."[30]

This principle of symbolism is important. For all Barthes's talk of music as "madness," as only saying and nothing else, he does, in his claim that "the body passes into music through no other relay than the *significant*,"[31] point toward an alternative semiology. As Middleton concludes:

> Barthes is writing of an extreme; but anyone who has participated actively or vicariously in intensely "executed" performance—who has felt the polyrhythmic interplay of hands in boogie-woogie piano, resonated with the intricacies of bluegrass texture, played along with a B. B. King guitar solo or the bass-line in Billy Ocean's "When the Going Gets Tough"—will recognize what he is pointing towards. At this extreme we would indeed find "a second semiology, that of the body in a state of music."[32]

We are fulfilling Henri Lefebvre's wish that clear correlations between signifiers and signifieds be abolished in attempting to understand music.[33] However, it remains important to maintain a certain conceptual distance between music as a social medium in sound, somatically and corporeally immanent, and individual subjectivity as socially constituted and somatically and corporeally mediated. The body, the "real" body, concludes Middleton, "cannot actually be grasped in music, but only by the *hands*; in music, it is necessarily represented, positioned, analogized, (its movements) traced. There is an absence as well as a presence, and the body in a state of music is not the same as—and must coexist with—the music in a state of psychic-somatic cathexis."[34]

This mode of signifying distinguishes music radically from language. Language, in its hegemonic visual forms and manifestations, makes an appeal that is essentially cerebral. Taking to its limits the capacity of thought to be independent of the world on which it operates, visual language, doubly arbitrary, eschews any tactile awareness, any direct awareness of the material world. Sound, the sense of touch "at a distance," as Murray Schafer has called it,[35] is effectively eradicated. In its hegemonic, visual forms and manifestations, language does not bring the body into play *directly*, either as a site for utterance or as a site for political struggle. Indeed, as we have seen, there is a strain of thought within poststructuralism that says that experience has meaning only when retrospectively located within the symbolic order—that is to say, retrospectively rationalized through language. The experience, knowledge, and meanings of the body cannot, according to this view of signification, speak *directly*, be spoken *directly*, or constitute *directly* the site of a politically efficacious awareness. There are resonances of this way of thinking in Middleton's comments on Baily's view that "music can be viewed as a product of body movement transduced into sound." This, says Middleton, "is moving us close to the limits of a semiotic approach. To some degree, the correlations or correspondences here seem so direct . . . that they have less to do with meaning than with processes in themselves, less with signs than *actions*."[36]

Yet it does not follow from this that music simply evokes unmediated experience subsequently to be rendered meaningful within the fabric of language. As I have attempted to demonstrate elsewhere in analyzing voice types as gendered through the mediations of the body,[37] the corporeal interface with music *is* quintessentially symbolic. Music *is* both structured and structuring. As Middleton concludes, "Human movement and human action are never culture-free; rather . . . there are differences in kind and extent of mediation through which pre-semiotic human interaction acquires symbolic, logical and significatory superstructures."[38] As Lefebvre concludes, "Musicality communicates corporeality. It renders the body into social practice . . . deploying their resources, music binds bodies together (socialises them)."[39]

Foucault perhaps seems to provide an exception to this trend within poststructuralism of separating experience from meaning when he claims that discourses constitute the body as well as the conscious and unconscious minds and the emotional lives of the subjects they seem to govern. The body, for example, is central to Foucault's analysis of sexuality in the modern world. He is concerned with how bodies have been perceived, given meaning and value, and with "the manner in which what is most material and most vital to them has been invested."[40] In the modern world, Foucault argues, sex has become a focal point of the exercise of power through the discursive constitution of the body. Yet if the body is constituted discursively, then it is constituted through language and visual inscriptions and placements in a way that implicitly denies the body's very essence and corporeality as a material site for utterance and political struggle. It remains the case that the body *is* spoken for *indirectly* through the conscious and unconscious processes of the mind. Music, however, goes behind the back of language and vision in speaking *directly to and through* the body. In so doing, it reminds us that while language may be fundamental to the symbolic nature of human worlds, it may also, in its hegemonic, visual forms and manifestations, elide from knowledge the fluid materiality of human relations with the world that it nonetheless symbolically mediates. If language can effect a certain separation from the world on which it operates, then it may delude us into forgetting that it is through material relatedness that we are moved to think. As Blacking has so eloquently argued:

> If there are forms intrinsic to music and dance that are not modelled on language, we may look beyond the "language" of dancing, for instance, to the dance of language and thought. As conscious movement is in our thinking, so thinking may come from movement, and especially shared, or conceptual, thought from communal movement. And just as the ultimate aim of dancing is to be able to move *without* thinking, to *be* danced, so the ultimate achievement in thinking is to be moved to think, to *be* thought . . . essentially it is a form of unconscious cerebration, a movement of the body. We are moved into thinking. Body and mind are one.[41]

Conclusion

This is the point from which popular music studies can, through an interrogation and influencing of cultural theory, make an impact on wider academic discourses that attempt to understand people as social and signifying beings. But to do this, popular music studies needs to face in two directions at once. It needs, first of all, to exploit the way in which texture and process are heavily foregrounded in most of popular music's genres to establish corporeal textures and corporeal processes—socially and culturally mediated—as the seat for the analysis of all musics. It is in this sense that the subject matter of popular music studies makes the discipline an excellent apologist for the examination, within the academy, of the nonlinguistic use of sound. It needs to draw music analysis away from its traditional preoccupation with the socially decon-textualized analysis of those parameters of music most susceptible to notational and therefore visual mediation: harmony, melody, and rhythm. This preoccupation still pervades much analysis within musicology and ethnomusicology. Analysis needs rather to concentrate on sound, and particularly the voice and the body in motion. Further, popular music studies needs to face ethnomusicology in drawing upon the work of figures such as John Blacking, Catherine Ellis, Charles Keil, and Steven Feld to force a cultural theoretical discourse to open up around their ideas and insights. Some of the most interesting work on the subject of music as a signifying practice within human communities has come from ethnomusicologists, yet their work has hardly begun to make an impact on understanding musical practices in the world in which we currently live.

Secondly, popular music studies needs to face cultural theory. It needs to subvert, forcefully, radically, and with vigor, the preeminence of the lin-guistic and the visual within poststructuralist and postmodern discourses. We are not, as scholars and academics, simply consumers, speculating cleverly over mute and silent sites about the kinds of meanings we like to think people construct around musical symbols. We must pay attention to the material ground of music, to the sounds that, in being structured, struc-ture our being by facilitating some possibilities and constraining others. Ul-timately, we must return to the empirical in grounding our analysis of meaning in music in (*inter alia*) the material substance of its articulation.

I would argue that we need a new kind of discipline to emerge out of the best of ethnomusicology and popular music studies. At the moment, the potential for that discipline lies within the new field of popular music studies, a field that, in studying a form of music that is undeniably social in its significance, is struggling to account for that sociality while at the same time not losing sight of music's specificity as a discursively constituted sig-nifying practice. The realization of this struggle will have consequences not only for musicology. It will also have consequences for cultural studies. In the words of Middleton: "Traditional musicology still banishes popular music from view because of its 'cheapness' while the relatively new field of cultural studies neglects it because of the forbiddingly special character of music. A breakthrough in popular music studies would reorient cultural studies in a fundamental way and would completely restructure the field of musicology."[42]

Precisely because popular music lies outside the established canon of musicology and inevitably raises questions that cannot be dealt with in terms of the traditional ways in which the canon is conceptualized, it leads the study of music into those areas envisaged by McClary as legitimate territory for a feminist critique. There need be no conflict in this respect. McClary does not see all the issues raised by a feminist critique of musicology as being reducible to questions of gender, although, in many cases, she would rightfully claim that they fall back on the invidious masculine/feminine dichotomy that so pervades our society at the level of culture. What a thoroughgoing critique of music education at the university level reveals, and this regardless of the origins and motivations of the critique, is that it remains remarkably exclusionary. The point here is *not* that the traditional canon should not be taught—in one way or another. And it is *not* that the benefits (and there are some!) of dominant modes of Western intellection should be jettisoned. The point is that if other musical traditions are not admitted to music education in ways that do not submit them to tokenism, peripheralization, and marginalization and if other ways of thinking about and engaging in the study of music are not seriously entertained, the public culture in which we all live will continue to live in ignorance of what it is music *can* be about other than unreflective leisure and pleasure or the uncritical maintenance of a particular form of musical capital. It is because music is placed in a "feminized" location in our world that it must be carefully controlled and monitored by the academy, subjected to the phallocentric and logocentric modes of intellection that McClary, in my view, so legitimately criticizes. But it is also because it is placed in a feminized location that it contains the residues of what it is that our culture, publicly, does not want to communicate with itself about. Blacking,[43] Catherine Ellis,[44] Charles Keil,[45] and Steven Feld[46] have argued persuasively, in studying the musics and cultures of other times and places, that music is centrally important to processes of social and cultural reproduction. Our education systems—not to mention our public cultures as a whole—have become very skilled at persuading people, young and not so young, otherwise.

A central concern of the philosophy of music education should be why we teach music in the first place. There are obviously some very practical answers to this question. There is a need for performers, teachers, radio and television producers, music librarians, and others whose professional lives require knowledge of music. However, the training of professionals itself begs the more central question.

I would submit that disciplinary alignments within academic music, as well as the ways in which music is traditionally taught, have become so entrenched and routinized that sight has been lost of the central questions as to why all human societies have music and why and how it should as a consequence be taught. Music is an inalienable presence within human societies for reasons that dominant Western cultures seldom admit to academic discourse: it is central to those processes within any society whereby individuals are collectively moved to think and organize themselves. I would submit that an important agenda for the philosophy of music education is to argue for readmission of these reasons as a basis for fundamental discussions about the role of music education. Music education has not traditionally been regarded as being in the intellectual forefront of academic music as a whole. Perhaps, for this very reason, it is the appropriate site from which to reinvigorate the academic study of music in such a way that it cannot only force meaningful dialogues with other disciplines, but constitute a platform from which the public in general can be made more aware of the central importance of music to the maintenance and recreation of human cultures.

NOTES

1. William Bennett, *Reclaiming a Legacy* (Washington: National Endowment for the Humanities, 1984).
2. Allan Bloom, *The Closing of the American Mind* (New York: Simon and Schuster, 1987).
3. Bill Graham, "Premier's Council Has a Narrow View of Education," *Forum* 6, no. 16 (November 1989): 2.
4. Russell Jacoby, *The Last Intellectuals: American Culture in the Age of Academe* (New York: Basic Books, 1987), p. 8.
5. Ibid.
6. Ibid., p. 5.
7. Simon Frith, "What Is Good Music?," in *Alternative Musicologies*, ed. John Shepherd, special issue of *The Canadian University Music Review* 10, no. 2 (Fall 1990): 97-98.
8. Susan McClary, "Towards a Feminist Critique of Music," in *Alternative Musicologies*, p. 14.
9. Ibid.
10. Ibid., p. 15.
11. See John Shepherd, *Music as Social Text* (Cambridge, U.K.: Polity Press, Cambridge, and Basil Blackwell, Inc., 1991).
12. Joseph Kerman, *Contemplating Music: Challenges to Musicology* (Cambridge, Mass.: Harvard University Press, 1985), p. 17.
13. McClary, "Towards a Feminist Critique of Music," p. 13.
14. Kerman, *Contemplating Music*, p. 174.
15. Ibid., pp. 174-75.
16. Line Grenier, "The Construction of Music as a Social Phenomenon: Implications for Deconstruction," in *Alternative Musicologies*, p. 32.
17. See Shepherd, *Music as Social Text*, pp. 9-74.
18. Jacoby, *The Last Intellectuals*, p. 5.
19. Frith, "What Is Good Music?," p. 92.
20. Richard Leppert and Susan McClary, "Introduction," in *Music and Society: The Politics of Composition, Performance and Reception*, ed. Richard Leppert and Susan McClary (Cambridge, U.K.: Cambridge University Press, 1987), p. xiii.
21. Kerman, *Contemplating Music*, pp. 72-73.

22. Grenier, "The Construction of Music," p. 28.
23. Richard Middleton, *Studying Popular Music* (Milton Keynes, U.K.: Open University Press, 1990), pp. 266-67.
24. John Blacking, "Towards an Anthropology of the Body," in *The Anthropology of the Body*, ed. John Blacking, Association of Social Anthropologists Monograph 15 (London: Academic Press, 1977), p. 9.
25. Middleton, *Studying Popular Music*, p. 262.
26. Johann Sundberg, *The Science of the Singing Voice* (DeKalb, Ill.: Northern Illinois University Press, 1987), pp. 154-55.
27. Middleton, *Studying Popular Music*, p. 264.
28. John Baily, "Movement Patterns in Playing the Herati *Dutar*," in *The Anthropology of the Body*, p. 330.
29. Roland Barthes, "Rasch," in *Langue, discours, société*, ed. Julia Kristeva, Jean-Claude Milner, and Nicolas Ruwet (Paris: Editions du Seuil, 1975), p. 222.
30. Middleton, *Studying Popular Music*, p. 243.
31. Barthes, "Rasch," p. 225.
32. Middleton, *Studying Popular Music*, pp. 265-66.
33. See Henri Lefebvre, "Musique et sémiologie," *Musique en jeu*, vol. 4, pp. 52-62.
34. Middleton, *Studying Popular Music*, p. 266.
35. R. Murray Schafer, *The Tuning of the World* (New York: Knopf, 1973), p. 11.
36. Middleton, *Studying Popular Music*, p. 243.
37. See Shepherd, *Music as Social Text*, pp. 152-73.
38. Middleton, *Studying Popular Music*, p. 243.
39. Lefebvre, "Musique et sémiologie," pp. 59-61.
40. Michel Foucault, *The History of Sexuality, Volume One, An Introduction* (Harmondsworth, U.K.: Penguin, 1981), p. 152.
41. Blacking, "Towards an Anthropology of the Body," pp. 22-23.
42. Middleton, *Studying Popular Music*, p. v.
43. John Blacking, *How Musical Is Man?* (Seattle: University of Washington Press, 1973).
44. Catherine Ellis, *Aboriginal Music: Education for Living* (St. Lucia, Australia: University of Queensland Press, 1985).
45. Charles Keil, *Tiv Song* (Chicago: Chicago University Press, 1979).
46. Steven Feld, *Sound and Sentiment: Birds, Weeping, Poetics and Song in Kaluli Expression* (Philadelphia: University of Pennsylvania Press, 1982).

Teaching Music as One of the Humanities

RALPH A. SMITH

In this article I address the question whether music can be understood as one of the humanities and accordingly be taught as a humanistic subject. When I speak of studying music in an educational context, I have in mind principally the experience of musical masterworks, especially those nonprogrammatic works that we listen to on what Aaron Copland calls their sensuous, expressive, and sheerly musical planes.[1] Masterworks are of course only a part of the world of music, but because they pose some of the more interesting problems of musical understanding they constitute the most important part.

Leonard Meyer: The Sciences, Arts, and Humanities

Any consideration of teaching music as one of the humanities must proceed from a definition of the humanities, and I honor custom by distinguishing the humanities from the sciences. In doing so I draw on a far-ranging and insightful essay by Leonard Meyer, which discusses such disciplines as creation, criticism, invention, and application in terms of their procedures and goals. Published in 1974, Meyer's essay reflects the tendency of the time to formulate taxonomies and classifications of knowledge. But I am less interested in Meyer's comprehensive classification of disciplines than I am in the ways in which he characterizes the sciences and the arts and understands the role of the humanities. Such distinctions are important inasmuch as teaching music involves conveying ideas about a way of organizing human experience that is unique and which in itself provides a ground for interpreting music as a humanity.

Ralph A. Smith is Professor of Cultural and Educational Policy at the University of Illinois at Urbana-Champaign and the editor of the *Journal of Aesthetic Education*. Among his recent publications are *Excellence in Art Education, The Sense of Art: A Study in Aesthetic Education, Aesthetics and Arts Education*, coedited with Alan Simpson, and *Art Education: A Critical Necessity*, coauthored with Albert William Levi.

How does Meyer proceed? He begins by locating the important differences between the behavior of scientists and artists not only in the nature of their respective accomplishments and in the relations of their achievements to their own traditions and to contemporary efforts, but also in the manner in which the structures and properties of the sciences and those of the arts affect audiences for science and art. I will put these differences in the form "Whereas X (science) is or does so and so, Y (art) is or does otherwise."

That is, whereas scientists discover relationships already present in nature, artists create works that never before existed; whereas scientific theories are propositional in form, works of art are presentational in character; whereas scientific theories tend to supersede, displace, or invalidate previous scientific hypotheses, great works of art remain continuous sources of vital experience; whereas science studies phenomena for purposes of framing theoretical generalizations, artists produce works the principal significance of which lies in their status as objects for aesthetic response and appreciation; whereas science strives to build an abstract edifice of scientific knowledge, characterized by systematic relations among its hypotheses, works of art are valued for their concrete individuality and particularities, for their nonrecurring as well as their recurring features; and finally, whereas the reputations of scientists are based on their creation of new paradigms for studying the phenomena discovered, usually early in their careers, artists' reputations have typically been based on their creative contributions to already existing styles, contributions that, moreover, generally became more meaningful and profound in the artists' mature years. Meyer provides numerous examples of these differences, as well as of a few points of similarity, but I pass over these and move on to his discussion of the humanities.

In his account of the humanities Meyer distinguishes understanding from explanation and describes three interrelated areas of humanistic inquiry: theory, style analysis, and criticism. Furthermore, he constrasts the role of the critic to those of the creative artist and of the scientist. Meyer believes it is the humanist-theorist or critic and not the artist who is most nearly comparable to the scientist. Just as the scientist formulates hypotheses to explain relationships among phenomena, so the humanist-theorist formulates explanations of the relationships in works of art as they are experienced by beholders. Once again I must pass over much of Meyer's interesting discussion of these points, especially his description of the role of tacit knowing in scientific research and artistic creation and his reasons for holding not only that understanding must precede explanation but also that it is possible to understand something without being able to explain it—positions implied, of course, in Michael Polanyi's assertion that we know more than we can tell.

When we do explain something, however, we must have recourse to general principles, and Meyer thinks three kinds of hypothesis are brought to bear in attempts to explain an artwork's structure and internal relationships and the ways in which they determine aesthetic experience. There are "(*a*) general laws, which are presumed to be constant over time and place; (*b*) restricted principles, derived from and applicable to the norms and procedures of a specific style; and (*c*) ad hoc reasons, which . . . are necessary adjuncts to the first two types when particular works of art are being explained" (pp. 191-92). General principles may be formulated by humanist-theorists themselves or taken from other disciplines and applied deductively, as Meyer illustrates in his borrowings from information theory.

The humanist-theorist, however, cannot rely solely on general principles when explaining works of art. There must also be reliance on ad hoc or commonsense reasons that command assent because of their congruence with a culture's beliefs and way of living. We can decide, for example, to convey an ordinary understanding of the impression of indomitable force and irresistible authority that issues from Michelangelo's *Moses* by associating these qualities with the statue's colossal size rather than by recourse to Freudian theory; similarly, we can explain the extension of a phrase in music not as the result of some quirk in the composer's personality but by saying that had the cadence come precisely at the point it was exected, it would have sounded too obvious and uninteresting. In short, we are obliged to engage in ad hoc or commonsense reasoning because general principles and style taxonomies do little to explain the nonrecurring features of a work of music and because no satisfactory account of music's capacity to move and affect us is as yet available.

I wish to draw attention to the part played by the restrictive principles of style analysis and ad hoc reasoning in music criticism as well as in the teaching of music. By "criticism" Meyer understands that activity which "seeks to describe and explain as precisely and explicitly as possible how the structures and processes peculiar to a specific work of art are related to one another and to the aesthetic experience of a competent audience" (p. 197). It is worth noting the twofold task of criticism: it attempts to describe and explain not only the musical character of a work but also the work's effect on the aesthetic responses of a competent listener, a point to which I return later.

To repeat, the humanist-critic is akin to the scientist in the effort to explain relationships; the vital difference between them lies in the fact that the scientist strives to develop hypotheses that account for relationships discovered among phenomena in the natural world. This involves isolating, limiting, and controlling the relevant variables, while the humanist is more concerned with the unique character of a work of art and its capacity to generate aesthetic experience. Given its focus on the idiosyncratic features of works of art, criticism transcends general theory and style taxonomies and asks what makes a particular work of art different from all the others, even different from other works in the same form, style, and genre.

I isolate the role of the humanist-critic because of its importance in a program of general music education that pursues the goal of developing percipience in matters of music and culture, that is, a state of mind characterized by a knowing appreciation of music and the atmosphere in which it exists. Like the humanist-critic, a music teacher working in such a program would also use general principles and ad hoc reasons when drawing attention to the processes, qualities, and structures of musical works, pointing out what is valuable and significant, and explaining how musical values impinge on aesthetic awareness. The difference is that teachers typically do not formulate the general principles they use; that is the humanist-theorist's job. As Meyer puts it, "Theorists and style analysts use particular works of art as exemplars—as data—for the discovery and formulation of general principles and for the description of the characteristics typical of some style; the critic [and, I would add, the teacher of music], working the other way around, uses the general principles and taxonomies thus developed to explain and illuminate particular works of art" (p. 199). As if in confirmation of a belief in the limited usefulness of general principles when it comes to explicating the idiosyncratic or nonrecurring features of artworks, Meyer adds that "there are many examples of antecedent-consequent structures, in common time, the minor mode, and with homophonic texture, whose melodies begin with an upbeat skip to the fifth of the scale and then descend to the tonic. But there is only one such combination of relationships which is Chopin's Prelude no. 4 in E Minor" (pp. 199-200). It is not only the critic's but also the teacher's task to explain why this is so.

The humanist-critic and the teacher of music appreciation thus occupy the middle ground between the composer and the performance of a work on one side and the audience for the work on the other; but they do their work somewhat differently. To be sure, the critic can also be said to perform an educative service for the public; but the critic's educational responsibility is less direct and stringent than that of the teacher. The music teacher's principal aim is the cultivation of musical percipience in young people to the point where they will be able not only to enjoy and particpate in music at a respectable level of comprehension but also to engage in intelligent conversation about it. Or we may say that the teacher of music is distinguished from the music critic by virtue of the teacher's self-image as an educator committed first of all to bringing about learning. A teacher of music, then, is not a philosopher or theorist or historian per se (except by analogy) but a professional pedagogue who draws on all these disciplines and specialized activities in order to develop appropriate degrees of musical awareness in students. This is what makes the teacher's task unique. The central pedagogical question thus becomes What models should guide the development of musical percipience? Here the music critic would provide what is perhaps the most important paradigm. Now the critic's connoisseurship is compounded of natural talent and disposition, performance skills or at least an advanced ability to assess them, and a vast knowledge of music's history and theory, not to mention love of and devotion to music. How far can education go in developing such critical finesse? Some distance, I think, but no farther than would be commensurate with the objective of general education to produce nonspecialists. An intelligent interpretive capacity is what I think we are after.[3]

But to suggest that the teaching of music should take music criticism as its model is in effect to say that music should be taught as one of the humanities. This raises the question of whether a broadly humanistic interpretation of music education can in fact show the aims of the field in a new and clearer light. It is one thing, and perhaps adequate for some purposes, to propose that music education should pursue the objective of developing musical percipience in the young so that they may realize the benefits that works of music at their best and most excellent are capable of providing. But it is another matter altogether to work out in detail what ought to go into building a sense of music adequate to attaining this goal. I believe we should start by looking for a definition of the humanities that would be especially suitable for music education, and indeed for arts education in general. Luckily such a definition can be extracted from the writings of the late Albert William Levi, particularly his *The Humanities Today* and subsequent discussions of the same topic.

Albert William Levi: The Humanities as Liberal Arts

In *The Humanities Today* Levi takes stock of the humanities in the contemporary world and asks how we can preserve the traditional aims and purposes of the humanities while adapting them to changed conditions.[4] How, for example, do we deal with the humanities' having become practically unmanageable as a result of their trying to encompass the works of all civilizations, non-Western as well as Western? How can a democratic society grounded in egalitarian ideals defend a tradition of learning whose origins are rooted in an essentially aristocratic culture? How, moreover, can we make good on the promise of a civilizing influence flowing from the study of great works? How can we maintain the claims of the humanities against their new rivals, the social sciences? For Levi these were not merely matters for idle philosophical speculation. As a charter member of the National Council for the Humanities he was sensitive to policy questions bearing on research and teaching, and he had a strong interest in the social role of the humanities. And in his three years as Rector of Black Mountain College, one of this century's interesting experiments in the liberal education of artists, he was required to address day-to-day problems of learning and administration. Levi was, then, a philosopher of the humanities with a keen interest in the uses of the humanities, and he believed that the taught humanities were meaningless unless they ultimately became the lived humanities.

Levi's persuasive redefinition of the humanities begins by recalling two traditions, one going back to the Middle Ages and the other to the Renaissance. The tradition dating from the Renaissance is most prominently characterized by a penchant for the rediscovery and recovery of ancient texts, which helps to explain why the humanities have become understood *substantively*, that is, in terms of literary artifacts or subject matter to be studied and mastered. This tradition lives on in the curriculums of higher education today where the humanities are thought of essentially as texts or works. The tradition dating from the Middle Ages defines the humanities *procedurally*, that is, in terms of methods, approaches, skills, or ways of interpreting human experience, and it consequently favors a conception of the humanities as liberal arts rather than as subject matters.

Levi's synthesis combines these two traditions, the substantive and the procedural, with the result that the humanities become the liberal arts of communication, continuity, and criticism. These arts, in turn, are associated with subject matters distinctive of each: the arts of communication are identified with languages and literatures, the arts of continuity with history, and the arts of criticism with philosophy in its ordinary sense of critical reasoning. Levi thus reconnects what E. D. Hirsch, Jr., thinks has become tragically separated in American schooling, skills and specific content.[5] For Levi then the aims of the humanities are three: to enable students to communicate successfully, to walk proudly with their cultural heritage, and to think critically. He writes that

> this has meant the presentation of languages as forms of enlarging a limited imagination and producing that mutual sympathy which Kant took to be the defining property of social man. In the case of the arts of continuity, comprehending both history proper and the use of the classics of literature and philosophy, presented as elements in a continuous human tradition, this has meant the presentation of a common past in the service of social cohesiveness and enlarged social sensitivity. And finally, in the case of the arts of criticism, this has meant the enlargement of the faculty of criticism, philosophically conceived as intelligent inquiry into the nature and maximization of values. A humane imagination, the forging of a universal social bond based upon sympathy, and the inculcation of a technique for the realization of values then become the ultimate goals of the liberal arts.[6]

Where do the arts of creation and performance fit into this picture? I think it is possible to subsume them under the arts of communication and criticism, if, that is, we are willing to tolerate some metaphoric license and stretch the meaning of language and communication to include artistic expression and performance and construe criticism as the disclosure of whatever it is that art communicates. Yet this may not be a satisfactory solution for those who attach great importance to creative and performing activities and who would consider them slighted by such subsumption. For this reason Levi and I in a recent volume agreed to add to the arts of communication, continuity, and criticism a fourth c, the arts of creation (which encompasses performance).[7] I am now ready to propose that for educational purposes arts education may be usefully conceived as the study of a distinctive mode of communication that has a history of outstanding accomplishments (i.e., exhibits continuity), challenges our appreciation of it with puzzling issues and situations demanding judgment (i.e., calls for critical reasoning), and cannot be fully appreciated in the absence of artistic creation and performance. To the standard definition of music education aimed at the development of musical ideas, concepts, and skills we have now added a number of larger humanistic objectives the attainment of which should be part of any liberal education.

It might be claimed that cultivating historical and critical capacities in music education takes time away from work toward the more immediate objectives of performing and listening, even that acquiring historical and critical knowledge serves extra-aesthetic outcomes and contributes nothing significant to musical percipience, that is, to the knowing appreciation of particular works. But such objections would be misguided. We need only recall that the music critic has been suggested as an important model for the music teacher. Now, there are probably few good music critics who are not also performers, and certainly none who does not bring to the task of criticism a strong sense of music's history (and usually the history of the other arts) and an intimate familiarity with the conundrums that beset discussions about the nature, meaning, and value of music. Indeed, ideas, concepts, and skills from relevant disciplines and practical activities are what the critic thinks with, and I cannot see why, to an appropriate extent, that should not be true of the teacher of music as well.[8]

Although the teacher need not command the full panoply of the critic's expertise, in certain respects the teacher's work is even more demanding than the critic's—or at least we can understand why someone would want to say so. In a discussion of teaching and learning in the arts Henry D. Aiken points out that the teacher's task is stricter and more austere than that of the critic because of the teacher's daily concern to help the young discern the form of being unique to works of art. This involves cultivating in students a fuller awareness of the idea that the creative life evident in artworks comprises one primary level of everyone's subjective nature. He goes on to say that teachers who perform this task through their talk, gestures, and attitudes provide a model of what it is to look for true possibilities in a work of art, what it is, for example, to discover a significant artistic form and to develop an authentic taste.[9]

Understanding Music

It is clear that teachers of music must draw on a number of disciplines and activities if they are to do a good job of developing musical percipience in young people. And although I suggest that music is a language that communicates something significant, I am fully aware of views that assert the contrary. What then, someone may ask, does music say? Does it really communicate anything at all? Consider Beethoven's Third Symphony. In this issue Peter Kivy holds that it is difficult to see not only how this symphony could be about anything profound but how it could be about anything at all. Indeed, he believes that it is nothing but "a magnificent abstract structure of sound: one big beautiful noise, signifying nothing." Although he thinks it is a deeply satisfying entertainment, he also believes that the Third Symphony totally lacks subject matter, content, and meaning. And if there is no message to be decoded, how can it teach or educate us about anything important? Let us therefore, says Kivy, enjoy music of this kind for what it is, a pure, contentless abstract form and stop burbling about its profundity. Let us find other grounds for justifying the study of music in a required program of liberal education.

Now I happen to believe that Kivy is one of the more interesting writers about the aesthetics of music today, and his works figure strategically in my teaching. For example, I show students the photograph of the sad-looking St. Bernard dog that serves as the frontispiece of Kivy's *Sound Sentiment*.[10] Why, I ask them, would a serious thinker begin a philosophical discussion of music with such an image? The St. Bernard, of course, introduces an analysis of expression in music in which Kivy argues the case for what he calls emotive criticism, a type of criticism that can reasonably assert, as Donald Francis Tovey did, that the second movement of Beethoven's *Eroica* "concludes with a final utterance of the main theme, its rhythms and accents utterly broken with grief" (pp. 5-6). Kivy's aim is to resolve what he calls the paradox of music description: the fact that the kind of music criticism that is the most objective and scientific is also the least humanistic and thus unable to say much about music's power to move us (p. 9). The value of emotive criticism for descriptions of the emotional qualities of great music notwithstanding, Kivy believes that music's lacking content and profundity disqualifies it from being taught as a humanity. A different case can be made for literature and the visual arts. Literature has traditionally been justified as one of the humanities because of its capacity to convey knowledge about the self and the self's proper relations to others and to culture, and among painters the great portraitists have been celebrated for their insight into human character. The theater arts likewise dramatize significant human relations. But compared to all that, what can music do?

Mindful of divergent theoretical positions on this topic, I suggest that music can after all provide us with deep understanding—an apprehension of reality no less—and that music can therefore be taken to teach and educate in its own way. My saying this, moreover, represents a shift in my thinking of a magnitude of perhaps a few more inches than the small distance that Bennett Reimer—to whom we are all indebted for his influential contributions to the philosophy of music education—admits to having moved his position on this question. For while I have always derived something I consider profound from listening to musical masterworks, I was persuaded, as Kivy apparently still is, that theories of musical meaning are undermined by both the facts of music and the requirements for something to count as a language. It is perhaps worth pointing out that the late Monroe C. Beardsley also did not take music to be any kind of symbol and that this position made him skeptical about semiotic theories of musical meaning. Instead, he regarded music simply as a process, as perhaps the closest thing to pure process that we have. In 1958, Beardsley wrote that "to understand a piece of music is simply to hear it, in the fullest sense of this word . . . to organize its sounds into wholes, to grasp its sequences of notes as melodic and rhythmic patterns, to perceive its kinetic qualities and, finally, the subtle and pervasive human qualities that depend on all the rest."[12] Consequently, Beardsley thought it a mistake to cast about for something outside music with which to connect or compare music. And although I was uncomfortable with the entailments of this view, especially for education—that since music cannot signify anything and therefore has no meaning, all interpretive statements about musical meaning are false and have no place in music teaching—I felt compelled to accept it. But as Kivy reminds us, a strong feeling or conviction about something is no substitute for an argument.

It was one of Beardsley's admirable characteristics that whenever possible he tried to accommodate new and challenging ideas. Thus in an essay titled "Understanding Music," published more than twenty years after his original views about musical meaning, he covers much of the same ground while reviewing the theories of musical meaning of Deryck Cooke, Donald N. Ferguson, Gordon Epperson, and Wilson Coker. He finds all of their efforts to explain musical meaning in semantic terms unsatisfactory.[13]

By then, however, aesthetics was reflecting the influence of Nelson Goodman's ideas about the nature and function of the arts as symbol systems. According to Goodman's theory, music has the ability to refer by virtue of a symbolic function technically called exemplification. It is not enough for Goodman, as it was for Beardsley, simply to say that music possesses aesthetic qualities and to leave it at that. For it seems to be Goodman's view that aesthetic qualities sometimes have elements of overt display, of active featuring, of drawing attention that are more fittingly captured by the term exemplification. In short, exemplification is claimed to be a form of reference and hence to perform a cognitive function. Goodman, then, is the fifth theorist Beardsley discusses in "Understanding Music." He judged Goodman's *Languages of Art* an enormously valuable book,[14] gave it a quite sympathetic reading, and then asked himself to what extent his thinking might be adjusted to a semantic explanation of art, that is, one in terms of art's cognitive function and ability to provide understanding.

Beardsley makes a number of illuminating observations about the way exemplification works, how, that is, certain properties and qualities can be referred to by a musical performance. His emendation of Goodman's theory would require that someone must actually put something on display or feature it before exemplification can occur. Thus a tree in the forest may possess qualities of majestic height and spread, but as long as no one is putting the tree on display, the tree cannot exemplify these properties. On the other hand, a fashion model who walks down a runway is putting something on display, is featuring, say, a trimly severe or a loose and billowy look. This is what is being exemplified. As Beardsley explains it: "Property-displaying is, or involves, reference when, and only when the property-displaying object is itself object-displayed."[15]

Now the performance of a piano sonata in a concert hall satisfies the condition of something's being put on display. The question is what, if anything, the sonata exemplifies, for a particular performance of a sonata need not exemplify all the properties of that sonata, only those that are noteworthy in the context of concert-giving and concert-going. These are the properties whose presence has a direct bearing on the sonata's capacity to interest us aesthetically. We may, of course, need the intercession of the music critic to realize which structures and relations of a musical work bear on our aesthetic response to it, and thus we would do well in this connection to recall Meyer's specification of the critic's role.

In order to help us understand how we might give a semantic explanation of a musical work in Goodman's terms, Beardsley asks us to consider a performance of Beethoven's Piano Sonata in A Major, op. 101. Which of the sonata's properties are exemplified for our aesthetic interest? The first movement's being in the key of A, with few restricted modulations, does not amount to a property that particularly enhances or inhibits the aesthetic effectiveness of the sonata. On the other hand, the first movement's uncommonly hesitant, diffident, and indecisive character does figure prominently in our aesthetic response; indeed, this quality plays a crucial part in the sonata as a whole, especially in the finale which we must await in order to experience the liberating resolution of the unusual musical business in the first movement. But what, to be more specific, is being referred to by the music? Beardsley emphasizes that reference is not being made to objects, events, processes, or emotional states as they occur in or belong to the external world. Rather, the reference is to qualities within the music itself. So far, I think, Beardsley and Kivy are in accord; the description of such qualities Kivy would call emotive criticism and Beardsley aesthetic criticism. Nor is Beardsley talking about the devices composers often use to establish some kind of connection with external reality—devices like sound imitation, conventional associations, and kinetic parallelism—for he does not construe these connections as instances of reference or meaning. What Beardsley has in mind is something more complicated, more profound, and it suggests a response to Kivy's claim that music—at least abstract instrumental music—has no meaning.

To illustrate his point, Beardsley follows an interpretation of the Beethoven sonata by Kay Dreyfus, an Australian musicologist who had made a study of Beethoven's last five piano sonatas. Dreyfus claims that the finale of this opus provides the clue to Beethoven's musical statement. "It is not a statement," she writes, "that is concerned with the conflict or confrontation of opposing ideas. . . . What the work *is* concerned with is the gradual discovery and unleashing of a capacity for growth and sustained development within the material introduced by the opening ideas of the first movement." As Beardsley puts it, the music moves from unexpected constriction and contraint in the first movement to great breadth of activity and assertiveness in the finale. From Dreyfus's description of the first movement, we learn that the movement employs a technique of delayed resolution as a substitute for development, that it is marked by tonal inconclusiveness, and that it is extremely brief in duration. All of these things are important, says Beardsley; but "so much happens so vividly, in a mere nineteen and one-half minutes, between the first notes and the last, in the way of musical growth, that the sonata can be said to show its 'concern' with growth in general, to exemplify that property" (p. 69).

But why should the exemplification of growth be so important? Beardsley thinks it is significant because growth is a basic kind of alteration found in human experience when it is at its most rewarding and especially when it is successful in overcoming obstacles; and music, being itself a form of change, can mirror or match this process. He goes on to say "that music exemplifies—indeed, exploits and glories in—aspects of change that are among the most fundamental and pervasive characteristics of living." As a mode of continuation, music in its movement toward completion "is marked by the sense that possibilities are opening or closing, that there is development or retrogression, that there is continuity or abruptness, doubt or decisiveness, hesitancy or determination, building or disintegration" (p. 70).

Such modes of continuation are features of all experience, and Beardsley thinks that if music has them, then it exemplifies them and therefore refers to aspects of reality in one of its humanly important dimensions. It is sometimes said—for example by Meyer in the essay I discussed earlier—that no satisfactory theory exists to explain music's power to move and delight; but perhaps part of the answer lies in music's ability to exemplify those modes of continuation that are so firmly woven into our personal and social destinies. Extrapolating from some of Meyer's remarks, Beardsley writes that "suspense is disturbing in whatever form it assumes, and the release from it correspondingly heartening and gladdening. So, too, disintegration is threatening, reversal astonishing, loss of power and drive unsettling, delayed fulfillment anxiety-producing, missed opportunity poignant; but growth is encouraging, revival inspiriting, arrival satisfying. Triumph over obstacles arouses confidence, and endurance, respect" (p. 71). Though none of these things is really happening to us as as we listen to music, says Beardsley, their distinctive forms of continuation nonetheless have great power to affect us.

Does music then provide knowledge after all? Can its profundity help us to a better understanding of ourselves and our relations to others and to the world? Does music afford us a kind of insight? To the extent that Beardsley came to believe in such possibilities he also accepted Goodman's argument for the cognitive character of music. "Music," writes Beardsley, "can make extremely delicate discriminations between kinds of continuation, between two slightly different forms of ambiguity or of headlong rushing or of growth. It thereby can sharpen our appreciation of such differences, and give us concepts of continuation that we might miss in ordinary experience, under the press of affairs, but yet that we can bring to experience (as 'models,' perhaps) with fresh perceptiveness and clearer cognitive grasp" (p. 72). I think Beardsley's interpretation offers us what we need for a humanities interpretation of music; it gives meaning to the notion of teaching music as a humanity.

If I have dwelled on the question of the cognitive status of music, it is because this is an issue difficult to avoid, especially in the context of a humanities interpretation of music education. Indeed, if, as Francis Sparshott believes, the problem of the cognitive status of art is the only one that keeps aesthetics alive, then I hope to have made a small contribution to that discipline's health and longevity. Music, we may now claim, not only has the capacity to provide magnificent enjoyment, it can also yield insight into human reality. It would doubtlessly be helpful at this point to sketch a curriculum designed around a humanities approach to music education, but this is a topic for another occasion. I'll merely indicate that such a curriculum would encompass roughly five stages of musical learning; that is, the phases of exposure to music's qualitative aspects and increasing familiarization with them; perceptual training; historical inquiry; the study of masterworks in some depth; and pehaps a seminar in which adolescents would have an opportunity to fashion an elementary philosophy of art, music prominently included. Performing activities would find a place at most levels, but their role and centrality would vary according to the learning phase in question. In other contexts I have variously called a curriculum of this kind an excellence curriculum, an art world curriculum, a percipience curriculum; here I refer to it as a humanities curriculum.[16]

Notes

1. Aaron Copland, *What to Listen for in Music*, rev. ed. (New York: Mentor Books, 1957), pp. 18-23.
2. Leonard Meyer, "Concerning the Sciences, the Arts—AND the Humanities," *Critical Inquiry* 1, no., 1 (September 1974).
3. In this connection, see Harry S. Broudy, B. Othanel Smith, and Joe R. Burnett, *Democracy and Excellence in American Secondary Education* (1958; New York: Robert E. Krieger, 1978)..
4. See Albert William Levi, *The Humanities Today* (Bloomington: Indiana University Press, 1970); "Literature as a Humanity," *Journal of Aesthetic Education* 10, nos. 3-4 (July-October 1976); and "Teaching Literature as a Humanity," *Journal of General Education* 28, no. 4 (Winter 1977). Cf. R. A. Smith, *The Sense of Art: A Study in Aesthetic Education* (New York: Routledge, 1989), pp. 127-32.
5. E. D. Hirsch, Jr., *Cultural Literacy: What Every American Needs to Know* (New York: Random House Vintage Books, 1988).
6. Levi, *The Humanities Today*, p. 85.
7. A. W. Levi and R. A. Smith, *Art Education: A Critical Necessity* (Urbana: University of Illinois Press, 1991). This is the introductory volume of a five-volume series titled "Disciplines in Art Education: Contexts of Understanding," published by the University of Illinois Press.
8. The notion of "thinking with" has been advanced by Harry S. Broudy in his extrapolations from Michael Polanyi's writings about tacit knowing. See Broudy's "On Knowing With," in *Philosophy of Education*, ed. H. B. Dunkel, Proceedings of the 26th Annual Meeting of the Philosophy of Education Society (Edwardsville, Ill.: Philosophy of Education Society, 1970).
9. Henry D. Aiken, "Teaching and Learning in the Arts," *Journal of Aesthetic Education* 5, no. 4 (October 1971): 107.
10. Peter Kivy, *Sound Sentiment: An Essay on Musical Emotions* (Philadelphia: Temple University Press, 1989). First published as *The Corded Shell: Reflections on Musical Expression* (Princeton, N.J.: Princeton University Press, 1980).
11. See, e.g., Bennett Reimer's *A Philosophy of Music Education*, 2d ed. (1970; Englewood Cliffs, N.J.: Prentice-Hall, 1989), the only systematic philosophy of music education as aesthetic education in the literature.
12. Monroe C. Beardsley, *Aesthetics: Problems in the Philosophy of Criticism*, 2d ed. (1958; Indianapolis: Hackett, 1981), p. 337.
13. Monroe C. Beardsley, "Understanding Music," in *On Criticizing Music: Five Philosophical Perspectives*, ed. Kingsley Price (Baltimore: Johns Hopkins University Press, 1981).
14. Nelson Goodman, *Languages of Art*, 2d ed. (Indianapolis: Hackett, 1976). Goodman has continued his analysis in *LA* in a number of subsequent books, e.g.,

Ways of Worldmaking (Indianapolis: Hackett, 1978); *Of Mind and Other Matters* (Cambridge, Mass.: Harvard University Press, 1984); and *Reconceptions in Philosophy and Other Arts and Sciences,* with Catherine Z. Elgin (Indianapolis: Hackett, 1988). Cf. *Journal of Aesthetic Education* 25, no. 1 (Spring 1991), a special issue titled "More Ways of Worldmaking."

15. Beardsley, "Understanding Music," p. 66.
16. R. A. Smith, *Excellence in Art Education,* updated version (Reston, Va.: National Art Education Association, 1987); *The Sense of Art*; and Levi and Smith, *Art Education: A Critical Necessity.*

Canonicity in Academia: A Music Historian's View

AUSTIN B. CASWELL

If music history textbooks are an accurate analogue of music historians' epistemological convictions, they reveal a clear set of priorities. Their largest proportion of space is devoted to an articulation of a body of works considered important to know as works, the next largest degree of attention is given to stylistic commentary, and the discussion of social context and reception comes in third by some distance. I suspect that this hierarchy and these proportions reflect the musical and pedagogical convictions of most academic musicians and their students as well: that knowledge of a canon of great works is most important, style comes next, and context and reception last. Most would agree that a student (1) should be able to identify Beethoven's Fifth Symphony and discuss its salient characteristics and (2) understand Beethoven's musical style, but (3) does not need to know as much about its genesis, first performance, and reception. Neither the canon nor canonicity[1] was invented by music historians, but both were embraced by them as givens; both reflect a consensus that has existed unchallenged in "classical" music study for more than a century and influences what classical musicians study and perform in their years of training as well as in their professional careers. This consensus is undergirded by the assumption that the canon's constituents, the great works of Western art music, are transcendent, that is, they (1) speak to all generations and (2) are the cultural soil for all subsequent compositional manifestations in Western art music.

I am disturbed by this picture because I am convinced that transcendence, the foundation of canonicity, cannot survive scrutiny. I am also convinced that the tyranny of canonicity as installed in the academy is destructive of our critical faculties—blinding us to a consideration of music's relationship to its cultural context, preventing us from making reasoned evaluations of our own music, and creating a false evolutionary model of history that leads us into grave errors of critical judgment. I am

Austin B. Caswell is a Professor of Musicology at Indiana University. His most recent major publication is *Nineteenth-Century Embellished Opera Arias.*

thus convinced that canonicity is a flawed paradigm for pedagogy and should be supplanted by another model.

I am not interested in mounting an in-house diatribe, but to find the flaws in transcendence and canonicity and to illustrate what they have done to our view of our musical culture. I enthusiastically concur that music in the care of the campus has accomplished much: it has convinced three generations of students that the heritage of Western music is as important as the same heritage of literature, painting, sculpture, and architecture. It has taken on the responsibility of providing performers for the concert hall and opera house and has explored hitherto ignored genres, works, and groups of composers (not the least of them women). Arguably, its most innovative accomplishment is expanding the canon backwards in time by exhuming the repertoire of the Baroque, Renaissance, and Medieval ages and demonstrating it to be a repertoire for performance by training performers to play it on the appropriate instruments and in the proper style.[2] But these accomplishments are all part of the job of training museum curators to take care of the established musical canon and thus have no relationship to the ongoing musical products of our own culture. Canonicity, by its very nature, offers us no way to approach the music of our time and place unless and until it has been judged canonic. Furthermore, canonicity, however much we may approve of some of its educational products, is ideologically ill founded.

I am convinced that transcendence, the basis of canonicity, is a notion we have appropriated in order to justify the works we choose to canonize, a procedure whose circularity seems obvious. It is so ingrained in our thinking that I might deal with it as a part of our collective unconscious but will do better to cite its use in a famous text. Donald Tovey, in his 1938 essay "The Main Stream of Music,"[3] makes use of the river metaphor to convey that the canon of transcendent music is a force shaped by a hand greater than ours and has the power to proceed on its course through history unchecked and unaltered by the changes of time or contextual judgment—a natural force to which humankind must accommodate itself. Once a piece of music becomes part of this stream, it must be accepted by all subsequent (read "downstream") civilizations; humanity ignores the stream or attempts to alter its course at humanity's peril. The relationship of all thinking people to the stream is that of an obligation—to respect it and care for it as an unquestioned cultural value. A transcendent artwork becomes a cultural icon that is to be revered by its inheritors; if they cannot understand it, they have the duty to learn how to do so.

We are taught that this transcendence is bestowed by history's gradual arrival at a verdict based on qualities found in the composition itself, dependent neither upon its functional role in its context, nor upon its contemporary reception. We learn that history's deliberations on transcendence depend upon the analysis of the musical text by experts working at a considerable distance in time and place in order to ensure removal from contextual involvement.[4] The corollary of this position is that music being composed here and now is not yet worthy of serious attention since we are too close to judge it for transcendence. As Tovey expresses it, "We of the twentieth century are in no better position than our ancestors to identify the main stream of contemporary music . . . [since] contemporaries are often pre-occupied with trivial matters."[5] The effects of this doctrine on the listening habits of educated Americans and the programming traditions of the musical institutions they support are too obvious to detail.

The weaknesses of this ideological construct are clear. First, its historical lineage is fabricated. A study of the history of musical criticism shows that the notion of transcendence doesn't appear before the very late eighteenth century and that it is largely a conceit invented by nineteenth-century criticism for the purpose of asserting a composition's ability to speak to all cultures and all times. Second, its assertions don't hold up historically. If a work achieves transcendence and a permanent place in the canon solely on the basis of its inherent qualities, then we ought to find great compositions, their excellences once perceived, maintaining their niches undisturbed by the passage of time and the changes of cultural values. I think such a search would be fruitless. In spite of its presumed immutability, the canon constantly changes by the application of criteria that change in response to the changes of cultural context. Not only do works once excluded on the basis of incomprehensibility (Beethoven's late quartets) enter the canon by their appeal to subsequent generations, but works once occupying a secure place (the operas of Meyerbeer) are dropped. The third, and perhaps greatest problem with transcendence is that of its means in conflict with its results: if transcendence (and thus canonicity) is determined by analysis, we must assume that analysis is unaffected by contextuality. But this asks us to accept that all analytical systems agree and that the critical evaluations resulting from them agree as well, a request that cannot be granted by any thoughtful reader of musical criticism of the past two centuries. As a fourth and final objection, I would suggest that the use of analysis to validate greatness is bankrupt since the assertion of greatness most often precedes the analysis.[6] The circularity of this relationship triggers the academic cyclone into whose vortex we draw our students: analysis creates greatness, which justifies continued analysis, which further validates greatness, which . . .

If the academy is to take on the responsibility of teaching, analyzing, and criticizing today's music, it should incorporate criteria that are consistent with its approach to the music of earlier Western centuries—its critical methodology should be the same as that used to study the Middle Ages, the Renaissance, and the Enlightenment. Rather than embracing the nineteenth-century aesthetic[7] that confers transcendence upon selected compositions, genres, and forms, we should embrace something even more fundamental: the belief that music's position in its own culture can be perceived by studying its reception in its own culture. A great deal of current research has pursued the implications of this principle, positing that musical meaning no longer can be seen to inhere in the score alone and that the score is but one part of a composite manifestation, other parts being (1) the performance and (2) the performance's reception by listeners of the time and place.[8] In such research context becomes a focus of study equal in importance to that of musical content—and by extension, context enters the realm of content. It is my belief that this contextual resonance is not only a focus of attention equal in importance to the study of the score and its performances, but also that it is the right name for the attribute we have falsely labelled transcendence. I am convinced that "masterworks" have been so judged *because* they demonstrated (within the culture for which they were composed) a contextual resonance of a high order, not because they were determined by analysis to exhibit compositional techniques that assured them a place in history.[9]

The sixteenth-century madrigal can be taken as a case in point: it enjoyed international success not because it incorporated compositional procedures valued by critical analysts, but because it met the needs of the leisured classes of the time, giving them a form of participatory musical entertainment that could involve both men and women in a portrayal of the rituals of courtly love. Because of this success it was seen (and analyzed) as a model of the union of poetry and music; our imposition on it of transcendence proceeds from its success rather than from any characteristics in the scores themselves.

The monuments of opera can be examined in the same light. Mozart, in *Don Giovanni*, used the compositional models of the eighteenth century not to meet critical standards, but to appeal to theatergoers of the time—that the opera succeeded caused it to be held up as a model of style, not the other way around. Mozart's and Haydn's symphonies were conceived as musical entertainment, not as demonstrations of the composers' command of canonized form; our consensus that they demonstrate consummate command of the form is achieved *because* they worked so well as entertainment.[10]

In applying this ideology to the music of our own time, we will need other critical bases, and in our search we will do well to examine those of scholars who have studied the vernacular musics of our own time in an attempt to determine the mechanisms by which their place in our contextual matrix is established. One such, Simon Frith, posits an aesthetic that consists of music's ability to do three things: (1) to help us create our identity, (2) to "give us a way of managing the relationship between our public and private emotional lives," and (3) "to shape popular memory, to organize our sense of time."[11] On his first point, Frith holds that rather than merely reflecting personality and identity, music has the power to create it. An individual creates her- or himself by deciding who she or he shall be (as well as who she or he shall *not* be) through the manipulation of many elements of external reality; dress, language, film, TV, and literature come into play, but music (because of its affective nature) creates the individual more strongly than any other medium. Frith's second function, that of defining our emotional lives, certainly overlaps with his first but can be separately articulated: he does so by citing the vernacular love song, which, while not used as a substitute for personal relationships ("pop singers do not do our courting for us"), serves to make "our feelings seem richer and more convincing than we can make them appear in our own words, even to ourselves."

The third function—"to organize our sense of time"—operates in two modes. One is music's ability to bring time to a halt, "to make us feel we are living within a moment, with no memory or anxiety about what has come before, what will come after." This phenomenon is experienced when music subverts our sense of the passing of real time and transports us to its own world. The other way music organizes our sense of time is by stamping events of the past with its brand. We are taken back to a significant past event through music more strongly than by any other association, so that the musical connection becomes that event. Frith concludes that by means of the operation of these three phenomena, music becomes a stronger part of the personality—he speaks of music as being "owned"—than any other external stimuli. Frith's phenomena are observed in popular music, but I propose that they are at work in any music and have indeed been the mechanisms that have selected the music of the classical canon.

We could examine the historical record at random to find clear evidence of Frith's aesthetic at work. The ecstatic ladies at Franz Liszt's concerts were not there to attend to musical form and style, but to define themselves as devotees of their sensual performer-hero and as Romantics sensitive enough to be transported to another world through the wordless art of sound.[12] They were there to label themselves as young, beautiful, and passionate at that particular time and place; in subsequent memory they certainly identified their younger selves by means of the music Liszt played. The London aristocrats who made Handel's operas successful may have been interested in *bel canto* and musical characterization, but they were doubtless more interested in demonstrating that they were sophisticated (and leisured and wealthy) enough to understand and patronize such an exotic and aristocratic form of entertainment.[13] And the upright mercantile audiences of the same composer's oratorios acted by a similar mechanism in choosing to define themselves not by means of Italian opera, but by the pious and moralistic oratorio.[14] My point is that any music demonstrates its integral relationship to a culture by its ability to create personhood and manipulate consciousness, and that this aesthetic is a more consistent and reliable tool for observation than are the ones we currently use.

Before investigating what transcendence's child, canonicity, has done to the way we look at music in academia, let me do a historical sketch of how canonicity became part of America's cultural and pedagogical fabric. Americans set their minds to developing musical institutions around the middle of the nineteenth century in an effort to establish the cultural trappings of a refined (and thus respectable) Western culture no longer totally engaged in survival and expansion. We did so by emulating the aesthetics and institutions of European high art and hiring European performers (or Americans trained by Europeans) to play European works for us. The institution we most consistently installed was the symphony orchestra; its pattern of establishment varied from city to city, but beginning with the founding of the New York Philharmonic in 1842 and spreading rapidly westward, every large northern American city created (or attempted) such an ensemble. American orchestras assumed leadership by presenting performances of significant European works as quickly as they became identifiable, and lesser orchestras followed the trail marked out by the leaders.[15]

But the European musical life we were copying was undergoing a profound change during this period. European performers and publishers who, up to midcentury, had responded to public taste by presenting the latest music, began, at the behest of audiences who defined themselves as "serious" and possessed of a discriminating musical taste, to concentrate on repeated performances of a smaller repertoire of revered compositions from the past—a canon. Within a very short time, the cultivation of new and immediately understandable works became a less prestigious branch of European musical life, its primacy taken over by another, that of serious attention to a few works of the past that the cognoscenti considered culturally significant. American musical institutions adopted this "serious" repertoire and its aesthetic and made little attempt to include anything else: the admission of new works into the canon was agreed to be the prerogative of the Europeans who had developed the institutions and the repertoire.[16] Native or popular institutions of musical entertainment, such as the concert band, were excluded from the perimeter of high art.

When, at the beginning of our century, American higher education began to accept music into a humanistic curriculum and to articulate philosophies to justify its inclusion, it embedded high art and its supporting aesthetics within a Platonic frame.[17] Music was seen as part of the cultural equipment of the eminent citizen: the leader of political, religious, educational, and commercial life who supported musical life as a patron. Following Plato, the training of such a citizen was to be that of the discriminating consumer rather than the professional. She (as women in America were allotted increasing responsibility for the direction of cultural life) was expected to develop powers of perception allowing her to discern good music from bad—the essential skill for the exercise of her responsibilities as cultural leader. In the American context, this discriminating taste was to be cultivated by a thorough exposure to the canon of Western European masterworks: a repertoire of forms and genres of the eighteenth and nineteenth centuries ranked hierarchically by genre and origin, so that, for example, symphony and opera were ranked numbers one and two among worthy genres, with Germany and (two paces behind) Italy and France the esteemed musical cultures. This hierarchy made it easy to decide what sorts of music a properly educated person should know and what sorts of critical criteria ought to be employed in musical judgments. In addition, it provided ready-made attitudes about other kinds (and provenances) of music: lesser genres, while not prohibited, were relegated to lower rank. It was acceptable for the properly educated person to enjoy the music played by the band in the Fourth of July parade, as long as she recognized that this enjoyment belonged to a different category of intellectual and sensory response than that accorded Beethoven's Symphony no. 5 or Wagner's *Tristan und Isolde*. This hierarchy was not only taught as an aesthetic credo, but shaped the curricula of higher education as well, so that the course that studied (but did not perform) the great German symphonies received credit while the glee club that performed (but did not study) American vernacular music did not. The effect of this curricular structure upon American critical faculties is essential to note: by unquestioningly accepting works Europeans valued, the American critical muscle atrophied and, when confronted with new American compositions, was able to render judgment only by rejecting everything except what sounded most European and most canonic.

It is interesting to compare this cultural and curricular development to another peculiarly American phenomenon: the study of Western Civilization. Both emerged and found a place in American college curricula at about the same time, and both were based on the same assumptions: that European culture represents the epitome of human civilization, that its history is an unbroken line culminating in present accomplishments, that its achievements comprise a canon of great deeds of great individuals, and that the goal of its study is to know those accomplishments and use them as models to build modern values and goals. As Gilbert Allardyce says in his study of the Western Civilization course, its aim was to portray all culture as pointing toward civilization's pinnacle—Western participatory democracy; its historiography was "the idea of history as the evolution of freedom."[18] The wide influence of the Western Civilization course may mean that it is not accidental that music textbooks of the period speak of music's historical development in the same terms and often adopt the same political/evolutionary metaphors.[19] The study of music literature built itself on the same foundation as did that of Western civilization: the conviction that culturally responsible education was based upon the study of the achievements of Western Europe, providing the student models by which to act and judge in his or her place and time. Thus music, like all products of the New World, was not to be judged by its validity in its own context but by its reflection of the cultural ideology of nineteenth-century Europe.

Degree-granting curricula in musical performance came into American higher education later and had to conform themselves to the canonic epistemology. Since professional preparation in music was incongruent with the Platonic model of the education of the ruling classes and involved a type of study that seemed suspiciously nonintellectual, musicians saw that if the study of performance were to be accepted at all, it would be by devoting it to the nonprofessional study of masterpieces, using the epistemology already established for music in the humanistic curriculum.[20] Thus American music majors studied the same music their nonmajor companions did—if for slightly different reasons. They saw their repertoire not only as classical models, but as transcendent masterworks that embodied beauty undimmed either by repeated hearing or changing cultural contexts. They learned that these pieces had stood the test of time, i.e., that they transcended the culture within which they were composed and formed a body of works essential for all musicians to know and repeatedly perform for the enlightenment of their nonperforming companions as well as for their own benefit as sensitive artists.

Instruction in musical composition was accepted by embracing the canon as well. But composition was even more difficult to fit into the Platonic model than was performance, since to treat it as the training ground for the professional composer was clearly contradictory of the nonprofessional goals of humanistic higher education. The solution was an interesting compromise—rather than training composers to write the marches, dances, parlor music, anthems, and musical shows America was consuming at the time, composition departments embraced the *raison d'être* of producing professionally trained (but noncommercial) artists whose works might some day qualify for history's accolade of transcendence by using the masterworks of Europe as models. Such activity was intellectually and artistically respectable whereas writing functional music for one's own time and place was not. Thus composition students, like their listening and performing colleagues, were weaned away from their own musical vernacular as from an inferior and perhaps dangerous food and made more serious artists by mimicking the aesthetics and techniques of the nineteenth-century European model.[21] One can argue that until very recently becoming musically educated in America, whether as listener, performer, or composer, meant putting one's own culture aside and adopting another.

This music curriculum settled into American colleges and universities and produced a distinct type of musician—one of the two deeply contrasting archetypes of American musician familiar to us today: one type academically trained to know and play the music of nineteenth-century Europe in the cultural museum of the concert hall and to teach it (often with no intervening period of exposure to musical life outside academia) to subsequent generations of music students, and the other type trained by means of the apprenticeship system and working in commercial musical life separate from academia and the cultural museum. Those in the first group have a knowledge of the canon of European music but often little interest in or experience with any music of their own time; the second group reverses these positions and has a thorough acquaintance with the vernacular music of their own culture but often little interest in the European canon. Most educated Americans are taught which literature (and group of players) is of greater value. Convinced that music with immediate, unexamined meaning is of lesser quality than the music that one must "learn to appreciate," they demonstrate disdain for what they consider low art.

As American musical academia took on a degree of responsibility for the care of the musical canon, it had to address its responsibility to consider the potential canonicity of American compositions. But the process involved a reliance upon European critical consensus to the exclusion of American critical opinion and music's relation to an American cultural context. These criteria extended to genres as well as works: symphony and opera were deemed canonic genres, and compositions cast in these molds might be found acceptable, while genres having American origins (Broadway musical theater, jazz, popular song) were seldom given consideration. That this matrix continues to dominate the cultivation of music in academia needs no further detailing; it controls what is studied in courses in music history, what orchestras and choruses perform, what the performer studies, and, eventually, what gets funding by government and private patronage.

What is the effect of this institutionalized canonicity upon the way academics view the music of our own time? I begin by listing the criteria I believe academics use when judging a new composition's value (i.e., its potential canonicity).

1. Its composer should have been trained in an academic institution.
2. Its techniques should reflect a study of the canon.
3. It is to be judged by analysis rather than by public reaction.
4. Its innovations should be those of structure and technique rather than of aesthetics.[22]

Where do these criteria come from? It is easy to assume that they are natural products of canonic thinking, but I hold that they are musical versions of the criteria applied to all academic disciplines—the ones by which all academic life is run and its products evaluated. Let us compare: in the evaluation of an academic's candidacy for promotion or tenure, his or her contributions must

1. manifest that they are the work of a trained scientist or humanist;
2. employ methodologies recognized by the discipline;
3. present demonstrable solutions to defined problems in terms understandable to members of the discipline;
4. offer evidence that they are significant contributions to established fields.[23]

The two lists are virtually the same; the first is couched in musical terminology while the second uses terms that cover all academic disciplines. Though the academic composer may claim to have brought high art (i.e., the criteria of canonicity) to the academy, he or she has actually been coopted by the academy and has accepted its criteria as the governing paradigm for the composition of new music. It is my conviction that these criteria urge us to dismiss the nonacademic music of our time to the detriment of the academy, the academically trained musician, the academically trained listener, and our culture's musical well-being.

The most famous instance of the composer embracing academia is that of Milton Babbitt and those associated with his thinking. Babbitt's case and especially his famous article of a generation ago, entitled (against his will) "Who Cares if You Listen?"[24] provide so well-known and so egregious a statement of position as to make them easy of dismissal, were it not for the fact that a generation of postwar composers was brought up under a credo closely connected to his. Babbitt, referring to his choice of title ("The Composer as Specialist"), describes the situation of the academic composer thus: "He is, in essence, a 'vanity' composer. The general public is largely unaware of and uninterested in his music. The majority of performers shun it and resent it. Consequently, the music is little performed, and then primarily at poorly attended concerts before an audience consisting in the main of fellow professionals. At best, the music would appear to be for, of, and by specialists." It is not the accuracy of this description that intrigues me: it is that Babbitt finds nothing disturbing in it. Rather than proposing that the composer alter his orientation or change his aesthetics, Babbitt defends the academic environment as the only worthy one: "It is my contention that, on the contrary, this condition is not only inevitable, but potentially advantageous for the composer and his music. From my point of view, the composer would do well to consider means of realizing, consolidating, and extending the advantages."

Babbitt speaks of the "revolution in musical thought" as parallel to that of "the mid-nineteenth-century revolution in theoretical physics," finding it to be similarly irreversible and, after describing the characteristics of his music in the language of a laboratory report, offers that there is no more need for a public understanding of "advanced" music than there is for the most recent developments in science: "After all, the public does have its own music, its ubiquitous music: music to eat by, to read by, to dance by, and to be impressed by. Why refuse to recognize the possibility that contemporary music has reached a stage long since attained by other forms of activity?" Babbitt's choice of rhetoric is as interesting as his stance; he speaks in terms of a progress normally associated with science or technology and expects that, like those disciplines, musical composition can best pursue advancement within the university, separated from contact with the public. "It is only proper that the university, which—significantly—has provided so many contemporary composers with their professional training and general education, should provide a home for the 'complex,' 'difficult,' and 'problematical' in music." He ends by calling for institutional support parallel to that undergirding the sciences in the fear that without it "music will cease to evolve."

What would happen to our view of the works of twentieth-century academic composers if, rather than seeing them as scientific research in need of support or as formidable intellectual edifices we must learn to decipher, we were to look at them according to Frith's criteria? Would we arrive at different insights if we asked of them the questions we feel it normal to ask of other musics: Whom is the piece written for? Who are its audience and how do they express themselves about it? What is the composer's relationship to her or his public? How does the piece function economically? How does it fit the social matrixes of the time? How does it serve (or attack) cultural institutions? Perhaps it is the realization that such questions provide telling insights that has influenced some trends in American musicology of late. Scholars concerned with American music are devoting increasing attention to the contributions of Gershwin, Ellington, Parker, Porter, Kern, and Berlin in response to clear evidence that the music of those composers is the music that provided cultural and personal identity for large numbers of Americans at midcentury, rather than that of Piston, Sessions, and Carter, in spite of the fact that the latter were valued in academia and the former were not.

What such studies represent is a search for a noncanonic approach to music, one that parallels the search for epistemological renewal going on in other humanistic disciplines. Returning to the comparison made earlier in this article, we find cultural historians concluding that the traditional Western Civilization course died because it focused upon an ethnocentric and monocultural elitism: the noble accomplishments of a select few from within a single culture. That this view can no longer serve our world is apparent. A new approach must be shaped, one that reflects

> the flowering of particularist cultures within American society, [one] directing attention to numerous levels of culture—not merely the *Kultur* of the "great ideas and great books" but also popular culture, mass culture, countercultures; and not merely culture in a public sense but culture as patterns in private relations. As a consequence, the generation now designing new, model introductory history courses is separated from the architects of Western Civ by a different understanding of civilization, one that embraces the Cathars of Montaillou as well as the Scholastics of Paris, the mothers of families as well as Founding Fathers.[25]

Milton Babbitt gave a set of lectures in 1983 at the University of Wisconsin and concluded them with the same subject he addressed in his 1958 essay quoted above—the relationship of the academic composer to the university. This time he uses a nonconfrontational tone even though his title, "The Unlikely Survival of Serious Music,"[26] indicates that his view has, if anything, become less sanguine. He has seen the composer integrated into the university but has learned from bitter experience that life there is not all it might be: "[Composers] have never been really admitted. . . . They are not provided the kind of academic positions that are awarded to those in other fields. Their professional needs are not satisfied in anything like the same way. Their music is not published as it should be by university presses. Their music is not recorded. They cannot communicate with their colleagues in the same way that most members of other fields can." He concludes, however, that the only place for the composer is in the university, because "to consign us to the great world out there, however seriously or however viciously, is to consign us to oblivion." His last sentence is a plea: ". . . music's being under the current egalitarian dispensation . . . [we] who've entered the university as our last hope, our only hope, and ergo our best hope, hope only that we're not about to be abandoned." Babbitt's plea is an abject one—while defending the academic composer as the most highly evolved organism of musical creativity, a form that can trace its lineage backward through generations of canonic masterworks, he admits that this most sophisticated organism is threatened by extinction. But what is he asking us to save: the Brazilian rain forest or the dinosaurs?

Recently, reading Stephen Jay Gould's *Wonderful Life: The Burgess Shale and the Nature of History*, the first book on paleontology I not only understood but was unable to put down, I was struck by a parallel to my dilemma. Gould has written an arresting account of how the evidence in a particular bed of shale in the Rockies of Eastern British Columbia has revolutionized perceptions of the processes of evolution. Darwin's version of evolution was heavily (if unconsciously) dependent upon the convictions of his society: he saw evolution as a rational, regular, step-by-step process by which unfit organisms died away (for apparent reasons) and fit ones survived. Each generation became a bit more sophisticated, complex, and thus a bit more distant from its crude and primitive ancestors. The process was seen as progressive and governed by the notion that the culmination of this ladder of ascent was the achievement of the greatest possible diversity of phyla, at the top of which was the pinnacle of the system: humankind, the goal toward which all selection aimed. All phenomena followed the same inexorable processes: Darwin's implication is that if we were to turn back the clock of time and start it again with any organic sample, the process would repeat itself identically and end up in the same place.

Gould, analyzing three generations of research on the Burgess Shale, makes a convincing case that none of these presumptions is borne out by the findings. Most of the Burgess fossils are unrelated to any organisms found later, and thus no lineage connecting them with today's species (including mankind) can be traced, and the diversity of species and their degree of complexity and specialization is much greater in the Burgess than in immediately subsequent strata. There is a decimation of species (thus a decrease in diversity) directly following this period for no discernible cause: no identifiable "unfitness" can be found in nonsurviving species. Gould proposes (1) that survival/extinction is more often dependent upon contingency through chance than upon "natural selection" of the "fittest," (2) that the ladder of sophistication and complexity cannot be posited as a governing process, (3) that the lineage from primitive precursor to a burgeoning multitude of more complex descendants does not appear, (4) that the cone-shaped diagram of increasing diversity is not only absent, but in this instance is supplanted by an inverted cone of shrinking diversity, and (5) that if the "tape recording of time were replayed" with an infinitesimal change in one or two contingent events, the scenario would go in any number of different directions, the end results of any of which would not be humankind. In Gould's own vivid style, "We came *this close* (put your thumb about a millimeter away from your index finger), thousands and thousands of times, to erasure by the veering of history down another sensible channel. Replay the tape a million times from a Burgess beginning, and I doubt that anything like *Homo Sapiens* would ever evolve again."[27]

I suggest that academic musicians, like Darwinian paleontologists, have been ruled by an inherited complex of assumptions that has led us to see ourselves as the highest, most sophisticated form of artistic evolution: the form toward which all previous musical species have been aiming. In enthroning ourselves thus, we have also enthroned what we deem the "fittest" compositional contributions of the present and called upon musically sensitive people to accept them as such and to dismiss other musics as "unfit." But just as Gould sees the need to revise evolutionary theory in the light of a contemporary evidence, so do we need to revise our thinking about the canonic theory of music. Maybe our canon (and its presumed heir, the academic composer's work) is not the trunk destined to serve as the nurturing stem of future musical evolution; maybe, like the burgeoning phyla of the Burgess Shale, it is one that is destined to disappear. We have convinced ourselves that the compositional qualities we have canonized are "fittest" and that others, though they may resonate with various segments of our culture, will not survive. But, to use Gould's paleontological terminology, this conviction is "overdetermined," and, like traditional Darwinists, we can no longer call this view into reality. Maybe the robust health of much vernacular music is evidence of its "fitness" and the affective sterility of much academic composition evidence of its lack thereof—maybe Babbitt is asking us to save the dinosaurs. If so, rather than respond to his plea, we ought to turn our attention to finding a remedy for our flawed relationship to our society's musical culture by adjusting our theory to fit the evidence rather than the reverse. But if Gould is right, the contingency of evolution means that we cannot know which organisms will prove fit enough to survive and which won't, which criteria are the ones that determine survival, nor even which kind of observation will reveal such things to us. Transferring Gould's conclusions to music, this means that no matter what music we value, by what criteria, and according to what system of observation, our esteem is irrelevant to what happens to that music in the future and to which music will prove influential upon future developments. The only conclusion I can arrive at is that evaluation of music's potential canonicity according to evolutionary models does a disservice to music as well as to our claims to intelligent cultural observation and should be rejected. We should stop worrying about which music has stood (and will stand) "the test of time" and devote our attention to which music speaks to whom and why.

How might this affect our work as pedagogues? For one thing, it would require us to operate more in the ethnological mode and less in the curatorial one. We would keep our "musical museum" intact up to c. 1900 and continue to train people to know it and play it, but would look at it not as masterworks transcending time and place, but as music that spoke strongly to a specific cultural context. Concerning the music of our own century, we will choose repertoire for study and performance by the same criteria that selected the successful works of the past: their ability to speak to a specific culture at a specific time. Our aim will no longer be to stuff our students with the regulation diet, but to ask them to become aware of how and why certain people at certain times became excited about certain musics and, by extension, how and why various peoples of our own times and places become enthusiastic about various musics.

How will this affect performer training and concert programming? With regard to the historical canon, not at all. The sounding manifestations of the musical museum (the symphony orchestra, the opera company, and the schools that train performers for them) need not be affected by this reorientation. With regard, however, to the study of the musics of our own time, it provides a rationale to include different bodies of literature representing the plurality of our culture.

NOTES

1. Throughout this article I will be using *canon* in the sense of a body of works considered essential for study as the masterworks of Western music literature. *Canonicity* is the belief in a canon, the set of ideas about how the canon functions in musical life, and the ideology governing how and by whom the canon is determined.

2. It is possible to argue that this last achievement could not have come about without the inclusion of a Music Appreciation and Music History course in the curriculum of American higher education—that academia (at least in this country) has not only created a new historical canon, but has created the audience for it as well.

3. Donald Francis Tovey, "The Main Stream of Music," in *The Main Stream of Music and Other Essays* (New York: Meridian Books, 1959).

4. "What they did all agree upon was that Western music should be viewed in terms of a canon and that some form of analysis of the scores was the means of determining what music belonged in." Joseph Kerman, "A Few Canonic Variations," *Critical Inquiry* 10 (September 1983): 114.

5. Tovey, "Main Stream," p. 344.

6. Joseph Kerman seems to agree: "This branch of criticism takes the masterpiece status of its subject matter as a donnée and then proceeds to lavish its whole attention on the demonstration of its inner coherence. Aesthetic judgment is concentrated tacitly on the initial choice of material to be analyzed; then the analysis itself, . . . can treat of artistic value only casually or . . . not at all." "How We Got into Analysis, and How to Get Out," *Critical Inquiry* 7 (Winter 1980): 313.

7. Throughout this article, I use the word "aesthetic(s)" in the sense of a doctrine or philosophy of beauty.

8. See Gary Tomlinson, *Monteverdi and the End of the Renaissance* (Berkeley: University of California Press, 1987); Jane Fulcher, *The Nation's Image: French Grand Opera as Politics and Politicized Art* (Cambridge: Cambridge University Press, 1987); and Pierre-Michel Menger, *Le Paradoxe du Musicien: Le compositeur, le mélodrame et l'Etat dans la société contemporaine* (Paris: Flammarion, 1983).

9. It will be objected that many works, such as J. S. Bach's *Art of Fugue* and even works of Charles Ives, demonstrate no contextual resonance since they were unknown at their time. I hold that such works should be considered according to their resonance for the later generations that discovered them.

10. See Leonard G. Ratner, *Classic Music: Expression, Form, and Style* (New York: Macmillan, 1980); Neal Zaslaw, *Mozart's Symphonies: Context, Performance, Practice, Reception* (Oxford: Clarendon Press, 1989), pp. 445-544; and Elaine Sisman, "Haydn's Theater Symphonies," *Journal of the American Musicological Society* 43, no. 2 (Summer 1990): 292-352. These researches operate within the assumption that eighteenth-century symphonies were functional music: music for theater, court festivities, dinners, dances, and so forth.

11. Simon Frith, "Toward an Aesthetic of Popular Music," in *Music and Society: The*

Politics of Composition, Performance and Reception, ed. Richard Leppert and Susan McClary (Cambridge: Cambridge University Press, 1987), pp. 133-49.

12. "He has been feted and has been serenaded; a woman knelt down in front of him and begged to be allowed to kiss the tips of his fingers—another embraced him in public in the concert hall—a third poured the remains of his cup of tea into her scent-bottle—hundreds have worn gloves bearing his portrait—many have lost their reason. They all wanted to lose it. An art dealer made glass-paste objects with Liszt's portrait and sold them as ornaments; thousands vied for his favours and begged for his money—and this is only the beginning. . . ." *Hell'sche Abendzeitung*, no. 88 (1842), in Ernst Burger, *Franz Liszt: A Chronicle of His Life in Pictures and Documents* (Princeton, N.J.: Princeton University Press, 1989), p. 142.

13. Evidence of the role of social rank in eighteenth-century opera is found in publicity, reportage, and private correspondence, as well as in theater architecture and audience behavior. The system of private boxes as extensions of the home, the publication of the names of (and frequently the amounts contributed by) the guarantors of an operatic venture, and the prominence given to the listing of notable persons in attendance at performances all demonstrate that "the quality" saw opera as a vehicle for affirmation of their position. See *Reminiscences of Michael Kelly . . .* (London: H. Colburn, 1826); *Musical Reminiscences . . . by the Earl of Mount Edgcumbe* (London: John Andrews, 1834); and *Musical Memoirs . . . by W. T. Parke* (London: Henry Colburn and Richard Bentley, 1830).

14. "Sir, I Beg Leave, by your Paper, to congratulate, not Mr.Handel, but the Town, upon the Appearance there was *last* Night at *Israel in Egypt*. The Glory of one Man, on this Occasion, is but of small Importance, in Comparison with that of so numerous an Assembly. The having a Disposition to encourage, and the Faculties to be entertain'd by such a truly-spiritual Entertainment, being very little inferior to the unrivall'd Superiority of first selecting the noble Thoughts contained in the Drama, and giving to each its proper Expression in that most noble and angelic Science of Musick. . . . Nothing shews the Worth of the People more, than their Taste for Publick Diversions: . . . Did such a taste prevail universally in a People, that People might expect . . . the same Deliverance as those Praises celebrate; and Protestant, free, virtuous, united, Christian England, need little fear, . . . the whole Force of slavish, bigotted, united, unchristian Popery, risen up against her, ..." *London Daily Post*, Wednesday morning, 18 April 1739. Otto Erich Deutsch, *Handel: A Documentary Biography* (New York: Da Capo Press, 1974), p. 481.

15. American orchestras of the first rank are still led, in the majority, by European conductors—a recognition of our sense of cultural obligation to the European canon as well as our insecurity to handle it on our own. The recent appointment of Kurt Masur as conductor of the New York Philharmonic continues this tradition, even though diluting it with no small amount of political opportunism.

16. I cannot blame everything I consider in need of repair on European developments; it is the nature of institutions everywhere to move toward entropy and self-preservation, and American musical institutions were acting no differently than were the European ones they were copying.

17. See Edmund V. Jeffers, *Music for the General College Student* (New York: King's Crown Press, 1944); and David Warren Seegmiller, "College Music: Programs and Their Administration" (Ed.D. diss., Teachers College, Columbia University, 1966), pp. 35-97. In the nineteenth century music first took a devotional role in U.S. higher education, followed by an avocational one.

18. Gilbert Allardyce, "The Rise and Fall of the Western Civilization Course," *American Historical Review* 87, no. 3 (June 1982): 696.

19. Titles often reveal the historiographical paradigm: C. H. H. Parry's *The Evolution of the Art of Music* (1893); George Dyson's *The Progress of Music* (1932); Marion Bauer's *How Music Grew: From Prehistoric Times to the Present Day* (1926); and R. H. Schauffler's *Beethoven: The Man Who Freed Music* (1934).

20. The incorporation of professional and humanistic curricula within the same in-

stitution is a uniquely American decision. Europeans separated the two by placing them in different institutions, establishing the conservatory for professional training.

21. There are notable exceptions to this pattern, such as the populism taken up by many American composers in the 1930s and 1940s. It is significant, however, that after World War II, this direction was seen as a temporary aberration and was rejected, especially by American musical academia, as being inappropriately political in its motivation. See Nicholas Tawa, *Serenading the Reluctant Eagle: American Musical Life, 1925-1945* (New York: Schirmer, 1984), chap. 1 passim.

22. These criteria show themselves clearly in juried competitions. In a survey I made of some fifty American competitions and announcements of grants-in-aid of composition, all but a few were found to be sponsored by academic institutions, address themselves to the academic composer, and make it clear that submitted works are to be evaluated by academically trained judges. They are also seen in the "Contemporary Music" event. This celebration is modelled after the meetings of scholarly societies and follows their protocol precisely. The performances of new compositions are clones of the presentations of research papers: the academic audience attends the compositions of its colleagues in a manner that makes it clear that a public audience would be inappropriate. Judgment is rendered rather by analysis, which often precedes or follows the performance.

23. These criteria have not been contrived for purposes of argument, but are taken from the statements governing the evaluation of research and creative activity in the promotion and tenure deliberations at Indiana University.

24. Milton Babbitt, "Who Cares if You Listen?" *High Fidelity Magazine* 8, no. 2 (February 1958): 38-40, 126-27.

25. Carolyn C. Lougee, "Comments," following Allardyce, "The Rise and Fall," pp. 728-29.

26. Milton Babbitt, *Words about Music* (Madison: University of Wisconsin Press, 1987), pp. 163-83.

27. Stephen Jay Gould, *Wonderful Life: The Burgess Shale and the Nature of History* (New York: W. W. Norton, 1989), p. 289.

Music Curriculum Development and the Concept of Features

This essay focuses on an issue with a philosophical and professional history in education, including more specifically music education. Under different guises and in various terminology, much has already been said and written on the subject in hand. Presumptuously perhaps, I think that it is now possible to go a little further. At least, that was my belief when I first decided to work on the problem for this symposium. Whether or not this article is really an advance in thinking is, of course, a matter for the reader to decide. I also felt it important to relate what I have to say to the literature already out there, thus avoiding hermetically sealing off my work from that of others. Music education has its fair share of intellectual hermits.

It is important to tackle a genuine educational problem, in this case a dilemma that every sensitive and thinking music teacher faces every day of the working week. Two brief quotations serve to highlight the issue, a no doubt familiar controversy.

> The outward and visible sign of the subject is the syllabus, a table of contents which lays down what the student is required to do and on what he is examined. . . . The syllabus narrows the student's vision at the edge of knowledge and cuts him off from precisely those fuzzy areas at the edges of subjects that are the most interesting and rewarding.[1]

> The moral of this fable is that if you're not sure where you're going, you're liable to end up someplace else.[2]

It seems that the question goes something like this: *Is it possible to structure a music curriculum without neutralizing musical experience?* To get this in perspective we need to stand back just a little before moving forward.

Keith Swanwick is a Professor and Chairperson of the Music Department at the Institute of Education, University of London. He is the author of *A Basis for Music Education*, *Music, Mind and Education*, and of many articles and research reports. He has also edited and contributed to *The Arts and Education*, published by the National Association for Education in the Arts, London.

When music making and music taking are abstracted from everyday psychological and cultural life, becoming institutionalized in schools and colleges, it becomes necessary to make decisions as to *what* music is included or excluded and *how* teaching and learning are to be managed. Through the selection of subject content and the organization of the learning environment, institutions (schools and colleges) are the makers and guardians of boundaries. They maintain their organizational subcultures by means of house rules, social order, age, and sometimes through gender specification and, most powerfully of all, by the way in which knowledge is selected, filtered, and structured. What counts as academic knowledge is largely defined by schools, colleges, teachers, and assessment systems. Music is particularly susceptible. It has a greater cultural or idiomatic "loading" than, say, mathematics or chemistry: it proclaims its social and value affiliations more loudly than geography, economics, or even art.

Two principal elements of my initial theme have already been isolated for us and, since in these preliminaries I have no intention of inventing the wheel, we may as well exploit an existing analysis: a conceptual map developed some years ago by the English sociologist, a friend and colleague of mine, Basil Bernstein.[3] I refer to the concepts of *classification* and *framing*, and I make no apology for here reviewing the essential import of these terms.

Essentially, *classification* has to do with the exercise of selection over curriculum content, the way in which certain activities, perhaps school "subjects," are marked out for inclusion in or exclusion from the curriculum. The idiomatic boundaries of music are a potential classification system. A teacher selecting for inclusion in the classroom only music from the nineteenth-century Western classical tradition would be working to relatively closed musical boundaries, to what Bernstein calls *strong* rather than *weak* classification. Weak classification presumes greater openness in the content of educational transactions, making room for alternatives of curriculum substance, giving some choice of *what* is to be learned. To furnish some scattered instances from music education, weaker classification would include the choice of idiom into which a person may opt for instruction, joining a rock group rather than the concert band or singing European sixteenth-century madrigals rather than "barber shop" quartet, or *vice versa*.

Framing, a different but related concept, has essentially to do with pedagogy or teaching style; with the degree of control that teacher or student possesses over the structuring, organization, and pacing of what is to be learned. Strong framing is identified with styles of formal instruction that are virtually always teacher directed. Weak framing would leave more scope for decisions on the part of students as to *how* and *when* they will learn a given *what*.

I said that there is a historical background to these issues, and the reader will immediately catch echoes of Dewey and other North American writers in what I have had to say. Certain characteristics of the important distinction before us have been brought out particularly well by Margaret Mead when reflecting on her anthropological work on Manus Island. She draws out some contrasts between the islanders' implicit concept of education and the then current educational practice in the United States.[4] Comparing the customs of Manus with education in the United States, Mead identifies a move from spontaneous choice to institutional coercion, from "freedom to power," where the emphasis "has shifted from learning to teaching." In other words, in formal or institutional education we can perceive stronger classification and framing.

> There are several striking differences between our concept of education today and that of any contemporary primitive society; but perhaps the most important one is the shift from the need for an individual to learn something which everyone agrees he would wish to know, to the will of some individual to teach something which it is not agreed that anyone has the desire to know.[5]

When someone *asks* how to balance a canoe or drive a motor car or finger a guitar, then strong framing may be desirable, necessary, and expected. But under these conditions there is an element of "student" *choice* as to what knowledge is appropriate; the person has already made a decision about classification, *what* is to be learned, and initiates a contractual arrangement with the teacher who will usually decide on instructional framing, *how* things might be taught. As Mead is pointing out, the problem with formal education in purpose-designed institutions like schools is that the instructional contract may be made indirectly with agents other than the student him- or herself; perhaps with a parent. A degree of classification is usually enshrined in the laws of countries or states. Beyond this, the finer detail of curriculum content and teaching method—what actually takes place—is ultimately left to individual teachers to decide. This is why the problem, though old, still affects us all.

We can see classification and framing (see figure 1) at work in music education in every session at all levels of teaching and learning. For example, running a church choir preparing for a Christmas carol service involves strong idiomatic classification—only certain types of music would be acceptable; *and* strong framing—the teacher is likely to function as a "director of music" rather than a facilitator of musical exploration. We might come to a similar conclusion about a class lesson in a school, where a teacher is organizing a classroom rehearsal of, say, the twelve-bar blues: once again, strong classification and framing. In both of these settings the teacher exercises considerable influence over the idiomatic content—what

Figure 1

THE TWO DIMENTIONS OF CLASSIFICATION
AND FRAMING

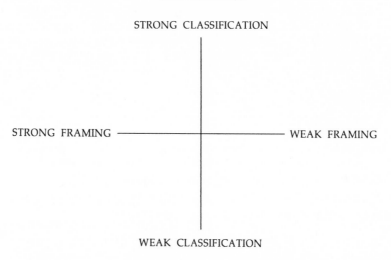

STRONG CLASSIFICATION

STRONG FRAMING ——————————————— WEAK FRAMING

WEAK CLASSIFICATION

counts as music—along with control over the pacing and mode of learning. But if work on the twelve-bar blues was individualized or in small groups with the teacher in an enabling role, we would then describe the transaction as strongly classified in musical idiom but more weakly framed in learning style. This is philosophically and educationally important: strong or weak classification does not necessarily or always imply a similar emphasis in framing; there are two quite different concepts here.

Any transaction in music education could be placed somewhere within these two dimensions, though in flexible teaching there may frequently be considerable movement between the extremes of weak and strong. In Britain, the music curriculum has moved increasingly toward students composing music—around 20 percent of available time in our secondary schools is taken up in groups or individuals making their own music. Here both classification—choice of idiom, and framing—style of teaching and learning, tend to be weaker. In North American high schools, on the other hand, the performance tradition of bands and choirs is more pervasive within the core music curriculum, generally giving rise to strong framing (the teacher directing) and fairly strong idiomatic classification manifested in the repertoire lists.

Now of course we must acknowledge that schools are committed to organize education, to classify and frame knowledge. They are not merely social gatherings where informal enculturation takes place but have placed upon them by society an ethical and contractual responsibility for the development of *mind*. And there are musical criteria in the world, musicians at work "out there," with an agenda of musical practices, procedures, and ideas which *in themselves* must contribute to the content and structure of music education.

The issue is, therefore, not *whether* but *how* musical knowledge might be classified and framed. How can the essentials of musical experience best be cultivated and structured within compulsory education systems when, as Mead says, we may be teaching something that it is not agreed that anyone has the desire to know?

In some cultures, a curriculum strategy for the management and notation of music education has been to identify "musical concepts," a procedure criticized by Thomas Regelski.[6] Concepts are cognitive processes "characterised by the thinking of qualities, aspects, and relations of objects, at which therefore comparison, generalisation, abstraction, and reasoning become possible."[7] Essentially, a concept is a kind of rule allowing us to cluster, classify, and categorize experience, seeing certain things as similar or different in a particular way; that is to say, seeing the world through the proffered conceptual grid. Thus my concept of red is likely to remain steady whether the object in view is a flag, a carpet, or a ruby.

I think it true to say that the conceptual basis of music curriculum design and practice of this type stems largely from the work of psychologists such as Seashore, who have isolated and classified musical experience into perceptual elements that to some extent are able to be isolated and tested. It is tempting to take so-called concepts relating to rhythm, pitch, timbre, and form and notate the music curriculum in an apparently progressive way, perhaps revisiting each concept area at different levels of achievement. But is this a valid way of proceeding?

The question is raised by M. L. Serafine.[8] She asks if it is indeed a correct assumption that musical cognition can usefully be broken down into the skills of discriminating pitches, identifying melodies, and so on: an assumption, she holds, that has permeated instruction and testing. These categories have, of course, been *invented* after the musical event. Concepts such as "triad" are the result of the theoretical analysis of certain aspects of music, usually after years of nonanalyzed and unlabelled practice. In many types of music, we do not easily divorce the concept of "melody" from its harmonic context, and it becomes nonsense if this is attempted.

George Bernard Shaw reports that the English composer Edward Elgar once heard someone refer to a phrase of Wagner's which contained the chord of the supertonic. Elgar responded with, "What *is* the supertonic? I never heard of it."[9] This is not to say, of course, that Elgar did not have a concept or image of supertonic chords but that it had not been important for him to talk about them.

Educators can also be perplexed as to how these "concepts" relate to musical experience; to what Michael Polanyi would call "dwelling in" music. Sam Reese suggests that any form of musical analysis, or talk *about* music, should be preceded and followed by experience of the whole work that is under scrutiny and suggests that we ought to concentrate on the expressive elements of music; though we would need some fairly sharp definition of "expressive" if teachers and students are to know what they are about.[10]

On analysis, musical "concepts" usually turn out to be either parcels of information, what some philosophers have called "knowing that," or they are specifications of pertinent skills. Thus the liberal and long list of concepts indexed in the *Manhattanville Music Curriculum Program* turns out to be, in essence, a catalogue of aural, notational, and manipulative skills, along with related information, including a knowledge of technical terms. These are the things that students should be able to demonstrate during a particular activity.[11] Nor does the interesting distinction made in the *MMCP* between "idiomatic" and "inherent" concepts resolve our specific difficulty. The acquisition of concepts, that is to say gaining skills and information, is not the sum of musical experience, which includes *personal knowing*, encounter with the particularity of this music, now, by direct acquaintance. Identification of concepts inevitably picks up only fragments of the total experience and can detract from the "thisness" of musical experience.

The philosophical problem has already been anticipated by Benedetto Croce, a philosopher by whom Susanne Langer was profoundly influenced. Writing from Naples at the turn of our century, the Italian puts his finger precisely on the difficulty.[12] His crucial position is that "knowledge has two forms: it is either *intuitive* knowledge or *logical* knowledge." These categories are further developed in the relationship shown in figure 2.

Figure 2

CROCE'S ANALYSIS

INTUITIVE	LOGICAL
IMAGINATION	INTELLECT
INDIVIDUAL	UNIVERSAL
INDIVIDUAL THINGS	RELATIONS BETWEEN THEM
AESTHETIC	INTELLECTUAL
IMAGES	CONCEPTS

Those seeking physiological correlates with psychological phenomena will recognize here a harbinger of brain hemisphere research. "What intuition reveals in a work of art is not space and time, but *character, individual physiognomy.*" It "gives us knowledge of things in their concreteness and individuality."[13] "Intuitions are: this river, this lake, this brook, this rain, this glass of water; the concept is: water, not this or that appearance and particular example of water, but water in general, in whatever time or place it be realised."[14]

Croce places intuitive or *aesthetic* knowledge at a more fundamental or prior level than conceptual or intellectual knowledge, saying that although the two forms of knowledge are different, they are not symmetrical but hierarchical in relationship. Aesthetic knowledge can stand alone, but conceptual knowledge depends upon a basis of intuitive knowledge. Similarly, intuition is not possible without experience of the basic "matter" of sensory impressions.

Croce is surely right: what we call the aesthetic is essentially our intuitive perception of the unique in the totality of its context; it has to do with the *particularity* of experience. In music education, identifying concepts does not easily meet this essential requirement, though obviously we need to have *some* generalized way of talking about both music and the music curriculum. The danger is that we and our students may come to imagine that this is what music is all about and that teachers will tend to work from and toward concepts, looking for music that exemplifies them. This can easily signal that music is merely an illustration of something else and not a significant experience on its own account. Did Mozart write the first movement of his 40th Symphony to illustrate "sonata form," and should we listen to it for this reason? So a teacher might choose to rehearse or present a song because it demonstrates the concept of changing meter or shows off a modulation to the dominant, whereas the ultimate reason for choosing any music is that it has the potential of significant engagement at the intuitive level.

But all the same, the dilemma remains; music educators do need *something* to talk about and to work at, informational handles by which to take hold of music and skills through which to make and perceive it. And there is an absolute requirement to have a structure for educational programs. My suggestion is a simple one, requiring only two prerequisites for curriculum making. The first is to find an alternative concept to "concepts." The second is to analyze the essential characteristics of musical knowing.

The alternative to concepts is already uncovered to a degree by Croce when he talks about "character, individual physiognomy." Let us pursue this analogy further. I have a concept of noses, I know roughly what physiological purpose they serve, that most if not all animals have them and that they come in a range of shapes and sizes. But the strong aquiline nose of a friend is a striking *feature*, not a concept. A feature is a distinctive and distinguishing element: a concept is a generalization. A concept draws attention to what is commonplace; a feature strikes us with what is unique in its context. There is nothing mysterious about this; a feature is what seems to be most apparent in a particular setting.

A falling semitone haunts the song about the dying rose with the worm in its heart from Britten's *Serenade for Tenor, Horn and Strings*. This is a strong feature. Repeated falling semitones are a common enough expressive device in Western music, but this song is *not* an illustration of the technique but a new embodiment of it in a special context. Of course we can abstract the procedure and think of it as a kind of motif that students might use for their own purposes. (I happen to have a recording of a group of eight fourteen-year-olds who had utilized the interval in an hour to make a first draft of a piece called *Mystery*.)

Over a period of time, we might build up a series of musical features into something that superficially *looks* like a list of concepts, perhaps even having a degree of progression. But under these conditions the attitudes of teachers will be different, for without a concern for musical features in every session, a music educator may be on the margins of what makes music musical, and music in school will be perceived to be an irrelevance to living musical experience. It is vital to notate the music curriculum (to classify and frame) in ways that optimize the possibility of significant musical encounters.

The second prerequisite for music curriculum making is to give an adequate account of the elements of musical *knowing*. I have had several stabs at this, and I am repeatedly driven to the same conclusions: first that it is indeed possible and second that there are four elements in the description. Crudely and boldly stated, these are as shown in figure 3.

Figure 3

THE ELEMENTS OF MUSICAL EXPERIENCE

1. Response to the Properties of Sounds

2. Perception of Expressive Characterization

3. Awareness of Structural Speculation

4. Experience of Symbolic Meaning as Personal Value

I am not here concerned to prove the strength of the model as a developmental chart but rather to view it as an experiential map of musical encounter. Here then are the basic processes, which can be best pictured as a spiral (see figure 4).

Figure 4

MUSICAL DEVELOPMENT

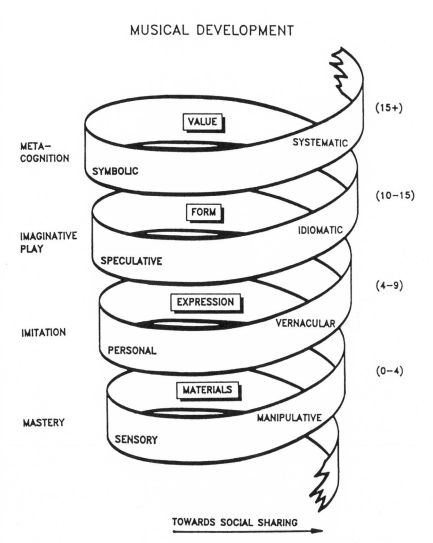

(15+)

META–
COGNITION

SYMBOLIC

VALUE

SYSTEMATIC

(10–15)

IMAGINATIVE
PLAY

SPECULATIVE

FORM

IDIOMATIC

(4–9)

IMITATION

PERSONAL

EXPRESSION

VERNACULAR

(0–4)

MASTERY

SENSORY

MATERIALS

MANIPULATIVE

TOWARDS SOCIAL SHARING

These nuances of musical *knowing* have their roots in fundamental psychological processes, and though I have no intention of justifying the model here, it is necessary to be somewhat specific as to the ideational sources. (The evidence is sifted elsewhere.)[15] All I will say here is that when we turn over the literature in aesthetic philosophy, we find that these four elements are logically discrete, even if some writers insist on stressing one rather than another, and of course everyone uses different terminology. The literature in psychology, though equally myopic and partisan, gives fairly strong evidence for details of the analysis. Let me give a short gloss here.

Mastery and Materials: It is possible to focus on the materials of any art, not only music; colors, duration, tones, words, gestures, and so on. These materials inevitably involve mastery of some skill, fluency with words or movements, ability with instruments, notations, brushes, knives, and so on. We may select and become sensitive to these materials, coming to control them. For example, we may work with or notice the use of black and white, hard and soft edges, movements that are smooth or that are angular. In music, the prescription of sets of sound materials has always been obvious. It seems essential for composers to limit available resources in order to make music manageable and get them started. The same is true for music linked to teaching. Thus we have the tonal system, twelve-note techniques, pentatonic scales, Indian *ragas*, and more limited sets of sound—as we find when Debussy makes a piano prelude out of the interval of the third, or when Bartók writes pieces in his *Mikrokosmos* based on "fifth chords" or "triplets in 9/8 time," or when jazz musicians improvise on the foundation of a well-known "standard" tune or a blues chord sequence.

Limited sets of materials are educationally invaluable in extending techniques, in sharpening discriminations, and in emphasizing particular relationships. Mastery may involve manipulative skills, perceptual judgments and discriminations, and, at times, handling notations in the form of scores, scripts, plans, and so on. I am not thinking merely of "exercises" but of ways in which we can actually get going in the arts. Nor does this analysis relate only to forming and performing. The spectator or listener may also focus on materials and techniques and become caught up in the way that certain colors, tones, techniques are handled. Just how does a painter achieve this or that effect? What types of sound give this music its character? We can even admire sheer virtuosity for its own sake.

Imitation and Expression: The more obviously representational an art object or event may be, the more it refers to events in life; the more it is imitative, having what I call *expressive character*. Teachers frequently take imitation as a focus for classroom or studio work. Thus, in drama we might initiate role playing, acting *like* someone else. In literature we might tell a story form another's point of view. In the visual arts we might try to represent a particular incident or person; or, in a more abstract way, seek to render an impression, a feeling, a quality of experience. In dance and music we might set the problem of communicating a particular dynamic process: the coming of darkness or dawn, the act of shrivelling up or of opening out, a sense of increasing stillness or activity. Though these imitative judgments are most apparent in the process of *forming* or composing, yet in the performance of written music, or in the theater, there is still scope for the player to make decisions about the detailed expression of the work; to take an active part in shaping the imitation, determining to some extent the expressive character. Only in larger and more mechanized performances—huge orchestras, bands, pageants—is there a necessity to work almost entirely "by numbers" and not make decisions about expressive character.

Imitation is not mere copying but includes sympathy, empathy, identification with, concern for, seeing ourselves as something or someone else. It is the activity by which we enlarge our repertoire of action and thought. No meaningful art lacks references, by imitation, to things outside of itself. Imitation is as inevitable as delight in the mastery of materials and is certainly not hostile to creative imagination.

Imaginative Play and Structure: If mastery directs us toward the materials of music and if imitation relates to its expressive or referential character, then imaginative play would have us focus on *structure*. By structure I mean bringing things into predictive relationships, creating tendencies that can lead us on expectantly or be broken off to surprise and delight us. Freud tells this little story:

> The Prince, travelling through his domain, noticed a man in the cheering crowd who bore a striking resemblance to himself. He beckoned him over and asked: "Was your mother ever employed in my palace?"
> "No, Sire" the man replied. "But my father was."[16]

Here our expectations concerning the relationship of king to commoner are turned right around, within a further relationship to the certain norms of sexual behavior. As Richard Wollheim says, in humor "a moment's mobility is granted to the mind."[17]

In classrooms, working with structure is perhaps the most sophisticated task. At the very simplest level, structure depends on recognizable repetitions and contrasts. How is this melody, or dramatic character, or passage of description, or dance movement different from that? Is the change gradual or sudden? Why does it change? Beyond this kind of thing we cannot go without invoking imitation, analyzing expressive character. What *kind* of change is it? Does it become more or less agitated, calmer, warmer, less or more aggressive? We shall also become curious about mastery of the materials. How is the change brought about? What is being manipulated, controlled, to bring about this effect?

My suggestion here is simply that all three elements will be activated in music education. It may be helpful to begin with a problem of mastery, or character, or structure, but once an activity is underway we shall be looking for a strong interaction between them; for how can we have any real experience of art without some level of mastery and some response to the elements of imitation and imaginative play? Only then are the gates of the mind open to the possibility of the ultimate meaningfulness of music.

Metacognition and Values: Value systems subsume the elements of mastery, imitation, and imaginative play. The emphasis here is on what psychologists call *metacognition*. Technically, metacognition is the term used to label the process of becoming aware of and articulating ideas about our own thought processes. I am using the term in a slightly more limited and special sense: indicating self-awareness of the processes of thought and feeling in a value response to music. Central to this awareness is the development of a steady and often intense commitment to the inner affective content of music. A strong sense of *value*, often publicly declared, permeates this mode of musical experience. Music has meaning for the individual at a high level of personal significance; I have used the term "symbolic" to denote this.

This transformation coincides with other developments that are frequently noted in the mid-teens: fervent religious commitment, zealous political affiliation, intense personal relationships, and ardent hero worship have all been observed; we may ourselves have experienced them. People are not only intensely self-aware at this time but may also need to reflect on, perhaps to talk with others about, their experiences, feelings, and emerging value perspectives. From a cognitive psychological perspective, Jerome Bruner puts it this way:

> Intellectual growth involves an increasing capacity to say to oneself and others, by means of words or symbols, what one has done or what one will do. This self-accounting or self-consciousness permits the transition from merely orderly behavior to logical behavior, so called. It is the process that leads to the eventual recognition of logical necessity—the so-called analytic mode of the philosophers—and takes human beings beyond empirical adaptation.[18]

It may be that such a level of response to music is rarely reached. Whether or not this need be so is another question, but I cannot escape the conclusion that not to be able to so respond is a form of musical underdevelopment. Of course it is true that everyone is potentially musical, in the same way that everyone is, to coin a word, "languagal"; but this is not to say that musical development can survive lack of stimulation and nurturing any more than language acquisition can. There have been cases of children deprived of linguistic and social interaction, such as Peter the "wolf" boy who, through odd circumstances, missed out on childhood in human society. Following this deprivation he was never able ever to converse at a later age. There is such a thing as musical deprivation too. Ultimately, we can only value what we know and understand, and this will depend on the richness of the musical environment and our cumulative interaction with the elements of music.

The ultimate development within the metacognitive, or value, mode might most appropriately be called the *systematic*. The evidence for this lies in the writings of musicians, especially composers, where a strong sense of personal value leads to the development of systematic engagement. New musical universes may be mapped out, and this creation of musical systems can be observed either in new generative musical procedures—we could think of Schoenberg and serial technique—or in talking and writing about music in a way that might be musicological, aesthetic, historical, scientific, psychological, or philosophical. Musicians in the West who have reflected systematically on the nature of music and its value would include Paul Hindemith, Tippett, John Cage, and Aaron Copland. India, China, and the Arab world also have an analytical and philosophical literature of this kind. Not only is the value of music strongly felt and publicly declared, but the field is subjected to critical analysis and development; musical potential is expanded by new processes or perspectives.

The best evidence for this model can be found in almost any responsive or critical account of a particular musical experience. Here is a report by a British seventeen-year-old of his first experience at an Indian sitar recital.

> After some time, insidiously the music began to reach me. Little by little, my mind—all my senses it seemed—were becoming transfixed. Once held by the soft but powerful sounds, I was irresistibly drawn into a new world of musical shapes and colours. It almost felt as if the musicians were playing *me* rather than their instruments, and so I too, was clapping and gasping with everyone else . . . I was unaware of time, unaware of anything other than the music. Then it was over. But it was, I am sure, the beginning of a profound admiration that I shall always have for an art form that has been, until recently, totally alien to me.[19]

Notice the sequence here: he is first impressed by sounds themselves; then he moves to an awareness of a realm of expression which he describes in metaphors of shapes and colors; then structural appreciation, the sense of surprise (essential in musical form) which has people clapping and gasping; ultimately he recognizes his enriched musical value system.

Consider also this narration by John Steinbeck. In his great novel *The Grapes of Wrath*, there is a fine description of a musical encounter among people driven from their lands by dustbowl conditions, living in camps by the roadside. He tells it this way.

And perhaps a man brought out his guitar to the front of his tent. And he sat on a box to play, And everyone in the camp moved in slowly toward him, drawn in toward him. Many men can chord a guitar, but perhaps this man was a picker. There you have something—the deep chords beating, beating, while the melody runs on the strings like little footsteps. Heavy hard fingers marching on the frets. The man played and the people moved slowly in on him until the circle was closed and tight, and then he sang *Ten-Cent Cotton* and *Forty-Cent Meat*. And the circle sang softly with him. And he sang *Why Do You Cut Your Hair Girls?* And the circle sang. . . . And now the group was welded to one thing, one unit, so that in the dark the eyes of the people were inward, and their minds played in other times. . . . And each wished he could play a guitar, because it is a gracious thing.[20]

We again notice the experiential sweep through the modes of musical knowing, from the anticipatory excitement of actually seeing the guitar brought out and the sensory impact of the beating chords and running melody, through to the vernacular and idiomatic songs and the expression of value.

The question is: can we devise a curriculum that guarantees such encounters? The answer has to be emphatically *no*, we cannot make such a promise. We can, though, safeguard both the integrity of musical experience and the explicit nature of music education by keeping in mind the essentials of what we are about, no matter what curriculum notation we use. Watch out, though, for particular forms of curriculum writing, evidence of classification and framing. Notations of any kind make some things explicit at the expense of others.

This is where the image of the spiral can have a corrective function. If we superimpose the intuitive-intellectual polarity of Croce on my helix, we notice a relationship. The intuitive, the aesthetic, the particularity of experience are similarly configured on the left side. The right side forms the background of skills and accumulated knowledge on which the creative imagination can shape or respond to unique events. This, the explicit part of education, the *non*-tacit, is where our network of music curriculum "concepts" can be found. And these will fall into the categories signalled in the four levels. Attention to the high/low of pitch, to sound length and quality, to gradations between loud and soft, these are a part of classroom or workshop conversation with younger children at the first level of manipulating "materials." Talk of and practice with such "concepts" as meter, phrase, beat, and syncopation takes us further; such skills and information are drawn from and give access to the common or "vernacular" elements of music. Conversations about form, style, and the social origins of music, along with the struggle for stylistic "authenticity," clearly belong to the "idiomatic"; while advanced work in musicology, aesthetics, psychology of music, or in devising new compositional processes heralds the possibility of "systematic" valuing. All this is fine and quite usual, but we neglect the left side at the peril of the integrity of musical experience.

Given a choice, my preferred curriculum formulation is to specify musical features drawn from music "out there." These might be at the level of materials (make a piece of your own with these five tones); in terms of expressive character (why is this piece called *Darkness*?); or as structure (how are we going to perform this piece to bring out its contrasts or surprises?). The simplest way, one which has obvious possibilities of curriculum sequential development, is to identify "sets of sound," units of materials ordered by level of difficulty and prerequisite experience, to be explored and controlled up through the levels of the spiral. A part, though not all, of this work would be weakly framed, with elements of student choice and decision making. At each level we would be looking for unique musical *features* rather than staying with generalizable labelling or *conceptual* classification; though by the end of compulsory schooling the students should have a pretty good conceptual map of what music is around and how it works.

The best curricula and the best music teachers already meet these requirements. I am, then, not suggesting anything new, but I *am* trying to say why they are the best.

NOTES

1. Christopher Small, *Music - Society - Education* (London: John Caldor, 1977).
2. Robert F. Mager, *Preparing Instructional Objectives* (Palo Alto, Calif.: Fearon, 1975).
3. Basil Bernstein, "On the Classification and Framing of Knowledge," in *Knowledge and Control*, ed. M. Young (London: Macmillan, 1971).
4. Margaret Mead, "Our Educational Emphasis in Primitive Perspective," *American Journal of Sociology* 48 (1942): 633-39; reprinted in *Tinker, Taylor*, ed. N. Keddie (Harmondsworth, U.K.: Penguin Books, 1973).
5. Ibid., p. 98.
6. Thomas A. Regelski, "Concept-Learning and Action-Learning in Music Education," *British Journal of Music Education* 3, no. 2 (1986): 185-216.
7. J. Drever, *A Dictionary of Psychology* (London: Penguin Books, 1952).
8. M. L. Serafine, "Cognitive Processes in Music: Discoveries versus Definitions," *Council for Research in Music Education Bulletin* 73 (Winter 1983).
9. George Bernard Shaw, "Music and Letters" (1920), in *Shaw's Music*, ed. Dan H. Laurence (London: The Bodley Head, 1981).
10. Sam Reese, "Polanyi's Tacit Knowing and Music Education," *Journal of Aesthetic Education* 14, no. 1 (January 1980).
11. *Manhattanville Music Program* (Bardonia, N.Y.: Media Materials, 1970).
12. Benedetto Croce, *Aesthetics: As Science of Expression and General Linguistic* (1900; London: Peter Owen, 1953, 1972).
13. Ibid., p. 5.
14. Ibid., p. 14.
15. Keith Swanwick, *Music, Mind and Education* (London: Routledge, 1988).

16. Sigmund Freud cited in Arthur Koestler, *The Act of Creation* (London: Pan Books, 1964), p. 66.
17. Richard Wollheim, *Freud* (London: Fontana, 1971), p. 105.
18. Jerome S. Bruner, *Towards a Theory of Instruction* (Cambridge, Mass.: Harvard University Press, 1966), p. 15.
19. I. Dunmore, "Sitar Magic," in *Nadopasana One*, ed. N. Varadirajan (London: Editions Poetry, 1983), p. 20.
20. John Steinbeck, *The Grapes of Wrath* (London: Penguin Books, 1939), p. 83.

An Introduction to African Views of Music Making

ELIZABETH OEHRLE

There are different concepts or notions underlying approaches to music making. In many parts of the world, however, formal music education focuses on those from the United States or England—notions which might be placed under the umbrella term of a Western approach to music education. The term Western requires definition, particularly if one is teaching at the southern tip of Africa. After all, when one is in the Far East, where, then, is the Far East? However obtuse, Western has become an easy term of reference. Few Western music educators have seemingly thought about other notions or approaches to music making or music education, for obvious reasons. Western notions of music education, however, have been and continue to be transmitted beyond the borders of the United States and England, and these notions are often accepted by other countries to the exclusion of their own particular and unique notion of music education.

Currently music education in a number of African countries is based mainly on a Western approach. This is the case in South Africa. The fact is that the traditional musical experiences of the many peoples in South Africa are grounded on different concepts about music making. For them music making is part of life, and life is music. The current situation in South African music education that has evolved has been described explicitly by a Xhosa music educator: "By the time the black child reaches the age of five he [sic] is a fully capable musician. The present school method of music soon knocks this potential out of him [sic]."[1]

One of my first experiences of the musical abilities of African children occurred when I had the unexpected good fortune to visit a Zulu student who was practice teaching in a mission school south of Durban. On arrival I

Elizabeth Oehrle is a professor in the Department of Music of the University of Natal, South Africa. She is the author of *A New Direction for South African Music Education.* Recent articles by her have appeared in such journals as the *British Journal of Music Education,* the *Education Journal,* the *International Journal of Music Education,* and *South African Music Teacher.*

found Bongani Mthethwa and another teacher in a large, dimly lit class-room with 160 primary school children. Using chalk and blackboard, Bon-gani was diligently following the prescribed syllabus and attempting to teach notation to 80 children, who faced his way as he stood at the north end of the classroom. English was being taught to the other 80 children facing the second teacher at the south end of the classroom. When I sug-gested to Bongani that his children might move outdoors for their music lesson, the children joyfully responded. They spontaneously formed into groups of five or six, and then it happened. Each group began to sing and dance with clicks, stamps, and claps in a manner that made this music educator smile from the inside out thinking, "This is what music education is about."

In the hope that music making like this will remain the rule and not be-come the exception, a research project aimed at finding a new direction for music education in Southern Africa is underway. It has been my experience and observation that the Western bias on which music education in South Africa is based is both narrow and exclusive. It is narrow because new con-cepts and ideas about Western music education are slow to reach Africa. It is exclusive because implicitly, and at times explicitly, students are taught that Western music is superior to other musics. In this regard Judith Becker's article "Is Western Music Superior?" comes to mind.[2] A Western bias may also be detrimental, as well as confusing, to African students whose musical background is based on different perceptual views of music making.

The philosophies and processes of music education used in South Africa have come mainly from England, originally introduced by the colonists, and from the United States, introduced by the missionaries and teachers, and they have been continually propagated by the availability of books, records, and articles. At the Fourth National Music Educators Conference held in South Africa in April 1990, not one keynote address focused on aspects of music from Africa. The generous funds that had been made avail-able were used instead to bring three outstanding speakers from the United States to South Africa.

The infusion of American music education ideas into Africa was prefaced by circumstances leading up to this. To illustrate we shall take a brief historical journey, beginning on the west coast of Africa, moving to the United States, and finally ending in Southern Africa. This excursion may cause us to wonder about, or perhaps to begin to imagine, what possibilities there might have been for American music education to have developed in other ways, had attitudes of tolerance and genuine interest been exercised with regard to the musical practices the West Africans brought with them to the United States.

Let us step back in time three and one-half centuries and recall that the

West Africans came to the United States as slaves. They brought with them virtually nothing other than their music and musical practices. This naturally influenced aspects of their lives in the New World. The different festivals that early Afro-Americans organized for themselves are but one example. Two such festivals were "Lection Day" and "Pinkster Day." On "Lection Day," along with parades, there were games and "singing and dancing to the fiddle, tambourine, banjo and drum." Missionaries described events like these and others as having "heathenish and savage manners,"[3] and they strove to put a stop to such practices.

The use of musical instruments by Afro-American workers on farms was sometimes suspect to the farmers because they feared that messages were being sent long distances when certain drums were played. The result was the passing of legislation which not only made it illegal for slaves to assemble without being supervised by whites, but "also banned the making and playing of drums."[4]

In the 1800s Protestant missionaries intensified their efforts to convert African slaves. The increased number of Blacks in congregations injected more spontaneous and emotional responses into church services. This generated critical comments from missionaries like Charles Colcock Jones who said, "The public worship of God should be conducted with reverence and stillness on the part of the congregation." Jones also advocated that one way of having Afro-Americans "lay aside the extravagant and nonsensical chants, and catches and hallelujah songs of their own composing"[5] was to teach them the proper way to sing hymns and psalms. One assumes then that what must have been considered improper in those days were dancing and other body movements, foot-stamping, clapping, shouting, interjections, and antiphonal singing. These were part of the Afro-American's church music stemming from traditional ways of making music in West Africa.[6]

What type of music education was Jones suggesting that the early Afro-Americans receive? In the eighteenth century Protestant ministers were particularly concerned with the need to improve the standard of singing at public worship services; thus the singing schools came into existence, and music literacy was of primary importance. Allen Britton's recent article about singing schools in eighteenth-century America gives vivid descriptions about the manner in which the schools were run by quoting from the writings of some of the early singing masters. Billings, one of the masters, advocated rules not unlike those of other singing masters or ministers of the day, and they are clearly intended to achieve *good order* in the society. To cite a few examples, it was decreed that each person must read and sign articles on which the society is based; that all must be punctual or a fine would be imposed; that the singing master's musical decisions were not to be questioned.[7] This then was the type of music education that Jones suggested that the early Afro-Americans should receive, involving instruction in singing and music literacy. However, both the rationale behind the schools and the manner in which they were run were totally foreign to the musical customs and ways of people coming from West Africa.

The Protestant church not only influenced the music making of the early Afro-Americans, but it also had an unprecedented effect on American music education. The churches' need to improve both the singing and the music literacy of their people actually give birth to music education in the United States. It was from these beginnings that music literacy has continued to assume a place of primary importance in American music education. This notion and a higher regard for Western music than for other musics were transmitted to Africa.

But a few results will be cited. One concerns replies given by three Zulu students at the university where I am teaching. Three questions, among others, were put to these students: What music did you listen to at home on the radio? What music do you prefer to listen to? What music do you prefer to perform? The answers in each case were—Western music. Another concerns a statement about African music education made by Professor Khabi Mngoma from the University of Zululand. In 1985, speaking about African music, he said: "The present emphasis is unfortunately on literacy only."[8] One final incident occurred during a conversation with a Zulu university student in his final year of music education, and what was said left me speechless. He told me that making music used to be part of his way of life before coming to the university, and he used to spend many hours playing the piano. Now, having spent nearly four years at the university, he had come to the realization that he was not good enough to play the piano.

Thus we have swung full circle. We brought Africans to America and discouraged their traditional ways of making music. We initiated a process of music education based on singing and music literacy, and then these notions, and others, were transmitted back to parts of Africa. The fact is that music making in parts of Africa may stand to lose more than it could hope to gain, because today these notions are being incorporated into music education, not only in South Africa, but in other African countries as well.

A section of my current research has entailed correspondence with approximately twenty-six African countries in an endeavor to discover the extent to which Western music and methods and African music and methods are being used. Some initial findings were presented at the Eighth South African Symposium on Ethnomusicology in 1989.[9] Among the six countries that have replied to date, Western music and methods are of primary importance in the educational systems of Ghana, Kenya, Uganda, Zimbabwe, and Nigeria. The most recent paper received from Dr. Okafor describes the situation in Nigeria. Speaking in October 1989 at the Annual Conference of the Association for Promoting Quality Education in Nigeria, he reminded the Association that "in the traditional society, music was integral not only with the arts but with life."[10] He went on to say:

> An examination of music education in Nigeria presents the observer with an immediate and glaring anomaly. The focus of music education itself appears to be on Western music—music transplanted or introduced into the culture of the indigenous Nigerian from an outside culture. The syllabus of the educational system, the curriculum content, and the philosophy and thrusts of the institutions which teach music, lay strong emphasis on Western music.[11]

Dr. Okafor stresses the need to rediscover the musical heritage of Nigeria as a basis for Nigerian music education.

Efforts to include African music are gradually beginning to surface in other African countries as well. Traditional music is being encouraged in Kenya, Ghana, and Zimbabwe, but indications are that the young people from the cities react negatively to traditional music. Gabon also replied, but though no mention was made of Western methods or music, educators are concerned with traditional methods of teaching, and they urge new music schools to adopt the type of teaching practiced by traditional music teachers in Africa. From Kenya, Nigeria, and Uganda, however, there is a clear indication of the importance of considering African concepts of music making.

I will now focus attention on African concepts or notions of music making. Though this does present difficulties for one trained in Western music, my motivation for making this start rests on a belief that the study of African concepts of music making will:

1. enhance music education generally;
2. question the assumption that music teaching, as it is now conceived, with its professions, methods, and activities applied to teaching classical Western music, corresponds to the needs of African music education based on a different logic;
3. help to stem the steady flow of Western music education ideas to Africa and perhaps bring about some sense of balance between an African approach to music making and so-called Western approaches.

This introduction to a few notions about African music making is by way of some organizing principles and characteristics of African music. As we are able to relate to what we know, perhaps that which is different will take on greater clarity through comparisons drawn between principles and characteristics of Western and African music. An oversimplification of Western characteristics is in no way intended to downgrade them or make them appear to be of lesser importance. Any such appearance results simply from our focus on an African approach. African music making, in the contexts of this article, is limited to traditional music making.

Many references are made to John Miller Chernoff, and the full depth of my indebtedness to his outstanding book will become apparent.

What is perhaps a most fundamental difference between Western and African music depends on whether importance is given to the product or the process of creation.[12] In the West priority is given to the product or the piece of music performed; the end result of a performance is most important. Furthermore, music is considered to be of real value if it withstands the test of time.[13] Criticism, when provided, is usually meant to improve the performer's actions or performance.

In Africa one can say that the process is far more important than the product. Emphasis is not on the artistic product, but rather on "the fashion in which the creative, form-giving process takes effect."[14] The essential aspect is its "functional integration" or community dimension. Criticism is "seen and offered as an act of participation and a gesture of support to help the artistic effort achieve its communal purpose."[15] More about the communal purpose as we progress.

Who makes music? In the West primarily professionals in concert halls or groups from "the top of the pops" hold center stage. Our dependence on specialization delegates the making of music to the professionals, and the vast majority are passive observers.

In Africa, music making is a group activity. More and more we shall come to realize that, for the African, "music's explicit purpose is, essentially, socialization."[16] Community life lays a great deal of emphasis on group music making, not on solo music making. "The cultivation of musical life in traditional African society is promoted through active participation in group life."[17] Among the Venda people, for example, the belief is that everyone has the ability to perform and make sense of music. The only reason some are better than others is that they are more committed or they work harder.[18]

How are musicians trained? In the West special colleges, universities, and schools of music provide opportunities for those having "talent" as musicians. In Africa "exposure to musical situations and participation are emphasized more than formal training." The basic principle is that of "learning through social experience."[19] The organization of traditional music in social life enables people to acquire their musical knowledge in slow steps from an early age.

In the West the artistic origin of music for the concert hall or on the popular stage is important. For the African, each new situation is a chance for artistic creativity because music may be both traditional and improvised.

In the West the visual aspect of reading and writing musical notation takes precedence when one learns about music making. One of the primary tasks of music educators in schools is to enable children to become musically literate. Concern about music literacy has even been voiced at the highest levels, but for nonmusical reasons. President Kennedy's Panel on Educational Research and Development recommended that the entire music curriculum "be examined to discover why public school music programs had not produced a musically literate and active public."[20] Their concern stemmed from the belief that serious study of the arts would enhance the sciences.

In Africa the oral/aural essence of music is fundamental to the process of music making. Concentrated and frequent listening enables learners to move from gathering simple to more complex musical ideas, techniques, and nuances which will enable them to take part in music making. Young players are encouraged to imitate the teacher or musician and, at times, to improvise or create their own music.

Looking more specifically at some characteristics of Western and African music, we see that for the Western musician melodic and harmonic development are of primary importance. For the African musician, rhythm is most important. Consider a few comparisons of the different concepts of rhythm.

Western music often has a main beat which might be the first and third. African music happens more on the offbeat and is shrouded in the metronomic beat. Richard Waterman coined the term "metronomic sense" in relation to African music: "[Metronomic] sense entails habits of conceiving any music as structured along a theoretical framework of beats regularly spaced in time and of co-operating in terms of overt or inhibited motor behavior with the pulses of rhythmic pattern whether or not the beats are expressed in these melodic or percussive tones."[21] Hand clapping for the African is "an undercurrent providing the free rhythms of the song with a metrical basis."[22]

Western rhythm is something to "get with." African rhythm is something to respond to. To play alone is meaningless. Cross-rhythms and shifting accents occur only when musicians are playing together. African drummers converse with one another; "in traditional African music, the rhythms themselves are a specific text."[23] A cardinal principle of African music is the clash and conflict of rhythms.[24] There are always two or more rhythms being played at the same time. Though each may be simple, in combination they are complex because they create cross-rhythms. The balance of rhythms is achieved through the total concentration of each player on one's own particular rhythm.

In the West synchrony is deliberate and normal. Time has a strict order and is a single objective phenomenon. For the African synchrony is incidental and derivative from cross-rhythms.[25] African children are "brought up to regard beating 3 against 2 as being just as normal as beating in synchrony, then you develop a two-dimensional attitude to rhythm which we in the West do not share."[26]

The way the rhythms are established in relationship creates a dynamic tension. The dynamics and power of the music are created by the repetition of the rhythms with varying accents. It is repetition which is used "to reveal the depth of the musical structure."[27] The difficulty is in realizing that "the music is perhaps best considered as an arrangement of gaps where one may add a rhythm, rather than as a dense pattern of sound. . . . A good rhythm, if it is to enhance itself, should both fill a gap in the other rhythms and create an emptiness that may be similarly filled."[28]

At concerts or performances in the West, the music being performed is the focus of attention of each listener. For the African the listener is actively engaged in supplying the fundamental beat at a performance. Waterman says: "The assumption by an African musician that his [sic] audience is supplying these fundamental beats permits him [sic] to elaborate his rhythms with these as a base."[29] One experiences African music only when more than one rhythm occurs at the same time. It is only in combination—when one rhythm defines another and when shifting accents seem to rearrange rhythmic patterns and create tensions—that we can experience the music.

These are but a few of the organizing principles and characteristics of African music, which differ from those of Western music. Having said that African "music's explicit purpose is socialization,"[30] what is the meaning of this basic idea?

The socialization of Africans is the manner in which persons internalize the values implicit in their society. It is education in the potentials and the limitations of society. Music's explicit purpose is socialization, and "the development of musical awareness in Africa constitutes a process of education."[31] It is important for those of us who are used to defining values in terms of abstract beliefs or concepts to realize that we are not thinking in terms of "implicit expectations." We are thinking in terms of actions that result, not from what one has been explicitly told to do or think, but in terms of implicit learning.

What are some of these implicit learnings, and how are they propagated through the process of music making? To rephrase, what are some desirable social characteristics, and how are they implicit in the process of music making? Approaching these questions as a non-African, one must be mindful of the danger of taking an all too simplistic approach to something of extreme complexity and depth.

Fundamentally, a sense of balance of relationships is inherent in all aspects of African musical aesthetics, a balance of aspects as well as of individual ability and communal growth.

The musical performer realizes the importance and value of balanced relationships; one balances what one hears with what one is going to add to the music in order to enhance the performance. The drummer, for example, must be able "to stand back from the rhythms of the scene and find an additional rhythm which complements and mediates those other rhythms."[32] The performer acts knowing, on the one hand, that what one is doing is "supported by . . . tradition and possibly the efforts of those who have played before." The performer knows, on the other hand, that one's contribution either limits or expands "the realization of a general concern, determining whether the people present constitute a community."[33]

Another implicit social value propagated through music making is striving for excellence, a phrase very familiar to Western educators. It has, however, other meanings in an African context. Excellence means quality with respect to the life of the society. "In their arts, Africans are directly involved in bringing quality to a social situation."[34] Music is considered to be good "if people participate in the appropriate way," and that is to sing, dance, or enjoy themselves. Music that is unacceptable is criticized by the community by pointing out limitations such as falling short of human qualities or acceptable aesthetics. The reason for the criticism is to improve the social situation.

The integrity of music as a social force provides the framework for an understanding of the use of technique and of individual expression in African music: "Expression is subordinated to a respect for formal relationships, and technique is subordinated to communicative clarity."[35] The player and the music come alive only by virtue of their relationship to the other players and music. Might this not have evolved from a Xhosa proverb, "Ubuntu ungamuntu ngabantu abantu," meaning, "A person is a person, by virtue of other people"? The people in attendance perceive the performer as "an exposition of their continuing involvement," and their criticism "is offered as a gesture of support to help him [sic] achieve his purpose."[36] The musician's performance is an attempt "to bring forth a fresh dimension of involvement and excitement to the community."[37] Aesthetically, the music involves people with their community. The nature of this involvement is the key to understanding the integrative power of the music.

There are indications that influential music educators from the United States and England are reaching beyond the bias of their own training and referring to African music makers to emphasize main points in their discussions. Two writers who provide me with professional intellectual stimulation are David Elliot and Keith Swanwick. Elliot, to illustrate his point that "the essential values of a culture are often reflected in the way music is learned and taught,"[38] refers, by way of Barbara Schmidt-Wrengler,[39] to the way the Tshokwe of Angola and Zaire make music. Their process of music making provides a model for social action; thus Elliot and the Tshokwe agree that music education embodies culture. Swanwick advocates musical encounters and instruction as a basis of music education in *Music, Mind, and Education*. To support the importance of musical encounters, he refers, by way of Blacking, to the musical practices of the Venda people from the northern part of South Africa.[40]

Catherine Ellis, researcher in Aboriginal music at the University of Adelaide, drew the attention of delegates attending the 1987 ISME Conference to the great, and virtually untapped, educational resource Australians have in the knowledge possessed by Aboriginal music educators. She also referred to the failure to recognize the contribution Aboriginal educators can make to the Australians' understanding of their own music systems.

She pointed out that the Australian music system is written while the Aboriginal is an oral tradition. The result is that one often forgets that education through music has primarily to be an aural awakening and an experiential voyage of discovery, not unlike thoughts expressed by Patricia K. Shehan in "The Oral Transmission of an Aural Art."[41] The Australian thinking about music "is geared to produce an elite circle of informed people," while the Aboriginal educators "have a keen awareness of the need to make education through music available to all." Finally, the Australian system separates music from the students' previous musical and cultural experiences, while the Aboriginal "knows the importance of keeping unreflective and conscious cognitive processes aligned so that the most profound, transcending level of learning remains an integral part of the overall scheme."[42]

Ellis's experience with Aboriginal musicians has taught her about the importance of musical life to a healthy community, and it has, "above all, taught her the significance of education through music as an agent for changing the world in which we live."[43]

African views or notions of music, like Aboriginal notions, could enhance music education generally by reminding those who provide the much sought-after literature for music educators of important values that tend to take second place in Western music education. We are reminded that music is for all, not only the talented; we are reminded of the relationship of music education to its community base; we are reminded of doing and learning along with telling and being taught; we are reminded of the integration of the arts. I recall that Bennett Reimer argued for this last point in his keynote address at the 1982 ISME Conference. The leader of the discussion following Reimer's address was from Ghana, and his immediate reply to the dictum that we must integrate the arts was that the people of Ghana have always done so.

Could it be that the time is ripe to rectify the insular attitude of our American forebears to the notions of music brought to the United States from West Africa? In the realm of fantasy, might we be encouraged to imagine how American music education could have evolved in other ways had the musical practices from West Africa been encouraged? In the realm of possibility, an appeal goes out to music educators whose books are marketed beyond the borders of the United States and England to set their visions beyond a unilateral declaration of Western music education. More particularly, there is an urgent need for those searching for a new direction in Southern African music education to take cognizance of underlying African concepts and views of music to insure that African children, who are music makers by the age of five, are able to develop their musicianship throughout their lifetime because of their music education.

NOTES

1. Christine Lucia, ed., *Proceedings of the First National Music Educators' Conference* (Durban, South Africa: University of Natal, 1986), pp. 197-98.
2. Judith Becker, "Is Western Music Superior?" *The Musical Quarterly* 72, no. 3 (1986): 341-59.
3. Portia L. Maultsby, "West African Influences and Retentions in U.S. Black Music: A Sociocultural Study," in *More than Dancing: Essays on Afro-American Music and Musicians*, ed. Irene V. Jackson (London: Greenwood Press, 1985), pp. 29-30.
4. Ibid.
5. Ibid., p. 31. Quoting Charles Colcock Jones, *Religious Instruction of the Negros in the United States* (Savannah: T. Purse, 1842), pp. 31-32.
6. Maultsby, "West African Influences," p. 33.
7. Allen P. Britten, "The How and Why of Teaching Singing Schools in Eighteenth-Century America," *Council for Research in Music Education* 99 (Winter 1985): 26.
8. Lucia, *Proceedings*, p. 119.
9. Elizabeth Oehrle, "Emerging Music Education Trends in Africa." (Unpublished manuscript).
10. Richard C. Okafor, "A Critique on the Place of Music in the National Policy on Education in the March towards Quality Education in Nigeria," October 1989. (Paper presented at Maiden/Annual Conference of the Association for Promoting Quality Education in Nigeria), p. 11.
11. Ibid., p. 20.
12. John Blacking, "Process and Product in Human Society," Inaugural Lecture (Johannesburg: Witwatersrand University Press, 1970).
13. John Miller Chernoff, *African Rhythm and African Sensibility: Aesthetics and Social Action in African Musical Idioms* (Chicago: University of Chicago Press, 1979), p. 13.
14. Jahkeinz Jahn, *Muntu: The New African Culture*, trans. Marjorie Irene (New York: Grove Press, 1961), p. 174.
15. Ibid., p. 154.
16. Chernoff, *African Rhythm*, p. 154.
17. J. H. K. Nketia, *The Music of Africa* (London: W. Norton, 1974), p. 50.
18. John Blacking, *Venda Children's Songs: A Study in Ethnomusicological Analysis* (Johannesburg: Witwatersrand University Press, 1967), p. 50.
19. Nketia, *Music of Africa*, p. 59.
20. Michael Mark, *Contemporary Music Education* (New York: Schirmer, 1978), p. 30.
21. Richard Waterman, "African Influence on the Music of the Americas," in *Acculturation in the Americas*, ed. Sol Tax. Proceedings and Selected Papers of the 29th

International Congress of Americanists, 2 (Chicago: University of Chicago Press, 1952), p. 211.

22. A. M. Jones, "African Rhythm," *Journal of the International African Institute* 24, no. 1 (1954): 32.
23. Chernoff, *African Rhythm*, p. 75.
24. Jones, "African Rhythm," p. 27.
25. A. M. Jones, *Studies in African Music*, 2 vols. (London: Oxford University Press, 1959), p. 193.
26. Ibid., p. 102.
27. Chernoff, *African Rhythm*, p. 112.
28. Ibid., pp. 113-14.
29. Waterman, "African Influence," pp. 211-12.
30. Chernoff, *African Rhythm*, p. 154.
31. Ibid.
32. Ibid., p. 125.
33. Ibid., p. 126.
34. Ibid., p. 153.
35. Ibid., p. 122.
36. Ibid., p. 126.
37. Ibid.
38. David Elliot, "Key Concepts in Multicultural Music Education," *Internatioinal Journal of Music Education* 13 (1989): 13.
39. Barbara Schmidt-Wrengler, "Tshiyanda Na Ululi—Boundaries of Independence, Life, Music, and Education in Tshokwe Society, Angola, Zaïre," in *Becoming Human through Music*, The Wesleyan Symposium on the Perspectives of Social Anthropology in the Teaching and Learning of Music (Middletown, Conn.: Wesleyan University, 1984), pp. 77-87.
40. Keith Swanwick, *Music, Mind, and Education* (London: Routledge, 1988), p. 128.
41. Patricia K. Shehan, "The Oral Transmission of an Aural Art," *The American Music Teacher Magazine* (February/March 1986): 16-17.
42. Catherine Ellis, "Aboriginal Education through Music: Complexity within Simplicity," *International Music Education Yearbook* 15 (1988): 56-57.
43. Ibid., pp. 64-65.

Whole/Part Relations in Music: An Exploratory Study

DOUGLAS BARTHOLOMEW

By way of introduction, I would like to state the theme of what is to follow: In order to have parts, one must have a whole. It is in the nature of parts to be related to a whole. It is from this simple idea that the rest of this essay follows.

Husserl's analysis of parts and wholes is at the heart of his phenomenological method, as Robert Sokolowski makes clear.[1] The following essay applies Husserl's analysis to musical situations. The traditional vocabulary of phenomenological analysis has been skirted in order to focus more on the phenomena in question instead of the technique. Husserl enjoins us to go to the things themselves. I will, by approximations, look to musical experience and invite you to do the same, describing carefully how music is present to us. At issue here will be the examination of musical phenomena in an attempt to see how Husserl's distinctions between types of parts and wholes shed light on musical structure, activity, and instruction.

Independent and Dependent Parts

A fundamental distinction can be drawn at the outset between two types of parts. Husserl defines a part as anything "that can be distinguished 'in' an object," and he draws a distinction between independent and dependent parts.[2] Independent parts are those that we think of normally, and their distinguishing feature is that they can be presented independently of the whole of which they are a part. In other words, they can be present separated from their respective wholes. Petals are independent parts of a flower. We can have the petals present apart from the flower.

Dependent parts, on the other hand, are inseparable from their whole. They can only be what they are in a more comprehensive whole.[3] A de-

Douglas Bartholomew is Associate Professor of Music Education at Montana State University, Bozeman. He has most recently contributed an essay to *Understanding the Musical Experience* and published an article in the *Bulletin* of the Council for Research in Music Education.

pendent part cannot be presented independently. A petal is an independent part of the flower, but the color of the petal is inseparable from the petal. To be sure we could have a yellow page, a yellow brick, or a yellow lemon, but we cannot have "yellow" present in perception without something that is yellow. Extension is another type of dependent part. We can have extended things physically present but not extension by itself. Husserl calls the "whole" to which a dependent part is connected its foundation. The petal is the foundation of its yellow color.

To have something present is usually to experience it perceptually, but we can also have things present by imagining or remembering them.[4] A petal is present to us when we see it, or we can remember this presence. We can hear someone perform a melody, or we can mentally hear a new or remembered melody. On the other hand, we can use words to talk about yellow without mentioning any particular yellow thing, and we can think about color apart from its foundation. Thinking and talking about dependent parts is abstract behavior. When we talk about a dependent aspect of something, we must abstract it from its concrete foundation. As we will see, the first tone of a melody is an independent part of that melody as an acoustical object, but the pitch of that sound is a dependent part of that sound. We can talk about pitch in an abstract way, whether it is higher or lower than another one, but this talk does not make pitch concrete. In fact, when we talk overmuch about a pitch dimension, we may begin to believe that pitch can be experienced without the mediation of sound. In order to have the pitch present we must, however, hear, remember, or imagine a sound.

A distinction between types of wholes can also be made. There are things made up of independent parts that have a structure something like a collection or an aggregate. The *ouevre* of a composer is like this. We come to know the parts as independent pieces and later collect them into a single unit. Another kind of whole, of which a melody is a prime example, is given as a "perceptual and continuous whole; its parts . . . are contained in it and only subsequently separated out."[5] The temptation, in musical instruction, to treat scales as aggregates of tones, measures as aggregates of beats, beats as aggregates of durations, form as an aggregate of phrases, periods, and episodes, and so on, is great. Before we can get clear about aggregates and continuous wholes, we need to explore the distinction between independent and dependent parts on its own.

Independent and Dependent Parts in Music

Traditional analysis distinguishes four dimensions to a sound that reflect measurable aspects of sound energy: timbre, loudness, duration, and pitch.[6]

Individual sounds have timbre, pitch, loudness, and duration as necessary components. These are all dependent parts of a sound and are founded by the sound of which they are a part. We cannot have these parts actually present without a sound. Timbre is the signature or personality of a sound: if we have a sound at all we have a timbre. Loudness lets a sound emerge from silence. A sound has to be of a sufficient duration for any other part to emerge.[7] Duration is a feature common to all temporal things. With respect to sound, duration is that which permits the moments of beginning and ending. Pitch presents a uniquely sonic space and, it might be noted, is also dependent on timbre and duration for its foundation. The pitch of a sound depends on its length. In fact, Fritz Winckel reports that tones shorter than 4 msec are perceived as clicks.[8]

The pitch a sound has depends on its timbre. At one end of the spectrum various "pink" noises can be produced whose pitch content is as much a timbral quality as a pitch quality. The complex sounds of everyday life, such a ticks, tocks, and machine sounds, seem to fall into this category. At the other end of the spectrum are tones—sounds of definite pitch content. Thus, while a pitch content is a necessary part of the sound-whole, this content depends for its clarity—its presentation—on the timbre of the sound-whole. R. A. Rasch and R. Plomp report that variations in the timbral features of a sound affect the perceived pitch.[9] Certain timbres obscure while others highlight the pitch aspect of a sound.

The duration of a sound can, with one exception, be subdivided into moments, but these moments depend on the duration of the sound and are inseparable from it. One is aware of the temporal extension of a sound and recognizes that it can be measured, but the sound itself is not like "pop-beads," it does not come segmented. It comes to us seamless, with a single beginning and ending. A single, sustained sound consists of smaller moments, moments that precede and follow one another. Were we to try to separate one or more moments, we would introduce new beginnings and endings. The beginning and ending of a sound are special moments in its extent and are not separately presentable: they are dependent parts which merge and blend with the intermediary moments to make up the extent of the life of the sound. The exception to this is that a sound can be so short that we cannot make out its beginning from its ending. A sound like this is formed, it would seem, of a single moment.

To summarize, a single sound is the smallest musical unit capable of independent presentation. It is the foundation for the concrete presence of timbre, loudness, and duration (though duration can be founded on other things). Furthermore, pitch is dependent on and founded by timbre and duration, and the moments that comprise the extension of sound are founded by duration and inseparable from it.

When we turn from individual sounds to combinations of sounds, more possibilities arise. The tones of a chord are all separable from the chord, as is each of the lines in a polyphonic texture. The words of a song do not depend for their presentation on the song. Variations can be separated and presented independently of their theme. Development sections can be performed without either recapitulations or expositions. None of this is startling. Musical works are made up of parts, many of which are independent parts and can be presented, as anyone who has played "drop the needle" knows, apart from their respective wholes.

Beat and meter are dependent on other things. Sounds can be the foundation of both of these features, but so can touch, movement, and a variety of other phenomena. Neither beat nor meter, however, can be perceived or imagined without being presented by some activity. Beat and meter do not stand by themselves. In his analyses of musical time Jonathon Kramer makes this point clearly. We use "information in a composition to understand where beats fall and how strongly accented they are, but . . . we do not literally *hear* beats."[10] Beats are inseparable from the sounds that present them. "Meter is not separable from music, since music itself determines the pattern of accents we interpret as meter."[11] Meter depends on a succession of beats and is founded on them, and both beat and meter depend on accentual relationships among sounds. Accents, in turn, depend on and are founded by variations, whether real or imagined, in duration, loudness, or pitch. Beat and meter are inseparable from accentual relationships, which are inseparable from other aspects of sound.

Tonal progressions and tonality in general depend on and are in separable from their presentation in or by means of pitch relationships. These relationships can be linear/melodic or simultaneous/harmonic, but in either case without hearing the pitch relationships, we can only think or speak about tonal progression and tonality. The sense of resolution that comes when a dominant harmony, however engendered, is followed by its tonic depends on the sounds involved, whether heard, remembered, or imagined. In a sequence of pitches, each pitch can be present by itself without regard to the others in the sequence. The sense of tonality, however, that comes from a certain series or collection of pitches cannot be perceptually or imaginatively present without the sounds involved. The sounds from which tonality emerges are not just an aggregate, a loose collection of sounds. Tonality emerges from a group of sounds, taken as a whole, in relation to each other. Tonality depends on pitch relationships and is founded on them. Tonal progressions are carried by pitch relationships and can be present in experience without these pitch relationships only in thought.

A scale, as a collection of tones, can be presented independently of other structures. Music books often present scales in this way. Students can practice scales and learn how to construct them without reference to other musical structures. The chromatic scale, for example, can be presented very much like a number line, extending infinitely far in either direction. There is no preferred tone in a chromatic scale, no place of rest, no sense of direction. While this scale enumerates the standard tones in a tonal system, it does not capture anything else about the pitch organization of this tonal system.

The major and minor scales of Western European music, however, reflect a tonal system. In these cases, the scales are not simply ordered collections of tones. If nothing else, they begin and end on particular tones, and this, unfortunately, is often where instruction ends. A major scale has a point of beginning and a point of closure or return. Each step has functional relations to the other steps. A minor scale is similar, but its steps have somewhat different functions. For a scale to present even this much of a tonal system, to be more than just a formalized arrangement dividing an octave in a particular way, it depends on a musical context. The tonal system, with its network of relations, founds the different functions associated with different scale degrees. A tonic is not a tonic without a felt relation to other tones. Without a foundation in what amounts to the concrete experience of music, a scale is at best an aggregate, a loose collection of sounds, lacking the felt sense of a tonal system.

When we turn our attention to melodies, things, at least at first, appear simpler. We can separate the individual tones from a melody just as we can pull petals off a flower. We indeed do damage both to the melody and the flower in this operation, but it is certainly possible to have an individual tone or a petal present without the melody or the flower from which it was taken. Likewise, we can pull the phrases of a melody apart. each phrase is presentable without the others. We can tap the rhythm of the melody without the pitch variation, or we can present the series of intervallic relationships in rhythms different from the melody which was the source of the intervals. While "gestaltists" might wince, there seems to be no way of denying that the individual sounds that go together to make up a melody can be presented apart from the melody.

There is more to this, however. The rhythm of a melody, narrowly defined as the pattern resulting from the durational relationships of the sounds, is an independent part of the melody: one can tap the rhythm without any pitch variation. A rhythm tapped like this, however, is the rhythm of a given melody only when one registers or notices the relationship between the rhythm heard and the melody not heard. We can tap a rhythm without pitch variation, but by itself this rhythm is not yet a part of anything larger than itself. It would only be a rhythm which may be equivalent to a rhythm of a melody, but which equivalence goes unnoticed.

How does "noticing" have anything to do with the equivalence of things? The equivalence in this case refers to durational relationships, the relative distances between attack points. Two rhythms, one having just been heard but without connection to a melody and the other the rhythm of a known melody, may be equivalent in this sense, but the two do not have the same network of whole/part relationships. The rhythm of a melody can be presented separate from the melody, but when presented in this way we can recognize it *as a part* of a given melody only if we already know the melody and connect the two in thought.

The sections into which we divide musical works are all separably presentable. We can hear a consequent phrase, theme, episode, or development without the remainder of the work from which each was taken. In music analysis we separate a work into parts by finding points of division based on musical events. As a result, the alphabet and terminology with which we describe musical form suggest that this form is an aggregate of parts. A development section, however, refers to, hints at, extrapolates from, and otherwise explores and enjoys material from its exposition. As developmental it depends on other things. A consequent phrase happens *in consequence* to an antecedent. To be a consequent, there must be an antecedent operating in at least an absent way. The whole can still work its magic on the parts even if we only hear a part. Without this magic, we could not separate a part form its whole and retain its connection to the larger unit. To have a part, even if we have it by itself, we have to have a whole.

It is obvious that individual sonic events can stand on their own, without context and in a very concrete presentation. When these same events are parts of larger wholes, however, they become colored with tints and hues of the larger context, tints and hues that depend on the context as their foundation. The first tone of the French Horn solo that opens the Finale of Stravinsky's *The Firebird* is not simply a sustained tone, of a certain pitch, timbre, loudness, and duration. It bears the content of the preceding and succeeding music to some degree. Without this content, and this is the point, the tone is not the first tone of this solo. It becomes the first tone of the solo when in thought we are able to supply its context or the actual context is presented with it. As the first tone of the solo, it must, of necessity, have a relation to its context. And while this relation is in place, this tone has a particular future, unlike the open possibility it has out of context. In this case, a sonic element becomes imbedded in a context that is framed by our perceptual field. It becomes an object of our consciousness and as such is involved in another set of whole/part relationships. What happens to the sonic events that are combined to make up musical works? Are they simply sonic events?

The answer to this latter question, I think, is quite simply "no." There is a shift that is introduced by the context, the "noticing" and the framing done in our perceptual field. Two rhythm patterns may have identical durational relationships, but this identity must be noticed, it must become a part of the consciousness of the rhythm patterns. The frame of consciousness, within which melodies are recognized, introduces contexts. As we look at larger wholes, contexts play an ever more important role. Context, a whole that has parts, is already at work in single sounds in the way timbre, loudness, duration, and pitch intermingle. Things get much less clinical, however, with more complex things. Melodies, for example, escape being streams of independent tones only by the grace of a listener for whom the sense of the melody comes only from the felt interdependence of the tones on each other. While the tones themselves are capable of independent presentation, as a part of a particular melody, each is flavored by the tones to come and the tones that have already occurred. The temporal context of a melody introduces a play between presence and absence. The now absent succeeding tones of the *Firebird* Finale are somehow present in its first tone. There is pitch content in the sounds we hear that is not accounted for by acoustical energy.

Presence and Absence in Music: Retentions and Protentions

The temporal profile of a melody provides another way to explore the play of presence and absence in a musical context. A melody consists of a sequence of tones, one following the other. It emerges from a quality of silence and passes into another silence. This is something we are all familiar with, but we are in error if we think that this analysis captures the temporality of a melody. If all that is present for us is the one tone actually sounding, then what we hear is not a melody but a sequence of tones. A melody has more connection to it, it has perspectives that are linked and that unite the series of tones. Husserl, in his analyses of time, referred to these perspectives as retentions and protentions.[12] These names identify some of the mixture of absence and presence that is at work in the experience of music.

When we are listening to a melody, there is only one tone sounding at a time. When the first tone is present and sounding, the rest are yet to come and absent. When the second tone is present, the following are absent, as is the first tone. This is a "one note after another" analysis, which is what we get when all we attend to is the actually present. We know that there is more to a melody when we hear people make music like this—just one note after another. What we need to add is our sense of how the not-sounding tones are absent, or rather, the way in which these not-sounding tones are present.

When we are listening to a melody and we pass from the first tone to the second, the first tone does not simply disappear; it is retained in our consciousness. Rather than its being simply absent, we have a retention of it. As we pass from the second to the third, we have retentions of the first two tones, and so on until at the end of the melody, the actually sounding tone being modified by the retention of all the previously sounded tones. The sense of the melody at this moment is not of a single present dimension, but includes this second dimension of retentions, absent aspects of the present sound that are part of the meaning of the present sound and are a part of what we hear just as the absent, unseen aspects of a desk are part of the meaning of this desk, and although not visible are still part of what we intend when we see this desk. Retentions are absent aspects that are inseparable parts of the present moment.

When we listen to a melody, and this is especially easy to grasp if the melody is one we know, at the very first moment of the melody, in fact, even before it begins, we have a sense of what is to come. This particular sense of an absent part Husserl calls a protention. Even though all the tones may be absent, part of the experience of a melody is having the meaning of the tones not yet heard infuse the presently sounding tone. Thus, as the melody moves from beginning to end, the meaning of each tone is affected by the protention of what is to come and is increasingly enriched by the retentions of what has already happened. Some of the perspectives of a melody come from the way in which the combination of protentional/-present/retentional profiles unfold in a series, and some of the varieties of perspectives come from the sizes and richness of retentional/present/protentional units one is able or chooses to attend to.

Retentions, however, are not recollections. When we come to the last tone of a melody, the tonic, we recognize this "tonic-ness" without having to recall anything at all. The tonal and metric meaning this or any sound has is a function of the profiles of the previous and succeeding sounds that are inseparable parts of this sound, laminated to the present sound. Nothing need be brought back to mind to feel this sense, nothing need be recollected. The felt presence of a gripping drama or a special person can be retained long after the physical sensations which "caused" this presence have disappeared. Tonality is a felt presence of other sounds.

Just as retentions are distinguished form recollections, so are protentions to be distinguished from acts that produce expectations. Like retentions, protentions are inseparable parts of our attending to a melody, they are not products of separate acts. Expectations and recollections are specific acts, things we do, while protentions and retentions are parts of each of our acts. Knowing what sounds are to follow permeates our experience of a present sound, but this permeation is simply a dependent part of the present act, part of the awareness of the full presence of a sound.

Retentions and protentions are inseparable parts of the present and are modifications of the present. Contrast the sense of V^7-I resolution with the return of the second theme in the recapitulation of a sonata form. The dominant chord infects the sense of the following tonic chord, it is no longer just a collection of tones. I do not have this same sense with respect to the key relations of themes in recapitulation sections, though I recognize that some may. For me, I recognize that both themes of the recapitulation are presented in the same key, that sometimes the transition between the themes turns into a secondary development area, but I *recall* that this is not as it was in the exposition. Given my skills, I do not *feel* a need for this kind of resolution. The changes in material in the transition of the recapitulation tip one off to something new, but they do not, again for me, play with a need for resolution. The transition to the dominant in the exposition is rarely, if ever, retained by me when it comes to the recapitulation. It is possible that sounds be retained over such long periods of time. As a piece becomes more well defined in listening, it is more likely that there will be retentions over longer periods of time. It is interesting to imagine how vivid these retentional profiles were for listeners of the eighteenth century, listeners who were just beginning to explore this kind of large-scale tonal progression.

An example from an instructional point of view may make this point more vividly. Anyone who has gone through elementary music theory classes, either as a student or a teacher, has likely found that an easy way to perform intervals accurately is to associate them with initial intervals of a song. For a rising perfect fourth, one sings the first two tones of "Here Comes the Bride," for a rising major sixth one sings "My Bonnie Lies over the Ocean," and so on.

While an interval can be presented in isolation from a melodic context, one tends not to sing just the first two tones of a melody in using this strategy. To get the initial interval, one tends to sing, whether aloud or in one's mind, the whole phrase of a song or at least more than the first two tones, not just the interval itself. Why might one sing more than just the first two tones? Because in order for the strategy to work, one depends on the initial tones of the song *to be a part* of the whole song and not independent of it. Having the protentional sense of the song, or at least the initial phrase, helps to define the initial interval. For some, then, it is necessary to sing more than the first two tones of a song to get the *sense* of the song. For others, the protentional profile of the first tones is strong enough to define the interval. To put it another way, without the relationship to the song, without the protentional profile of the rest of the song, someone using this strategy may not be able to sing accurately the interval comprised by the first two tones of the song without singing the whole phrase. It is the relation to the whole song that solidifies this interval. In practice, this switching from one context to another works against all sense of context, relationship, and consecution that are functions of a characteristic protentional and retentional framework. One is left singing only an aggregate of tones and singing them one at a time.

Melodies, and musical works in general, are not aggregates. They are perceptual wholes whose parts, even when the parts are independent, become, as particular musical works, bound by webs of internal relationships. As has been said, "Bach uses the same seven notes my students did, but, oh, how he used them!" How the notes are used makes the difference it does precisely because musical things are not aggregates. It is precisely the way a protentional/retentional framework can be elaborated that provides much of the richness of musical experience.

Other Forms of Presence and Absence

The contrast between independent and dependent parts plays on the contrast between presence and absence. Having a melody present is to hear it, whether we actually have the sound present or if it is only present in our inner hearing, the object of an act of remembering or imagining. It should be clear that when we remember a melody, we are experiencing it in an absent way, relative to actually hearing someone perform it. When we talk about a melody, the music is that to which we refer, it is what we mean, but we are not experiencing its temporal dimension as we do in perception, imagination, or remembering. When we talk about a melody, refer to it, or describe it, we have it in the way that language presents things—we experience it in its absence; we have it *as* present.[13] We can talk about the difference between $\frac{3}{4}$ and $\frac{6}{8}$ meter without having to hear, actually or imaginatively, an example of either of these meters, though it should be clear that meaningful talk about music is dependent on the possibility of a concrete experience of the music in question.

Music notation can present a melody in two ways. While we can let the music sing through the notes, we can also, at least in some situations, see the notes and recognize the song without bringing it to auditory presence. The score, like language, directs our attention to the melody, but we do not necessarily listen to it. In Husserl's language, we intend it in an empty way. The music (sound) may not be present, but we have it as present.

Not every musical part in perception is clearly present or distinct.[14] When we are listening to a melody, some tones stand out more clearly, others are sensed only vaguely and indistinctly. Sometimes our attention drifts, and the music becomes something like a sonic background to whatever has caught our figural attention. In this case, though the music is present, we do not articulate it. We do not pay attention to its parts, and they become indistinct. When the music is complex, we may be unable to make the parts distinct. Unfamiliar collections of pitches, thick textures, complicated rhythms can make it difficult to sort things out. A child might confuse things and try to sing the piano or guitar accompaniment when unsure of the melody. An alto might lose her entrance tone when the soprano part suddenly crosses below her part. A student can clap the rhythm of a song accurately when the song is present perceptually, but cannot when forced to remember or inner-hear the song. Vagueness is a form of absence, but it is not like the absence used when we refer to things. Vagueness can infect something perceptually present, imagined, or something referred to with words.[15] We do not always attend to the interrelationships of parts and articulate them in listening or performing.

Protentions are typically less determined in terms of content than are retentions. The retentions have just happened and impinge directly on following events. Protentions arise from assumptions and things taken for granted. When we assume the melody that we are about to hear is one that we know, certain protentions are called into play. We can be fooled: the melody may start out the same but change, or the performer could trick us. But it is on the basis of the protentional and retentional framework that we can judge whether we've been tricked at all.

Parts of a melody vary in terms of clarity and impact also. The pitch content may be very striking and pull our minds away from the rhythm. We can become so enamored of the rhythmic drive that we cannot recall accurately the melody that went with it. Here, too, we do not articulate the parts of what we are hearing.

Within a simple melody some tones seem to draw attention to themselves, while others seem to recede. When we feel that one tone is more important or is the focal tone of a passage, we are not being lazy in our articulation of parts. On the contrary, when we notice that our attention is drawn to some tones rather than others, we are attending to parts at work within this passage. Captured in the protentional and retentional profiles might be the tonal code of the passage, its pitch contour, the relative durations of the sounds, and so on. These are inseparable features of the passage, but they are not always noticed clearly. When we do attend to these parts, structures other than simple linear patterns emerge.

The highly articulated diagrams devised by Heinrich Schenker, for example, describe complex and long-range tonal structures. Musical surfaces, in the Schenkerian view, are prolongations and elaborations of underlying musical structures.[16] In the musical surface we find that certain tones are of pivotal or focal importance. The tones surrounding these focal tones attach themselves to the foci in subordinate ways. The focal tones emerge at analytical levels below the surface. Because of the way these tones are arranged and related, certain of them remain dominant and are moved to deeper levels. A part of each tone in a musical work, under this theory, is its relation to the fundamental structures at the deeper levels of analysis. In order for this analytical approach to be founded in concrete experience, there must be present in each sonority a profile of these fundamental structures. The initial sonority of a work must contain a protentional profile of the remainder of the work. For an intermediate sonority, the complete work will be present either retentionally or protentionally. Without this content, one will always be having to *recall* previous sonorities, to shift one's attention away from the present musical flow in order to attend to the tonal structure. Without the protention and retention of structural tones, one would not be able to connect one structural tone to the next. These tones could still be more conspicuous than their neighbors, but they would not be related in perceptual presence. The sense of the relations described by Schenker requires that the relation *be a part* of the tone. The relationships a tone has within a musical work, whether as a member of the *urlinie* or simply a momentary neighbor tone, is an inseparable part of the tone and is founded on the work *as a whole*.

In accounts of musical movement and progression we can see the tension between presence and absence at work: for a sense of connection, of consecution,[17] or of movement between tones or sonorities, there must be the profile of other sounds at work in the felt presence of the sounds we are now enjoying. Whether it is a long-range connection or a simple passing tone sequence, without the protentional profile of the latter tones in the immediate present of the former there will only be succession, one isolated sound of certain dimensions followed by other sounds of other dimensions.

A multilayered Schenkerian diagram presents the music in an abstract way. If we cannot keep the music in mind while we examine the diagram, discussion about the diagram becomes empty. We need, through memory or imagination, to be able to let the sound of the music sing through the diagrams. The protentional and retentional profiles of a sonority, which are founded on the context from which the sonority emerges, is part of its perceptual presence. In these profiles, certain tones may stand out, others may recede. It is these profiles, this rich fabric of present and absent sound and sound relationships, that is the foundation for the structures that theorists detail. The sense of shape, the flow, growth, movement, progression, and similar attributes that we experience when we listen to musical works likewise depend on and are inseparable from the protentional and retentional contents of the sounds we hear.

On the basis of such a presence, we can also think about relationships not present, not a part of a series of protentional and retentional profiles. This thought, however, takes us away from musical presence. This is neither good nor bad, in and of itself. Not all the meanings present in musical experience need to be an immediate part of the temporal profiles of the sounds. Ultimately, the thought has to be grounded in musical presence, but musical presence includes human experience as well as acoustical information. The guarantor of the thought is the possibility that the connections and relationships between and among the tones and the experience of the listener could provide the foundation for that which is now just thought. For them to be other than pure possibility, thoughts and talk about music, whether occurring in the immediate presence of the music or not, need to be capable of being cashed in, of being felt in a present musical experience.

Musical works are highly articulated wholes. Like material objects, in any presentation they can be experienced in one of a variety of perspectives. We attend to each presentation of a musical work with a particular perspective. Sometimes we hear it in one way, sometimes another. Each perspective emphasizes some of the possible relational profiles of the work and discounts others. The protentional and retentional content of a tone can be ambiguous, but once clarified, it can only be what it is. It will take a new presentation to let it be otherwise. The relational profiles of a work are not just possibilities but are founded in an intentional content, a particular network of protentional and retentional relationships. This felt relational content depends on the richness and integration of the temporal profiles of the musical work in question.

Music and Feeling

When we begin to appreciate the relationships of parts in musical works, we do not yet understand how they work, but we feel them working. We are responding to the sensibility of music. The feelings connected with melodic shape, tonal movement, rhythmic flow, timbre and texture, contrasts and returns, and other parts are dependent upon the presentation of these parts. The parts, on the other hand, depend on their unfolding in experience, on the integration of temporal profiles, and on the sense resulting from the retentional and protentional profiles of this integration. The musical relationships depend on the feeling, as determined by the retentional and protentional content, and the feeling depends on the relationships presented in sound.

Dance and movement can highlight the mutual association of feeling and sound. Dance and movement can be presented apart from music, but when added to music, they can develop their own temporal profiles that either emphasize or create tension with the musical profiles. Dance and movement can provide a commentary on the musical relations and the feelings arising from and as a result of them.

Song and words provide for a similar possibility. Words, as we mentioned earlier, are separable parts of vocal music. The interaction between the sound of the language, the meanings presented by the words, and the sense of the music provides for a complicated network of whole/part relationships.

The combination of words and music and of movement and music does not necessarily imply aggregate relationships. Texts can be learned apart from music and added to it later, as can dances. In social dancing, it would seem that an aggregate relationship might be the norm. Whether it be polka, jitterbug, waltz, or watusi, it does not seem that the music and the dance participate in a continuous whole as much as they find themselves together because of certain shared features, such as meter, tune, and style. In ballet and song, the combination presents more of a unity. In these cases the typical presentation is of a continuous whole. There are shared relations between the pairings that emphasize the continuity. While it is not necessary, this continuity can even extend into less sophisticated forms.

Feelings associated with a musical work can arise from a story or program. The program of a piece of music is separable from the music. We can recite the program without the presence of the music. The same is true of any story associated with the music. The music and its program are more like an aggregate than a continuous whole. We come to know the program separately from the music, often by reading about the music. In hearing, we may recognize an aptness or correspondence between the music and the program, and the two may fuse together, but the connection does not seem necessary.

Feelings associated with a musical work can result when the music and the feeling are part of a larger whole. Music, in its role as an accompaniment to human activity, whether social, religious, economic, or political, is connected to and plays a part in stimulating a range of human feeling and accompanies a range of human activity. Music contributes to the feelings involved in situations like these, but it is *as a part* of a larger context. It plays a role, supporting other activity, other meanings, and adding its own temporal commentary. This is not to say that the music in these cases is demeaned or that the value of music is any less because of the part it plays in these various contexts. As I hope has been made clear, music depends on context. At a minimum, a musical work must play itself out, in its temporal profiles, to a listener. This context, that of sound and listener, is the foundation of musical activity. The child who listens to the sounds of pots and pans, who improvises songs, the laborer who sings work songs, the serenade, the hymn (whether patriotic or prayerful), the dance, all of these illustrate this human context, a context in which music serves human needs. The separation of music from this human context cuts music off from its foundation. A mistake we make is to think that the dependent parts, melodies, tonal progressions, structural relationships, and so on, are independent of the human context. They are founded in that context.

Music Instruction

With what are we left? What can the analysis of whole/part relationships mean for music education? Formal music instruction often begins with single notes: pitch names, rhythm names, quarter notes, whole notes, pitch matching, and so on. These identification skills are important and are roughly comparable to alphabet skills in language learning. The comparison is revealing. The alphabet no more introduces the child to language than do these note identification strategies introduce students to music. These are the smallest parts of music, and the musical context that is established by them is minimal at best.

Scale and intervallic recognition and construction are also skills that are taught as fundamental or basic to musical development. These, like the identification skills described above, are typically taught out of musical contexts rather than in them. While it is possible to learn intervals outside of musical contexts, they will still have to be put back into context. Major thirds, while all the same size, do not all sound the same. Context makes the major third, fa-la, different from do-mi. They are the same interval, but they have a different function. Students can learn to construct scales in general music classes, but without the musical context, whether heard or remembered, that imparts a tonal content to the scales, these constructions will be little more than formal exercises. The tonal sense that can be so much a part of a scale will not come from constructing scales. As Thomas Clifton puts it, "Tonality is the result of neither a simple stipulation, nor an objective examination of tonal functions as syntax, but the presence of the body behaving in and with the musical situation. Without this bodily behavior, all talk about the piece being tonal because of such and such structural relations, or because it begins and ends in the same key, indicates something of a cart-before-the-horse kind of thinking."[18] The horse is the felt relationship between and among the tones. The cart is the notation and verbal description.

Learning rhythm from the mathematics of fractions does not invoke musical experience. Spelling words with note names does not involve melody. Strategies like these move us away from the musical experience *even when they involve sound.*

A rich and valued musical life is what is required. It is this that will be the foundation of musical understanding. If we are to respond to meter, motive, motion, contrast, tonality, growth; if we are to learn a musical vocabulary, a vocabulary of textures, chords, scales, patterns, a vocabulary of terms we can use in the absence of music; if we are to be able to imagine the presence of sound when we look at notation; and if we are to value musical experience in the midst of instruction, then we will have to learn to respond to these parts in the musical whole. We will have to sense these parts working in musical contexts, because it is the musical context, a context that includes sounds and listeners as inseparable elements, that lets them work.

We need to cultivate teaching strategies that maintain and respect musical contexts. Solfege, Curwen/Kodaly handsigns, and rhythm syllables are strategies that can be used within a context. They articulate relationships in musical flow. They can be used to focus on particular relationships without the loss of context. When we lose context, we lose those parts that depend on the context for their presence.

By the same token, we need to be careful not to treat music as if it were an aggregate of parts. Tones are not aggregate parts of a melody, phrases are not aggregate parts of a musical form. Neither melody nor form consists of parts that are collected into a single unit. They are continuous wholes. The parts of a melody are separable from the melody only when treated as acoustical objects. As a melody, each tone contains, as an inseparable part, the mark of its kindred tones in the melody, and so it is with form. When we reduce form to an alphabet, without the felt connection between the parts, we reduce music to acoustical events. In instruction, we need to honor the felt connection between tones and between phrases.

We need to beware of strategies that present musical works as acoustical, historical, aesthetic, or theoretical objects, that abstract the music from its human context. These descriptions of music are founded on musical works and musical activity. Their basis has to be in musical experience and not the other way around. It is all too easy to describe music in acoustical, historical, aesthetic, or theoretical terms and lose sight of the musical experience that founds them. The instructional question would be how to help students find the evidence of the theoretical, historical, aesthetic, or acoustical point in their own musical experience.

This much sketches, in terms much too brief, some of the pedagogical considerations that might follow from the distinctions made above concerning whole/part relationships. What is the object or goal of these strategies? Musical understanding is rooted in the felt awareness of musical contexts. Musical feeling is rooted in musical experience. The core context is the human experience of sound. Music needs to be kept a part of human experience. In order to have parts we must have a whole. Music instruction is just a part of a student's life. The foundation of musical instruction is the place that music enjoys in the life of one's students. How rich a place do we make it?

NOTES

1. Robert Sokolowski, *Husserlian Investigations: How Words Present Things* (Evanston, Ill.: Northwestern University Press, 1974), p. 8.
2. Edmund Husserl, *Logical Investigations*, 2 vols., trans. J. N. Findlay (New York: Humanities Press, 1970), p. 437. The following discussion draws on Husserl's analysis found in the Third Investigation, "On the Theory of Wholes and Parts," pp. 435-89; and Sokolowski, *Husserlian Investigations.*
3. Husserl, *Logical Investigations*, p. 453.

4. Sokolowski, *Husserlian Investigations,* p. 24. For a treatment of imagination in this regard, see Edward S. Casey, *Imagining: A Phenomenological Study* (Bloomington: Indiana University Press, 1976).

5. Sokolowski, *Husserlian Investigations,* p. 10; see also Husserl, *Logical Investigations,* pp. 480-81.

6. Jean-Claude Risset, "Musical Acoustics," in *Handbook of Perception, Vol. IV, Hearing,* ed. E. C. Carterette and M. P. Friedman (New York: Academic Press, 1978), p. 522.

7. It can almost seem that duration is the foundation of sound, but this is a confusion of parts. It is because sound, among other things, has length that we are able to have the presence of duration. See Thomas Clifton, *Music as Heard: A Study in Applied Phenomenology* (New Haven, Conn.: Yale University Press, 1983), pp. 51-56.

8. Fritz Winckel, *Music, Sound, and Sensation: A Modern Exposition,* trans. Thomas Binkley (New York: Dover, 1967), p. 111.

9. R. A. Rasch and R. Plomp, "The Perception of Musical Tones," in *The Psychology of Music,* ed. Diana Deutsch (New York: Academic Press, 1982) pp. 1-24.

10. Jonathon D. Kramer, *The Time of Music* (New York: Schirmer Books, 1988) p. 97.

11. Ibid., p. 82.

12. Edmund Husserl, *The Phenomenology of Internal Time-Consciousness,* ed. Martin Heidegger, trans. James S. Churchill, intro. by Calvin O. Schrag (Bloomington: Indiana University Press, 1964). See also Izchak Miller, *Husserl, Perception, and Temporal Awareness* (Cambridge, Mass.: MIT Press, 1984).

13. Robert Sokolowski, *Presence and Absence: A Philosophical Investigation of Language and Being* (Bloomington: Indiana University Press, 1978).

14. Sokolowski, *Husserlian Investigations,* pp. 19-21.

15. Ibid., p. 21.

16. Felix Salzer, *Structural Hearing: Tonal Coherence in Music,* 2 vols. (New York: Dover, 1961).

17. The term is from Edward A. Lippman, "Progressive Temporality in Music," *Journal of Musicology* 3, no. 2 (1984): 121-49.

18. Clifton, *Music as Heard,* pp. 35-36.

Essential and Nonessential Characteristics of Aesthetic Education

BENNETT REIMER

I have chosen to discuss the concept of aesthetic education for two reasons. First, it has been, with little question, the most visible, most widely acknowledged philosophical orientation in music education for some three decades. That is why, no doubt, Michael Mark was recently led to suggest that we are now living in the period of Aesthetic Education, which began around 1960.[1] While that judgment can be and has been disputed,[2] it is significant that it could have been made at all and even more significant, and interesting, that it is the only period among the five he proposes that is based on a philosophical position. None of the others even remotely relates to a particular philosophy as its basis, nor do any of the nine periods previously suggested by Edward Bailey Birge in his *History of Public School Music in the United States*.[3]

We seem to be getting some message from this, but the message is far from clear. On the one hand, music educators devoted to philosophical scholarship should rejoice that philosophy—*any* philosophy—has exerted such influence that it seems at all feasible to name a period of our profession's history after it. On the other hand, being involved with philosophy, we are likely to have a great mixture of responses to such an occurrence. That is partly, no doubt, because philosophers tend to have a great mixture of responses to everything, simplicity being anathema to their characters. But there are, I think, good and substantial reasons for having a great many perplexed thoughts about this unprecedented elevation in music education of a particular philosophical orientation to the status of a historical era. So the second reason I have chosen this topic relates to my conviction that it would be fruitful for us as a community of scholars to pay attention to some of these perplexing thoughts about aesthetic education and that, in fact, it would be fruitful for music education as a whole if we

Bennett Reimer, John W. Beattie Professor of Music at Northwestern University, is the author of *A Philosophy of Music Education*. Among his recent publications are articles in *Design for Arts in Education*, *Music Educators Journal*, and this journal.

were to achieve better understandings about them. My discussion will make abundantly clear how ambitious this agenda actually is.

In this article I want to explore some of the important features of this concept. I must make it clear at the outset that not only is this task not easy, it is also to some very real extent incapable of being accomplished authoritatively. This stems from the fact that there exists no accepted, definitive definition or explanation or even interpretation of what aesthetic education actually is. There is no holy writ we can consult or no constitution to which we can refer.

Philosophers should not be discomfited by that fact because few philosophical positions which have achieved the status of having had a name attached to them have had clear, incontrovertible "first sources." But the irony of our situation as people who do philosophy of music education is that our profession—music education as a whole, that is—is characterized, to a remarkable and some would say pathological degree, by the propensity to reify anything with a name attached to it. This tendency is not limited to nonphilosophers in music education who, perhaps, should not be expected to know better. It extends, I am afraid, to the philosophical community, in which aesthetic education is sometimes viewed as a set of dogmas incapable of being breached and doctrines incapable of being changed.[4] I want to argue that there are no such dogmas or doctrines, although I will suggest my own candidates for what, in my opinion, are typical characteristics of aesthetic education. I will propose that aesthetic education is not a body of immutable laws but instead provides some guidelines for a process that, by its very nature, must be both ongoing and open-ended.

Fourteen years ago, at one of the Aspen conferences sponsored by the Central Midwestern Regional Educational Laboratory as part of its Aesthetic Education Program, one of the influential early thinkers about aesthetic education, Harry Broudy, addressed the general topic I am addressing now. He began by saying, "No consensus on the meaning or the usage of the term 'aesthetic education' being discernible, what follows refers pretty much to my own concept of it."[5] I am in the position now of echoing those words precisely. Broudy then listed five generalizations about aesthetic education frequently made by various groups that have shown an interest in the concept. These remain pertinent today, so I will use them to structure my discussion.

First, many believe that all children should be educated about the broad family including all the arts, and that it is possible to structure a curriculum to provide such an education. Second, there is a shared hope that the arts will achieve a more solid position in the schools than they have been able to in the past, even to the extent of being a required rather than an elective subject. Third, there seems to be a widespread belief that an aesthetic education is possible and desirable for all students in schools and need not be limited to those with special artistic talent. Fourth, there is continuing debate and disagreement among aesthetic education advocates on the degree to which "extra-aesthetic" values—moral, political, economic, social, and so forth—should be attended to as part of arts study. This lack of agreement extends to the use of aesthetic learnings to facilitate learnings in other subjects. Fifth, the least agreement is to be found about the aesthetic and educational theories by which aesthetic education could be explicated and justified.

I will comment about each of these five generalizations about or descriptions of or characteristics of aesthetic education, with somewhat more concentration on the fifth, which is the most complex and troublesome and which is also most germane to the interests represented in this special issue. But any discussion of aesthetic education must range more broadly than within aesthetic theory alone, because the ramifications of the concept of aesthetic education are very broad, covering most if not all aspects of educational theory, educational practice, and philosophy of education. In fact, a major point I will try to make is that aesthetic issues as such—that is, issues associated with the field of professional aesthetics—while they are essential to any viable concept of aesthetic education, are not sufficient for an understanding of its nature and are not the sole determinants of what it might be or might become.

Item one, having to do with teaching all the arts rather than just one or a few, has generated a whole literature of its own, so my treatment of it here will have to be very selective. I want to make a point about each of three levels of this issue—the political level, the curriculum level, and the philosophical level.

At the political level, we should remind ourselves that aesthetic education in one of its dimensions began as a political movement—that is, as an attempt to win for the arts the support, money, school program time, staffing, and prestige which its advocates dearly desired but had had a notable lack of success achieving in American education. In unity, perhaps, there might be political strength. So in the middle 1960s, when the term "aesthetic education" had begun to enter the lexicon of educators in the arts, the term was appropriated by a major initiative to build a comprehensive arts program—the CEMREL Aesthetic Education Program. That program, given its multiart focus, and given that it then was, while not the only game in town, certainly the major one, and given the political clout wielded by a well-funded program in which major figures from all of the art education fields participated, cemented in the minds of many the view that "aesthetic education" automatically means "arts education."

I have never held that view, despite my having been the official music education participant in the initial, definitional stage of the Aesthetic Education Program leading to the publication of its *Guidelines for Aesthetic Education*,[6] and despite my involvement since that time in a host of arts education endeavors at both the theoretical and practical levels. I have certainly been an advocate of comprehensive arts programs, partly, of course, for political reasons in that I tend to believe that each of the arts would be more secure in education under the aegis of a comprehensive program than is possible when each stands entirely alone. My point here is that such a position is a political position, not a theoretical one. There are, of course, theoretical *implications* of this position, which have for many years fascinated me because I find them so challenging and so enlightening. But it has been my view that music education in and of itself as a professional entity can be conceived as aesthetic education, as can each art in and of itself. It is debatable whether music education and the other art education fields *should* cooperate politically, but no position in that debate depends on the prior assumption that, in order to be aesthetic education, the arts must be conceived as a unified political body.

The second level of item one concerning the issue of arts education is an extension of the first to include more than the political dimension. The curriculum, as I conceive it, includes the broadest possible range of all the issues impinging on the nature of education and how it can be provided, and the nature of various subjects within education and how they can be provided. The question here is, Can a *bona fide* curriculum, fulfilling all the multiple demands of both theoretical and practical curriculum issues, be achieved by a single art? Or are such demands so inclusive that no single art could reasonably or possibly fulfill them all, so that at this level of the aesthetic education endeavor more than one art or, perhaps, all the arts, would be required to be treated together rather than individually?

I have taken the position that music, by itself, can fulfill all dimensions requiring to be addressed in a total curriculum and be, by itself, an instance of aesthetic education. It is certainly possible to build a comprehensive curriculum for all the arts, but the decision to do so and the attempt to do so are not, in my view, in any way required in order for aesthetic education to be achieved.

But what about the philosophical level of the issue beyond the political and the educational? Is there anywhere within the philosophy of art or aesthetic theory a set of principles or a persuasive argument which would cause us to believe that music would be misrepresented, or falsely understood, or deprived of essential characteristics, if it were not studied as part of the larger field including the other arts?

This is a very difficult and complex question, because it raises the issue, so heavily debated for so long in history, of the nature of the interrelations among the arts. As I understand that historical debate, it seems to take place across a continuum of arguments. At one end of the continuum is the view that the arts are essentially unitary, the various arts being different only in insignificant features. At the other end of the continuum is the position that the arts are essentially autonomous, any similarities being quite inconsequential. And, of course, between these extremes are arguments at every point along the way.

The continuum in theorizing about this point is reflected in the continuum of positions adopted by educators in the arts. At one end have been those who assume that to teach art one must capitalize the word, treat it as homogeneous, and demonstrate that any seeming differences among the arts are essentially trivial. At the other end (usually ulcerated by their irritation with the position I have just described) are those who regard any fraternization among the arts as being tantamount to artistic depravity, in that each art can only be destroyed in its veracity (not to mention its virginity) by consorting in any way with any of the others.

I hope I will not disappoint by not providing the correct theory, finally, as to whether and how and to what degree the arts are interrelated. But I need not disappoint as to articulating where I stand on the education continuum, because I only need to reiterate what that stance has been from the beginning of my involvements with arts programs and continues to be to this day. If one envisions the continuum of positions as a yardstick, with the "arts as unitary" view on the right and the "arts as independent" view on the left, I am positioned about an inch and a half to two inches from the left end of the stick. I am persuaded that the essential value and meaning of each art must be attained within the domain of value and meaning that particular art exemplifies. As I put it in *A Philosophy of Music Education*, for arts programs to be effective, "*the distinctive ways that each art operates must become progressively clearer.* . . . Glossing over the uniquenesses, diluting them by forced combinations, dulling them by constant equating of one with another, making them more obscure by ignoring the peculiar, particular flavor of each, can only weaken aesthetic sensitivity and limit the capacity to share aesthetic insights in the wide variety of ways they are available."[7]

Nevertheless, I have allowed myself that inch and a half or two, because I also believe that similarities among the arts exist and that those very similarities provide a powerful opportunity to explore below their surfaces to the level at which each art manifests them distinctively. That opportunity to appreciate fully the maxim I have long followed—that the arts are not redundant—is presented only when more than one art is being examined, one of them serving as the foil to understand better the particularities of the other. So my advocacy for comprehensive arts programs includes, in addition to my beliefs in their political efficacy and their curriculum feasibility, the theoretical conviction that the arts as a totality constitute a meaning domain sufficiently different from others to be counted as a genus, and in which the nature of the domain derives from the accumulative contributions of each of its exemplifications.

My conclusion from this aspect of the issue is that it is certainly not necessary for music education as aesthetic education to be pursued within a structure including other arts. However, doing so would not be counterindicated by theory, and there may be good practical reasons for doing so. The essential point is that a cooperative arts program should never, in any way, threaten the integrity of any of the arts it includes.

The second of Broudy's five generalizations about aesthetic education raises the issue of whether it is essential to the nature of aesthetic education in any single art that the philosophy be used as the primary advocacy basis for helping that art achieve a more solid position within the education establishment. Many music educators, when first encountering the ideas connected to aesthetic education, seemed to have thought so and came to regard aesthetic education as a means for demonstrating, in a more solid, more defensible, more thoughtful way than previously, that music education was a necessary subject in schools.

Now here I must make an important distinction. It is between philosophy and what it attempts to do, and advocacy and what it attempts to do. The distinction is subtle because a philosophical position can be used for advocacy purposes—that is, purposes intended to persuade others to give more support to a particular endeavor than they are likely to do otherwise. But the fact that it *can* be used to do so does not mean that it is required to do so or even that it be conceived that it would ever be used to do so. A professional philosophy—that is, a coherent position about the nature and purpose of a professional field providing a set of principles on which actions can be based—serves a function that is essentially "intramural." It forms and shapes the belief system and value system of a field so that the field can be guided in its actions and in its growth in coherent ways and in ways founded on its most distinctive aspects rather than on its superficial aspects.

The function of advocacy, on the other hand, is essentially "extramural." It exists to achieve a particular purpose with a variety of constituencies with which a field must interact. That purpose—winning support—can often be served most effectively by arguments *ad hoc* and *ad hominem*. The danger with such arguments, of course, is that they can be made with no connection to an underlying belief system which provides a sufficient level of restraint and veracity to keep those arguments from becoming fallacious. When that occurs, the unintended effect is to weaken or demean the field in either the short or long run. So a philosophy, while capable of providing direct advocacy arguments, must be used for that purpose circumspectly; that is, when it is felt that it will be more effective than other possible arguments or when it can provide a useful dimension to other arguments. In short, a philosophy is necessary but not sufficient for effective advocacy.

But there is a different sense of "advocacy" for which a professional philosophy is essential and should be sufficient. That sense has to do with a profession's self-understanding of its inherent character and its fundamental reason for being. In this sense, the word philosophy means not just "the critical study of the basic principles and concepts of a particular branch of knowledge," but also "a system of principles for guidance in practical affairs." (Both definitions are given under "philosophy" in the *Random House Dictionary*.) This distinction, I would suggest, is profound, and to treat it with the seriousness it deserves would require, at the very least, a separate essay of the sort being published here. So I must limit myself to a few observations.

Music education existed in the United States from the days of the early colonists until around 1960 with little cohesion at the level of an explicit set of philosophical principles guiding its actions. Aesthetic education was the first movement to attempt to articulate a substantial and coherent set of such principles, to demonstrate their efficacy for practice, to speak to and to be determined by the implicit intuitions about music and music education long held by the field, and at the same time to attempt to satisfy the requirements of critical, analytical philosophy. That it attempted—and attempts—so much accounts for its strength in having provided a working philosophy for so many practitioners of music education as to have won a place for itself as a plausible symbol for a period of the profession's history.

But that very breadth, which has made it so influential throughout the profession, also has its price in requiring that continual clarification and correction take place in its underlying premises at the level of analytical scholarship. The creative tension here is to keep in dynamic balance the need for a viable philosophy—one that is applicable to the broadest possible range of activities and programs in music education—with the equally pressing need for it to be valid at the level of the most exquisite analytical-critical refinements in its infinite details. It may be impossible to achieve complete success at both ends of this rather long continuum, especially in that each end tends to require specialists who focus on the particular tasks each end entails—robust application at one, meticulous scholarship at the other. In all such continua the tendency is for each end to lose sight of the other and to go its separate way. Avoiding that professional disaster requires that some people specialize in keeping the ends connected. Having so specialized for most of my career, having experienced the pleasures and rewards of doing so but also the abiding frustrations in attempting to do so because of the inevitable inadequacies in being as expert at both ends as one would like to be, I am in little need of instruction as to the difficulties entailed in building an intellectually valid philosophy that is also professionally useful across the entire spectrum of applications to the teaching and learning of music.

It is an essential characteristic of aesthetic education, I think, that it attempts to fulfill both needs. One may dispute any and all philosophical principles and educational applications proposed in its name, but it is my sense of its essential character that aesthetic education is founded on the premise that sound scholarship and sound practice depend on each other in mutually supportive, necessary ways, and I think that is a major reason aesthetic education has had such an important impact in the history of music education.

Item three in Broudy's list of generalizations frequently made about aesthetic education is that, whatever it is, it is applicable to all children in schools and not just the small percentage at the tail of the curve who demonstrate unusually high competencies in the arts. Now this generalization, I have always believed, is the easiest to which to give assent as an essential characteristic of aesthetic education, although there has been a conviction on the part of some that aesthetic education implies an elitist view of both art and education—a view I have spent a fair amount of energy disputing. I would propose that aesthetic education should clearly be conceived to apply to all students no matter their level of interest or talent in the arts. Ironically, the tough issues here have to do with curricular applications. If aesthetic education is conceived to be for all students, what are the essential learnings with which all should be provided?

In music education this question immediately translates into the issue of performance versus appreciation or, if you prefer, expression versus impression. Our history in regard to this issue as to which of the two is essential has been to offer both, but in what I would roughly estimate would be a 90-10 split overall in favor of performance. We have had very few people arguing for a reversal of that ratio, except, perhaps, in regard to high school humanities courses and appreciation-type courses. But we have had many who would be comfortable with more like a 99-1 split in favor of performance and who, in fact, practice methodologies based on pretty much that kind of split. The interesting question is, Where on that scale should aesthetic education be conceived to be?

Characteristically, aesthetic education has taken a comprehensive stance to the curriculum dimension of this issue. A useful music curriculum, in this view, is one that includes all possible ways people interact with music—listening, performing, improvising, composing. It also includes all the ways people think about and know about music—its history, its social contexts, how to criticize it in relevant ways, its many functions, the many issues related to how we can best understand its nature, and so forth.

But it is not just in being comprehensive that an aesthetic education curriculum achieves its purpose—it is also in promoting an interaction with music of a characteristic sort, and that interaction can be achieved in any and all aspects of a total program. A performing group concentrating on performance as such can be, and should be in my opinion, an instance of aesthetic education because it is or should be providing an engagement with and an experience of—one kind of experience of—music itself. How that experience can best be provided in a performing group is a valid, important question, but if it is being provided at all, it is, to that extent, an instance of aesthetic education as I conceive it. Exactly the same can be said for a course devoted entirely to listening—say, at the high school or college level. So the essential characteristic of aesthetic education in relation to this particular issue is not that there always must be one particular balance among the many ways people can be engaged with music, although inclusiveness or comprehensiveness should be a feature of the total program. What seems to me to be essential to aesthetic education is that any engagement at all with music must include—and, it is to be hoped, emphasize above all else—a quality of interaction that we as professionals would recognize as being inherently "musical." What is that quality of interaction? I will attempt to answer that question in my discussion of item four.

Broudy's item four, you will remember, has to do with the degree to which aesthetic education should be linked with extra-aesthetic—moral, political, economic, religious, civic—values. It also extends to the question of whether aesthetic materials could be used to facilitate the teaching of other subjects. Now these may seem to be rather simple matters, to be disposed of summarily. In actuality, they raise some of the thorniest, most intractable problems in the entire field of aesthetics, to which whole literatures have been devoted and about which there exists a tremendous diversity of opinion. Again, I am forced to tackle an infinitely complex problem—whether various modes of knowing or experiencing exist, whether the aesthetic is such a mode and why, and if so, whether it relates in any way to others—as but one item among several others in my discussion. I will offer some thoughts about this matter and use those thoughts as a segue to item five, because they launch me directly into issues of aesthetic theory proper.

It is possible to view music as having no connection whatsoever with "extramusical" matters. Such matters would be conceived as anything other than sounds organized to be intrinsically meaningful or significant or compelling in that they form a perceptible or potentially perceptible self-determined and self-contained structure of interrelations. Such a view, dismissing anything but interactive sonorous events as being musically meaningful, has been called "absolutism" in the aesthetic literature, and as with all such "isms," proponents for it may be found as supporting more or less pure versions of it. I, personally, have spent a great deal of intellectual and psychic energy attempting to alter my seemingly natural propensity to be an almost pure absolutist. I have been influenced to make some small degree of modification by the opposing view, generally called "referentialism," which tends to downplay or dismiss musical form (in the sense I am using the term) as being the essential determinant of aesthetic meaning or significance and concentrates, more or less exclusively, on associative or representational content in works of art as being the essential factor in how they achieve meaning. But I have been much more heavily influenced to soften my absolutistic bent by the rather persuasive set of arguments one confronts when dealing with thinkers whose home discipline has not been music—that is, people trained in the other arts. They tend, if I may be so bold as to generalize, to be much more suspicious of what they construe as "formalism" than those in music, more easily seduced by referentialism, but usually quite convinced that neither can account as fully as is necessary for the range of meanings the arts can mediate. I have, therefore, succeeded in budging myself about an inch and a half to two from the end of this particular yardstick. I would argue that so-called "extra-artistic" matters can indeed be and often are important determinants of the aesthetic meaning available from works of art, but that in every case a necessary transformation in their nature must take place in order for that meaning to qualify as being aesthetic. That transformation—and I mean the word in its literal sense as a change in form "across" or "beyond"—is caused by and is a function of that quality or set of conditions which characterizes art and sets it apart as a genuine meaning domain.

That quality, I am convinced, is indeed its capacity to create intrinsically meaningful structures and to transform anything else it chooses to incorporate, such as conventional symbols, political statements, moral exhortations, stories and icons and whatever else, by setting such material as one dimension of—often an important dimension of—its intrinsic structure. The transformation of meaning through formed interrelationships occurs particularly and necessarily with emotions, I would argue. Emotional states or moods, like any other incorporated materials, can influence aesthetic expressiveness, but such expressiveness always transmutes, through the structures into which it is cast, any representation of an emotion as it might exist in experiences outside art.

The "beyondness" or "transcendence" achieved by intrinsically meaningful form is, I think, the essential characteristic of the aesthetic. This transcendence is achieved in all arts of all cultures at all times in history. Each culture achieves it in ways characteristic of that culture, ranging from Western concert halls to Balinese group ritual dances to African drum ensembles. Whatever the social context, art shapes and molds individual and communal experience into meaningful forms sharable by those participating in that culture.

That realization, that art is not the property of any one particular culture such as that of Western Europe, opened music education in the 1960s to all the musics represented by our polycultural society. The long-held, entrenched idea that the music studied in schools should be "school music" began to be replaced by a far more liberal attitude toward what is musical. While a good deal of conservatism still remains in music education about this matter, aesthetic education, I think, has gone a long way toward helping music education become more comprehensive in what music it includes as well as more comprehensive in the ways it engages students with music.

It would follow that an essential characteristic of aesthetic education is its attempt to enhance people's ability to gain the meanings available from culturally embedded expressive forms. Everything in our world can be regarded as potentially yielding such meanings; that is, regarded as and responded to as an instance of meaningful form (which is another way to say "to be aesthetically experienced"). Art is the activity of creating objects and events and processes that yield such meanings, and therefore art adds the crucial dimension of human engagement in the processes of generating, capturing, and sharing the cognitions available from this mode of representation. So aesthetic education is likely to deal primarily, although not necessarily exclusively, with works of art. It is important to understand that the word "work" in "work of art" functions as both noun and verb. In some cultural settings a "work" is generally understood to be the product of an artistic endeavor. In other settings it is more likely to be conceived as a process engaged in by people during the act of creating an expressive form ("forming"). Both meanings are equally valid, I believe, and both are included in my concept of "work of art."

Engagements with works that emphasize their meaning as art—their ability to yield meanings from their structures of interrelated sounds and to transform words, images, ideas, emotions, and any other socially shared human values by incorporating them as meaningful aspects of musical structure—may be understood to be aesthetic education. We would recognize engagements of the sort I have described as being "musical," I feel reasonably sure, no matter what the particular kind or type of music is in question, ranging from music completely lacking in material other than form through the most non-form-laden examples one might choose. So long as a structure of sounds both incorporates and to any degree envelops additional content it can be conceived as musical and responded to as such. There is no "correct" or "desirable" standard, as far as I know, for what the ratio of form to content should be, some genres or types or styles of music around the world having high form-to-content proportions and others low.

In the Western classical music tradition, of course, composers throughout history have chosen to incorporate a great variety of materials but have been careful to remind us that their music must be considered to be more than any such incorporated content. A recent striking example is given by the composer John Corigliano, whose Symphony No. 1 was premiered by the Chicago Symphony Orchestra in March 1990. The piece reflects Corigliano's anger, despair, and sense of impotence in having lost so many friends to AIDS. The symphony is "a cry 'Of Rage and Remembrance' [the subtitle of the first movement] for those I have lost and for those I'm still losing," says Corigliano. But the composer insists he does not wish for the piece to be known as an "AIDS symphony."

> That is why I assigned the subtitle "Of Rage and Remembrance" only to the first movement. I want it to be known as a symphony because it is a major work of art and should be heard that way. I want the human part of it to be part of the subtext, but I don't want it to be the only thing with which people identify this piece. I wanted this to be an abstract work, because I think that abstract music can touch the deepest and most basic emotions.[8]

In his review of the performance in the *New York Times* (18 March 1990), John Rockwell said:

> There are all kinds of reasons why the current Chicago Symphony subscription concerts at Orchestra Hall are significant. But the most compelling is that they mark the arrival of a major new orchestral score, one that addresses a terrible crisis of our time and also manages to make impressive sense on abstract esthetic terms. . . . Music is the most abstract art, and its application to topical issues can sometimes seem forced, a too-easy purchase on the emotions. This symphony sounds almost overwrought at times in its emotional extremism. Yet it is also full of an esthetic coherence that could convince even one utterly ignorant of its inspiration. Knowing that inspiration only lends it a greater poignance.

Corigliano and Rockwell are struggling here to articulate the principle I have tried to articulate and that so many aestheticians have also tried to articulate—that art transcends referential content through its form and that that transcendence yields meanings "deeper and more basic" than the meanings of the content it incorporates, meanings specifically and characteristically "aesthetic." So I am attempting here to argue that there is an identifying set of characteristics, or conditions, or symptoms, or values, or ways to experience, or ways to exercise percipience, or to be phenomenally aware (and on and on depending on whom you are reading) that particularly pertain to the aesthetic domain; that works of art from any place and of any sort—classical, popular, or whatever—are determined in their nature as art (or, as some would suggest, as "art enough") by such characteristics as they are understood to exist among members of a cultural community cognizant of them; that music is one instance of "works of art"; and that attempts to provide tuition about how to interact in relevant ways with musical phenomena can be construed as aesthetic education. Moral, political, religious, and any other cultural values can indeed be implicated in such tuition in the way I have explained, and often *must* be, or a particular piece of music or musical process could not be understood appropriately.[9]

It is difficult for me to imagine how such tuition would facilitate the teaching of other subjects, except, of course, as an excellent way to help students understand such things as that other subjects go about creating meaning in other ways, that there are interesting and often puzzling overlaps among those ways, that cognition can be understood to be multifaceted with aesthetic cognition as one of the several genuine, intersecting facets, and so on. That would indeed be fruitful, I would feel, as educational material, so long as that which is most characteristic about the aesthetic domain, or any domain, is not misrepresented or forced to serve functions not characteristic of it.

These considerations and recommendations bring me smack up against the final item in Broudy's list—the lack of agreement about the aesthetic and educational theories on which a concept of aesthetic education might be built. What I have just proposed about the essential characteristic of what is musical and the way people engage themselves with music "musically" and therefore what would count as musically educative under a consequent notion of aesthetic education, all represent a particular point of view founded on a particular segment from aesthetic theory, translated into recommendations for educational practice equally founded on a particular view of educational theory.

I would go so far as to say that any coherent position taken by anyone on the issue in question would be equally so founded on some one or other theoretical base. "Eclecticism," for example, is not just a random assortment of bits and pieces from any and all philosophical positions, but requires a painstaking selection and coordination and reconciliation of aspects of several views, forging a position of its own from diverse sources. If it does not do that, but is simply a smatter from any and all *bona fide* philosophies, it is mindless and therefore useless, degenerating into a kind of free-form pluralism. Philosophical pluralism states a truism—that there are many contending philosophies—and is incapacitated by that truth. Any viable philosophy of music education must take into account the fact of cultural-artistic pluralism, attempt to make some sort of sense of it by explaining its nature, and attempt to suggest how education might most reasonably contend with it. A philosophy might explain why musical heterogeneity should be ignored, or celebrated, or undermined, or strengthened, or whatever that particular philosophy led one to do about it. It would be a strange philosophy indeed that simply did not take it into account. It is not a philosophy, but an abdication of the philosophical imperative, I believe, to take no theoretical position about the nature of musical diversity so that one can act coherently according to that position, but simply to maintain that no position is possible because of the fact of that diversity. Not only is that a philosophical evasion, it is an educational one as well. A philosophy, I think, is obligated to carve out a position—not to avoid taking one—and that position, by virtue of its being a position, must be positioned somewhere along the spectrum of all possible theoretical bases.

That spectrum has itself widened exponentially in recent years. In 1970, in the first edition of my A *Philosophy of Music Education*, I commented, with no small measure of frustration, that in the face of the diversity of views in aesthetics "one is tempted to throw up one's hands in despair, turn one's back on the entire field of aesthetics, and proclaim that in aesthetic education one might as well do whatever strikes one's fancy, since there probably exists plenty of justification for whatever this happens to be."[10] Twenty years later that comment almost sounds optimistic. An increasingly tightening inward spiral of critical analysis has taken place, not only of every aesthetic issue but of the notion that the concept "aesthetic issue" is itself viable. This has been accompanied by an increasingly loosening outward spiral in which the field of aesthetics, by concentrating on an examination of its own products rather than of the objects and events it had previously presumed to explain (and therefore having become meta-aesthetics or, one is tempted to say, megalo-aesthetics in its narcissistic self-absorption), has so gnawed at its own carcass as to have led some to suggest that it is time we abandon the beast as being moribund.[11]

I often feel (in fact, it is getting to the point where I usually feel) that this is a blessed suggestion. Unfortunately, I'm afraid it can't be followed. The great color-field artist Barnett Newman no doubt had a point when he quipped, "Aesthetics for artists is like ornithology for the birds." But I think music educators with a philosophical bent are stuck with having to think carefully about such things as music and its nature, and I would generally call the careful articulation of such thought "aesthetics." The question becomes, Is it possible to avoid being sucked so strongly into the exploding and imploding forces of contemporary Western theoretical-formal-analytical aesthetics as to be rendered sterile as functioning music educators by them, while at the same time continuing to seek enlightenment and even guidance from the field of aesthetics so that we can do more intelligently what we think it is important to do?

The form of my question indicates my suggested answer. It is that we as music educators have no alternative but to do aesthetics ourselves and also to seek guidance from professionals in aesthetics proper. But it is also that we who seek in aesthetics must know where to look. Much of aesthetics has, in fact, little if anything to do with what music educators must attempt to deal with in order to create a viable professional philosophy, and that is because much of aesthetics is simply not interested in the issues we need to address. I would not go so far as to say we should be oblivious of the larger field of aesthetics within which we must conduct our goal-directed searches, because we do need to be aware of the struggles going on even at the borders of that discipline (and that, of course, is where the bloodiest battles always take place). We may not want to go so far as Francis Sparshott did, in the preface to his monumental *The Theory of the Arts*, when he said, "My concern is to develop a coherent line of thought, and little of what other people have written proves to be of actual use when one's own direction has become specific."[12] But we can certainly sympathize with the feeling that our own agenda should guide our scholarship. That agenda, I want to suggest, requires us to focus on the needs of our field—music education or, if one chooses, music education as aesthetic education—as providing us with our obligatory issues, about which aesthetics can then, perhaps, give us some guidance. Harry Broudy said this very well, I think, in the chapter I have used to structure this essay:

> It is especially difficult to make the connection between aesthetic education and the kind of writing that is concerned primarily with the discourse about aesthetics, "meta-aesthetics." The logical properties of aesthetic judgments and definitions are not themselves aesthetic objects. This is not to say that speaking precisely is not important to aesthetic education. On the contrary, if one is to distinguish aesthetic experience from other kinds, if one is to defend one attitude toward the aesthetic object rather than another, then discussions of definitions and criteria for usage cannot be avoided. But, whereas in formal aesthetics this can go on as an end in itself without engaging in concrete transactions with particular aesthetic objects, this cannot be the case in aesthetic education. Accordingly, aesthetic theory has to be given educational relevance, a task that is not quite the same as generating either aesthetic or educational theory.[13]

This argument has been updated recently to reflect the tangled situation in professional aesthetics over the past decade or so to which I referred above. In a 1987 article in the *Journal of Aesthetics and Art Criticism* entitled "The Liveliness of Aesthetics," Marx W. Wartofsky presents a point of view in consonance with Broudy's and with what I am attempting to propose. He begins by saying that his essay is not "in" aesthetics but is "about" aesthetics. If it were "in" aesthetics, he says, it would be about such matters as "art (artworks, the artworld, art talk, art biz, artists, etc.) or about criticism or the theory of art, or the experience (reception, evaluation, appreciation) of art; or if not about art, then about the aesthetic, or aesthetic concepts like Form, Beauty, Style, Taste; or if none of these, then about representation in art, or depiction, or semblance, or about expression, and more and more." I quote this sentence to make the point that despite a decade or more of some attempts to either discredit or dismiss such matters, they remain, with little question, the enduring foundation for the great majority of scholarly efforts in aesthetics.

Wartofsky discusses the variety of claims in recent analytical aesthetics, the fashions and styles of discourse they adopt, and the distance they have generated between their concerns and the basic issues relating to how and why we value art, leading, he says, to the derivativeness and dreariness of this segment of aesthetics. What is the antidote? To pay attention, Wartofsky asserts, to art.

> Art, in its career, its changes, its corruptions and failures as well as in its successes and epiphanies, is a naturally vital source of problems and insights in aesthetics. . . . The fact is that, analytic or not, the liveliest range of books in aesthetics, as well as essays, symposia, etc. has been stimulated by an immediate relation with and competence in the arts, and a close knowledge of their present state and of their history. . . . the arts constantly provide one with something to say—to understand them, to make them accessible to others, to engage the practitioners and performers in reflection on their *metiers*, to submit one's own work to their criticism, and that of one's colleagues. Enough and more to do in full aesthetic autonomy. The liveliness of aesthetics lies, I think, in such intercourse with the arts.[14]

I want to propose that the liveliness of music education philosophy lies in its relevance to problems and issues of learning and teaching the art of music in valid ways; that is, in ways that scholarship can help us validate. More than ever before, and certainly more than twenty years ago when I first expressed the thought in the first edition of A *Philosophy of Music Education,* the formation of a useful and tenable philosophy of music education "must start with an acquaintance with the field of music education: its problems, its needs, its history, its present status. Aesthetics must be used by music educators to serve their own purposes. Otherwise they are likely to lose themselves in the history and problems of aesthetics, never to emerge with a workable philosophy."[15] I added to this thought in the second edition of A *Philosophy* the sentence "Aesthetics must never be the master of music education—it must be its servant."[16] Music education, I am proposing, must be regarded to be a "music educationworld." The world it represents and creates is just as real and as valid and as stipulative of what can go on in it as is the "artworld" with which it intersects and with which it engages in a great variety of influences and counterinfluences. I would assert, therefore, that an essential characteristic of aesthetic education is that it attempts to address the philosophical issues of the world or culture of music education by seeking helpful, relevant, and intellectually defensible resolutions from whatever sources it can, including, necessarily and importantly, the field of professional aesthetics.

That endeavor requires, first, that the fundamental philosophical problems arising within music education be articulated clearly and, second, that solutions be sought that are relevant not only to the nature of those problems but also to the nature of music education as a social-cultural institution. Both conditions require a philosophy amenable to and dependent on change as an essential characteristic, because it is a given that the philosophical problems considered to be fundamental to music education will change over time, the availability of viable solutions to them will also continually change, and the social-cultural nature of music education will also continue to change. It must be an essential characteristic of aesthetic education as a professional philosophy, then, that it not consist of one particular set of problems or issues, resolved in one particular fashion, relevant to one particular institutional Zeitgeist as it exists at any one particular period in history.

This principle applies as well to the maintenance of a recognizable political-cultural entity such as a nation. The United States, for example, has existed as a characteristic entity despite enormous changes over time in its philosophical self-understandings, the available resources for addressing its self-definitional issues, the social-cultural contexts within which the issues must be addressed. Longevity and identity are both essential for the viability of a cultural institution, and both can be achieved only if mechanisms for change are built into the institution's guiding principles. Aesthetic education, as I understand it, is an attempt to articulate a philosophical orientation that can be both temporally pertinent and progressively developmental.

The philosophical agenda for music education, under this view, remains constant while its contents evolve. The agenda is to articulate what the most pressing issues are, to attempt to resolve them in light of the most useful and persuasive available scholarship, and to use the resolutions as the basis for applications to the teaching and learning of music as it is embedded in the existing overall culture as well as within the existing culture of the field of music education. Debate within the music education philosophical community can then take place in a context of both theoretical and practical significance. What are the central philosophical issues now facing us? That question will always provide music education philosophers plenty to deal with. What are the most viable and defensible solutions to those issues? Again, a question allowing a great deal of room for healthy argument. How can suggested solutions be translated into helpful practices in educational settings, and how do those translations reflect back on and validate or invalidate the solutions? Another fruitful domain for scholarly efforts.

What has been missing in the history of music education has not only been an active, ongoing philosophical community, but also a structure within which such a community could flourish as an integral part of the larger music education endeavor. Perhaps we are now ready to begin establishing such a community and a cooperative structure within which individuals, while retaining their intellectual independence, can also contribute to shared goals.

What might such shared philosophical goals be at this point in history? It would be impossible to articulate any unless there existed for the person doing so a sense of what music education now consists of as a profession and a philosophical orientation that would be pertinent to that sense. Given my image of what music education has become as an institution, and my philosophical orientation based on several essential characteristics of what I term aesthetic education, I would like to focus briefly on just two important philosophical goals (among many others that might be mentioned) now very much needing to be better achieved.

The first has to do with our understanding of the relation between music and feeling. This is not only because this relation continues to be as much of an enigma for contemporary aestheticians as it has been throughout history, but because any philosophy of music education neglecting or disclaiming this dimension of musical experience will not speak to a major if not the major personal and professional value of music to music educators. Largely because aesthetic education in its earliest formulations took the nature of musical feeling to be one of its most important topics, this philosophy seemed relevant to the profession at large. That situation has not changed, in my view, nor is it likely to, so a viable philosophy of music education needs to continue to clarify this issue so that educational practices can more validly and effectively reflect our better understandings.

That will not be a simple task, as history has shown us. One of the important early contributions of aesthetic education was to clarify that music did not function as emotional expression; that is, as a translation into sound of a composer's or performer's present affective state. The key to unlocking this new set of ideas was provided at that time in history by Susanne K. Langer, who was a pioneer in formulating a different basis for understanding feeling in music than the prevalent "expression of emotion" theories and therefore helped us turn attention inward, to musical form and the experience of it rather than outward, to emotions music was ostensibly referring to by means of sounds as conventional symbols. As Francis Sparshott explains, "According to her theory, it is just because the artist's (and other people's) repertory of 'knowledge' of the possibilities of feeling is not available as knowledge but exists as a sort of empathetic capacity that art is necessary to symbolize the modes of sentience. The conundrum that her critics pose for her, that we cannot know that art does this unless we can already recognize the symbolized modes of sentience, so that the symbolization is unnecessary, is readily solved: all that we know is that the work of art before us gives form to *some* form of sentience; *what* form that is we can say only by describing the work."[17] Such a description, Langer would have added, must be of the musical form (or "forming") as such—the "work"—rather than of affective states of being, which are incapable of being mediated by language. Her insistence on this point had the further effect of turning attention in music teaching to sounds as such and to the experience of those sounds as being affectively dependent on their form and therefore incapable of being more fully experienced except by more and more refined perceptual awareness of their intrinsically musical form (including, of course, whatever other social-cultural materials were implicated as determining components of that form).

Langer's seminal yet partial contribution did not still the outpouring of debates on this issue (I hardly need say), and we continue to read, in a great many books and journal articles on the matter, still more tortured attempts to explain why and how and wherein a sad piece of music achieves its sadness. This is important work, no doubt, but I want to call attention to what I think is even more important—the increasing recognition that affect, or feeling, is not just a concomitant of musical experience but is an active ingredient in the intelligence with which such experience is mediated. I refer here to Nelson Goodman's claim that to experience a work of music aesthetically is a cognitive achievement in which "the emotions function cognitively: in organizing a world, felt contrasts and kinships, both subtle and salient, are no less important than those seen or inferred."[18] Further, one cannot discern the musical properties of formed sounds without an engagement of feeling. "Emotional numbness," says Goodman, "disables here as definitely if not as completely as . . . deafness."[19] Roger Scruton puts it this way: "To understand musical meaning, therefore, is to understand how the cultivated ear can discern, in what it hears, the occasions for sympathy. I do not know *how* this happens; but *that* it happens is one of the given facts of musical culture."[20] It is certainly, I would add, one of the essential facts of music education culture, and it would seem to me, therefore, an essential characteristic of a professional music education philosophy such as aesthetic education aspires to be that it continue to attempt to clarify for the larger profession how feeling is implicated in musical experience as insights about that implication continue to deepen.

These considerations lead me directly to the second philosophical issue to which I think we must pay particular attention as part of our professional agenda—the issue of musical cognition. Musical knowing, as both Goodman and Scruton imply, seems to be intimately connected with the phenomenon of musical feeling, the former being incomprehensible without the guidance and formative powers and phenomenological pervasiveness of the latter. It may very well be the case, and I would argue that it certainly is the case, that musical meaning or knowing depends on or dependently implicates feeling. Mikel Dufrenne's explanation seems to me apt. "Simply described," he says, "feeling reveals an interiority. It introduces us to another dimension of the given. It is not only a state or mode of being of the subject, it is a mode of being of the subject which corresponds to a mode of being in the object. . . . Aesthetic experience will show us that feeling . . . is an immediacy which has undergone mediation. . . . Furthermore, such feeling, in which perception is realized, is not emotion. It is knowledge. . . . This feeling has a noetic [cognitive, mindful, reasoning] function. It reveals a world. . . . Feeling . . . is a capacity of receptivity, a sensibility to a certain world, and an aptitude for perceiving that world."[21]

Dufrenne is focusing here on "knowing of"—one of what I conceive to be two essential and interconnected modes of knowing in music. The second mode of knowing essential to musical experience is, I think, "knowing how," which is the engagement of the self in creating music whether by composing or performing or improvising. "Knowing how" entails feeling, of course, and depends on "knowing of" as the *sine qua non*, but adds the dimensions of active imagination and employment of the competent body—in itself, I would argue, as would many others, a realm of experience with cognitive resonance. I would also argue, but cannot take the time to do so here, that listening entails a particular kind of "knowing how" also to be conceived as creative, in the sense David Best proposes when he says that the term creative "applies equally to the creator and spectator, for it requires imagination to understand a work of imagination."[22] We particularly need to learn much more than we know at present about the "knowing how" entailed in composing, which has been largely neglected in music education but over the next several decades may become as important in our programs as performance has been.

In addition to the two essential aspects of musical cognition—"knowing of" and "knowing how"—two supplementary modes exist—"knowing about" (or "knowing that") and "knowing why." The former deals with verbal and symbolic conceptual knowledge about music as a phenomenon; the latter with the same kind of knowledge but about the cultural-historical belief systems in which music as a social institution exists. The philosophical agenda in regard to musical cognition is to clarify what each dimension consists of so that each may be taught more carefully as both an entity and as one aspect of the larger whole to which it contributes. Especially complex is the precise nature of the interface between the exteriority of "knowing about" and "why," on the one hand, and the interiority of "knowing of" and "how," on the other, in that, while a great deal of empirical evidence exists that the former does indeed influence the latter, we know too little about how, precisely, that occurs and therefore cannot arrange our education strategies as intelligently as we need to. I am aware, when I suggest that we explore that interface more intensively, that it raises profound and difficult issues relating to the nature of the human mind and the nature of

consciousness itself. That those issues are, in fact, issues so deeply important to the field of music education attests to the centrality of our field in the
larger domain of cognitive scholarship. It is time we both recognize and
proclaim that centrality.

Given the assumptions I have made about several essential and nones-
sential characteristics of aesthetic education, the question arises as to
whether it is important or helpful to retain the term "aesthetic education" at
all. Of course, none of us owns the term, and people will or will not use it as
they wish. But what should we desire about it? Obviously some will want
very much to continue to use it while others have long since said good rid-
dance to it.

I confess to a good deal of ambivalence in this matter. On the one hand,
one grows accustomed to a much-used phrase as to a comfortable pair of
old shoes, its tears and scuffs and loose threads and worn spots being perceived not so much as imperfections but as signs of its adaptability to the
rough-and-tumble to which it has been subjected and the durability of a
wise initial investment. On the other hand, one is tempted by some of the
snappy new styles. Conceived this way, one vacillates.

Conceived differently, however, and in a more rigorous intellectual
manner, aesthetic education can be taken to symbolize a process rather than
an entity. In that sense I suspect it might serve a useful or even essential
function, reminding us as scholars and practitioners to keep our eye on
what matters and helping us define what it is that matters. For me, the most
essential value of aesthetic education is not its name but its agenda. It is as a
reminder and symbol of that agenda that the term "aesthetic education"
may continue to prove useful.

NOTES

1. Michael L. Mark, "A New Look at Historical Periods in American Music Educa-
    tion," *Council for Research in Music Education*, Bulletin 99 (Winter 1989). The pre-
    vious periods Mark identifies are 1. The Colonial Period (1620), 2. Public School
    Music (1800), 3. Curricular Development (1864), and 4. The Expansion of Musi-
    cal Performance (1920).
2. J. Terry Gates, "*Fermez la porte?*: On Michael L. Mark's 'A New Look at Histori-
    cal Periods in American Music Education,'" *Council for Research in Music Educa-
    tion*, Bulletin 103 (Winter 1990).
3. Edward Bailey Birge, *History of Public School Music in the United States*
    (Washington, D.C.: Music Educators National Conference, 1928). The periods
    Birge proposes are 1. The Development of the Singing School, 2. The Magna
    Charta of Music Education in America, 3. 1838-1861—The Period of Pioneering,
    4. The Beginnings of Method—(1861-1885), 5. Concentrating on Music Read-
    ing—(1885-1905), 6. The Turn of the Century, 7. The Twentieth Century, 8.
    Music Teachers' Associations—The Conference Movement, 9. Recent Trends
    and Developments in Music Education.
4. For a clear example of such a view, see David J. Elliott, "Structure and Feeling in

Jazz: Rethinking Philosophical Foundations," *Council for Research in Music Education,* Bulletin 95 (Winter, 1987).

5. Harry S. Broudy, "Some Reactions to a Concept of Aesthetic Education," *Arts and Aesthetics: An Agenda for the Future,* First Yearbook on Research in Arts and Aesthetic Education, ed. Stanley S. Madeja (St. Louis: CEMREL, Inc., 1977).

6. Manuel Barkan, Laura H. Chapman, and Evan J. Kern, eds., *Guidelines: Curriculum Development for Aesthetic Education* (St. Louis: CEMREL, Inc., 1977).

7. Reimer, *A Philosophy of Music Education,* 2d ed. rev. (Englewood Cliffs, N.J.: Prentice Hall, 1989), p. 230.

8. John von Rhein, "Absent Friends," *Chicago Tribune,* 11 March 1990.

9. An excellent example of how music is influenced by, absorbs, and transcends a theatrical story is given in Roger Scruton, "Analytical Philosophy and the Meaning of Music," *Journal of Aesthetics and Art Criticism* 46 (Special Issue on Analytical Aesthetics, 1987): 175. For a careful explanation of how conceptual information is made to yield aesthetic cognition, see Kenneth Dorter, "Conceptual Truth and Aesthetic Truth," *Journal of Aesthetics and Art Criticism* 48, no. 1 (Winter 1990).

10. Reimer, *Philosophy,* 1st ed., p. 12. Not succumbing to that temptation, I added, "The question is, can one accept this condition and at the same time develop a point of view which helps one's efforts to be as consistent, as effective, as useful for one's purposes as intelligence and modesty allow? There is really no alternative but to answer yes."

11. Francis Sparshott suggests an alternative to the notion of music as art in *What is Music?,* ed. Philip Alperson (New York: Haven Publications, n.d.).

12. Francis Sparshott, *The Theory of the Arts* (Princeton, N.J.: Princeton University Press, 1982), p. viii.

13. Broudy, "Some Reactions," pp. 254, 255.

14. Marx W. Wartofsky, "The Liveliness of Aesthetics," *Journal of Aesthetics and Art Criticism* 46 (Special Issue on Analytical Aesthetics, 1987).

15. Reimer, *Philosophy,* 1st ed., p. 13.

16. Reimer, *Philosophy,* 2d ed., p. 15.

17. Sparshott, *Theory of the Arts,* p. 321.

18. Nelson Goodman, *Of Mind and Other Matters* (Cambridge, Mass.: Harvard University Press, 1984), p. 147.

19. Nelson Goodman, *Languages of Art,* 2d ed. rev. (Indianapolis: Hackett, 1976), p. 248.

20. Scruton, "Analytical Philosophy," p. 174.

21. Mikel Dufrenne, *The Phenomenology of Aesthetic Experience* (Evanston, Ill.: Northwestern University Press, 1973), pp. 376-79.

22. David Best, *Feeling and Reason in the Arts* (London: George Allen and Unwin, 1985), p. 76.

What Should One Expect from a Philosophy of Music Education?

PHILIP ALPERSON

There is a puzzle about music. On the one hand, whether we are performers or members of an audience, whether in the rarified atmosphere of a recital hall or in the confines of the shower stall, whether our interest is in Mozart or in the blues, whether we study music in the structured context of a university classroom or chance upon it on a car radio, whether we have years of concert performance behind us or have difficulty carrying a tune, hardly a day goes by when we are not engaged by some sort of musical experience. Music is our constant companion.

Moreover, music seems to be a source of genuine enrichment without which our lives would be considerably diminished. For some, this enrichment comes through the composition of music. For others, musical performance is the chief source of musical delight. Others take pleasure in some of the ancillary aspects of music making, such as musical instrument design or working as a musical engineer. Still others write about music. Most of us enjoy listening to music. And for many, music provides enjoyment through some combination of these activities.

And yet, questions about the nature and function of music and why music ought to be a subject of education remain for most of us as perplexing as they seemed to Aristotle, who long ago remarked that unlike reading, writing, and even physical training, "It is not easy to determine the nature of music, or why any one should have a knowledge of it."[1] As Aristotle observed, music is not necessary to human existence, nor is it even useful, at least in the sense of utility that clearly applies to other subjects of education such as reading and writing, which are useful in the management of a household and the acquisition of knowledge and in political life and in money making, or even gymnastics, whose benefit to strength and

Philip Alperson is Associate Professor of Philosophy and Chair, Division of Humanities, at the University of Louisville. He has edited *The Philosophy of the Visual Arts* and *What is Music? An Introduction to the Philosophy of Music* and contributed articles to such publications as the *Journal of Aesthetics and Art Criticism*, the *International Journal of Music, Dance, and Art Therapy*, and the *Council for Research in Music Education Bulletin*.

health is evident enough. How do we justify an expenditure of time and money for education about an activity which, on the surface of things, seems so utterly dispensable?

The situation does not appear to be quite so desperate in the case of literature and the visual arts. At least there we can fall back on the bromide that art imitates life. Not that the question of the usefulness of art is settled with such a claim. We should still want to know why the imitation of life should be regarded as a valuable endeavor. As one critic so well put it, "Art is not a copy of the real world. One of the damn things is enough."[2] Plato put the matter even more acutely in Book X of the *Republic*, where he insists that we put the question to Homer.

> Friend Homer . . . if you [are] able to discern what pursuits make [people] better or worse in private or public life, tell us what State was ever better governed by your help? . . . [W]ho says that you have been a good legislator to them and have done them any good? . . . [W]hat city has anything to say about you? . . . Is there any war on record which was carried on successfully by [you] or aided by [your] counsels, when [you] were alive? . . . Or is there any invention of [yours] applicable to the arts, or to human life? . . . Must we not infer that all the poets, beginning with Homer, are only imitators; they copy images of virtue and the like, but the truth they never reach?[3]

Plato was under no illusion, of course, concerning Homer's reputation. Indeed, Plato himself admits to having "an awe and love" of Homer. What worries him is the question just what the value of poetry—and by extension most of what we would today call "the arts"—really is. Perhaps, Plato suggests acidly, people devote themselves to the arts of image making because they can't do anything better with their lives. In fact, the accusation of uselessness is among the more benign of the charges that Plato levels against the arts. Imitative artists, producing objects that are thrice removed from the truth, create deceptive and dangerous illusions. They present the false as true. They feed and water the passions. We need to cast a suspicious eye on the behavior of artists, Plato warns, as well as on their potentially damaging effect on society.

Nor is this kind of thinking far removed from the thoughts of many today. We have only to examine the feelings many parents try valiantly to suppress when they discover that an otherwise intelligent daughter or son has decided to attend art school to see how pervasive the suspicion of the artistic life is. Art is fine as a hobby, but surely reasonable people would not choose to make art a career. As Garrison Keillor is reported to have remarked, "Today, no American family can be secure against the danger that one of its children may decide to become an artist." Or, if we want a less psychological indicator of the disrepute in which the artistic life is held in many quarters, consider the level of budgetary support for arts programs in colleges and universities as compared with, say, business, engineering, medical, or technical programs. Ah, but these programs make tangible and beneficial contributions to society. Doctors heal people. Engineers build bridges. What *is* it that poets and painters do?

The situation is even worse for musicians. At least the poets and painters can fall back upon a 2,000-year tradition of collective amnesia regarding Plato's criticisms. Poetry and paintings are imitations of life, we continue to insist, or at least they should be. Their value, attendant upon their mimetic capability, lies precisely in the fact that these arts hold the mirror up to nature. Or, if we wish to be more charitable, we might say that it has not been so much a matter of forgetting Plato's criticisms of imitative art as accepting Aristotle's defense of it. Poetry, says Aristotle, describes "not the thing that has happened, but a kind of thing that might happen. . . . Hence poetry is something more philosophic and of graver import than history, since its statements are of the nature rather of universals, whereas those of history are singulars."[4] Since Aristotle's time, a virtual industry has grown up around the project of extending Aristotle's compliment to poetry to the entire range of imitative art.

But music—instrumental music in particular—is not mimetic art.[5] Or if it is, it is not mimetic in the clear and distinct ways that poetry and painting are. It is true that the study of music theory found its way into the curriculum in virtue of its historical connections with mathematics, metaphysics, and astronomy, but few mathematicians, metaphysicians, or astronomers feel the professional need to study their musical scales these days. Education administrators typically regard music education programs as frankly peripheral, especially in the schools, where often the best they can say about music education is that it provides students with recreational diversity and that it sometimes serves as a means to soothe the tempers of unruly children.[6] Is it any wonder that those who are involved in music education today feel continually pressed to defend even the relatively meager time and resources devoted to music education? How can we justify using limited educational resources to support music education courses in the schools or in the context of a university general education program? Or worse, to support professional schools which produce more musicians? Do we really want—or need—such programs? What should we expect from those programs that already exist?

It is at this point that the music educator might well look expectantly to the philosopher. Philosophy—which for present purposes I shall take to be the sustained, systematic, and critical examination of belief—helps us to comprehend and assess the presuppositions and content of our understanding of the world. The philosopher, one would think, would be in a position to provide, first of all, a philosophy of music, which, ideally would consist in the critical examination of our beliefs about the nature and function of music, including a philosophical consideration of the various aspects of music making and the production of music generally, an inquiry into the nature of musical works and other musical productions, an account of the appreciation and evaluation of music, and an assessment of the role of music in society and the status of music as a form of human activity. An adequate philosophy of music, in other words, would provide an understanding of what we might call the "musicworld," by which I mean the set of practices related to the making, understanding, and valuation of music and the social, institutional, and theoretical contexts in which such practices have their place.[7] If we could arrive at something like an adequate philosophy of music, we would then have a base on which we could build a philosophy of music education, whose task it would be to provide a reasoned account of the goals, techniques, and values of music education in particular. This would involve, among other things, an explanation of what there is to be learned about musical practice in its widest sense, how such things are learned, and how they might be taught. Such a philosophy of music education would go some way toward defending music education from its detractors by indicating the positive value—if there is such—of music education and would therefore help to justify our continuing, if not increasing, support of the enterprise.

But on what grounds do we build our philosophies of music and music education? This amounts to asking not only, What is the history of the philosophy of music? but also, What should the history of the philosophy of music be? For reasons that I hope will become clear as we proceed, I believe that we must in fact ask both these questions if we are to hope to arrive at an adequate philosophy of music.[8] In the present article, however, my aim shall be much more modest. On this occasion I would like to outline three general strategies upon which philosophies of music and music education might be built and assess the prospects of each. My selection of these three strategies is based upon both programmatic and pragmatic grounds: we have to start somewhere, and the strategies I shall discuss represent what I take to be three important directions that contemporary music education might take.

I should also note at the outset that in speaking of music education, I shall have in mind that variety of music education which occurs in a more or less systematic way in the school or university setting. In saying this I do not mean to imply that the school or the university is the sole locus of music education in our society. Quite to the contrary, many of our habits and expectations relating to music are formed in a more or less willy-nilly way in the home and in nonacademic settings, influenced by what we see and hear on radio, television, and musical recordings, by what we read in magazines, journals, and newspapers, as well as by our transactions with established institutions of music such as the band shell and recital hall. We shall have to bear this in mind as we proceed in our thinking about music education in more strictly academic settings.

It is probably fair to say that music education in North America has, since the middle of the twentieth century, been dominated by the idea of "aesthetic education,"[9] and it is with that notion that I should like to begin. Conceptually speaking, the idea of music education as aesthetic education is driven by several theoretical suppositions about art that dominate much modern thinking about the arts. This line of thought revolves around certain basic concepts, especially notions of the "fine arts," the "work of art," "taste," "aesthetic experience," and "disinterested pleasure."

An adequate treatment of these concepts is beyond the scope of this essay.[10] I shall instead rest content with a somewhat schematic and dehistoricized representation of the array of interlocking concepts on which the modern view is based. On this view, music is understood as one of the so-called "fine arts" whose chief characteristic is said to be that they issue in the production of objects the main value of which derives from their very contemplation. The linchpin of the view thus becomes the notion of *aesthetic experience*, a subjective state whose chief feature is said to be *disinterested perception*, which is understood as a pleasurable interest in something for the sake of its contemplation alone, apart from any personal, moral, political, or otherwise practical interest or purpose it might have. The *aesthetic attitude* is understood as those mental states thought to be necessary for the having of aesthetic experiences. An *aesthetic object* is understood as anything, natural or artificial, that can occasion the aesthetic experience. *Works of art* are artifacts created especially for the purpose of providing aesthetic experience. The *"fine arts"* are those arts that address themselves primarily to aesthetic experience. *Creation* is understood as the process of bringing works of art into existence. The *artist* is the agent who creates the work of art. The artist is generally thought to possess a particular talent for creating works of art which is called *genius*, the mark of which is *originality* (sometimes *creativity*). A *masterpiece* is an exemplary work of art, usually the product of genius. *Taste* (sometimes *imagination*) is the aesthetic faculty, the faculty of disinterested perception. *Aesthetic appreciation* is the process of responding to works of art or natural objects aesthetically. *Connoisseurship* is the possession and practice of refined taste. *Criticism* is any kind of discourse about the arts, its two most important components being *interpretation* (judgments about the meaning or significance of a work of art considered as an aesthetic object) and *evaluation* (judgments about the success or failure of a work of art considered as an aesthetic object).

Now I have presented this set of concepts in a relatively minimalist way in order to stress their relations to each other and to show how much of the art world is encompassed by this array of terms and concepts. Further, we can see that the most substantive term among them is "aesthetic experience," which is here defined in terms of a specific state of mind: "disinterestedness" or, as it sometimes called, "disinterested pleasure." It should be pointed out that this is not the only way to conceptualize the notion of aesthetic experience. One might define aesthetic experience in terms of a special class of objects with the capacity to provide aesthetic experience; or one might define aesthetic experience in terms of a special class of properties (such as beauty and the sublime) which seem to be distinctively aesthetic. But for our purposes we need not concern ourselves with these alternative strategies. There is also considerable philosophical dispute about the very intelligibility of the notion of aesthetic experience. I shall come back to this question; but, again, my aim at this point is not to rehearse contemporary debates about the concept, but rather simply to identify certain fundamental conceptions central to our thinking about art.

Let us return, then, to that pivotal notion in this cluster of concepts: the "disinterested" mode of contemplation which is said to be the defining feature of aesthetic experience. One way of explaining the disinterested state of mind is to define it along *formalist* lines, which is, roughly speaking, how Kant understood the term in the *Critique of Judgment*. The aesthetic experience was for Kant essentially a contemplation of "purposiveness without purpose," which is to say attention to the design, delineation, form, or structure of something, without reference to concepts or to the practical significance of what might be represented or expressed in a work or, indeed, whether we would wish such a thing to exist at all. We derive pleasure in such experience, Kant argued, from the harmonious free play of the cognitive powers of the imagination and the understanding.[11]

Here we arrive at what we might call a "formalist aesthetic" view of art or "aesthetic formalism" for short. The formalist aesthetic view understood as a general theory of art leads us to the first two of the basic strategies for music education which we shall consider here. According to each of these strategies, music education should consist in the training of the ability to produce works capable of evoking the aesthetic experience as just described and in the training of the ability to respond in the appropriate way to such objects. In both cases, the specifically aesthetic qualities are construed as qualities of form. The first of these strategies, however, construes the notion of form in a relatively narrow way as perceptual properties of a certain sort: the sensual, syntactic, and structural properties of the works themselves. Let us call this view of art the "strict" version of aesthetic formalism.

It might be noted that the strict formalist emphasis is also pronounced in visual art education in American public schools, where its influence may be traceable to a particularly influential book, Arthur Wesley Dow's *Composition* of 1898, which provided a system of instruction to produce harmonious compositions, as well as to the pressure exerted on art programs in the public schools to discover talent for use in industry. We see the strict formalist emphasis at the university level as well, especially in the stress put upon courses in "design," "composition," and "form" in the "fine arts" and "commercial arts" programs of many departments of visual arts. In the field of the visual arts, the philosophical connection between aesthetic form and aesthetic experience is made most explicitly by Clive Bell, who defines art in terms of the objective spatial quality he calls "significant form," which is in turn defined by its capacity to evoke a uniquely aesthetic experience which he calls the "aesthetic emotion." Significant form in the case of the visual arts is describable in terms of "lines and colours combined in a particular way, certain forms and relations of forms."[12]

In the case of music education, the influence of strict aesthetic formalism can be seen in programs of study that stress a variant of musical analysis which emphasizes what is sometimes called "structural listening," the main point of which is to teach students to attend to formal and functional relationships in musical compositions. The philosophical foundation for this approach is to be found in Eduard Hanslick's classic *On the Musically Beautiful* which offers accounts of musical composition, performance, and appreciation based upon the notion of a musical work as a composition of autonomous "tonally moving forms."[13] The musically beautiful, Hanslick argues, lies in the tone structure of the work. Composition is a working upon purely musical material. The composer is (or should be) concerned with the creation of a piece whose beauty, sense, and logic derive from "the after-effects of audible tones."[14] Indeed, says Hanslick, from a philosophical point of view, "the composed piece, regardless of whether it is performed or not, is the completed artwork"[15] (which goes a long way in explaining Hanslick's equivocal treatment of musical performance). The pleasure of listening is the pleasure of following and anticipating the design of the musical composition, an activity which requires a certain degree of vigilance but which, Hanslick says, "can, in the case of intricate compositions, become intensified to the level of spiritual achievement."[16]

The appeal of a philosophy of music education based upon strict aesthetic formalism is considerable. First of all, it identifies and provides methods to train students to attend to musical qualities and relationships the appreciation of which, as Hanslick rightly notes, can genuinely enhance the enjoyment of music.

It also gives teachers something to do in the classroom. Akin to the so-called "principles of design" in the visual arts pertaining to contrast, gradation, theme-and-variation, restraint, and so on,[17] strict aesthetic formalism gives music educators a subject matter, a standardized vocabulary, and a methodology. Hanslick's view that the "logic" of musical development and relationships is based upon "certain fundamental laws of nature governing both the human organism and the external manifestations of sound, . . . mainly the law of harmonic progression"[18] may sound quaint to some (though by no means all) modern ears, but we are a long way from giving up the notion that a central part of musical meaning comes from the understanding of musical materials, forms, techniques, and styles and their historical development. Students are given something which in principle they ought to be able to learn and something which in principle can and should be taught. The strict formalist understanding of aesthetic experience also supplies a set of standards to which one can appeal: these are the achievements in the canon of works enshrined by the history of music.

The strict formalist understanding of "the aesthetic" is also conveniently democratic. It provides a kind of training that at least in some rudimentary sense is accessible to all, even if it should turn out that in practice the appreciation of purely musical form is something reserved for the few. "Accessible" here means two things. First, the skills involved are thought to be fundamentally human, involving basic human faculties, so that in principle no one is excluded from such training. On Kant's view, for example, every rational being has at least the capacity to feel, under appropriate conditions, the harmony of the cognitive powers involved in the exercise of taste.[19] Of course, some people will be more sensitive to aesthetic qualities than others. The artistic "genius"—the paradigm of the exquisitely sensitive human being—is at one end of the spectrum, possessing the productive talent to create works of art; the clod is at the other. But presumably no human being is utterly without the capability of at least some elementary appreciation of aesthetic qualities. To be totally incapable of aesthetic satisfaction is, we think, to be not fully human. The idea that music is a universal language is a commonplace, even if there is no widespread agreement on what that language says.

Strict formalistically based music education is also accessible in the sense that this sort of appreciation of music does not require sophisticated or esoteric contextual knowledge about music. Aesthetic qualities are, in the first instance, qualities of *perception*. Hanslick stressed that musical contemplation is an "intellectual" enterprise, but by this he meant a discriminating appreciation of the sequence of tonal forms. Music is addressed to the faculty of imagination which is educable but not, in the case of music, concerned with concepts that may be adventitiously attached to musical structures. In particular, the aesthetic appreciation of music can have no truck with musical or cultural history when these are understood as the study of musical works in relation to the ideas and events of the times that produced them.[20] The appeal of this kind of approach to some students and some teachers is obvious.

The strict formalist understanding of "the aesthetic" has another important consequence for music education. It identifies at least two positive values that might provide a justification for music education. First, insofar as it draws attention to aesthetic qualities in music, music education might foster the cultivation of taste by enhancing the capacity to respond to aesthetic qualities such as beauty, harmony, order, and so on. Second, art may be a "free play" of the cognitive powers, as Kant thought, but it might be play with a purpose. Art educators, especially in the visual arts, frequently argue that aesthetic education seeks to refine and sharpen the sensitivity of our faculties. Kant himself argued not only that the judgment of taste is satisfying on its own account and that it "quickens" the cognitive powers (without actually providing knowledge), but that it provides a link between knowledge and desire, serving as a symbol of the morally good.[21] It might be claimed, then, that art, and music in particular, involves far more than a refinement of an interest in pleasing forms,[22] a point to which we shall return shortly.

But it is important to note at this point what the strict way of understanding "aesthetic experience" excludes when it is taken at face value. As we have seen, it is normally thought that "aesthetic" qualities or values are to be distinguished from moral, religious, personal, or other "practical" concerns. But notice that the strict formalist gloss of aesthetic experience imposes a further restriction. It deemphasizes or entirely excludes expressive or representational qualities in music and any other properties that might be thought to contribute to extramusical meaning in musical works. Of course it may be argued that musical analysis is a means to the enhanced enjoyment of music, and this is undoubtedly so. In that sense the view implicitly makes reference to an aesthetic pleasure we might derive from musical contemplation. But this approach to music does not concern itself directly with the expressiveness or evocation of the so-called "garden-variety emotions" such as love, pathos, fear, and so on, per se or of the expressiveness in music of other sorts of qualities which in fact play an important part in the compositional, performance, and listening practice of many music lovers. Nor does the approach take as its object the representation or symbolic reference to particular individuals, entities, events, or conditions, real or imagined, which, again, seem to be musically significant for some people some of the time.[23] These exclusions are commonly, if somewhat inchoately, noticed by those students who are resistant to the strict formalist focus. This resistance often melts away (at least temporarily) after it is branded as naive or philistine by their teachers. "Good taste" is, after all, defined precisely in terms of a "refined" ability to appreciate things from the aesthetic point of view.

But let me say a bit more on behalf of the Philistines. Few people really believe in the strict formalist version of the aesthetic hypothesis as I have been presenting it. Most of us think that musical meaning goes beyond the aesthetic qualities of sense perception as the strict formalist would describe them to include expressive meaning (and often representational meaning) in some sense or other. In fact, the formalism of the strict formalists allowed for a certain degree of expressive (if not representational) meaning. Bell not only described the appropriate aesthetic response to visual art as the "aesthetic emotion," but he went on to make several rather vague and quasi-religious pronouncements about what he took to be its real significance.[24] Hanslick seems to come close to Bell's description of aesthetic experience when he says that "the ultimate worth of the beautiful is always based on the immediate manifestness of feeling."[25] He also qualifies his otherwise relentless attack on expression theories of music in two ways:[26] he allows that which he calls "the basic ingredients of music" (tonalities, chords, timbres, etc.) can represent specific states of mind, and he argues that music can, by virtue of the dynamics of its tonal motion, reproduce the dynamics of feeling, an observation which looks backward to Schopenhauer's claim that music can express emotions "in the abstract . . . without the motives for them"[27] and forward to Susanne Langer's expressivist view that musical form can symbolically present the "logical pattern" of emotive life.[28] We must remember, too, that strict aesthetic formalism arose in the late nineteenth and early twentieth centuries as a polemical corrective to the excesses of Romantic emotionalism. As with all polemics, we should try to separate the rhetorical strategy from the substantive argument. Indeed, it may be the case, as Peter Kivy has argued, that we have no choice but to hear music expressively, in part because of a basic human tendency to anthropomorphize the world around us.[29]

Strict aesthetic formalism leaves us with another peculiarity that we cannot explain away. One aspect of musical practice in particular, which plays an important role in the music world but which seems to be attenuated to the point of oblivion on the strict formalist aesthetic point of view, is music criticism, understood here to include interpretative and evaluative judgments about music. The paradigm of critical discourse for Hanslick is description of the movement of tonal forms. Hanslick even provides an example of the type to show the skeptical that it can be done.[30] But much critical discourse about music—including Hanslick's own[31]—makes frequent use of nontechnical expressive and representational terms and allusions which the strict formalist regards as "extramusical." To be told by Hanslick that these references—to the extent that they are about the music at all—are properly to be regarded as merely figurative ways of describing without remainder purely tonal movement seems counterintuitive, to say the least. It seems, then, that we are left either with a technical discourse which eschews the sort of meaning that has long been seen to be at the center of musical experience or with a musically and intellectually dishonest gibberish. Kivy offers a wry description of the dilemma: "Music, after all, is not just for musicians and musical scholars, any more than painting is just for art historians, or poetry for poets. It seems to me both surprising and intolerable that while one can read with profit the great critics of the visual and literary arts without being a professor of English or the history of art, the musically untrained but humanistically educated seem to face a choice between descriptions of music too technical for them to understand, or decried as nonsense by the authorities their education has taught them to respect."[32]

We might therefore try to save the notion of aesthetic experience by construing it somewhat more liberally by saying that the appropriate mode of contemplation of works of art is indeed an aesthetic attitude of disinterested contemplation, but that this is an attitude that can be taken toward a broader range of subject matter. Schopenhauer, one of the most influential of the aesthetic attitude theorists, widened the notion of the aesthetic attitude in just this way. Let us call this the "enhanced" version of aesthetic formalism.[33] The enhanced version of aesthetic formalism forms the basis of the second main strategy I wish to consider for developing a philosophy of music and a philosophy of music education.

What is important to bear in mind here is that, on the general view of art we are now considering, only such expression or representation as is presented and appreciated aesthetically is considered to be appropriate to a work of art, properly so-called. A person's screaming in pain in a hospital would not likely be counted as a musical performance, in part because we would typically regard such an action as an immediate report of actual pain, whereas a song about pain or a song about a person screaming in pain in a hospital might be considered a musical work—if the experience or event were presented in such a way that it could be contemplated from an aesthetic point of view.

The enhanced version of aesthetic formalism has important consequences for aesthetic education. First, it allows under the artistic umbrella a wider range of expressive and representational meaning, an expansion which must be dealt with by art educators. It also enables us to say that what we are concerned with is not so much the subject matter of a work of art per se, but rather the formal working out of the content which can have expressive and representational aspects, a topic which is the subject of countless thousands of slide presentations in art appreciation and art history classes. What art offers us is a presentation of a world, and what we are interested in is the aesthetic quality of that presentation: its order, coherence, and degree of integration; its richness, intensity, and complexity; its unity in variety—in general its internal relatedness. The methods and content of art criticism are widened accordingly but in a way that retains an important place for at least the spirit of strict aesthetic formalism.

We are also able to say that art can provide us with a surrogate world—a kind of laboratory in which a world is created and experience examined. This last consequence is also extremely important for art education, for it is but a short step to the claim that this aspect of aesthetic experience has some further instrumental cognitive value which might be seen to justify the practice and discipline of art education, specifically, that art provides knowledge about the world.

This last step, it should be stressed, is not a necessary consequence of the enhanced version of aesthetic formalism. One might agree with Plato that there is no positive sense in which the created worlds of art provide knowledge about reality or, what is worse, that art provides only dangerous falsehoods. One could argue that to connect art to any such instrumental value is to violate the necessary condition of aesthetic experience that it be disinterested or nonpractical. Or one might argue that the referentialist implications of such a move call into question the very idea of a formalist theory, and one might plump for the formalism.

However, if it *could* be shown that the created worlds of art do provide knowledge about the world and that the cognitive function and enhanced aesthetic formalism were not incompatible, then the art educator would be in a position to say that aesthetic experience is valuable for the disinterested contemplative pleasure it provides *and* that aesthetic experience has an important extrinsic value which enhances the utility of art. Such arguments are in fact common among visual art educators. Some argue that visual art has cognitive value insofar as it is a means by which we refine our specifically visual perceptual abilities.[34] We had in fact already seen the same sort of argument made on behalf of strict aesthetic formalism. But the enhanced version of aesthetic formalism makes possible more ambitious claims. Rudolf Arnheim, for example, argues that explorations in the visual arts amount to a kind of "visual thinking" vital to the expressive and social development of individuals and which can be seen as easily in the works of Rembrandt as it can in the finger-painting of children.[35] Others extend the claim to the entire cultural landscape, including the fine arts, arts of design, architecture, and urban planning.[36] Art thus becomes a means of understanding oneself and one's world. The enhanced version of aesthetic formalism thus allows art educators to claim as their own an educational domain that is important and perhaps unique.

Now we have seen before that general claims made on behalf of the arts do not always apply straightforwardly to music. Nevertheless, the same sort of claim has become increasingly prevalent in justifications of music education. In 1970, for example, Bennett Reimer asked in his very influential book *A Philosophy of Music Education*, "Why should every person be given the opportunity to understand the nature of the art of music?" and he answered, "Because the art of music is a basic way of 'knowing' about reality."[37] In a recently revised version of that book, Reimer reaffirms the view:

> [M]usic and the other arts are a basic way that humans know themselves and their world; they are a basic mode of cognition. . . . The idea now gaining currency is that intelligence exists in several domains, such as the linguistic, the musical, the logical-mathematical, the spatial, the bodily kinesthetic, the interpersonal, and intrapersonal. . . . [Music education] must be conceived as all the great disciplines of the human mind are conceived—as a basic subject with its unique characteristics of cognition and intelligence, that must be offered to all children if they are not to be deprived of its values.[38]

Reimer then goes on to specify that the knowledge one gets from musical experience is knowledge about the domain of human feeling. This is a claim that was much favored by Romantic philosophers, musicians, and literati, though Reimer himself adopts an essentially Langerian expressivist view of musical meaning to support his case, emphasizing in particular Langer's claim that the knowledge of the life of feeling provided by music is uniquely "presentational" and nonconceptual (as opposed to the conceptual knowledge of discursive symbolic systems such as verbal language).

Since this view of music education is so widespread, it deserves a name. In keeping with our previous terminology, we might call this "the cognitivist version of the enhanced aesthetic formalist view of music education," but since that formulation is too ungainly to be worth preserving, let us refer to the position simply as the "aesthetic cognitivist" view of music education. My use of the term "cognitivist" here needs some qualification. One could quite plausibly argue that strict aesthetic formalism was already a cognitivist view: one has knowledge (by acquaintance) of formal properties and relations. Indeed, the same can be said of enhanced aesthetic formalism: we come to recognize expressive and representational qualities *of the music* (say). This is in fact a commonly accepted usage of the term in philosophical literature. I am reserving the term "cognitivism" here, however, to refer to the notion that musical properties and features provide *extramusical* knowledge.[39]

Here, then, we have the elements of the second basic strategy for developing a philosophy of music and a philosophy of music education which I wish to consider. To recap, the basic tenets of the aesthetic cognitivist view of music education are as follows. The view rests on an enhanced aesthetic formalist approach to music. That is to say, the aesthetic cognitivist view of music education roots musical practice in a particular (aesthetic) view of musical experience and the pleasures to be derived from the contemplation of musical form. Its account of musical experience is more inclusive than that of strict aesthetic formalism, allowing for the aesthetic apprehension of expressive, representational, and symbolic properties in music. The view is cognitive insofar as it asserts that one gains knowledge about reality in the apprehension of these properties. The most prevalent version of the view is *expressive* aesthetic cognitivism, according to which the salient musical properties are said to be expressive ones. Musical works, on this view, not only exhibit expressive properties, they provide insight about human expression and human subjectivity. The main purpose of music education on the expressivist version of the aesthetic cognitivist view is to make these insights accessible and to refine the understanding of feeling. Music education, then, is a means to the education of feeling.[40]

What are we to make of this view? Aesthetic cognitivism, even in its more exclusive expressive variant, certainly represents a more wide-ranging approach to the art of music than strict aesthetic formalism, and the view of music education which flows from it is accordingly broadened. Aesthetic cognitivism answers to an undeniably important aspect of musical experience. Most composers, performers, listeners, and critics believe that music has some sort of content which cannot be reduced to qualities of musical form as understood by the strict aesthetic formalist. It is probably also safe to say that many musicians and nonmusicians agree with the expressive aesthetic cognitivist that a main kind of musical meaning is expressive meaning.

The view is especially appealing to many musicians insofar as it promises to resolve what Langer had called the "paradox of feeling and form."[41] Our experience of works of art seems centrally and inescapably to involve, on the one hand, qualities of form which we suppose to inhere in the object, but at the same time qualities of feeling which we normally attribute only to sentient beings. The solution that musical works express emotion *through* their form by means of symbolic presentation seems to preserve proper respect for musical form while giving it a human face, so to speak.[42] (It is because of this respect for the importance and integrity of musical form that I have chosen to preserve the label "formalism" instead of calling the view a "referentialist" view, a term that would not be wholly inappropriate.)

The expressivist aesthetic cognitivist view of music education also provides a coherent account of the goals and methods of music education. It provides prescriptions for the sort of music to be taught (expressive music), for the sorts of experience to be encouraged and cultivated (the aesthetic apprehension of musical expressiveness through formal elements), and even the appropriate critical vocabulary to be used in the classroom (language that calls attention to expressive musical events).[43] These suggestions can be applied to both general music and professional programs of study and have implications for various aspects of musical practice, including composition, performance, listening, and criticism.[44]

Whether the claim for the cognitive value of music can be sustained in a way that would support the kind of justification of their profession that music educators might hope for, however, is a difficult problem. There are several questions to disentangle, and it would take us too far afield to deal with them adequately here. The main issues are these. (1) From a phenomenological standpoint, can the description of aesthetic experience, with its emphasis on sustained attention to the immediacy of musical form, be reconciled with the demand that in musical experience (whether we think about composing, performing, or listening to music) we simultaneously learn about "the inner life" and thereby educate feeling?[45] This is one of the issues connected with the general question posed earlier of whether this view is more properly construed as a formalist or a referentialist theory.[46] (2) What constraints must be placed on the sense of "knowledge" required by the theory? If this sort of knowledge is nonconceptual, as the theory insists, are verdicts of "true" and "false" appropriate? If they are and if, as the theory claims, this knowledge is ineffable, how would we support a claim that what we have learned is true (or false)? If notions of truth and falsehood are not appropriate in this context, what is left of the idea that we gain knowledge about reality? It should be remembered here that normally we think we can allow for the possibility of direct knowledge (by acquaintance) of perceptual qualities, feelings, and so on, and still retain the concepts of "true" and "false" because we do have recourse to intersubjective criteria according to which we can describe, verify, or disconfirm the veracity of another person's description of the world. The problem arises when we abandon the ideas of truth and falsity. If the required notion of knowledge becomes too severely constrained, the justificatory aspect of the expressivist cognitivist theory is eviscerated. (3) Supposing that we do gain knowledge from musical experience, how profound is that knowledge? According to Langer's theory, for example, what we are presented with are musical dynamic structures that have the same "logical pattern" as certain domains of felt subjective life. Reimer quotes with approval Langer's remark that music gives us knowledge, not of the nature of definite emotions, but rather of "how feelings go."[47] But what have we really learned about how emotions go from listening to or performing Beethoven's *Eroica* symphony or Ravel's *Bolero*, to take two highly expressive pieces of music?[48] Let us say that the logical pattern of *Bolero*, for example, is a musical "picture" of a gradual and steady increase in energy, tension, and conflict, leading to a final climactic eruption. No doubt the ineffability of experience renders the preceding discursive description hopelessly inadequate, but what insight is gained about human feeling through repeated listenings, except perhaps the recognition of a general form that might be shared by an indefinite number of experiences? It might be replied that musical experience leads to the improvement of sensibility, serving to enhance our understanding of feeling or perhaps actually refine the capacity to feel.[49] These claims are in fact quite common features of expression theories of art, but the epistemological and methodological problems involved in confirming these hypotheses are quite forbidding.

It might be noted that these questions are not necessarily dispensed with by the claim that musical experience involves a particular kind of musical "intelligence." Musical intelligence might easily be understood as a skill in creating or understanding musical form, not necessarily a claim about the acquisition of knowledge about "how feelings go." This is in fact just how Howard Gardner characterizes the situation in his widely cited treatment of "musical intelligence" in his book *Frames of Mind*.[50] It is true that Gardner offers the passing remark that music "can serve as a way of capturing feelings, knowledge about feelings, or knowledge about the forms of feeling, communicating them from the performer or the creator to the attentive listener."[51] But his approach to musical intelligence is basically as a species of "human problem-solving and product-fashioning skills,"[52] a matter of working with and understanding specifically "musical ideas," by which he means tones, tonal and harmonic relationships, rhythms, musical contours, larger musical patterns, and so on. This is the sense in which music becomes an object of cognition on Gardner's view. Gardner is in fact careful to say that while there may be "superficial links" between musical intelligence and other intellectual systems, "the core operations of music do not bear intimate connections to the core operations in others areas; and therefore, music deserves to be considered as an autonomous intellectual realm."[53] If this is so, the expressivist aesthetic cognitivist would still need separate arguments to show (1) that the exercise of musical intelligence results in the acquisition of knowledge (and knowledge about emotion in particular) and (2) that musical intelligence, among all the other intelligences, is a human faculty to be actively cultivated, given that life is short, budgets small, and the number of "intelligences" multiple. It may be that musical intelligence stands as a basic human potential, a potential that music education is uniquely equipped to develop. But allusions to a specifically musical intelligence do not in themselves amount to a justification of the cognitive value of music education.

Apart from the question of the viability of the cognitive claim about musical experience, we should also want to know how adequate enhanced aesthetic formalism (and, *a fortiori*, the more restrictive expressivist version of enhanced aesthetic formalism) is as a general view of musical practice. There are both philosophical and cultural sides to this question. It turns out, for instance, that though examples of "aesthetic" predicates and categories come easily to mind, the question of what makes a property an "aesthetic" property is not an easy one. One reason for this is that there may be no such thing as a pure "aesthetic" judgment about a work of art. Our habits of perception are hardly innocent. They are affected, if not in large part determined, by historically and culturally specific conventions and expectations. This is true even in the case of what we normally consider to be relatively pure and nonproblematic aesthetic categories. This point has been widely recognized in the case of the visual arts, with much discussion focussing on the work of Ernest Gombrich and Nelson Goodman.[54] But the point can also be made with regard to music. The sonata-allegro form, for example, is not a "natural" musical configuration which one perceives in a cultural vacuum but rather a culturally encoded musical form with a particular history. Learning to compose, perform, or appreciate fully music in which this form is an important compositional element is a matter of having learned to recognize, even if subconsciously, the features of that musical form which became a part of the vocabulary of a particular musical culture at a particular time.[55] That is to say, aesthetic judgments cannot in the end be separated from questions about their origins and the histories of the categories upon which they depend. This means that, however we understand the idea of "disinterested" contemplation, we must construe it to mean contemplation that is to a considerable degree culturally informed. As it turns out, that is a qualification, in fact, on which most enhanced aesthetic formalists and aesthetic cognitivists would insist. Our appreciation of musical works will be affected, not only by talent, but by preparation.

The aesthetic cognitivist, however, faces another problem which is less easily overcome. On the one hand the aesthetic cognitivist eschews "practical" functions which are taken to be extramusical. Yet the main justification of music education ends up being the eminently practical functions of the acquisition of knowledge and the improvement of sensibility. But if we allow this, why stop here? Music has functioned in a variety of ways in human society, as ethnomusicologists are fond of reminding us. Alan Merriam famously lists ten functions of music: aesthetic enjoyment, emotional expression, entertainment, communication, symbolic representation, physical response, enforcement of conformity to social norms, validation of social institutions and religious rituals, contribution to the continuity and stability of culture, and contribution to the integration of society.[56] Merriam is at pains to emphasize that this is not a list of mere "uses" to which music might be put, but rather a list of "functions" in the technical sense of a "specific effectiveness of any element whereby it fulfills the requirements of the situation, that is, answers a purpose objectively defined."[57] I shall not attempt the daunting task of establishing the didactic, iconic, moral, and social meaning or cultural significance generally of music, much less attempt a critique of the anthropological investigations from which Merriam's list is derived. But it does seem reasonable to hazard the view that though the aesthetic function has played a central role in the cultural heritage of the

West, the understanding of music as an art of the aesthetic (even in the enhanced sense) does not exhaust everything we would wish to say about the cultural importance or utility of musical practice in the West or in the culture of other people.[58]

Even with respect to Western culture, we would do well to remember that the idea of understanding art under the rubric of "the aesthetic," which seems so natural and commonsensical, is actually of relatively recent origin. This notion has its roots in antiquity but really gains currency only in the eighteenth century with the development of modern theories of taste under the influence of philosophers such as Shaftesbury, Kant, Hutcheson, and Hume; and in the nineteenth century when the investigation of a faculty or internal sense of taste gave way to theories of "aesthetic attitude" and the mode of attention thought to be appropriate to works of art, as well as in various Romantic reformulations of these notions. It is only in the eighteenth and nineteenth centuries that the modern "system" of the five major arts—painting, architecture, sculpture, music, and poetry—comes into being.[59] It is no coincidence that the rise of instrumental music as an art in the West is contemporaneous with these theoretical developments.

We are very much the children of this line of thinking, in that we are heirs to this historical tradition and the main theoretical tenets remain widespread among artists, critics, teachers, and the general public, while at the same time we rebel against the authority of our elders. It is commonly argued, for example, that the actions of certain twentieth-century visual artists have challenged, if not undermined, this approach to art. The so-called "ready-mades" of Marcel Duchamp are often taken to be prototypical of this moment of modern artistic practice. Duchamp's notorious *Fountain*, the urinal which he submitted to an art exhibition in Paris, has, to be sure, formal properties that might (arguably) serve as the object of aesthetic contemplation. But to concentrate on these properties (so it is argued) is to ignore the significance of Duchamp's act of submitting to the jury an object that was clearly not the product of the usual artistic intention to create something appropriate to the aesthetic response. It is this challenge to prevailing aesthetic theory that earns *Fountain* its status as a "work of art" (if it deserves it at all).

It is an intriguing question whether a parallel case exists in the music world. Perhaps we can identify something of a continuum here. The so-called "breakdown of tonality" witnessed in the last century and subsequent developments in polytonality and dodecaphony make use of new and challenging compositional principles, but these developments are radical only with respect to prevailing rules and conventions of the tonal compositional tradition of the West. Modern experiments with unconventional sound sources such as the prepared piano or electronically produced or manipulated sounds have introduced new timbres into musical practice and have greatly expanded our sense of what counts as a musical sound, as, more radically, has the employment of sounds from the entire pitch continuum (as opposed to the use of relatively distinct pitches and intervals in tonal music) as we hear in the music of Harry Partch, for example. More radical still are contemporary works (if we may use the term) that feature indeterminacy as a compositional or performance principle. This is not as revolutionary as one might at first suppose, since musical practice has always had its indeterminate features, whether we think of musical elements (such as dynamics and tone color) for which notation is seriously deficient or practices that allow for considerable discretion in performance (such as the provision for "optional" instrumentation or improvisation). Perhaps the work of composers such as Stockhausen and Cage is the closest we get to the innovations of Marcel Duchamp. Insofar as they have insisted upon the entire realm of the audible as the proper object of musical attention, these musicians have sought further to enlarge the conception of musical material and, perhaps more importantly, have pushed the notion of indeterminancy to the extent that the idea of music as the production and appreciation of composed thematic "works" is seriously weakened. I shall leave open the question of the extent to which these developments challenge other basic conceptions that go to make up the conceptual matrix of "the aesthetic" which we sketched earlier. I shall also leave open the question of whether these developments in the music world should be regarded as having the sort of revolutionary force often attributed to modern developments in the visual arts. But I shall not shirk from suggesting that a strong case can be made for so regarding them.

For all of these reasons, we might now turn to the third basic strategy for understanding music and music education, an approach that is based on what might be called a "praxial" view of art. The praxial view of art resists the suggestion that art can best be understood on the basis of some universal or absolute feature or set of features such as, to take the example closest to hand, aesthetic formalism, whether of the strict or enhanced variety. The attempt is made rather to understand art in terms of the variety of meaning and values evidenced in actual practice in particular cultures.

This does not mean abandoning the idea of aesthetic experience and its related notions as applied to works of art. That approach does, after all, answer to an undeniably important kind of cultural significance. But it does mean placing the aesthetic approach to works of art alongside other "non-aesthetic" functions that art can serve and has served. The approach is contextual but not relativistic, either in the sense in which it might be thought that no truths about artistic realities can be had or in the sense in which it is claimed that no standards of artistic value can be enunciated. The truths and values of art are seen rather to be rooted in the context of human practices, which, as Alasdair MacIntyre has pointed out, are forms of human activity that are defined (in part) precisely in terms of the specific skills, knowledge, and standards of evaluation appropriate to the practice.[60]

A praxial philosophy of music applies this theory of art to musical practice in particular. The basic aim of a praxial philosophy of music is to understand, from a philosophical point of view, just what music has meant to people, an endeavor that includes but is not limited to a consideration of the function of music in aesthetic contexts.[61]

One of the main consequences of taking such a reformulation of aesthetic theory seriously is that the face of music education as many of us know it would be changed in significant ways. The range of music investigated would be enlarged, though not in the way that one might at first expect. It would be wrong to think of the praxial approach as adding a consideration of, say, "popular," "folk," or "indigenous" music to the canon of "serious" music studied in the curriculum of aesthetic formalism, since it is wrong to think that aesthetic formalist approaches are appropriate only to "serious" music[62] (which in the minds of some means Western instrumental music roughly from 1650 to 1900). The aesthetic formalist approach will be rewarded by any kind of music capable of providing aesthetic experience of the requisite sort, and a praxial philosophy of music would continue to take this aspect of musical practice as an object of study (without the restriction that music be *expressively* aesthetic). The issue is not that of changing the emphasis from "high art" to "low art." The difference is more radical, since a praxial philosophy of music will consider the production, study, and appreciation of music in contexts where the aesthetic qualities of music are less central to the practice, whether we are thinking of music in the context of social rituals, the function of music as a heuristic device for scientific and philosophical theories,[63] the use of music for the communication or enforcement of social norms, the use of music in music therapy, and so on.

It is important to realize also that the aesthetic and nonaesthetic functions of music are often inextricably linked. We need only think of the development of religious music in the West to see that this is so. Or consider the case of jazz. The term "jazz" of course does refer to a certain musical style which can be characterized in more or less formalist terms: there are certain recurring compositional patterns, harmonies, and performance practices (such as the emphasis on improvisation), and so on. But jazz is also a musical practice that suffers from a kind of marginality in society, and there is in fact a dialectical relationship between the formal stylistic features of jazz and its cultural setting. It can be argued quite plausibly, for example, that vocal inflections, the emphasis on improvisation and antiphonal response, harmonic patterns that sound "dissonant" to some ears, the choice of nonstandard musical instruments, and the "studio talk" which identifies significant features of jazz style and performance are formal and technical aspects that are closely tied to the fact that jazz has come to be seen as an assertion or badge of membership and pride in a Black community which has been seriously marginalized itself. White jazz players, too, understand this marginality and the musical practices that reflect it. To be a jazz musician, White or Black, is almost by definition to engage in deviant behavior. This situation is caught in a particularly poignant way in Bernard Tavernier's film *'Round Midnight*, whose extraordinary evocation of a musical life of the jazz musician Dale Turner ranges over technical matters such as the communication between musicians on the stand (Turner's use of hand signals during performances, for instance, to tell soloists to "trade fours"), the care and attention to detail that Turner lavishes on his improvisations (which we see in the long sequences in which entire musical compositions are superbly played and sensitively filmed), to the squalor of Turner's surroundings and his outsider status as an American in Paris (caught beautifully in a shot of a bidet loaded with dirty dishes), Turner's total devotion to his night music, and the stark contrast between the freedom that Turner's music holds for him and some of his listeners and the manipulation and constraint placed on Turner's life by those who live off that music. A praxial philosophy of music education would take this dialectic between the musical and the moral as a serious object of study.[64]

Also, since the goal of music education is taken to be the understanding of musical practice in a generous sense, the general effect of instituting a program based on a praxial view of music would be a less compartmentalized approach to music education, both in general music and in professional programs. In general music appreciation classes, for example (which for many students are the only formalized study of music at the university level), in addition to an exposure to the materials and forms of music, the inculcation of good listening habits fostered by practice in the contemplation of the musical work regarded as a *fait accompli*, and an introduction to the cultural context of musical works, we would find a greater emphasis on the direct aquaintance with the production of musical works, or if that sounds overly ambitious, at least a little bit of time at the keyboard. The term "art" does, after all, have an important ambiguity: it refers both to a set of objects (as when we speak of "works of art") as well as to a correlative range of human activity (as when we speak of painting, sculpting, writing, music making, and so on, as "arts"). One may or may not agree with Kristeller's suggestion that one reason modern aesthetics has largely analyzed works of art from the point of view of the spectator or listener rather than of the producing artist is that the origin of modern aesthetics is in amateur criticism in the eighteenth century.[65] But on the praxial view, a music education program which aims to educate students about musical practice in its fullest sense must take into account, not only the history and kind of appreciation appropriate to the musical work of art, but also the nature and significance of the skills and productive human activity that bring musical works into being, if for no other reason than the fact that the results of human action cannot be adequately understood apart form the motives, intentions, and productive considerations of the agents who bring them into being.

It is certainly true that the kinds of education that are possible vary not only with the time of life, but with the specific backgrounds and environments of individual students. One must therefore be realistic about the sequence in which different skills and concepts are introduced into a general curriculum. But this is only to say that one must strive to achieve a progressive introduction to artistic skills, concepts, theories, and cultural studies in the schools and at the university level, and there do exist programs that incorporate into the general education program a broadly based and contextually informed notion of artistic practice, one that combines an interest in aesthetic appreciation with an interest in the productive aspects of artistic practice and the cultural (including extra-aesthetic) contexts in which the arts are created, deployed, and enjoyed.[66]

The praxial approach to music education would also have implications for the education of music professionals. We would find in composition and performance programs, for example, a greater attention to the social, historical, and cultural conditions and forces in which practices of musical production arise and have meaning. Professional schools of music at the university level are notorious for failing to allot sufficient time to their students for general cultural studies. It is not uncommon to find undergraduate programs of study in composition and performance allowing less than 10 percent of a student's total course time to cultural studies outside the field of music.[67]

There are, however, two sorts of difficulties that a praxial view of music and of music education must face. The first is the question of the adequacy of the praxial view of art as a philosophy of art, a question that goes to the heart of how one conceives of the philosophy of art. For it will be seen that the implicit notion of "art" (and in the present case, "music") has been greatly extended beyond its customary understanding. Indeed, the praxial view calls into question our understanding of philosophy itself, for it represents not only a shift away from philosophy conceived as a foundational discipline, but perhaps even a move from philosophy to anthropology, or so its critics might argue. These are important and difficult questions which I shall not take up here, except to indicate in the broadest of terms the likely reply that a philosophical analysis of a human activity must begin with the complexities of the activity as it practiced and that in the case of specifically artistic practice those complexities embrace more than merely formal, technical, or, indeed, aesthetic concerns.

The second major set of questions concerns the appropriateness of such a view for the philosophy of art education and, in the present context, the philosophy of music education in particular. The question here is whether art education (and music education in particular) should make space for the kind of inquiry suggested above, especially the concern for moral, psychological, sociological, and political questions in professional school curricula. This question may be advanced on philosophical grounds. But it may also be based on practical considerations, since programs of professional training already place heavy demands on students' time simply for the development of the requisite technical skills. Indeed, it is quite likely that the practical argument is the one that will be heard most often.

Here I think at least two responses are possible. First, one can argue that any program of education that aspires to introduce students to something of the complexity of the subject must strive to address the subject in all its intricacy. The praxial understanding of what "the subject" is brings us back to the first set of questions. But, beyond that, one can insist that questions about art education be placed within a larger canvas: the education of the human being generally. If one wishes to take responsibility for the education of one's students in the fullest sense, a concentration on the purely aesthetic will not suffice. Art education, both in the context of general education and in the professional school, must, it will be argued, concern itself not only with the skills that will enable one to become a competent artist or critic, but, more profoundly, with the enlargement of the mind and the development of character. For, as Aristotle argues, "To be always seeking after the useful does not become free and exalted souls."[68] And that is the real reason why, in the end, we shall have to tie the concept of aesthetic education to the concept of education through art. I will not try to disguise the normative character of these last remarks. But that, it seems to me, is the sort of insight one should expect from a philosophy of music education.

NOTES

1. Aristotle, *Politics*, 1339a, trans. Benjamin Jowett, in *The Basic Works of Aristotle*, ed. Richard McKeon (New York: Random House, 1941), p. 1309.
2. Attributed to Virginia Woolf, in Nelson Goodman, *Languages of Art* (Indianapolis: Bobbs-Merrill, 1968), p. 3.
3. Plato, *The Republic*, X, 599-601, trans. Benjamin Jowett (New York: Modern Library, 1941), pp. 367-68.
4. Aristotle, *Poetics*, 1451a-1451b, trans. Ingram Bywater, in *The Basic Works of Aristotle*, pp. 1463-64.
5. I shall be concerned in this article for the most part with instrumental music and problems relating to education in that context. I believe that much of what is said in the article has application to music that is not purely instrumental (song, music drama, music video, and so on), but these arts introduce complexities that require a more extended treatment than is possible here.
6. The justification of music education as a form of recreation can be traced back to Plato and Aristotle, though in America the more direct influence is Sir Thomas

Elyot's *The Boke Named the Governour* (1531), which argued that the appropriate education of future rulers would include time for pleasant recreation, such as playing a musical instrument. Elyot's book set the tone for educational patterns in colonial New England. Educational reformers in the nineteenth century regularly advocated the inclusion of music in the curriculum, but primarily as means of maintaining discipline.

7. I am here striving toward a specifically musical understanding of the notion of an "art world" which ranges over the theoretically and art-historically based understanding of this term advanced by Arthur Danto ("The Artworld," *Journal of Philosophy* 61, no. 3 [1964]: 571-84) and the social-institutional understanding of the term advanced by George Dickie (*Art and the Aesthetic—An Institutional Analysis* [Ithaca, N.Y.: Cornell University Press, 1974]). I do not mean to imply agreement with the respective theories in which these concepts are situated.

8. I am therefore inclined to disagree with Bennett Reimer's methodological suggestion that in developing a philosophy of music education, "the field of aesthetics must be approached in a highly selective way. It would be beside the point (and quite impossible) to investigate indiscriminately the writings of every aesthetician in history . . . . Instead, the search must start with an acquaintance with the field of music education; its problems, its needs, its history, its present status . . . . Only those portions of aesthetics useful for this purpose need be used. Aesthetics must never be the master of music education—it must be its servant." (*A Philosophy of Music Education*, 2d ed. [Englewood Cliffs, N.J.: Prentice-Hall, 1989], p. 15). Of course, no one wishes to be accused of indiscriminacy, but how can one know in advance of investigation which areas and developments in aesthetics will be beneficial and which will not? Some areas may turn out to be heuristically valuable. Nor can music education rest content with an examination of its history or its present status, unless these are linked to the dynamics and transformations of actual musical practice.

9. Cf. Reimer: "If music education in the present era could be characterized by a single, overriding purpose, one would have to say this field is trying to become 'aesthetic education'" (p. 2). See also Michael Mark, "The Evolution of Music Education Philosophy from Utilitarian to Aesthetic," *Journal of Research in Music Education*, 30, no. 1 (Spring 1982: 15-21).

10. For a thorough examination of these and related concepts, see Francis Sparshott, *The Theory of the Arts* (Princeton, N.J.: Princeton University Press, 1982), esp. section 1, "Arts," pp. 23-280.

11. Immanuel Kant, *Critique of Judgment*, trans. J. H. Bernard (New York, Hafner, 1951), §§1-15.

12. Clive Bell, *Art* (London: Chatto and Windus, 1914), chap. 1, "The Aesthetic Hypothesis," pp. 22-23.

13. Eduard Hanslick, *On the Musically Beautiful*, trans. Geoffrey Payzant (Indianapolis: Hackett, 1986). In the musical literature, the progenitors are Schenker, Salzer, Adorno, and Schoenberg.

14. Hanslick, *On the Musically Beautiful*, pp. 31-2.

15. Ibid., p. 48.

16. Ibid., p. 64.

17. See Stephen Pepper, *Principles of Art Appreciation* (New York: Harcourt, Brace & World, 1949).

18. Hanslick, *On the Musically Beautiful*, pp. 30-31.

19. Kant, *Critique*, §§18-22.

20. Hanslick, *On the Musically Beautiful*, p. 38.

21. Kant, *Critique*, §49 and §59. I am here speaking of Kant's view about the judgment of taste in general. His assessment of music in particular was at best mixed. Music, on Kant's view, is neither an art of speech (such as poetry) nor a formative art (such as painting), but rather an art of the play of sensations. Kant concludes that if "we estimate the worth of the fine arts by the culture they supply to the mind and take as a standard the expansion of the faculties which

must concur in the judgment for cognition, music will have the lowest place among them (as it has perhaps the highest among those arts which are valued for their pleasantness)." Kant further observes that whereas one can avert one's eyes from a disturbing work of visual art, one cannot avert one's ears from unpleasant music. Music in that regard can be compared to "a smell which diffuses itself widely" (Kant, *Critique*, §53, p. 174). For an argument that Kant's conceptions of genius and taste should have led him to conclude that music has the highest position among the arts, see Herbert Schueller, "Immanuel Kant and the Aesthetics of Music," *Journal of Aesthetics and Art Criticism* 14, no. 2 (1955): 218-47.

22. Cf. Halbert Britan, *The Philosophy of Music* (New York: Longmans, Green, 1911): "To pass judgment upon a composition as to its originality or its strength demands the highest degree of exact discrimination, of comparison, and of mental synthesis. The appreciation of gracefulness betokens a sensitiveness to fine distinctions of form and meaning which may prove most beneficial, not only in art, but in mental processes both intellectual and moral" (pp. 239-40).

23. For a critique of the notion of "structural listening" as a goal of music education, see also Rose Rosengard Subotnik, "The Challenge of Contemporary Music," in *What is Music?: An Introduction to the Philosophy of Music*, ed. Philip Alperson (New York: Haven Publications, 1987), pp. 375-81.

24. Bell, *Art*, chap. 3, "The Metaphysical Hypothesis."

25. Hanslick, *On the Musically Beautiful*, p. xxii.

26. Ibid., pp. 11-12.

27. Arthur Schopenhauer, *The World as Will and Representation*, vol. 1, trans. E. F. J. Payne (New York: Dover Publications, 1969), p. 261.

28. Susanne Langer, *Feeling and Form* (New York: Charles Scribner's Sons, 1953).

29. Peter Kivy, *Sound Sentiment* (Philadelphia: Temple University Press, 1989). This is a revised and expanded version of Kivy's *The Corded Shell* (Princeton, N.J.: Princeton University Press, 1980). See especially chap. 7, "The 'Physiognomy' Defended."

30. "Let us listen, for example, to Beethoven's 'Prometheus' overture. What the attentive ear of the music lover hears, in continuous sequence, is something like the following: The tones of the first bar, following a descent of a fourth, sprinkle quickly and softly upward, repeating exactly in the second. The third and fourth bars carry the same upward motion further. The drops propelled upward by the fountain come rippling down so they may in the next four bars carry out the same figure and the same configuration. So there takes shape before the mind's ear of the listener a melodic symmetry between the first and second bars, then between these and the next two, and finally between the first four bars as a single grand arch and the corresponding arch of the following four bars." (Hanslick, *On the Musically Beautiful*, p. 12.)

31. The "fountain?" A "grand arch?"

32. Kivy, *Sound Sentiment*, pp. 8-9.

33. It can be argued that Kant's discussion of "dependent" (as opposed to "free") beauty places him in this camp as well. See Kant, *Critique*, §16.

34. "The central purpose of art instruction is to assist students in achieving reasonably full aesthetic experiences with works of art and other visual phenomena which are capable of eliciting such experience. Aesthetic experience is defined as an open and active confrontation with an art object or event during which the individual performs a visual analysis of the multitude of qualities and aspects present in the situation. He attends to sensory qualities and their formal composition, media, technique, mood and feeling, literal and symbolic meanings, and also to the relationship of these aspects to his own feelings toward the situation. This active exploring and relating of aspects ends with a fusing of these aspects and with a determination of total character and significant meaning of the object or experience. The experience may also include an evaluation of aesthetic merit based on whether or not the aspects form a firmly integrated

whole, whether the object or event has a uniquely vivid quality about it, whether the experience with the object or event leads to pleasureful feelings, or whether the object or event is well-crafted, represents the time in which it was done, and seems to get at essences. . . . Art is the only subject commonly taught in the schools which has concern for developing the visual ability to experience aesthetically." Brent R. Wilson, "Evaluation of Learning in Art Education," in *Handbook of Formative and Summative Evaluation of Student Learning*, ed. B. Bloom, J. T. Hastings, and G. F. Madaus (New York: McGraw-Hill, 1971), pp. 510-11.

35. Rudolph Arnheim, *Visual Thinking* (Berkeley: University of California Press, 1969).

36. See, for example, Richard M. Carp, "The Role of the Arts in the Humanities and Liberal Arts Classroom," *Art & Academe* 2, no. 1 (1989): 69-84.

37. Bennett Reimer, *A Philosophy of Music Education*, 1st ed. (Englewood Cliffs, N.J.: Prentice-Hall, 1989), p. 9.

38. Reimer, *A Philosophy*, 2d ed., pp. 11-12.

39. This is why I shall not use Reimer's own label of choice, "absolute expressionism." The term "absolute" disguises the genuinely referential aspect of the theory. I shall proceed on the supposition, however, that the referentialism of the theory can be reconciled with enhanced aesthetic formalism as I have described it.

40. Cf. Reimer: "Every art 'reveals the nature of feelings' in its own, particular way, and the major function of every work of art is to do precisely that. . . . Every good work of art . . . is good because its artistic qualities succeed in capturing a sense of human feeling. . . . The major function of education in the arts is to help people gain access to the experiences of feeling contained in the artistic qualities of things. Education in the arts, then, can be regarded as the education of feeling. . . . The deepest value of music education is the same as the deepest value of all the arts in education: the enrichment of the quality of people's lives through enriching their experiences of human feeling" (pp. 50-53).

41. Langer, *Feeling and Form*, chap. 2.

42. Cf. Langer: "The function of music is not stimulation of feeling, but expression of it; and furthermore, not the symptomatic expression of feelings that beset the composer but a symbolic expression of the forms of sentience as he understands them. It bespeaks his imagination of feelings rather than his own emotional state, and expresses what he or she *knows* about the so-called 'inner life'" (p. 28); and Reimer: "What is the value of such experience? First, if any experience in human life can be valued intrinsically . . . then surely artistic experience is of this sort. . . . But in another sense we can reflect about the value of artistic experiencing as a major way to fulfill our capacities for richness and depth in our lives. . . . Because experiences of art yield insights into human subjectivity the arts may be conceived as a means of self-understanding, a way by which our sense of our human nature can be explored and clarified and grasped" (pp. 52-53).

43. Reimer, *A Philosophy*, pp. 53-54.

44. See ibid., chaps. 4 and 6-9.

45. Cf. ibid., "We can, by examining the melody (etc.), *improve the feeling itself by improving the melody*" (p. 35, italics original).

46. Langer is careful to distance herself from the notion of a rare and pristine disinterested aesthetic attitude (Langer, *Feeling and Form*, pp. 37ff), but the phenomenological question remains.

47. Reimer, *A Philosophy*, p. 63.

48. The problem for Langer is even more complex, given her claim that what music presents is "virtual time," a symbolic presentation of "psychological time." See Philip Alperson, "'Musical Time' and Music as an 'Art of Time,'" *Journal of Aesthetics and Art Criticism* 38, no. 4 (Summer 1980): 407-17.

49. Cf. Reimer, *A Philosophy*: "The act of improving the objectification of the feeling—the melody—actively improves the feeling we now have. . . . Experiencing

the clarified feelings another has composed gives us clarified subjectivity to share. . . . Experiencing and creating art *refine* feeling and *sensitize* feeling in the same ways" (pp. 35-37).

50. Howard Gardner, *Frames of Mind* (New York: Basic Books, 1985).
51. Ibid., p. 124.
52. Ibid., p. xii.
53. Ibid., p. 126.
54. See Ernst Gombrich, *Art and Illusion*, 2d ed. rev. (Princeton, N.J.: Princeton University Press, 1961), and Goodman, *Languages of Art.*
55. The example comes from Kendall Walton. See his "Categories of Art," *The Philosophical Review* 79, no. 3 (1970): 334-67.
56. Alan P. Merriam, *The Anthropology of Music* (Evanston, Ill.: Northwestern University Press, 1964), chap. 11.
57. Ibid., p. 218. Merriam is here following a formulation of the social anthropologist S. F. Nadel.
58. I therefore take issue with Reimer (*A Philosophy*) when he says, "[W]hile music has many important nonmusical or nonartistic functions, its musical or artistic nature is its unique and precious gift to all humans. . . . [W]hen music itself, with its universal appeal to the human mind and heart, is bypassed or weakened in favor of nonmusical emphases that submerge it, we have betrayed the art we exist to share. It is that simple" (p. xii).
59. See P. O. Kristeller, "The Modern System of the Arts," *Journal of the History of Ideas* 12, no. 4 (1951): 496-527, and 13, no. 1 (1952): 17-46; and Jerome Stolnitz, "Of the Origins of 'Aesthetic Disinterestedness,'" *Journal of Aesthetic and Art Criticism* 20, no. 2 (1961): 131-43.
60. "By a 'practice' I am going to mean any coherent and complex form of socially established cooperative human activity through which goods internal to that form of activity are realised in the course of trying to achieve those standards of excellence which are appropriate to, and partially definitive of, that form of activity, with the result that human powers to achieve excellence, and human conceptions of the ends and goods involved are systematically extended." Alasdair MacIntyre, *After Virtue* (Notre Dame, Ind.: University of Notre Dame Press, 1981), p. 175.
61. A praxial philosophy of music is laid out programmatically by Francis Sparshott in "Aesthetics of Music: Limits and Grounds," and Nicholas Wolterstorff in "The Work of Making a Work of Music," both in Alperson, *What Is Music?* The book also contains praxial treatments of more specific topics, including musical meaning, composition, performance, and the evaluation of music.
62. Cf. Reimer on "Aesthetic Experience and Elitism," *A Philosophy*, pp. 110-13.
63. I have discussed this possibility in "Music as Philosophy" in Alperson, *What Is Music?*
64. For a more extended analysis of philosophical issues pertaining to jazz education, see my "Aristotle on Jazz: Philosophical Reflections on Jazz and Jazz Education," *Council for Research in Music Education Bulletin*, no. 95 (Winter 1988): 39-60.
65. Kristeller, "Modern Systems" (1952), p. 44.
66. The curriculum at Alverno College, for example, identifies "aesthetic responsiveness" as one of eight abilities in which students must satisfy minimum standards of achievement in general education. It identifies several "increasingly complex" levels of aesthetic responsiveness: first, the ability to respond to formal and expressive elements of individual works of art, developing the vocabulary appropriate to such a response, and engaging in the creative processes of certain art forms by composing simple tunes, drawing, in linear perspective, acting out anecdotal situations to come to appreciate the intricacies of plot, and so on; second, the ability to appreciate stylistic interrelations among works of art within a particular art form and among art forms themselves; third, the ability to relate artistic works to the historical, philosophical, theological, and

cultural contexts from which they emerge; fourth, the ability to make and defend judgments about the quality of selected artistic processes and products; fifth, the ability to choose and discuss artistic works that reflect a personal vision of what it means to be human; and sixth, the ability to demonstrate the impact of the arts on one's own life to that point and to project their role in one's future. All students are required to satisfy minimum standards in each of the first four levels. Students who choose one of the arts as a major or area of specialization must satisfy standards at the fifth and sixth levels. See Timothy Riordan and Judith Stanley, "Assessing for Hard-to-Asses Abilities" (Paper read at the AAHE Assessment Forum, Third National Conference on Assessment, 8 June 1988, Alverno College, Milwaukee, Wisconsin).

67.   I take my own university's programs to be representative. The percentage of credit hours allotted for cultural studies outside the School of Music for bac-calaureate degrees are as follows: Instrumental, Keyboard or Voice Performance (9 percent), Theory or Composition (9 percent), Music History (7 percent), and Music Education (7 percent, counting one sociology course).

68.   Aristotle, *Politics*, *The Basic Works of Aristotle*, 1338b, p. 1308.

I would like to thank Edward Berman, Peter Kivy, and John Kratus for their very helpful comments and suggestions. I am especially indebted to Acton Ostling, Jr., for his astute comments and criticisms of this article. His example of a musical life has meant much to me over the years.

Language, Metaphor, and Analogy in the Music Education Research Process

HILDEGARD C. FROEHLICH and GARY CATTLEY

This article is guided by the belief that the purpose of research lies in the discovery of laws by which the workings of the universe may be explained. We describe seemingly disjoint events and phenomena, classify them according to observed recurrences of same events, and then organize them into patterns of causal relationships. From those patterns we formulate theories as to why the events and phenomena may have come about in the first place. We assume our theories to be valid when they allow for the prediction of same or similar phenomena in the future. As the description provides the evidence needed to test the theory, the latter is only as good as the descriptors underlying that theory are meaningful.[1]

The relationship between evidence and theory formation becomes of particular importance when—as is the case in music education—the nonverbal evidence, musical behavior, requires verbal description. By naming an observed phenomenon, researchers in music education select from their repertoire of words a label that appears to give meaning to the observed phenomenon. We "handle" the evidence in a way most appropriate to our own understanding of the phenomenon; in a sense, we manipulate that which we do not know.

To find labels for describing musical behavior and learning, music psychologists and educators look for, or sometimes even invent, terms by which to make sense of what they observe about the relationship between music and the learner.[2] Some of the terms that have become common in our field are learning and teaching style; auditory images; musical thought and musical processing; musical style and taste; conservation, musical growth, learning sequence, and stages of musical learning. We categorize sounds ac-

Hildegard C. Froehlich is a Professor of Music Education at the University of North Texas. She is coauthor of *Research in Music Education: An Introduction to Systematic Inquiry*, has published recent articles in *Internatonal Music Education* and the *Music Educators Journal*, and has contributed essays to *What Works: Instructional Strategies for Music Education* and the *Handbook for Research on Music Teaching*.
Gary Cattley is a Ph.D. candidate in Music Education at the University of North Texas.

cording to such terms as pitch, rhythm, harmony, texture, form, and tone color and classify their respective characteristics as musical concepts and elements. We derive meaning from such concepts and elements by exploring the learner's reaction to them. If we can show a relationship between specific perceptual tasks and the concepts/elements established by us, the terms describe "reality."

Many scholars, among them linguists, semioticians, philosophers, and scientists, have suggested that language not only facilitates but also limits that which it communicates.[3] Consequently, verbal choices impact the validity of the theory by which we hope to predict nonverbal behavior. The proficient music education researcher would be that person who is sensitive to the impact verbal choices exert on what we believe to know about the learning and teaching processes in music. One of the many responsibilities of a philosopher in music education should be to lay the groundwork for that sensitivity.

The Problem

To state that one phenomenon resembles another one without it being the same brings us into the realm of metaphor and analogy as basic linguistic research tools. For example, when we speak of music *processing* we refer to mechanical images common in the world of technology. Most recently, the term has been primarily associated with the world of the computer. We thus imply a relationship between the reality of the computer (invented by us, therefore understood by us) and the brain (that which we seek to understand). Although the concepts invented by us for developing the computer seem to serve us well, they may not be valid when explaining how children and adults respond to musical sound.[4]

There are many writers in the areas of metascience and philosophy of science who seek to define and delineate the meanings and roles of analogy, metaphor, model, and theory in any pursuit of knowledge.[5] Judging from the extant body of literature, many writers use the terms analogy and metaphor interchangeably. Other writers have shown a similarly close connection between analogy and model.[6] Despite such disagreements, however, the authors seem to concur that the concepts are essential for understanding the scientific process and the place of theory formation in it.

Few scholars in music education have carried out such theoretical explorations, although they have articulated the need for theory development in music education and have described approaches toward the testing of specific theories about music perception and learning. Little writing exists, however, on the relationship between theory development and language. We need a research agenda that (1) describes what images, analogies, and metaphors researchers in music have employed to explain musical be-havior; (2) clarifies the relationship between analogies, metaphors, and models germane to musical learning; and (3) determines what models have been most useful for the purpose of theory development and testing in our field. We hope to contribute to such an agenda by exploring whether and how researchers have used analogy and metaphor as descriptors of percep-tual learning in music.

Defining Analogy and Metaphor

Both analogy and metaphor require the juxtapositioning of two objects (or concepts) to each other. The difference between the terms lies in the relationship we establish between the two objects/concepts. An analogy is generally believed to imply that two objects should correspond to each other in function, position, or properties. Apples and pears, for example, are analogous to each other since they are both fruits, grow on a tree, have a skin, and are eatable. A metaphor is commonly defined as a figure of speech in which the original meaning of a term is transferred to another object in order to provide a new context for that object. Take, for example, the term *evening of life*. The first object, *evening*, ordinarily not connected to the second, *life*, gives the latter added descriptive power.[7]

Theorists in the sciences debate primarily whether the distinction be-tween analogy and metaphor as described above is sufficient when em-ployed for the purpose of theory development. The greatest disagreement among various writers appears to exist between those who maintain, as W. H. Leatherdale does, that analogies should always be empirically verifiable and those who stress that analogies are, in A. I. Miller's terms, perceptual metaphors [sic!], i.e., "the means by which people imagine processes in the same way as if they were actually occurring."[8]

Analogy. P. A. Angeles reminds us that what once was a mathematical term only, signifying "a common or reciprocal relationship between two things or a similarity of two proportions," has later become a linguistic "comparison of similarities of concepts or things."[9] M. B. Hesse points to several types of analogues simply because the number and type of alike properties among the objects differ.[10] She suggests the use of analogy is most productive when one does not have *a priori* knowledge of the struc-ture of that which one wishes to explain.[11] This lack of knowledge, however, also makes it possible to be in error when choosing a particular analogy.[12] One such error may occur because of possible incongruencies be-tween the two compared structures. Incorrect assumptions about the struc-ture from which we draw the analogies (source domain) may cause misconceptions about the structure we wish to describe (topic domain). To illustrate: a part of the concrete operational stage of Piagetian cognitive development theory is that of reversibility. As many writers have pointed out, when applied to music learning, reversibility either takes on a different meaning or has no meaning at all.[13]

Erroneous assumptions may also be drawn when a specific attribute of the source has no equivalent representation in the topic domain but, due to its presence in the source domain, is retained as a descriptor. Errors may further occur as a result of the way we weight certain attributes in the source domain and give them the same importance when describing the topic domain. Similar surface features may exist in source and topic domains, but the features may have different causes.[14] For example, when we describe the learning-teaching process according to a model taken from information theory and speak of the teacher as the sender/operator and the learner as the receiver, the source domain is the input-output model common to cybernetics. Extending these characteristics to describe operations of individuals in regard to psychological responses means to look only at surface features. The reality of communication as an interactive and causal relationship is being ignored.

Leatherdale goes one step further than Hesse and distinguishes between three types of analogues: (1) analogy as "resemblance of relations," the most commonly found and important analogy for science; (2) analogy as an often intuitive approach toward finding resemblances between groups of properties; and (3) analogy as "resemblance in an ensemble of qualities, or of properties or attributes (not relations) given in immediate sense experience." This third group divides into manifest and imported analogy.[15]

Using manifest analogies means to classify an experience according to readily perceived properties, such as "colours, tastes, sounds, and tactile sensations." Based upon properties and relations readily discernible from sense experiences, manifest analogies not only would be empirically verifiable but also would lead to different explanations, or models, than would imported analogies. The latter are analogies "based upon abstract or esoteric relations."[16]

Metaphor. Accepting the commonly used definition of metaphor as 'figure of speech,' Angeles defines the term as a "word (phrase, statement) that denotes one thing [and] is applied (transferred) to another thing to suggest a likeness between them." He suggests to judge the usefulness or quality of a metaphor by such criteria as the number of similarities (resemblances, correspondences) that exist between the things compared and the number of similarities brought to awareness which were previously unnoticed.[17]

Leatherdale, and with him several other writers in the field, criticizes this definition and similar ones mostly found in the literary arts. He proposes to differentiate between simile and metaphor, and he warns of the commonly found term 'figure of speech' as a definiens for metaphor. To become effective as a figure of speech, a simile must have a necessary element of novelty. A new context or perspective is thus required to make a simile "more actual" or real to the reader or listener than it was in its original context.[18]

The place where, according to Leatherdale, simile as figure of speech and metaphor touch each other lies in their context-dependent nature, each of them requiring novel juxtapositions or comparisons. Metaphor, however, mandates interpretation of meaning. For example, to say that a child conserves rhythm requires knowledge of the term conservation in the original Piagetian theory as well as in its application to music research. Therefore, the reference to conservation could be interpreted differently dependent upon which kind of context knowledge is being applied to the reference. The statement could signify that the child has reached a certain level of musical learning. The statement also could be a cue for the act of the child having properly manipulated a given rhythm pattern according to a given task. The statement could conjure up a particular image of the child as an accomplished music learner; serve as a trigger point for the reader to make inferences about the difficulty of the learning task at hand; or invite a comparison to other experiences or learning situations we have encountered.[19]

Four important functional relations of metaphor to context must be considered. (1) Not only metaphor requires context; all words, when strung together, do. The way different audiences interpret the meaning of the context in which the words are imbedded determines the difference between metaphorical and literal meaning. In the example given above, to explain rhythmic learning by verbal terms foreign to the context of music performance makes it metaphorical when members of different target groups hearing the statement may bring to it different expectations and, thus, would give the statement different contextual meaning.

(2) There is a contextual tension between the topic domain (in our example, what the child does musically) and the source domain (Piagetian theory based upon observations of mathematical-spatial manipulations).[20] This tension can be resolved only if the implications of the metaphor are fully understood. In music, many researchers interested in the application of the Piagetian concept of conservation to music learning concern themselves with this "tension." They ask whether it is valid to apply terms derived from observations in one subject matter area to the description of another. In terms of theory development, they ask whether conservation is an appropriate metaphor for explaining musical learning.[21]

(3) To resolve the tension between metaphor and context requires full awareness of the difference between words with literal and metaphorical meaning. At times, the words make sense only if they remain metaphorical; they turn nonsensical if they are taken literally. It thus becomes nonsensical to say that a child is too young to conserve a musical concept or pattern.

Conservation is not an act, that is, a concrete behavior; rather, it is a name invented by us for the verbal description of a mental process about which we know merely that it takes place over a certain length of time.

(4) A metaphor can be understood only within a joint cultural community or reference group. This means the persons using the metaphor and the audience to whom the metaphor is directed must share the same experiences, language, and contextual meaning implied by the metaphor.[22] Consequently, the images and pictures used in metaphorical language must be familiar to those to whom the explanations are directed.

Because of the variety of meanings one can derive from a metaphor, Leatherdale distinguishes between literal and contextual meanings. Literal meaning is present when one can either readily accept or deny the truth of a sentence because its meaning is relatively invariant and unambiguous. A meaning becomes contextual when there is "a disharmony between words and context—or, essentially, between one word and another." This disharmony must have been created on purpose as we describe observations "in unfamiliar ways or ascribe to them attributes, properties, behaviour and relations which cannot be located among the . . . literal meanings of the words used." At times, they may even "seem . . . incongruous or incompatible with these literal meanings."[23]

Questions

Applying the above constructs of analogy and metaphor to research on perceptual development in music, our questions are:

1. What language have music education researchers used to describe the musical behavior of children?
2. What qualities, properties, attributes, and contextual meaning does the language imply?
3. What realities are alluded to by the employed analogies and metaphors, and are these realities compatible with each other?
4. Does the use of analogy and metaphor limit or strengthen our ability of asking pertinent research questions in music education?

The Description of Conceptual Learning in Music According to Analogy and Metaphor

One of the basic questions about musical development is at what point the learner can label heard sounds, compare such stimuli to each other, and determine relationships between them. This threefold task has been used (a) to determine the constructs of musical ability and musical achievement, and (b) to answer questions about the relationship of age and musical learning.

Many researches, too numerous to list, are aware that inexperienced learners lack the verbal vocabulary to describe musical experiences. Often music educators have documented this lack of vocabulary.[24] They have drawn specific attention to the ongoing dilemma of asking children to solve musical tasks of tone and pattern recognition when the terms used for such identification were taken from contexts of life experiences outside the reality of sound. The focus of our analysis does not lie on the language used by the subjects to label what they heard, but rather on the language used by the researchers to describe that process of perception. What resemblances of qualities, properties, and attributes have been employed to explain verbally the musical development and auditory perception of learners of different ages?

The Use of Internal and Language-Bound Images to Explain the Processing of Musical Sound

When researchers in music education study the musical perception of learners of different ages, they often analyze the learner's ability to iden-tify rhythmic and pitch pattern relationships in altered melodic con-texts.[25] This is done because auditory perception in music involves the extraction of information from the total of the musical structure to which the listener attends. To describe the process of how the learner selects a particular musical phenomenon from the total of the composition, source domains have been either visual-spatially or language oriented.

Visual Source Domain. In music teaching and research, many of our analogies to describe musical sound derive from the written score. Our source domain is that of musical notation. We label pitch relationships as "high and low" and "up and down" and pitch-rhythm relationships in terms of melodic "contour," "line," and "shape." We refer to "figure and ground" to address the relationship between the musical element to be at-tended to (pitch, rhythm, melody, tone color, etc.) and the configuration of the sound structure (which could either be melody alone or a fully or-chestrated score). Whether the descriptors are analogies or metaphors would depend upon the view we hold about our Western system of music notation.

Take, for example, melodic contour. Literal meaning of the term would exist for all those individuals who are familiar with music notation and who believe that the phenomenon of musical sound is preserved and repre-sented accurately through the written score. Under this condition, the term might be, in Leatherdale's terms, a manifest analogy. As long as the as-sumption were upheld that our musical terminology derives in all cases from notated music, the properties of melodic contour would be com-parable to the property of visual contour and would be empirically verifiable.

When viewing music notation as an already abstracted form of musical sound, the description of melody as having contour would fall either under abstract analogies (in Leatherdale's terms, imported analogy) or under perceptual metaphor (Miller's terminology). Indeed, if musical notation were viewed as a specialized, esoteric body of knowledge familiar to only a relatively small group of people, melodic contour would become metaphorical, requiring contextual understanding to be of explanatory value. Thus, whether *melodic contour* is an analogy or a metaphor depends upon our knowledge of and the appropriateness of musical notation as the guiding principle for music terminology.

Contextual meaning is most certainly present when researchers explain sound perception in "figure and ground" images. These images suggest spatial-physical relationships between the properties in a composition. The image implies perspective in a three-dimensional space. Even if we accepted the reality of musical notation as the basis of our terminology in music, the reality of a three-dimensional score has not yet become common practice. Thus, the "figure-ground" terminology requires a very special and particular kind of experience in and knowledge of musical analysis. Currently, only those musicians might share this specialized knowledge with each other who master Schenkerian analytical procedures. More importantly, for the analogy to be of more than surface value, such related terms as positive, negative, and ambiguous space, foreground / middleground / background, picture plane, implied and actual lines would also have to be applicable to the phenomenon of music.

Suggesting that there is an analogue between visual and musical comprehension, some researches have attempted to document alike properties between spatial and musical perception.[26] One example is the study by D. J. Nelson and A. L. Barresi who sought to investigate children's age-related intellectual strategies for dealing with musical and spatial analogical tasks. Beyond wanting to know "whether there [was] a common level of logic and spatial analogical tasks," the researcher wondered "whether the levels of logic could be characterized by similar intellectual strategies across the two domains."[27]

Focusing on analogical reasoning as the form of logic under study, Nelson and Barresi correlated spatial analogy tasks (SANTs) with musical analogy tasks (MANTS), both sets developed by the researchers. The spatial analogy tasks required the identification of same-colored and same-shaped figures in a progressively more difficult context. The children presented their answers by selecting from four possible choices the shape they believed provided the correct equivalent ("If shape A belongs to shape B, then shape C must belong to which of the possible choices?") The musical analogy tasks required a "yes-no" response mode from the children. The task administrator played a musical example and said: "This example goes with example 2, does example 3 go with example 4?"

The results showed "a relationship between age and the children's responses to analogical tasks using either musical or spatial relationships,"[28] but they also suggested that the learners did better in the spatial analogy tasks than in the musical ones. This, we believe, was at least partly the case because the tasks were not comparable, that is, analogous. Solving the analogy tasks in music required memory and abstract (mental) sound imaging. The visual-spatial tasks remained at the concrete level of choosing shapes visibly available to the learner. Manifest, concrete analogies in the visual test became imported, that is, abstract analogies in the music test. At this point, we question the use of analogues from the visual arts as desirable metaphors in the reality of musical perception.

Language-Bound Source Domain. Some researchers have long advocated looking for useful analogies and metaphors in the areas of language learning and speech perception since language and speech have in common with each other the use of short- and long-term memories as well as the symbolic representation of sound.[29] C. P. Schmidt's study on aspects of cognitive style and language-bound/language-optional perception is a case in point.[30] He designed the study to examine "the predictor variables of field dependence/field independence, reflection/impulsivity, and language-optional/language-bound perception."[31]

Schmidt operationalized all variables "through tests of Group Embedded Figures, Matching Familiar Figures, Temporal Order Discrimination, Fusion, and Aural Skills. Data were analyzed through multiple regression and analysis of variance procedures."[32] The measurement tool designed to assess language-optional/language-bound perception was that developed by S. W. Keele and D. R. Lyon.[33] Essentially, word components of twenty-two different words are constructed by eliminating either the first or the second letter of a word (for example, the word "blanket" becomes banket/lanket). The respondent is asked to identify in a given time frame (1) the consonant that was sounded first ("b" or "l") and (2) the fused word ("blanket").

Schmidt found that of all the relationships identified in the study, temporal-order discrimination accounted for the largest amount of variance (16.1 percent). Because of the number of tests employed in the study, Schmidt considered this variance an important finding. We concur to the degree that we believe he provided some evidence that temporal-order discrimination in language study can provide useful descriptors for music discrimination. Stated differently, language perception may be a potentially important source domain for analogues that describe music perception.

Whereas this idea is not new, we emphasize linguistics as a source domain for analogies and metaphors in music rather than as an *equivalent* to musical learning. Images drawn from the contextual meaning of language acquisition may, indeed, come closer to the phenomenon we call musical learning than images drawn from spatial-physical relationships between objects. However, the question is not whether music learning *equals* language learning but rather whether it may be *likened* to it, and if so, to what degree.

Thinking of Learning As Progressing in "Stages" or "Plateaus"

As a result of Piaget's work, music researchers often have referred to "stages" within which children progress musically. Another term introduced by R. Petzold and E. Gordon, and confirmed since then by many other researchers, has been that of a learning "plateau."[34] It is not our purpose to enter into a debate about the validity of such findings, but rather to examine the meaning of these terms as being analogous or metaphoric.

To determine whether the word stage is a useful analogy for the description of musical learning, we would have to ask whether the term brings with it qualities, attributes, or proportions that are equal or common to the phenomenon under study. To ask whether the term is a useful metaphor, we would need to ascertain whether the word and the context within which it occurs are literal in that everybody readily understands and shares the contextual meaning. Or are the word and the context somewhat unusual, or even disharmonious? If so, is there a community of likeminded individuals who would benefit from a highly context-dependent metaphor?

The answer to all questions depends on the definition of learning. If one assumes that musical learning is a linear and one-dimensional progression toward a preestablished and agreed-upon goal, the image of an upward-bound progression may serve as an appropriate analogy for musical learning. The child is learning toward "something"; the top, once reached, is an improvement over the bottom from where the individual came. The analogy of "stage" would be concrete, and the metaphor of "stagewise progression" would have nearly literal meaning. If, on the other hand, one were to understand musical learning as the result of a nondirectional, exploratory series of "encounters" with music, the case would be different. The learners could choose their own musical activities at their own pace, and the acquisition of predetermined musical skills and knowledge would become secondary to the sharpening of the learners' senses in different experiential contexts. The properties and attributes between the analogy of learning stages and the observed phenomenon would not be the same any more.

At least for now, education, and particularly formal schooling, has the purpose of a one-directional enterprise: the learner is to gain specific skills and knowledge at increasingly higher levels of refinement. Therefore, both researchers and teachers probably subscribe to learning stages as a metaphor relevant to the learning process in music. But in no case should the metaphor become a manifest analogy. The meaning should not be taken literally to the point either that music curricula are being planned "in stages" of two-year intervals or that we study the behavior of five-, seven-, and nine-year olds to the exclusion of four-, six-, eight- or ten-year-old children.

Limitations and Strengths of Analogies and Metaphors in Music Education Research

The use of analogy in the explanation of the unknown has been beneficial in music education as it has triggered much research and debate on the nature of musical learning. Specifically, the use of spatial relationships in efforts to explain the process of identifying and discriminating between musical contours has resulted in valuable inquiries, and a number of good insights and ideas for new research avenues have resulted from those inquiries. However, the structure of musical discrimination itself is still not fully known, and we must therefore be prepared to accept that only surface similarities may exist between the source and the topic domains used thus far. Once we find serious incongruencies between the two domains, we must modify or replace the analogy. If we retain an analogy even if we have reason to believe that it is deficient or misleading, its use becomes an impediment to our efforts of seeking to understand what we observe. It is somewhat paradoxical, therefore, that the strength of employing analogy can also become its weakness.

Beyond the literal juxtaposition of and comparison between topic and source domains lies the metaphoric use of verbal descriptors. Here, each domain has attached to it its own set of images. These images carry with them their own contextual meaning, that is, terms in the topic domain are seen differently from those in the source domain because of the different connotations and associations affiliated with both sets of terms. This means that the associated ideas of the topic domain are affected by those of the source domain, and vice versa. To repeat: the research content of conservation is common only to those people who concern themselves with Piagetian epistemology as applied to musical learning. The explanation of musical learning, however, should come from familiar metaphors, not unfamiliar ones. Otherwise, we defeat the purpose of seeking to explain the unknown.

Most researchers in music education hope to accomplish two goals: (1) they want to satisfy their own curiosity about the unknown in music learning and teaching; and (2) they hope to give the profession new insights into the learning-teaching process. The relationship between seeking to understand that which one does not know and the improvement of everyday life through research results, however, is ambiguous due to the fact that we describe musical learning processes primarily by the use of analogies and metaphors.

As may have become evident, one cannot draw a sharp line in music education between analogies and metaphors because both types of descriptors require contextual understanding. This fact has ramifications for their usefulness in music education research. Specifically, the question arises whether the descriptors help the practice of music teaching. We would answer with a qualified "no."

First, there is a danger in music education research of turning metaphorical terms into manifest analogies and of treating them as concrete reality. This becomes apparent, for example, when textbooks in music do not allow for musical transfer tasks at an early age because "the child is too young to conserve."[35] Secondly, the contextual meaning necessary to understand many of the metaphors used in music education research is different for the various groups involved in music-instructional pursuits. Contextual understanding thus is group specific and dependent upon the knowledge any of the groups has of, and the relationship it sustains with, the source domain from which the analogies and metaphors were drawn. For this reason, to practitioners in the field the understanding of research reports ceases to be a simple matter of translating research jargon. At issue is instead whether the terms used reflect analogies and metaphors that lie within a source domain familiar to the group with whom we wish to communicate.[36] Thirdly, analogies may have concrete/literal meaning for some individuals but may have metaphorical meaning for others. The difference between both lies in the degree to which those who share in wanting to know the unknown and those who are interested in improving instructional practice share in the same contextual understanding. One group may take literally what for the other is highly metaphorical; a metaphor knowingly employed by the researcher may become practiced reality for the teacher. Here lie both the boundaries of and the facilitators for understanding research in music education.

NOTES

1. Deanna Kuhn, Eric Amsel, and Michael O'Loughlin, *The Development of Scientific Thinking Skills* (San Diego: Academic Press, 1988), pp. 3-4. See also Bertrand Russell, *Human Knowledge: Its Scope and Limits* (New York: Simon and Schuster, 1948, 1976); E. D. Klemke, Robert Hollinger, and A. David Kline, eds., *Introductory Readings in the Philosophy of Science* (Buffalo, N.Y.: Prometheus Books, 1980); Arne Naess, *The Pluralist and Possibilist Aspect of the Scientific Enterprise* (Oslo: Universitetsforlaget; London: Allen & Unwin, 1972); and Cyril S. Smith, "Struc-

tural Hierarchy in Science, Art, and History," in *On Aesthetics in Science,* ed. Judith Wechsler (Cambridge, Mass.: MIT Press, 1978), pp. 9-54.

2. See, for example, the term "audiation" in Edwin Gordon, *Learning Sequences in Music: Skill, Content, and Patterns* (Chicago: G. I. A. Publications, 1984).

3. Ludwig Wittgenstein, *Tractatus Logico-Philosophicus,* with an introduction by Bertrand Russell, 6th impression (London: Routledge & Kegan, 1955). See also Basil Bernstein, *Class, Codes and Control,* 2d. rev. ed. (Boston: Routledge & K. Paul, 1977); Peter L. Berger and Thomas Luckmann, *The Social Construction of Reality: A Treatise in the Sociology of Knowledge* (Garden City, N.Y.: Doubleday, 1967); Noam Chomsky, *Language and Problems of Knowledge. The Managua Lectures* (Cambridge, Mass.: MIT Press, 1988); Umberto Eco, *Semiotics and the Philosophy of Language* (London: Macmillan, 1984); Barry Gholson, William R. Shadish, Jr., Robert A. Neimery, and Arthur C. Houts, eds., *Psychology of Science: Contributions to Metascience* (Cambridge: Cambridge University Press, 1989); Patrick A. Heelan, *Space Perception and the Philosophy of Science* (Berkeley: University of California Press, 1983); Paul A. Komesaroff, *Objectivity, Science and Society* (New York: Routledge & Kegan Paul, 1986); and Thomas Kuhn, *The Structure of Scientific Revolutions,* 2d ed., enlarged (Chicago: University of Chicago Press, 1970).

4. The term "processing" implies a sequential time-line of the sound travelling from the ear to the brain. There might be some evidence that would dispute such an explanation. See Jerry D. Wallace, *An Investigation of Extrinsic Laryngeal Muscle Responses to Auditory Stimulation* (Ph.D. diss., Music Education, North Texas State University, Denton, Texas, 1985), pp. 143-46.

5. Max Black, *Models and Metaphors* (Ithaca, N.Y.: Cornell University Press, 1962); Max Black, "More about Metaphor" in *Metaphor and Thought,* ed. A. Ortony (Cambridge: Cambridge University Press, 1979), pp. 19-43; Mary B. Hesse, *Models and Analogies in Science* (Notre Dame, Ind.: University of Notre Dame Press, 1966); Mary B. Hesse, *Revolutions and Reconstructions in the Philosophy of Science* (Bloomington: Indiana University Press, 1980); W. H. Leatherdale, *The Role of Analogy, Model and Metaphor in Science* (Amsterdam: North-Holland Publishing Company; New York: American Elsevier Publishing Company, 1974); Arthur I. Miller, "Imagery, Metaphor, and Physical Reality," in *Psychology of Science: Contributions to Metascience,* pp. 326-41; Arthur I. Miller, *Imagery in Scientific Thought: Creating 20th Century Physics* (Cambridge, Mass.: MIT Press, 1986); and Frans van Zetten, "Abstract Terms as Denatured Metaphors," *Philosophical Investigations* 11 (October 1988): 315-35. On language, metaphor, symbolism, and science, see Lawrence LeShan and Nehry Margenau, *Einstein's Space and Van Gogh's Sky* (New York: Macmillan 1982); Allan Paivio, *Imagery and Verbal Processes* (New York: Holt, Rinehart and Winston, 1971); and David Smail, *Illusion and Reality: The Meaning of Anxiety* (London: J. M. Dent, 1984).

6. For a review of literature, see Leatherdale, *The Role of Analogy, Model and Metaphor in Science.*

7. *The American Heritage Dictionary of the English Language,* p. 825.

8. Miller, "Imagery, Metaphor, and Physical Reality," p. 328.

9. Peter A. Angeles, *Dictionary of Philosophy* (New York: Barnes and Noble, 1981), pp. 8-9.

10. Hesse, *Models and Analogies in Science,* pp. 57-67. She calls all alike properties and functions between the two objects positive analogues. Properties that set the two objects apart from each other, i.e., unlike properties, would be negative analogues.

11. Ibid., pp. 130-56.

12. One might be tempted to view Bohr's model of paths of electrons around an atom's nucleus as equivalent to the orbits of the planets around the sun. However, the positions of planets are subject to laws of motions. The orbits of electrons (as viewed in quantum theory) are best described statistically in terms

of probability position. Points of departure between two nonphysical (i.e., conceptual) systems are often more difficult to detect.

13. See note 26.
14. Hesse, *Models and Analogies.*
15. Leatherdale, *The Role of Analogy, Model and Metaphor in Science*, pp. 3-4.
16. Ibid.
17. Angeles, *Dictionary of Philosophy*, pp. 168-69.
18. Leatherdale, *The Role of Analogy, Model and Metaphor in Science*, pp. 92-93.
19. See Leatherdale, *The Role of Analogy*, pp. 97-98.
20. Leatherdale's equivalents to topic and source domain are principal subject matter (that which we want to explain) and subsidiary subject matter (the area from which we draw the descriptors).
21. Douglas Bartholomew, "Problems with Piagetian Conservation and Musical Objects," *Bulletin of the Council for Research in Music Education* (Late Summer 1987): 27-40; David J. Nelson, "An Interpretation of the Piagetian Model in Light of the Theories of Case," *Bulletin of the Council for Research in Music Education* 92 (Summer 1987): 23-34; Mary L. Serafine, "Cognitive Processes in Music: Discoveries vs. Definitions," *Bulletin of the Council for Research in Music Education* 73 (Winter 1983): 1-14; and Mary L. Serafine, *Music as Cognition: The Development of Thought in Sound* (New York: Columbia University Press, 1988).
22. Leatherdale, *The Role of Analogy*, pp. 101-103.
23. Ibid., p. 98.
24. Harriet Hair, "Children's Responses to Musical Stimuli: Verbal/Nonverbal, Aural/Visual Modes," in *Applications of Research in Music Behavior*, ed. Clifford K. Madsen and Carol A. Prickett (Tuscaloosa: University of Alabama Press, 1987), pp. 59-70; Serafine, *Music as Cognition: The Development of Thought in Sound;* W. W. Zimmerman, "Verbal Description of Aural Musical Stimuli," *Journal of Research in Music Education* 19 (Winter 1971): 422-31; Robert Walker, "Educating in Thoughts Too Definite for Words," *Bulletin of the Council for Research in Music Education* 77 (Winter 1984): 20-29; and Robert Walker, "Children's Perceptions of Horses and Melodies," *Bulletin of the Council for Research in Music Education* 76 (Fall 1983): 30-41.
25. The reader is referred to the studies published during the last twenty years in the standard research publications of music education and music psychology as well as in the documentary reports of the two Ann Arbor symposia, "Applications of Psychology to the Teaching and Learning of Music," 1981 and 1983.
26. See, for example, Kai Karma, "Selecting Students to Music Instruction," *Bulletin of the Council for Research in Music Education* 75 (Summer 1983): 23-32, where he stipulated, "If spatial ability is an ability to comprehend visual figures, musical aptitude is an ability to comprehend acoustic figures." See by the same author "Musical, Spatial, and Verbal Abilities," *Bulletin of the Council for Research in Music Education* 59 (Special Issue, Summer 1979): 50-53. See also J. Bamberger, "Revisiting Children's Drawings of Simple Rhythms: A Function of Reflection in Action," in *U-Shaped Behavioral Growth*, ed. S. Strauss (New York: Academic Press, 1982), pp. 191-226; Harold E. Fiske, "Musical Cognition: Serial Process or Parallel Process," *Bulletin of the Council for Research in Music Education* 80 (1984): 13-26; and others cited previously.
27. David J. Nelson and Anthony L. Barresi, "Children's Age-Related Intellectual Strategies for Dealing with Musical and Spatial Analogical Tasks," *Journal of Research in Music Education* 37 (Summer 1989): 93-103.
28. Ibid., p. 100.
29. See, for example, R. S. Day, "Music Ability and Patterns of Cognition," in *Documentary Report of the Ann Arbor Symposium: Applications of Psychology to the Teaching and Learning of Music* (Reston, Va.: Music Educators National Conference, 1981), pp. 270-83.
30. Charles P. Schmidt, "The Relationship among Aspects of Cognitive Style and Language-Bound/Language-Optional Perception to Musicians' Performance in

Aural Discrimination Tasks," *Journal of Research in Music Education* 32 (Fall 1985): 159-68.

31. Ibid., p. 161.
32. Ibid., p. 159.
33. Steven W. Keele and Don R. Lyon, "Individual Differences in Speech Fusion: Methodological and Theoretical Explanations," *Perception and Psychophysics* 32 (November 1982): 434-42.
34. The meanings of *plateau* and *stage* are not interchangeable, but for the purpose of this article their differences are negligible.
35. Personal communication with a textbook author whose publisher/editor argued against the inclusion of transfer tasks for five-year-olds on the ground that they could not conserve at that age level.
36. Anthony P. Cohen, *The Symbolic Construction of Community* (Chichester, U.K.: Ellis Horwood Limited; New York: Tavistock Publications, 1985).

Teaching and Learning Philosophy in the Music Education Doctoral Program

GERARD L. KNIETER

Contemplation never comes easy for Americans of the North. Whatever our ethnic origins or the quality of our cultural baggage, we are doers first and reluctant contemplators. We even prefer to fund "action research"! Thus we are prone to accept all forms of free-floating anti-intellectualism in the arts and in daily life. Even our intellectuals often pose as anti-intellectuals, citing in defense of their own mucker pose Goethe's oft misused comment about grey theory and the "green tree of life."

Doing philosophy requires very high-order thinking; but one must always use the Tao test: it has to be absolutely simple if the tool is to be acute. This is a variation of William of Occam's razor—"Do not multiply your entities beyond necessity."

American society has a long tradition of anti-intellectualism. Its roots are deep in our history. It is a product of the rugged individualism, the sense of manifest destiny, and the successful heroism it took to forge our nation.

Anti-intellectuals reject theory as impractical, intangible, and unrelated to success. They are not aware that theory and practice are critically interdependent. While theory provides the intellectual and substantive basis for a discipline, practice offers us the applied knowledge of that discipline in useful ways. Academic disciplines have structure, syntax, an epistemology, and a special method of investigation. Yet, academics are viewed with suspicion, as are all professionals, because they speak a technical language available only to the initiated. While many works in the social sciences document this well-known truism, it is interesting to note that although our society appears to endorse the educational process as a social value, it offers relatively little economic support for the enterprise, on a *per capita* basis, when compared to many European and Asian nations.

Gerard L. Knieter is Professor of Music at the California State University, Northridge. He has contributed essays to *Music Education for Tomorrow's Society* and *Readings in General Music*, coedited *The Teaching Process and the Arts and Aesthetics*, and published articles in such journals as the *Music Educators Journal* and the *National Association of Secondary School Principals*.

American teachers and professors do not have the same social, economic, and professional standing as the European or Asian teacher and professor. Education is regarded as a vehicle to achieve the better life. Yet, if one compares the salaries of teachers and professors with those of athletes and entertainers, operational pragmatic values emerge. *American society provides economic support for that which it values.*

Popular movements, fads, and cycles will continue to dominate American education because, as a microcosm of American society, it reflects the social, political, and economic ethos of the larger culture. For example, it is monumental nonsense for there to be a preoccupation with assessment today (as there was in the thirties, fifties, and seventies), when in terms of intellectual quality many who are selected to teach do not come from the upper percentile of the most intellectually talented students in our colleges and universities. The majority of our brighter students enter business and the other professions because they know that their beginning salaries and potential earnings far exceed the average salaries of teachers and professors. Both American educators and the public are often lost in an irrelevant reflection on how one should improve a troubled corporation, assuming that these procedures would be appropriate for solving problems in education. However, it is not widely understood that education is a process, not a product. Those procedures which are appropriate for corporate America, and which are often properly driven by the "bottom line," do not work well with children who are being taught to think critically and master several bodies of organized knowledge, while also acquiring the aesthetic and cultural heritage of a pluralistic society. National goals for education are often suggested to us by the well intentioned and by government officials who are not professionally prepared.

Philosophy does not provide either all the answers or all the solutions for American education or for music education. However, it is a discipline that when skillfully employed has the capacity to assist us in identifying cogent questions which can focus the intellectual potential of our students and teachers upon critical issues. Philosophy bakes bread, it asks all the embarrassing questions we never like to answer, and it is good company for the lonely and distressed. Today we are repeating the errors of the past. We seek counsel through imprecise democratic processes from those who are not professionally competent, and we employ slogans rather than basic research to support our efforts.

This essay will deal with the role of philosophy in the doctoral program in music education in the hope that some relevant and functional options will emerge that may have the potential to extricate us from both the national confusion and the lack of leadership and direction in our profession.

The Role of Philosophy in Music Education

The study of philosophy in music education provides the focus for identifying the *assumptions* upon which various music education and educational views rest. In general, music teachers teach the way they were taught. This process appears to work because those who are successful impart both the process and the content of their knowledge to their students. The students who acquire this knowledge in turn transmit it to their students. In fact this process enjoys the tradition of "lineage." Many students and teachers of the piano trace their teaching approach back to Liszt. Why would anyone today want to study the way Liszt was taught? Would we want to study law, medicine, and business the way they were taught in the nineteenth century? If Liszt were alive today, it is probable that he would seek the newest approaches since he was an innovator. Why then do we look backwards for our models? The *assumption* is that the past is better.

The study of philosophy in music education provides the opportunity to identify the *values* we impart. It has been held by many that the study of music stimulates creativity. If this is desirable, and if this is so, we should be prepared to demonstrate this special uniqueness. If other *values*, such as developing aesthetic sensitivity or cultivating nonverbal intelligence, are also significant, then the instructional process should be organized to emphasize their systematic cultivation.

The study of philosophy in music education enables one *to select a point of view*. One cannot be neutral in the arts or in education. Emotions run high in fields where the affective domain is organically generic to the substance and process. *Selecting a point of view* for doctoral students involves exposure to all available options. While it is true that no single institution can be prepared to examine all approaches with equal competency, it is critical for these programs to attempt to identify the widest variety of options that are professionally viable. Unfortunately, many institutions tend to indoctrinate their students. It is useful to distinguish between indoctrination and institutional orientation.

It is vital that those who teach philosophy have a point of view. It is equally critical that they demonstrate an intellectual open-mindedness which encourages the expression of all divergent points of view provided that such views are systematically based, logically developed, internally coherent, epistemologically sound, and relevant to the inquiry being pursued. The professor should always identify a personal bias and present both its the strengths and weakness. It is my supposition that since all views in education are based upon assumptions about human behavior, they should be held tentatively—open to modification in the light of experience and the outcomes of operational testing.

Each view will have strengths and weaknesses. Those with philosophical integrity will be able to acknowledge the limitations as well as the advantages of their positions. Those who present a philosophy of music education that is final and complete will by definition be presenting an intellectually dead position. Since the art of music is evolving, and since our understanding of the nature of human behavior and education is also evolving, it follows that music education must also be in a dynamic state of evolution. Those who present us with final answers fail to understand epistemology, philosophy, music, and the field of education.

The study of philosophy in music education provides the opportunity *to assess* the impact of each position. One *assesses* an educational position in order to provide definitions, to determine relevance, to judge coherence, to devise strategies, to propose options, to construct curriculum, and to evaluate educational quality. But this is hardly a comprehensive list.

The Goals of Philosophical Study in Music Education

Every profession should have a purpose, a destiny, a direction. Music educators, as all professionals, have goals in order to focus their energies, prioritize their resources, and determine the relevance of emerging and competing issues. It is from a knowledge of philosophy of music education that one develops the capacity for selecting appropriate goals. The goals that are discussed below are not presented in any particular order. They are viewed as mutually significant but hardly comprehensive. Such a discussion would go beyond the scope of this article.

To demonstrate the importance of selecting goals, an example of an appropriate goal might be *to develop the aesthetic potential of all students*. Having such a goal would mean that there would be opportunities both for the general student and for those who are musically talented to study music in a curriculum that is developmentally systematic and exhibits vertical articulation, kindergarten through grade twelve. Such a course of study would provide both intensive and extensive opportunities so that the music education of all students would move beyond musical literacy to musical expressiveness through composition, performance, and appreciation (evaluation and criticism). Unless we make every effort to build musically informed audiences, there will be little need for musical performance.

One of the fundamental goals basic to the study of philosophy in music education is learning *to identify significant issues*, for it assists us in prioritizing our resources, both human and fiscal. Music educators have many concerns. Our national meetings have workshops and seminars ranging from teaching composition to nonmusicians to the selection of woodwind mouthpieces. While there has been some evidence to indicate that performance has been slowly increasing in society, music education in the schools still faces considerable difficulty. The problem is the same now as it was when Lowell Mason brought music education to the schools in New England. Music and the other arts are still not viewed by many educators and many communities as important as some other academic subjects. While the attitudes and values of educators and members of the community vary throughout the nation, and generalizations always run the risk of inviting the defensive to identify some of our best programs, the fact still remains that very few elementary schools in the United States have even one music teacher for the several hundred or several thousand students within their individual buildings.

The ability *to think critically* is another important goal. Music educators have been debating the issue of whether or not the general student should be taught to read music. This debate began decades before this writer's appearance on the planet; however, it continues into the present. To the best of my knowledge, the same arguments are still presented on both sides. Yet, the issue seems abundantly clear from a philosophical orientation. The fundamental question is not whether or not we should teach music reading, but what the purpose of teaching music reading is. We know that there are many who attend concerts who do not read music and who enjoy their season tickets. There are also others who can read music and appear to derive great satisfaction from their experience with music. From a critical and philosophical perspective, one should teach music reading to the general student to the degree that it enhances musical understanding and clarifies musical meaning. There appears to be little virtue in teaching major and minor tetrachords to students if they cannot hear the difference between them and do not understand how these particular relationships work musically.

Another goal that will enhance music education is the ability *to think creatively*. The obvious applications involve composition and performance. The formal process of teaching students to compose is usually postponed until the upper division of the undergraduate curriculum. If, however, we are committed to developing the aesthetic potential of all students, opportunities to study musical composition will begin in the elementary school in the same way we study English composition. This process will continue throughout the grades for those students who appear to have the ability.

Performance will be taught with more musical insight than mere dedication to the right notes and the right rhythms. Students will be able to study the various interpretations that are given to a variety of musical styles so that when they arrive at the university fewer of them will still be "typing" on their instruments. The quality of their creative interpretations will be appreciated by a more informed musical audience.

The general student has the most to gain. For example, this student can develop the ability to hear theme and variations and the use of stretto and fragmentation in thematic development. The ability to recognize these musical relationships illustrates a process of cognitive integration that is the same in kind for the nonmusician as it is for the musician. To paraphrase Jerome Bruner, anything we can teach them, they can learn. The non-musician learns the same way as the professional musician does; the difference is in degree of complexity, not in kind. Musicians who are schooled in eighteenth-century counterpoint, for example, will be able to identify inversion and augmentation in a Bach fugue. It is exciting to note that junior high school students also have been taught to do the same thing. The listening process is one of the centers of nonverbal intelligence; it provides music educators with a unique opportunity to cultivate this most significant dimension of cognition.

To be knowledgeable about the various schools of philosophy is another important goal. Philosophy has been viewed as the "mother" of all subjects. It has provided a process of problem solving that scientists refer to as the scientific method, it forms the model for all spheres of professional criticism, and it provides the field of education with several systematic ways of explaining and evaluating both content and process. There are also schools of philosophy that provide the basis for understanding how the various arts function as discrete academic disciplines comparable with mathematics, history, and biology.

As we debate the ever-emerging role of education and the role of the arts in education, it is vital that we be knowledgeable about the impact these various positions have on our field and the community. If one subscribes to certain views held by a recent secretary of education, for example, the arts could be viewed as a form of elitism. Yet if we recognize that this nation evolved and continues to evolve from a global immigration, then it is even more important to understand the nature of pluralism as a philosophical option.

It is also necessary for music educators to understand the nature of music as it impacts on the ethics and morals of human behavior. There are those philosophers who have stressed the relationship between music and ethical or moral behavior; among the most famous of those are Plato and Confucius. The idea that music can influence behavior has been scientifically established in the field of music therapy. However, the idea that music (the sound) can cause people to act with either the milk of human kindness or the wrath of the barbarian is still at the very best an assumption. This assumption or belief caused many people in the 1920s to view jazz as a corrupt musical style.

Today, the notion that music has the capacity to influence ethical and moral behavior is still operative. There are many who believe that some of the recent styles of commercial music exert a powerfully negative force on children. Hence, the idea of musical censorship is a theme at the time of this writing. Such discussions are usually wrought with deep emotion, and few seem able to distinguish between the message in the lyrics and the message in the music. What seems abundantly clear is that every adult generation denigrates some of the music of its contemporary youth. It always predicts the extinction of that segment of humanity exposed to the music in question. While it is tempting to see the humor in a series of predictions that have recurred from ancient times, it is simultaneously frightening to bear witness to the observation that failure to know history dooms us to repeat it. The idea that music, which is inanimate, can be anthropomorphized is an intellectually primitive construct, yet it "lives" in the minds of some well-meaning citizens.

It is also important *to be knowledgeable about the various schools of aesthetics.* For those who are not familiar with the various aesthetic positions, it may be difficult to explain: (1) how music is similar and unique with respect to the other arts; (2) how music should be compared to the hard sciences, social sciences, and humanities; (3) how music functions both as an academic discipline and a performing art; and (4) how music should be employed in the educational enterprise. If one is to teach music and prepare teachers of music, discussions of the nature of musical meaning, the significance of music, the role of the symbol, sign, and metaphor cannot be avoided. While there are thousands of books and articles on this subject, one does not have to become an expert. It is, however, critical that a sophisticated basis for musical understanding be acquired so that one has the credentials to present a cogent explanation of music to a professional colleague or an intelligent layman, for such an explanation may save the life of a music program.

To understand the relationship between music and the other arts is another goal. There is a movement in all fields of education toward the interdisciplinary. This movement finds a parallel in the other professions, business, science, communications, and technology. It therefore becomes necessary for us to be literate in the other arts. There are some fundamental constructs that should be considered. For example, which of the arts exist in time, in space, or in time and space? What structural components can be generalized across all of the arts without violating their respective epistemologies? What aspects of human nature and experience can be found in all of the arts? Are these factors unique to experiences in the arts? Or can they be found in experiences with other subjects? When constructing an interdisciplinary curriculum in the arts, what are the several ways in which one can proceed? How does one evaluate the different arts? What are the differences between an interdisciplinary and a multidisciplinary curriculum?

If we are to understand our uniqueness, we should also understand our similarities to the other arts. Is the aesthetic experience the same in all of the arts? How is it different from the religious experience? Why are music and religion and mathematics and speech often compared?

The intersections that occur in this study overlap one's philosophy, one's aesthetic position, and one's educational orientation. The questions that have been posed are the ones most often raised by laymen and by professional colleagues. It is necessary for our profession to be able to address our relationship to the other arts with cogent and sensitive insight.

To understand the relationship between music and the other academic subjects can provide empowering insight into the nature of knowledge. In an age of science and technology there appears to be a tendency for society to expect that unless academic credibility can be established for a subject, it may not be considered significant for inclusion in the curriculum. The question then becomes, What criteria are essential for academic credibility? In the past, answers to this question have largely been drawn from the field of epistemology. For example, subjects have been considered academic disciplines when they have had a minimum of the following: (1) a syntax; (2) a theory of knowledge; (3) a history of significant literature; (4) a method of research particular to the discipline; and (5) academic authenticity. For example, although music has proportional relationships (rhythm), its internal logic is based upon a systematic organization of sound, growing out of a cultural history in which aesthetic considerations are preeminent. This analysis allows us to state quite clearly that while music and mathematics share some similarities, the study of one does not substantially affect the understanding of the other. Mathematics teaches us abstract thinking. It is a science used to express the nature of the universe in measurement, properties, and relationships. It does not deal in the affective domain. In music we do; we deal in emotion. We trade in feelings, and we are not scientific, we are aesthetic. We experience music through time, and because it affects our emotions, it causes physiological changes and is therefore a concrete tangible experience. It is not ephemeral, it is simply nonverbal.

It is also important that musicians understand other disciplines in order to explain and to clarify the importance of musical study and the uniqueness of musical meaning to those who are educated in a thoroughly different universe of discourse. Music is similar to other disciplines to the degree that it shares the qualities of all academic disciplines. It is unique because it is a performing art existing in the dimension of time. It is also necessary for us to understand colleagues in other fields in order to enhance our own intellectual credentials. As musicians we cannot be narrow, if we are expected to explain our discipline to others.

To assess the quality of research and clinical practice is another important goal. Sometimes there is confusion between evaluating the quality of a research design and the significance of the hypothesis under study. It is perfectly possible to examine a relatively trivial hypothesis by utilizing very sophisticated statistical treatment. A statistical treatment gives the impression that something scientific and important has taken place. Part of the problem associated with what this writer will call the "trivial dissertation" is the fact that many doctoral students approach the dissertation as an academic hurdle, viewing it as a different type of qualifying or comprehensive examination. Hence they examine previous dissertations that have already been accepted and simply model their own on the same format, thinking that all they need to do is to change the hypothesis. Furthermore, the advisor is also concerned that the student choose a topic and a format for the research that will fall within the student's capacity, while being acceptable to the academic and personal eccentricities of other members of the committee. Bearing all this in mind, a continuing variation on an "auld Gothic" plot appears to have been emerging in our journals and institutions.

This situation became alarming when the writer's doctoral students complained about the difficulty they had in finding innovative, original, or creative professional articles or dissertations for review. Possible approaches to this problem will be examined later in this article.

A case could be made that there is too much publication, not only in music education but in all of education. The reason for this situation may be that many colleges and universities will not grant tenure or promotion to faculty who do not publish. Hence, as soon as doctoral students have completed their dissertations, they seek to publish a series of articles in order to achieve tenure or promotion. While it is beyond the scope of this essay to comment with any depth on this situation, or to propose alternatives, it is clear to this observer of our professional journals that we are engaging in a mindless rehash of previous movements under new names. It appears that the greatest number of publications are produced first by doctoral students and then by young college and university faculty. It is also interesting to note that once academic advancement is achieved, most of the publication by this population stops. In general, publication seems to be carried on by the same small percentage of individuals who have continued to be productive throughout their careers. This could be an important strength.

In general, there seems to be little interest in connecting the research and the practice of music education. Although one should acknowledge the *Music Educators Journal* for beginning to cope with this issue, it is not a dominant theme in our profession. It may be that our field, as so many others, also suffers from the same anti-intellectualism discussed at the beginning of this article.

The evaluation of clinical practice, music teaching of any kind, is primarily based upon the degree to which the instructional process accomplishes its objectives. There are many ways available to those whose responsibility it is to evaluate instruction, and they need not be reviewed here. However, if one is preparing doctoral students, it is appropriate to expect not only that such people will be familiar with standardized instruments and practices, but that they will also be intimately acquainted with ways to evaluate the quality of the philosophy, goals, and objectives set for the instructional program. Furthermore, it would be reasonable to expect that a more intensive knowledge of the research on creative teaching should be important. We have all seen inspirational teaching, and many of its characteristics are well known. These characteristics should form the normative criteria for the best teaching in our profession.

The Content of Philosophical Study in Music Education

Each teacher of philosophy of music education will have an individual approach to this area of study. The approach will have very naturally emerged out of a synthesis of formal education, significant life experience, and the psychodynamic integration of personal and professional values as they impact on the subject. Hence, one who does this teaching is engaged in a deep commitment. It follows that each course will be unique while exhibiting certain similarities with others. The uniqueness will be manifest in the very special talent that the professor has developed as an academic scholar, teacher, and musician. Similarities will exist to the degree that the fundamental properties of music, education, human behavior, and their philosophical examination will present some inevitable parallelism.

The following course of study was successfully presented for over a decade in the doctoral program at Temple University. It makes several assumptions: (1) that students range in age from their early twenties through the mature years; (2) that experience ranges from just completing the masters degree to many years of public school and university teaching; (3) that some students can hardly write a literate sentence in the English language while others have published in professional journals; (4) that musical maturity and experience range from acceptable to professional and artistic; and (5) that knowledge of the other arts and academic disciplines also demonstrates the broadest possible range. Until doctoral students complete most of their course work and examinations, the majority of classes are heterogeneous. Seminar courses are often the place where homogeneity can be found.

The various topics are presented in the context of students': (1) reading assigned textbooks and other materials; (2) writing critical analyses of journal articles and selected works; and (3) preparing a comprehensive research term paper. The assigned readings do not always parallel the presentation of the course materials, for it is felt that the lectures, readings, and writing assignments should provide the widest possible exposure and academic challenge for those who are to assume leadership positions in music education. The amount of time spent on each topic depends upon the experience of the class, and it is appropriate to acknowledge that any single topic could be a course in itself. One simply attempts to balance intellectual depth with a wide variety of topics, a thoroughly frustrating compromise. The following are among some of the topics or areas that may be included.

The course can begin with a discussion of *the nature and function of philosophy*. By considering the various definitions of philosophy, students can become aware that all systems of philosophical thought are based upon fundamental assumptions which are considered pragmatically operative. They briefly examine the various fields of philosophy: aesthetics, ethics and morals, metaphysics, epistemology, logic. Next, students can become acquainted with the philosophical approach, aim, method, purpose, language, and at least one philosophical construct not necessarily related to education or the arts.

Truth is a useful illustration. Oscar Wilde said, "Never allow fact to stand in the way of truth." It comes as a shock to most students that truth is a pluralistic construct. For example, a particular event, which is in conformity with actual fact, when experienced by two or more people, can be described differently by each observer. Yet each is telling the truth, although the particular event is described differently by each individual. Trial attorneys learn about eyewitness testimony early in their education, for they know that truth is in the eye of the beholder. This becomes a vital tool for cross-examination. Although this philosophical idea is hardly new and was not chosen for its potential application to music education, it becomes pretty obvious that the commercial promotion of any educational approach as the "true" way or the "best" way to success reflects a considerable degree of superficiality.

The nature of education can be the next area for consideration. Students again use philosophical methods to uncover the characteristics of education from which they derive a working definition. It is critical, of course, that they comprehend the definition of definition so that they have the professional knowledge to be able to present a propositional statement that will qualify the particular universe of discourse.

Education can have universal application in a variety of situations. Therefore, the sequence of instruction moves to *philosophy of education*. Students examine the ways in which one can study or derive a philosophy of education. This exposes them to several traditional methods: (1) history of ideas; (2) types of educational philosophy; (3) selections from general philosophy; (4) problems of education; and (5) systematic philosophy of education.

The nature of art is a most significant focus for the course. It is at this point that students confront the epistemological uniqueness of art as compared to and with all other subjects. In this context all of the arts are dealt with generically. It is also at this time that students are reading various aesthetic theories so that the richness of intellectual activity is enhanced through the use of the best minds that have written on this subject. However, a discussion of specialized reading will be delayed until later in this article.

It now seems logical to pursue a discussion of *the nature of music.* At this point it is critical for students to develop a personal and professional conception of what music means to them. It should be a position supported with logic and research that they can articulate with precision and conviction. Closure in this area is vital, for it is this discussion that finally leads to the focus of the course of study: *a philosophy of music education.* Students have been led to a point where they can see that it is imperative to have a philosophy of music education. They will have reviewed a wide variety of contrasting views, they will have analyzed the research supporting these various views, and they will have synthesized a position that represents the best and most cogent thinking of which they are capable. While the selection of a particular point of view is always left to the student, all students should be able to articulate a position to their peer group at a level of professional coherence so as to withstand the most challenging academic and scholarly scrutiny.

Epistemology is a very useful area of study since it has a wide variety of applications to music education, particularly in the area of curriculum development. It is also useful to select at least one area of philosophy for some intense examination so that music educators can return to this field for stimulation and refreshment.

A study of the theory of knowledge is logically the concern of all those who teach. It is helpful for students to be able to contrast the various aspects of knowledge: (1) knowing and having knowledge; (2) knowledge of and knowledge about; (3) perceptual and conceptual knowledge; (4) propositional and nonpropositional knowledge; and (5) knowledge as subjective and objective. Sources of knowledge provide additional insights: (1) the senses; (2) reason; (3) existence; (4) tradition; and (5) revelation. Studying the validation of knowledge involves a penetrating examination of the nature of meaning, truth, and how these can relate to the evaluation process in education. The organization of knowledge involves an examination of: (1) classes of objects; (2) aspects of experience; (3) methods; (4) theories; and (5) communities of discourse.

In view of what we know about the way knowledge is organized, it is very interesting to observe that the favorite American sport is still revising the curriculum. This is because we are afraid to ask the real questions. What kind of a world do we want? What kind of teachers do we need to have this world? What kind of experiences do students need to bring about the world we want? Hence, each year new curriculum texts propose alternative ways of designing the curriculum. Since epistemology has to do with the nature of knowledge, and since curriculum has to do with the organization or sequence of the knowledge to be learned, it seems reasonable for doctoral students to become familiar with the literature and thinking of those who understand the philosophical nature of knowledge. By the time they have completed a study of this area, it may be easier for them to discover the cyclical as well as the innovative in curriculum theory.

The study of *readings and analyses from significant philosophers* involves an examination of significant contributions from those whom the philosophy teacher feels to be helpful. This writer believes that a basic minimum should include: Dewey, Whitehead, Langer, Broudy, and Greene. An in-depth consideration of these views of the philosopher and the educational philosopher tends to highlight the basic assumptions that music educators must cope with when they select and chose a position. Furthermore, it is often inspirational for students to confront the intellectual excellence that is found in the writings of the above representative group as compared to typical educational publications. An additional advantage is that students have the opportunity to seek application of the views of the various philosophers to contemporary educational issues. It may be, for example, that a certain philosopher provides us with an elegant rationale for music. Yet, this rationale may find little application in either teaching or learning music. The opposite may also be true; it is possible for one to read a wonderful rationale for education only to find that it holds little appeal for music education.

The selection of a reading list and the texts that go with it will individualize each philosophy course. This is an important strength since, if it is one goal of philosophical instruction to develop independent thinking, we would not want all courses in the field to be the same.

Teaching, Learning, and Evaluating Philosophical Study in Music Education

The present literature on college teaching is sufficiently impressive so that those who are interested can examine a large variety of publications. Works by Cross, Eble, McKeachie, and the Jossey-Bass publications would make a good beginning for these not familiar with this literature. We who teach philosophy of music education represent a fraction of the music teaching population, and it is doubtful that we can expect an outpouring of publications in this area. The following discussion is, therefore, offered as a synthesis of both experience and the study of the above literature.

Part of the biggest challenge in teaching this course is to get the students, as Maxine Greene would say, "to do philosophy." The idea that philosophy is a process that uses language to transform, to clarify, and to bring greater depth to understanding all human experience is often a frightening consideration for some who have spent the greater part of their time leading musical organizations and teaching general music. Yet one cannot learn philosophy without becoming philosophical. Hence, rather than talking about *philia* meaning love and *sophia* meaning wisdom, we can begin with the assumption that all of philosophy will appear to be "Greek" to our students.

It is easier and more practical to begin with the basic tools of philosophy: the "dialogue" and the question "why." It is useful to start these courses with a series of questions that are basic to music and to education. At the very beginning it is also helpful to require a precise use of language and definitions of all terminology used by either student or teacher. If this practice becomes habitual, it is not threatening; it simply provides the clarity and specificity frequently lacking in educational discussions. Students learn that establishing definitions makes informed communication possible, even if the definition is operative only for that class.

Hence, while the instructional process can be organized in terms of a series of topics (the curriculum), the teaching and learning environment can emphasize the Socratic dialogue. Although the average music student is accustomed to taking notes, the challenge of explaining why the study of music is as important as learning English usually requires an effort that makes performance anxiety wane by comparison. Students should be involved in all forms of classroom activities so that their ability to debate and to discuss at a professional level can be systematically cultivated.

Students should also be reading and writing analyses of journal articles in the style of the professional critic. While most reviews in our field are an exponentiation of the table of contents, summaries cannot be acceptable for these assignments. Students should select journal articles that are approved by the professor and should not be more than two years old. Students should be required to: (1) state the author's basic assumptions; (2) evaluate the degree to which the author's position is developed through logic, internal coherence, evidence, research; and (3) indicate the reasons why the reviewer agrees or disagrees with the author. If students submit one a week (no more than two to three typed double-spaced pages) for the first half of the semester, substantial growth can take place since the procedures used in class will be employed in the weekly written assignments. The quality of written work for these assignments should be fairly close to publication level. While many students will have problems with written English, it is perfectly acceptable for them to have their work edited for English. In view of the fact that all professional writers have their works edited, it is important for doctoral students to get used to submitting work that reflects the professional quality appropriate for their dissertations.

The evaluation process begins with the first class and continues with each class through participation and through weekly written assignments. The final examination should not only cover the assigned readings, it should cover the class discussions as well. These examinations are most useful when they are in essay form. Students should be asked the types of questions that will not allow them to repeat memorized information. For example, if they are asked to compare or to contrast two positions as they apply to a particular music education situation, then students will be forced to synthesize the information so that integrated learning can be demonstrated.

The term paper should illustrate philosophical research through the exposition of a particular problem. It may also be helpful for the professor to approve the topics so that students who have difficulty identifying an appropriate problem will not waste this opportunity on an unrealistic project. Grading is a topic that has caused unbridled debate since its inception. Philosophy courses are seldom limited to doctoral students, they often have masters students in them if they are foundation courses. This writer believes in two standards: one for masters students and one for doctoral students. Course criteria should be given the first day of class. Doctoral students should be expected to do extra reading, to write better critical analyses, to develop probing term papers, and to provide more searching final examinations.

Consideration of the lecture as an instructional device has been left for last. Considerable research concerning the nature of the lecture is available in the literature on college teaching and, therefore, will not be repeated here. This large body of research tends to indicate that lecturing may be one of the most ineffective ways to share information. Yet experience informs us that in selected situations it appears to be the most efficient way we know. What makes the most sense is to assume that the professor has read widely and is able to synthesize a great deal of information in a relatively short period of time. This process of sharing information can be exciting, stimulating, thought provoking, and creative. Here is where the research is most useful since it indicates the ways in which such presentations can be organized. The lecture can also be a deadly bore! It is an individual decision for each professor to select the appropriate combination of teaching strategies so that the instructional climate enhances learning opportunities.

Current Observations

The impact of philosophical study in music education should enhance the entire field. However, while many colleges and universities offer courses in this genre to graduate students, it appears that such courses do not have a great deal of impact. This impression is created by the sparsity of intellectual debate of a substantive nature in our national professional journals or at our national professional meetings. For those who want a functioning example of a national professional dialogue, examine the research journal *Studies in Art Education* for the past several decades.

There is a difference between music scholars presenting alternative views in history, literature, theory, composition, performance and music educators' failure to debate significant policy issues. While our music scholars are active, there is no dialogue to speak of in music education. To cite an example, my distinguished colleague Bennett Reimer has written a first-rate text on philosophy of music education. While he would be the first to confess to human fallibility, at the time of this writing I have not read a reasonable intellectual challenge to his work. If that is the case, there are two logical conclusions: (1) the work is profoundly excellent and should be viewed and hailed as such; or (2) our colleagues do not have the intellectual credentials to find the imperfections in a fallible though still quite excellent work.

Since we appear to have no intellectual challenge to a standing philosophy of music education, and since it is unlikely for that position to demonstrate absolute perfection, it is possible that we hold membership in a profession that is intellectually bankrupt! Alternatively, ours may be the only profession in which final answers have been achieved.

The writer is concerned that although basic research is difficult to fund in the hard sciences, it is even more difficult to fund philosophical research in music and the arts. Furthermore, until and unless the educational establishment understands that there is an intellectually demanding and substantive base upon which music rests, the level of their support will continue to be primarily symbolic. The absence of a national dialogue concerned with profound issues reveals a serious weakness in our profession.

Some Options for Consideration

The future can be bright. If we educate our students to think, to be able to express themselves, and to communicate their thoughts to policymakers throughout the nation, we can look forward to a society in which music and the arts will be a primary force. We know that the experience of music is seductive, compelling, inspirational, healing, and instructive. The public also knows that there is magic in the experience of music and that it has the capacity to entertain.

Why not begin with the obvious. One generic goal to mobilize our profession could be to develop the aesthetic potential of all Americans. The more specific goal would be to develop the musical potential of the entire population. Since most educational activities in music have the potential for accomplishing this goal, and since all educators and social institutions can benefit from a musically literate population, this goal may be one way to begin a national dialogue. Such a dialogue may assist our society in achieving many of those humanistic qualities that are generically inherent in our population.

Other options can also be explored:

An ongoing series of conferences that will seek to identify and prioritize significant issues to develop a national agenda.

An in-depth consideration of the development of a national music curriculum K-12.

A new examination of psychology which removes the old "theories of learning" approach still used by some but discarded by most psychologists.

An examination of the research in teaching that can be used for applied music and music ensembles.

A systematic attempt to open an ongoing dialogue with other academic disciplines, guidance counselors, administrators, board members, legislators, and state superintendents of instruction.

A fundamental commitment to basic research in music and music education.

A fundamental commitment to applied research in music and music education.

Development of interdisciplinary and multidisciplinary programs of research with the arts and other academic disciplines at all levels of instruction.

Development of interdisciplinary and multidisciplinary programs of research with other professions.

The above options could hardly be described as comprehensive. Yet they could be a beginning. If the options could be considered, refined, and replaced by a more cogent, better focused, and more appealing list for music educators at all levels of instruction, we might develop a national agenda. While the writing of each generation claims its own time to be critical for commitment and decision making, such claims should be considered valid since that generation always lives in the present: that organic continuum between the future and the past. Therefore, what we do, or fail to do, will have a significant impact on the future quality of music education and American life.

This article was supported, in part, by the Office of the Dean, School of Arts, California State University, Northridge.